The Truth About Shylock

THE TRUTH ABOUT
SHYLOCK

BERNARD GREBANIER

Random House :: *New York*

Ah, love, let us be true
To one another! for the world, which seems
To lie before us like a land of dreams,
So various, so beautiful, so new,
Hath really neither joy, nor love, nor light,
Nor certitude, nor peace, nor help for pain;
And we are here as on a darkling plain
Swept with confused alarms of struggle and flight,
Where ignorant armies clash by night.

Contents

Preface

Some honest members of the audience at the New York production of Jean Genet's *The Blacks* have informed the director, Gene Frankel, that they did not understand the play. "I tell them," says Mr. Frankel, "not to try to understand it all. There are parts of this play even I don't understand as the director." *

Our times are getting to be more and more remarkable. A graduate student at Columbia University has just learned from an electronic computer the answer to a question which has been argued for decades by classical scholars: Is *The Iliad* the work of one poet or several poets? The machine has settled the matter: There was only one Homer. Over a period of four years, we learn, the young scholar "translated" the poem for the computer; the machine gave him his answer in only five hours.

If audiences and directors are not to trouble themselves to understand the plays on view and if, on the other hand, matters requiring the subtlest esthetic awareness are to be relegated to machines, are we to anticipate the total discrediting of human understanding and sensibilities? Will the course of progress inevitably lead to the installation of devices at theaters and opera houses for determining with mathematical accuracy what we are to feel about the works and performances presented?

Such a day may arrive. But while it is still in the future, I have felt obliged, with the full knowledge that at any moment such machines will render obsolete my and all preceding speculations, to contribute my own and (with shame I confess it) merely human conclusions on a question as much disputed as the Homeric one: What did Shakespeare mean by Shylock?

When he created him Shakespeare could not have anticipated that Shylock would become the emblem about which so much contention would rage. Shakespeare's money-lender is now the symbol for those

* *New York Herald Tribune*, July 3, 1961.

who love and those who hate anti-Semitism. In addition, Shylock is held up as a reason for praising or condemning Shakespeare as a defender or defamer of the Jews.

I am convinced that he thought neither of attacking them nor of defending them when he wrote *The Merchant of Venice*. The play, I believe, was composed as a dramatic statement of a great and noble idea which has nothing to do with the other issue. Shylock is not only a Jew, he is also a prototype of the banker; and what Shakespeare has to say on that head applies equally to Christian, Jew, or Moslem.

Misconceptions about Shylock are owing to confused notions about both historical fact and the play itself. Commentary and acting traditions have increased the disorder. To come at Shakespeare's meaning, it is exigent first to know some important things. Shylock was a money-lender; what did it mean to be a usurer in Shakespeare's day? Shylock was also a Jew; how did the Elizabethans feel about Jews? And how did Elizabethan attitudes on both subjects affect Shakespeare?

This work undertakes to trace the great idea expressed in *The Merchant of Venice*. It seemed necessary, therefore, to supply an answer to these questions by gathering together, as indispensable to an understanding of Shakespeare's purposes, a background of copious facts which would speak for themselves. They reveal quite clearly, among many other things, that it is not at all the case—as is always assumed—that what was true of the Middle Ages in general was necessarily true of Shakespeare's England; they say, moreover, that what was true of Shakespeare's contemporaries in England was not necessarily true of Shakespeare. This background, itself fascinating, makes it possible to approach *The Merchant of Venice* without becoming lost in the mists of abstract speculations and inherited platitudes.

But what Shakespeare meant by his Shylock can be discovered finally only within the confines of the play in which he figures. To understand him it is essential to understand the play, not as a sociological treatise, but as a dramatic entity. For that comprehension the historical background is invaluable. But it is even more necessary to approach this magnificent play with an understanding of human values and with esthetic sensibilities. To approach *The Merchant of Venice* without them (lacking our electronic computer) would be as wasted an endeavor as a blind man's confronting a Titian or a deaf man's sitting through a Beethoven symphony. Knowing the background, we must discover the play's great idea in the play itself.

The Truth About Shylock

1

To Begin with an Elephant

A point is the beginning of magnitude.—Proverb.

: :

Contention is a hydra's head: the more they strive the more they may: and as Praxiteles did by his glass, when he saw a scurvy face in it, brake it in pieces; but for that one he saw many more as bad in a moment.—Burton, *The Anatomy of Melancholy.*

: :

The first, the Retort Courteous; the second, the Quip Modest; the third, the Reply Churlish; the fourth, the Reproof Valiant; the fifth, the Countercheck Quarrelsome; the sixth, the Lie with Circumstance; the seventh, the Lie Direct.—*As You Like It,* IV, iv.

: :

Those who in quarrels interpose,
Must often wipe a bloody nose.—Gay, *The Mastiff.*

: :

O we fell out I know not why,
And kissed again with tears.—Tennyson, *The Princess.*

: :

The Elephant, like Infinity, may be held to be symbolic of the vast resources of genius.—Ibn Gareer, *Imitation of the Prophet.*

It is related that a certain Rajah of India in olden times, bored with the routine of his sensual pleasures, decided to enjoy some intellectual fun for a change. He therefore ordered his Chamberlain to collect in the courtyard of the palace all the blind men in town. At the same time he caused the noblest of his elephants to be conducted there.

When the subjects of this diversion were assembled, it turned out by good luck that there were thirteen of them. The Rajah disposed his person comfortably under a canopy in the courtyard, and bade the blind men come close to the elephant. "This, O blind men," said he, addressing them, "is an elephant. Approach and discover what an elephant is like."

Two of the blind men began to feel the elephant's trunk, three his tusks, one his ear, one a side, two his belly, two his legs, and two his tail.

One who felt the trunk announced that the elephant is like a snake, the other that it is like a pole. One who felt a tusk thought the elephant like a sword; another, like a spear, the third, like a plowshare. The blind man who felt an ear was sure that the elephant is like a fan; the one who felt a side protested that the elephant is like a wall. One who felt the belly decided the elephant is like a granary; the other, like a filled sack. One who felt a leg proclaimed the elephant to be like a tree; the other, like a pillar. One who felt the tail agreed that the elephant is like a fan; but the other, the thirteenth, insisted that the elephant is like a rope.

Thereupon they began to beat one another with their fists and to call one another terrible names. The Rajah, at first delighted at their contention, soon wearied of them, and dismissed them. Each blind man returned to his post convinced that he alone knew what an elephant is like. And to all the world passing by, each blind man declared at the top of his lungs his knowledge: "The elephant is like a snake!" "A pole!" "A sword!" "A spear!" "A plowshare!" "A fan!" "A wall!" "A granary!" "A filled sack!" "A tree!" "A pillar!" "A rope!" And each also cried to every passerby: "Pay no attention to my colleagues! They are completely ignorant! I alone have felt what an elephant is like!"

Shakespearean commentary and scholarship have tended to be as accurate as were the blind men about the elephant—and little more so. Not that scholars have not often had a point. For that matter, each of the blind men had a point too. At some moments an elephant's trunk *is* like a snake, at others it is like a pole; his tusk may with reason be compared to a sword, a spear, or a plowshare; his ear or tail, when in motion, is something like a fan; his belly does resemble a granary or a filled sack; his leg is like a tree or a pillar; his tail is sometimes like a rope. But the trouble with the verdicts of the blind men was that though the elephant has a trunk, tusks, ears, sides, belly, legs, and tail, the elephant is not a trunk, a tusk, an ear, a side, a belly, a leg, or a tail.

It is a similar inability to see either Shakespeare or any one of his plays as a whole that has been the chief shortcoming of scholars and critics. A true definition of the elephant must naturally take into account the trunk, the tusks, and all the other members of the animal;

but it is absurd to generalize the characteristics of any of these members into a description of the animal as a whole.

Yet this is precisely what criticism and scholarship are forever doing with Shakespeare. And, indeed, there was less likelihood of the blind men's being led deeply into error, if only because an elephant's trunk has some meaning as a trunk, a tusk as a tusk. Whereas, no line of a play can be isolated and described this way independently of the whole organism, which is the play as a totality. With the exception of its opening lines, every line of a play derives its meaning only in terms of what has already been done and said in the play, and of what is happening at the moment onstage. Thus, when Lady Macbeth greets Duncan before her castle:

> All our service
> In every point twice done, and then done double
> Were poor and single business . . .
> (*Macbeth*, I, vi, 14-16)

although her words say that there is nothing that she and Macbeth can do for Duncan which will be hospitable enough, we are not asked by the dramatist to say to ourselves: "Lady Macbeth is truly a gracious and loyal subject to her king." On the contrary, we are asked to remember that she has already plotted with her husband the murder of Duncan; we are also asked to observe how well she masks her purposes with a hypocritically cordial welcome to him. That is, in view of her earlier talk with Macbeth on the subject of the projected murder, we are expected to interpret this greeting as being really an invitation to Duncan to enter and be murdered.

No commentator has thus far interpreted this greeting as proving that Lady Macbeth is truly a gracious and loyal subject to Duncan. But should such an interpretation ever be made public, no one ought to be astonished. For scholarship has made thousands of judgments on Shakespeare quite as chargeable with distortion. The villain of *Hamlet*, for instance, has been misjudged on the basis of chance words in the play. It is perfectly true that Hamlet does describe his uncle as a satyr, a bat, a filthy moor, a clown, a toad, a cutpurse. But that he does so is no warrant for one critic to consider this "abundant evidence that he [Claudius] is unattractive, even repulsive," [1] or for another therefore to conceive Claudius as of

"small nature, . . . a man of mean appearance—a mildewed ear." [2]
On the contrary, we are expected to remember that when Hamlet
makes these judgments they emanate from a long-standing dislike
and current loathing of Claudius. Taken as a whole, the play presents, rather, the evidence that Claudius is a highly intelligent man
capable of real affection for his wife, not a monster, and probably
a very attractive-looking man at that.[3]

Shylock has been called, with Hamlet, the most disputed of all of
Shakespeare's characters. [4] Certainly, few of the dramatist's creations
have been more subject to misinterpretation because of a simple-
minded overconcentration on isolated lines or speeches, and an unwillingness to remember that the play must be taken in as a totality.
The temptation to err with such an approach is particularly great—
and all the more dangerous—just because Shylock is so complex a
character.

One passage shall, at this point, suffice to illustrate. When Bassanio is asking Shylock to make the loan to Antonio, we read:

SHYLOCK.   May I speak with Antonio?
BASSANIO.   If it please you to dine with us.
SHYLOCK.   Yes, to smell pork, to eat of the habitation which your
           prophet the Nazarite conjured the devil into: I will buy with
           you, sell with you, talk with you, walk with you, and so follow-
           ing: but I will not eat with you, drink with you, nor pray
           with you.

(I, iii, 27-34)

Now, if you take this passage out of context, a favorite vagary of
scholars, and moreover disregard Shylock's later behavior, you could
easily build upon it the notion of a Shylock who, as a pious adherent
to the precepts of the religion of his people, is a typical Jew. You
might go further and exclaim with one popular writer, that Shakespeare here shows a most extraordinary partiality towards this Hebrew: "No Christian writer, before or since Shakespeare, has dared
to put such 'blasphemy' into the mouth of a 'heretic.' " [5]

But alas! Read the play Shakespeare wrote and you will find that
the unalterable fact is that Shylock soon *will* be going to dine with
Bassanio; that then he will presumably be perfectly willing to smell
pork, to dine and drink with Christians. And he is very explicit,
when he does go, about his reasons for going—reasons which are far
from admirable.

In view of the fact that Shylock will go to dine with Bassanio, we are required, therefore, to reinterpret his earlier remarks on the subject of his unwillingness to accept the invitation, in the light of this later conduct (and this we shall presently do). Our example indicates the pitfalls of generalizing the whole man on the basis of any one of his remarks. Such is the error of mistaking the tail for the elephant.

But scholarship has also been guilty of equipping the animal with features which Nature never bestowed upon it. The blind men, after all, did not supply the elephant with a horn like the unicorn's; what they felt, the elephant actually possessed. But scholars are forever adding features to a play, not to be found in what Shakespeare actually wrote. Thus, one scholar says of Shylock that he "is not villainous when thought of at his hearth with Leah and the infant Jessica, nor in the synagogue beside Tubal." [6] Such a pronouncement, if accepted, ought to move one with sympathy for Shylock— were it not that it is not consistent with some inconvenient facts. We never see Shylock at his hearth; we never see him with Leah; we never see Jessica as an infant; we are never inside the synagogue. None of this is in Shakespeare's play. And therefore none of it may justifiably be brought in to soften Shylock's portrait. We do see him, when Jessica is a young woman, in his house with her and his servant; and then he reveals himself as a harsh, brow-beating father and a miserly master. We do hear him later wish that Jessica were dead at his feet, if only he could have his money and jewels back (III, i, 80). He does make one reference to Leah, and it reveals that somewhere in the recesses of his warped being Shylock retains a tender memory of her—that, and nothing more. As for Shylock in the synagogue, we have no reason to assume that there he would show himself to be a pious Jew; on the contrary, we should have perhaps more reason (as we shall see) to assume that he is merely a hypocritical one. But since we are not permitted to be present when he is in attendance at his place of worship, we had better assume nothing about his conduct there.

The honest lover of Shakespeare must be constantly on guard against these extensions contributed by other people to the play —extensions which often quickly become accepted as authentic tradition, and which often turn the work into a monstrosity. Such, for example, are the insertion of a new stage-direction in *Hamlet* (II, ii, 162-4) to cause the Prince to overhear Polonius' plan to "loose" Ophelia to him; the preposterous interpretation that Gertrude drinks the poisoned drink to save her son from drinking it; the many absurd suggestions which have been offered for staging the fencing-match in the last scene.[7] In the Fall of 1961 the Iago at Stratford-upon-Avon introduced the idea that that villain was a homosexual: he was forever kissing Roderigo passionately, he draped Desdemona's handkerchief on Cassio's head, he stroked Othello's hair as the Moor lay in a swoon. This is indeed a *new* Iago!

Now, it is a fact of natural history that a giraffe is particularly fond of munching on the leaves of the mimosa tree. Does it follow that his neighbor, an elephant, will therefore be devoted to the mimosa tree too? Yet this is the kind of analogy which is constantly being made by scholarship to account for Shakespeare. No better instance of this can be cited than the ends to which the Lopez case has been put.

Dr. Roderigo Lopez was a converted Jew of Portuguese descent, who was much esteemed in London as a physician and scholar. He served as medico to the Queen. When in 1590 Antonio Perez, claimant to the throne of Portugal, fled to England with his entourage, there to be welcomed as an enemy to Philip II, Lopez was assigned to him as interpreter at the English Court. It appears that Lopez did not get on very well with Perez. A plot against Elizabeth's life came to light, and Lopez was implicated in it and found guilty. After some delay Elizabeth signed his death warrant, and he was hanged at Tyburn in the spring of 1594. He was subjected to peculiarly savage tortures, quite possibly because he had been a Jew, quite possibly because he was thought to be an agent of the fiercely hated Philip II. In any case, because he had been a Jew, some monumental conclusions have been made by scholars concerning *The Merchant of Venice*. For example, although there is every reason to believe that the play was written in 1596 or even in 1597, there have been some frantic attempts to push the date to an earlier year so that it might seem to have been written almost immediately after Lopez' execution, and to have been inspired by it.

Characteristically, but without a shred of proof, one scholar blandly remarks: "It is not improbable that Shakespeare witnessed the butchery at Tyburn." (It is equally not improbable that Shakespeare may have been visiting with his family at Stratford at the time. Or that he may have chosen deliberately not to be a witness to the butchery at Tyburn.) On this slight hypothesis, the same commentator allows his fancy to rove wildly: he advances as proof that "Shakespeare had Lopez in mind when he set out to portray Shylock" that Bassanio should exclaim to Portia before making his choice of the caskets:

> Let me choose,
> For as I am, I live upon the rack.
>
> (III, ii, 24-5)*

Lopez, this scholar points out, had pleaded at his trial that his earlier confession had been a series of lies "to save himself from *racking*." Unless Shakespeare were thinking at the moment of Lopez, the commentator concludes, "there is no reason why Shakespeare when Bassanio is professing his love for Portia, should suddenly think of the rack." [8] † (This scholar, by the way, overlooked the opportunity to fortify his case, such as it is; when Antonio urges Bassanio to look everywhere for the money needed, he says:

> Try what my credit can in Venice do:
> That shall be rack'd even to the uttermost.
>
> (I, i, 180-1)

Here our scholar might have also declared: "There is no reason why, when Antonio is assuring his friend of the loan, Shakespeare should suddenly think of the rack" unless the dramatist had Lopez in mind.)

Indeed, arguing in the same way, one could make an imposing brief to prove that Shakespeare could never get the Lopez case out of his mind for the rest of his career! In his last play, *The Tempest*, which everyone agrees was written in 1611, seventeen years after Lopez' hanging, Prospero threatens Caliban with:

> I'll rack thee with old cramps . . .
>
> (I, ii, 369)

(Or have I herewith started a new vogue to prove, despite the overwhelming evidence for 1611, that *The Tempest* too was written around 1594?)

---

* The line-numbers as given throughout this book are those of the Cambridge Edition.
† But in that case, why should not the image have been assigned to Shylock?

How that Lopez affair must have haunted Shakespeare's days and nights, if we reason in this fashion! Earlier the same year, in *The Winter's Tale* (1611), when Paulina comes in to announce the reputed death of the Queen, she cries out to Leontes:

> What studied torments, tyrant, hast thou for me?
> What wheels? racks? fires?
>
> (III, ii, 176-7)

Menenius in *Coriolanus* (1609) accuses the demagogues, Sicinius and Brutus, of being

> A pair of tribunes that have rack'd fair Rome
> To make coals cheap!
>
> (V, i, 16-17)

Near the end of *King Lear* (1606), Kent murmurs concerning the dead Lear:

> Vex not his ghost; O, let him pass! He hates him
> That would upon the rack of this tough world
> Stretch him out longer.
>
> (V, iii, 313-15)

In *Measure for Measure* (1604), the Duke apostrophizes "place and greatness" with:

> thousands escapes of wit
> Make thee the father of their idle dream
> And rack thee in their fancies.
>
> (IV, i, 63-5)

Escalus, incensed at the accusations of the "friar," cries:

> Take him hence, to the rack with him!
>
> (V, 1, 313)

and the "friar," enjoying the double-talk, retorts:

> Be not so hot. The Duke
> Dare no more stretch this finger of mine than he
> Dare rack his own.
>
> (315-16)

How the Lopez case must have weighed upon Shakespeare during that particular year of 1604, ten years after the event! For he was not free of it with all this. *Othello* belongs to the same year; in it Othello cries out to Iago:

> Avaunt! be gone! thou hast set me on the rack.
>
> (III, iii, 335)

Pandarus, talking of Helen to Cressida, in *Troilus and Cressida* (1602), admits that Helen has a lovely "white hand, I needs must confess—" and Cressida interrupts with:

> Without the rack.
>
> (I, ii, 152)

In *Twelfth Night* (1600), Sebastian cries, on seeing Antonio again:

> How have the hours rack'd and tortur'd me,
> Since I have lost thee!
>
> (V, i, 226-7)

The Friar, during the church scene of *Much Ado About Nothing* (1598), philosophizes:

> it so falls out
> That what we have we prize not to the worth
> Whiles we enjoy it, but being lack'd and lost,
> Why, then we rack the value.
>
> (IV, i, 219-22)

Falstaff, in *I Henry IV* (1597), when called upon to give his reasons for recognizing the color of Kendal green "when it was so dark thou couldst not see thy hand" indignantly refuses:

> What, upon compulsion? 'Zounds, an I were at the strappado, or all the racks in the world, I would not tell you on compulsion.
>
> (II, iv, 261-3)

Indeed, arguing from the use of "rack," why not attempt to prove, as one easily could, that Shakespeare had a clairvoyant foreknowl-

edge of the Lopez execution from the outset of his writing plays?
As early as 1591, in *I Henry VI*, we find Mortimer saying to the
Gaolers:

> Kind keepers of my weak decaying age,
> Let dying Mortimer here rest himself.
> Even like a man new haled from the rack.
>
> (II, v, 1-3)

Later in the same year Shakespeare's premonitions seem to have increased; for in *II Henry VI* we discover two references. Cardinal
Beaufort thus charges Gloucester:

> The commons hast thou rack'd.
>
> (I, iii, 131)

Speaking of John Cade, York says:

> Say he be taken, rack'd, and tortured,
> I know no pain they can inflict upon him
> Will make him say I mov'd him to those arms.
>
> (III, i, 376-8)

And on the very eve of the Lopez execution, twice again in *Love's
Labour's Lost* (early 1594), despite the lightness of the play, Shakespeare had forebodings. Holofernes comments upon Don Adriano
de Armado that he abhors

> such rackers of orthography.
>
> (V, i, 21)

Rosaline assures Biron:

> You must be purged too, your sins are rack'd,
> You are attaint with faults and perjury.
>
> (V, ii, 828-9)

It is to be hoped that this little excursion into absurdity will have
shown the futility of erecting scholarly pyramids of theory by the
simple device of ignoring all the inconvenient facts.

Of course, many other scholars have had a merry time of it

identifying Shylock with Lopez on other grounds just as tenuous.
Ever since Furness in a footnote gave them the hint, a considerable
number of commentators have consented to find the clue in the passage, just before the trial, where Gratiano abuses Shylock:

> thy currish spirit
> Govern'd a wolf, who, hang'd for human slaughter,
> Even from the gallows did his fell soul fleet,
> And whilst thou lay'st in thy unhallowed dam,
> Infus'd itself in thee.
>
> (IV, i, 133-7)

The argument runs that since the Latin for wolf is *lupus*, Shakespeare is "probably punning on the name Lopez: Lopez-Lupus-
Wolf." [8] But there is no justification for taking these lines to mean
more than they say. Animals were sometimes hanged in Shakespeare's day when proved to be killers. Moreover, Shylock is a usurer,
and usurers were frequently spoken of as wolves.[9] They still are. The
attempt to discover Shakespeare's intentions in *The Merchant of
Venice* by calmly assuming that Shylock is another Lopez is in the
last degree frivolous.

To return to our friend the elephant. Suppose that because he
wanders the same terrain as do zebras and tigers, the elephant were
to be declared authoritatively an animal possessing stripes? A manifest absurdity. Yet this is the sort of absurdity which scholarship is
forever asking us to accept concerning Shakespeare. It is doubtless
interesting and useful to know that the same land which can nurture animals which are striped also nurtures the elephant. But we
must be careful not to jump to the conclusion that such a land
nurtures only striped animals.

Scholarship has done much to elucidate Shakespeare's times. We
know a great deal, in consequence, about the manners, customs,
superstitions, prejudices, conventions, law, sports, games, language of
his contemporaries. All of that is extremely valuable to know for
its own sake, and invaluable to the reader and student of Shakespeare—up to a point.

Unfortunately, this aggregation of knowledge concerning the Elizabethan age and theater has resulted in the assumption that Shakespeare was a sort of run-of-the-mill Elizabethan, and no more than
that. E. E. Stoll always implies this to be the basis of his thinking

about Shakespeare: he goes so far as to say that Shakespeare "more than any other poet reflected the settled prejudices and passions of his race." [10] He seems willing to grant that the dramatist was a very clever one, though prompted by an unfailing "opportunism" to take short cuts by turning to account popular traditions and predilections. Thus, according to such reasoning, though there is no very good excuse in the play itself why Hamlet should pretend to be mad, Stoll finds that this was Shakespeare's intent because the Elizabethan audience was familiar with "feigned madness as an artifice and a natural employment of the avenger." Shakespeare therefore, according to Stoll, was content to pass "lightly, carrying the audience with him, over the reasons" for the pretended madness.[11]

If it were true that Shakespeare wished his audience to understand Hamlet to be feigning lunacy, but could not be bothered to explain why Hamlet should play such a role and left it to his audience to supply their own reasons—why then, honest critical judgment would have to brand the play the product of botched workmanship. It were feeble exoneration of the playwright that he could count on his audience's adding to the play what is not to be found in it. Instead of explaining for Shakespeare why a pretended madness which he himself never explains—and nowhere indicates!—is in the play, it is surely more profitable and to the point to ask whether or not there *is* any assumed madness in the play at all. An investigation of the action of *Hamlet* will reveal no place where Hamlet pretends to be mad.

This is but one example. But mountains of idle speculation have been amassed from the highly untenable point of departure that what Shakespeare's fellow-dramatists were doing or trying to say, Shakespeare himself perforce was doing or saying.

If scholarship be granted this right to interpret everything in terms of what some contemporary was doing, any writer's work quickly degenerates into a kind of jigsaw design of popular conventions fitted together to pass as a piece of literature. What writer of talent, not to speak of genius, could be tempted to create merely to do that sort of empty thing?

We shall present evidence aplenty that the Elizabethans were fairly generally (though by no means universally) hostile toward the Jews. If we allow ourselves the same kind of "scholarly" predisposition in trying to understand Shakespeare, we jump to the false conclusion that as an Elizabethan he was inevitably hostile to the Jews. One critic goes so far as to say that in *Titus Andronicus* Shakespeare gave his heartless Moor the name of Aaron because it was a Jewish name, with the express purpose of making him "more hateful." [12] No doubt the parents of our own unloved Aaron Burr, with a clairvoyant foreknowledge of the undelectable life their offspring was to lead, named him Aaron for the same reasons!

Certainly too much has been made of this dogged search for signs of the epoch in the works of a writer, particularly when the writer is one of the world's greatest. For example, Shakespeare undoubtedly employed Elizabethan English. He could hardly help doing so. But at his finest he was more likely to be writing Shakespearean English than Elizabethan English. Were it otherwise should we be prizing him as our greatest poet?

Again, Elizabethan audiences liked to have their clowns, in tragedy as well as comedy. And Shakespeare therefore gave them their clowns. But where in Elizabethan drama are to be found the other Launcelot Gobbos, the Dogberrys, the Grave-diggers, the Touchstones, the Festes, or Fools like the immortal one in *King Lear*? And, moreover, why is each of these so utterly different from the other—if only convention were involved?

No, it will not do to paint Shakespeare with the stripes his contemporaries may have worn, however Shakespearean scholarship has labored to do so. If any writer in any age stood both in the age and at the same time far above it, Shakespeare was that writer. He is constantly setting the reader who knows him well, back on his heels by the complete modernity, vision, and timelessness of his understanding. The attempts of the researcher to deprive him of all that makes him nonpareil are a futile waste. For this reason one ought to be vexed at the presumptuousness of such scholarly arrogance as Schucking's when he says, "Little good can result from even the most sagacious verdict of the mere amateur." [13] This is to forget that Shakespeare wrote not for future scholars, but for the human beings who were his audience. The "mere amateur," unencumbered by the lumber of that kind of scholarship, through love of Shakespeare often understands him more profoundly. How much closer to the truth is the attitude of Bradley who, with all his learning, could admire "that native strength and justice of perception, and that habit of reading with an eager mind, which make many an unscholarly lover of Shakespeare a far better critic than many a Shakespearean scholar." [14]

Whatever scholarly materials it brings to bear upon *The Merchant of Venice* and the character of Shylock, this work attempts never to forsake a "justice of perception" as to what this play and Shakespeare's other plays reveal in themselves. We must see Shakespeare, of course, as an Elizabethan. But we must also see what in him was uniquely his own in that age. We must also remember our story of the elephant and never be turned aside by the phrase or line out of *dramatic* context. We must see the play and the characters as entities and as the creation of the most far-seeing and compassionate and the least sentimental of the world's writers. If we will settle for no less, we may find it possible to arrive at a notion of what the truth about Shakespeare's Shylock is.

2

Prick Them and They Do Not Bleed: Englishmen and the Jews

Sir Roger made several reflections on the greatness of the British Nation: as, that one Englishman could beat three Frenchmen.—Addison, *Spectator*, 383.

::

All prejudices may be traced back to the intestines.—Nietzsche, *Ecce Homo.*

::

If Christians were Christians, there would be no Anti-Semitism. Jesus was a Jew. There is nothing that the ordinary Christian so dislikes to remember as this awkward historical fact.—J. H. Holmes.

::

Ignorance only is maker of hell.—Sir. W. Watson, *England to Ireland.*

::

I've no kind of prejudice against any kind of people meself, especially if they're Irish.—Kevin O'Toole.

::

Tantum religio potuit suadere malorum!*—Lucretius, *De Rerum Natura*, I.

::

Si les Juifs n'existaient pas, il faudrait les inventer.†—Baniergré, *Quoi de Neuf?*

Any attempt to arrive at Shakespeare's intentions in creating Shylock is likely to be frustrated just because the money-lender in *The Merchant of Venice* is a Jew. Jewish people and unbigoted people generally tend to be extremely sensitive the moment anything with a Jewish connotation is brought up. It is not odd, of course, that this oversensitiveness with its attendant loss of perspective should exist—least odd in our own century, when the savagery meted out to Jews has been of nightmarish proportions. Nevertheless, one could

* How many evils has religion induced!
† If there weren't any Jews, it would be necessary to invent them.

wish that everyone would be a little more objective. To assume immediately the defensive about everything Jewish is self-defeating, unfair to multitudes of unbigoted non-Jews, and sometimes too indulgent of the shortcomings of those who are Jewish.

It would surely be absurd to maintain that every time a Jew is represented in literature he must be depicted as an archangel. After all, like members of all groups, some Jews are saints, some are devils, and the majority are decent but humanly fallible. To refuse to admit this much is certainly to enroll oneself in the service of error, not truth. Yet many commentators have got into a lather of indignation because Shylock's character has been depicted as less than angelic. Shakespeare, they reason, to have so created any Jew must have been a bigot. [Harbage has come up with an interesting statistic, which indicates that Shakespeare's view of human nature was more than charitable. In 38 plays of Shakespeare he finds 775 characters whose moral quality he feels it possible to estimate:

Number of characters	Morally	Percentage of 775
378	Good	49%
158	Good "in the main"	20%
106	Bad "in the main"	14%
133	Bad	17%[1]

Shakespeare, thus—if we may generalize upon Harbage's findings —mirrors half the world as good, and almost three-quarters of the world as good or nearly so; the villains among us seemed to him to have been of a sizeable but not overwhelming proportion, and in the minority.] Calish blames Shakespeare for giving "world-wide currency to the conception that Jews are a class of people, of whom the hard-hearted, loveless usurer is the type." [2] (If his Shylock indeed could be blamed for having lent currency to such a conception, it nevertheless would be as unjust to upbraid Shakespeare for this perversion of his own meaning as it would be to lay at the door of Jesus some of the perversions of His teachings which masquerade as Christian practice.) A number of years ago, while I was rehearsing *The Merchant of Venice* for a college performance, I received several abusive letters charging me with wishing to aid and abet the cause of anti-Semitism. I received almost as many thanking me for my undertaking to present a play "which so nobly defends the Jews." I felt indebted to neither attacker nor thanker, since I view

Shakespeare's play as neither an assault upon the Jews nor a defense of them. I was interested in presenting the play as I understood Shakespeare to have meant it.

Many scholars have been equally eager to discover intentions hostile to the Jews in Shakespeare's mind. Charlton, for example, declares the portrait of Shylock to be "a composite production of Shakespeare the Jew-hater and of Shakespeare the dramatist." [3] And Neilson and Hill observe: "There can be no doubt that Shakespeare intentionally endowed Shylock with traits which have fostered the traditional antipathy to his race." [4]

It may by this time be suspected that I completely doubt that such were Shakespeare's intentions. It is perhaps not beside the present point to listen to Harry Golden; he notes that the German Nazis never employed Shylock as part of "their gigantic propaganda campaign" against the Jews, but preferred to give wide distribution to Budd Schulberg's *What Makes Sammy Run?*—because, Mr. Golden concludes, the Nazis were aware that the Germans knew their Shakespeare too well to admit of such a use of Shylock.[5]

It would, of course, be idle to deny that Shylock was created against a background of a long antecedent history of hatred for the Jews and of injustice to them. The Christian record is appalling enough. It is all the more appalling when it is remembered that, from the Christian point of view, Jesus, as part of the divine plan, was born a Jew.

Some of this appalling history we must trace.

After the destruction of Jerusalem, the Jews at first enjoyed a considerable amount of tolerance among the Romans; the Constitution of Caracalla (198-217) insured them, no less than others dwelling within the Roman Empire, the rights of Roman citizens.[6] The Hebrew patriarchs "enjoyed almost royal authority" and "were often on terms of intimate friendship with the emperors." But this comfortable state of affairs altered with Constantine when Christianity became the official religion in 312. The Theodosian Code degraded the Jews as inferior and depraved (*inferiores, perversi*), a sect godless and dangerous (*secta nefaria, feralis*), their meeting for worship a blasphemy (*sacrilegi coetus*).[7] While their worship at synagogues was protected against intrusion, they were strictly forbidden to admit Christians into their numbers or to hold Christian slaves. Marriage between Christian and Jew was made punishable by death in 423.

The attitude of the Church Fathers kept pace with the official

Roman position. At first the Church Fathers were charitable enough in their attitude. For example, Hippolytus, Schismatic Bishop of Rome (second-third century), no bigot, paid the Jews the tribute that "they earnestly aim at serious habits and a temperate life." But changes begin to appear in the words of the Father of Church History, Eusebius, Bishop of Caesarea (third-fourth century); he held circumcision a disgrace, and urged that measures be taken against what he called the Jewish "heresy." Ephraem Syrus (fourth century) called the Jews the "circumcized vagabonds." Ambrose, Bishop of Milan (340-397), revealed himself to be openly a foe of the Jews: he endorsed the destruction of a synagogue in Mesopotamia on the grounds that the house of worship was "a home of depravity in which Christ is daily blasphemed"—though he granted that "some Jews exhibit purity of life."

From this time forth, animosity against the Jews was recurrent in the stand of early churchmen. Earlier the objections had been largely in the realm of abstract argument. Now there entered a note of violence which unquestionably led to violence of action, and encouraged persecution. St. Augustine (354-430) lumped Jews, Arians, and heathens together as one group. Cyril, Bishop of Alexandria (fifth century), was responsible for the expulsion of Jews from Alexandria in 415. Gregory the Great (Pope from 590 to 604) declared the Jewish religion to be a "superstition, depravity, and faithlessness," but he protected the Jews from mistreatment. One of his bulls reads: "Just as no freedom may be granted to the Jews to exceed the limits legally set for them, so they should in no way suffer a violation of their rights." [8]

Centuries later the Angelic Doctor, St. Thomas Aquinas (c. 1227-1274), was not of this generous frame of mind; he said of them that they are "doomed to perpetual servitude, and the lords of the earth may use their goods as their own." [9] Such, indeed, was the widespread practice of the lords of the earth. Nor was the father of Protestantism gentler. Luther urged that synagogues and houses belonging to Jews be burned, that the Jews be deprived of all their wealth, that their books and prayer-rolls be destroyed, and that they be put to work with a spade.[10]

The Emperor Justinian in 553 forbade the use of the Talmud, and he denied to Jews and all heretics the right to appear as witnesses in civil courts against Christians.

But it was in the Middle Ages that the lot of the Jew became intolerable, particularly in England, France, and Germany. The Crusades saw a furious augmentation of persecution on the part of the mobs who, for the sake of pillage, accompanied the crusaders. Numerous cities of the Rhineland witnessed massacres of Jews in 1096. Bernard de Clairvaux protested against similar acts during the Second Crusade (1145-47). During the Third Crusade, most famous of the three because of Richard the Lionhearted, hatred of the Jews was whipped to a new frenzy.

The account in Holinshed's *Chronicles* under the year 1189 requires no comment:

Upon this daie of king Richards coronation, the Jewes that dwelt in London and in other parts of the realme, being there assembled, had but sorie hap, as it chanced. For they meaning to honour the same coronation with their presence, and to present to the king some honourable gift, whereby they might declare themselves glad for his advancement, and procure his friendship towards them, for the confirming of their privileges and liberties, according to the grants and charters made to them by the former kings: he of zealous mind to Christes religion, abhorring their nation (and doubting* some sorcerie by them to be practised) commanded that they should not come within the church when he should receive the crowne, nor within the palace whilest he was at dinner.

But at dinner time, among other that pressed in at the palace gate, diverse of the Jewes were about to thrust in, till one of them was striken by a christian, who alledging the kings commandement, kept them backe from comming within the palace. Which some of the unrulie people perceiving, and supposing it had beene doone by the kings commandement, tooke lightlie occasion thereof, and falling upon the Jewes with staves, bats and stones, beat them and chased them home to their houses and lodgings. Heerewith rose a rumor through the citie that the king had commanded the Jewes to be destroied, and thereupon came running togither, to assault them in their houses, which when they could not easilie breake up nor enter, by reason the same were strongly builded, they set fire on them, so that divers houses were consumed, not onelie of the Jewes, but also of their neighbours, so hideous was the rage of the fire. . . .

The king being advertised of this riotous attempt of the outragious people, sent some of his councellours . . . to appease the tumult: but their authoritie was nothing regarded, nor their per-

* fearing

suasions any whit reverenced, but their thretnings rather brought themselves in danger of life among the rude sort of those that were about to spoile, rob, and sacke the houses of the Jewes. . . . The Jewes that were in those houses which were set on fire, were either smoldred and burned to death within, or else at their comming foorth most cruellie received upon the points of speares, billes, swords and gleaves of their adversaries that watched for them verie diligentlie.

This outrage of the furious and disordered people continued from the middest of the one day, till two of the clocke on the other; the commons all that while never ceasing their furie against that nation, but still killing them as they met with any of them, in most horrible, rash and unreasonable maner. At length, rather wearied with their cruell dooings, than satisfied with spoile, or mooved with respect* of reason or reverence of their prince, they withdrew themselves from their riotous enterprise, after they had executed manie unlawful and horrible enormities.

This great riot well deserved sore and greevous punishment, but yet it passed over without correction. . . . The most part of men . . . liked the dooings hereof well inough, interpreting it to be a good token, that the joifull daie of the kings advancement to the crowne should be dolefull unto the Jewes, in bringing them to such slaughter and destruction. . . .

The occasion of this tragedie and bloudie tumult . . . sprang principallie from the king, who if he had not so lightlie esteemed of the Jewes when they repaired unto him with their present, . . . this hurlie burlie had not ensued.

It is worthy of remark that Holinshed, although he based his narrative upon earlier records which were highly prejudicial to the Jews, in 1577 was writing of them in a style which is not without compassion for them. It is worthy of remark because Holinshed who was so widely read in his own times is plainly an Elizabethan who could stand above the bitter hatred againt Jews which scholarship pretends was utterly universal during Shakespeare's lifetime.

By the time of Richard I, the Jews were victims of the slanderous myth of ritual-murder. During their early days the Christians themselves suffered heavy persecution because they were charged with offering human sacrifice in their religious ceremonies. Justin Martyr (c. 150) found it necessary vehemently to defend his fellow-Christians against the accusation; and Tertullian, Origen, and other

* consideration

Church Fathers were equally indignant against the widespread notion that human sacrifice was connected with the Eucharist. Later, various heretical sects had to face the same charges from the orthodox.[11] But during the Middle Ages, the imputation of such sacrificing of human beings as part of their religious observance settled upon the luckless Jews.

One of the earliest "cases" of ritual murder on record was the so-called murder of a Christian child in Norwich, England, in 1144. The Jews in that city were supposed to have purchased the child before Passover, and during the Passover festivities to have tortured him with all the tortures visited upon Jesus, and then to have buried their victim.[12] Similar episodes are recorded in 1168 at Gloucester and in 1181 at Bury St. Edmunds.

The twelfth century in England ended with a shocking instance of how far hatred for the Jews had progressed. The Jews of York were so gravely threatened in 1190 that they sought the protection of the Warden of York Castle, who permitted them to take refuge in Clifford Tower. But Richard Malebys, who was heavily in debt to them, collected a mob which stormed the tower. As William of Newburgh (died c. 1198) tells the story, the beleaguered Jews saw only two alternatives: death at the hands of the mob or conversion to Christianity. Most of them decided it was better to take their own lives, and did so. Those who surrendered to the fury outside asked to be baptized as Christians; instead they were put to death.

No legend ever fabricated at the expense of the Jews did them more damage than the story of little Hugh of Lincoln, best known to literature in Chaucer's version, *The Prioresses Tale*. The legend was spun around the disappearance in August 1255 of an eight-year-old boy from the town of Lincoln. There are numerous accounts of what occurred, and patient scholarship has reconstructed the actual happenings.

Hugh was a son of a widow named Beatrice. One day while playing ball, Hugh ran after the ball and by accident fell into a cesspool in the yard of a house belonging to a Jew. There his body remained for twenty-six days. Unluckily, it happened that during these days a great many Jews from other towns had convened at Lincoln for important festivities: the daughter of an honored scholar, the Chief Rabbi of Lincoln, was to be married. On the day after the wedding-ceremony the body of the child, having risen to the surface of the cesspool, was discovered. The Jews must have been only too well aware of what havoc that little corpse could cost them; understandably, they lost their heads and foolishly tried to dispose of the body elsewhere. Three days later, a woman passing the place where little Hugh's corpse had been laid, saw the body. Inflamed by the suggestions of John of Lexington, canon of Lincoln Cathedral, the populace at once accused the Jews of a ritual murder. It mattered not that the month was August and that Easter is never later than April: the Jews were charged with having made of Hugh a "Paschal offering"—and so Matthew Paris solemnly records it.

Hugh's remains were deposited in a stone coffin and, with much pomp and ceremony, interred in the south aisle choir of the Cathedral. It chanced that, en route to Scotland, Henry III was at Lincoln at this time. The case was presented to him.

Now, Henry had just sold the Jews for a large sum of money to his brother Richard. [The Jews, however much hated, had proved invaluable as financial assets. The church had forbidden the practice of usury to Christians, and a number of Jews had seized upon money-lending as the only profession open to them (see Chapter III). The constant seizure of their wealth and the heavy taxation imposed upon them by the Crown led them to charge enormous rates of interest. Thus they became, unwillingly, the "sponges by means of which a large part of the subjects' wealth found its way into the royal exchequer." [13]] Henry saw that the affair at Lincoln offered him a fine opportunity for seizing Jewish property. It was therefore pretended that the gathering at Lincoln for marriage festivities had been actually for the express purpose of murdering a Christian child. All the Jews in England were held, in consequence, equally culpable, and were ordered either to submit themselves to a jury or to be hanged. Those who were willing to be tried were thrown in jail, from which they were allowed to ransom themselves with fines of exorbitant amounts.

Little Hugh's story, as officially presented, seized upon the popular imagination, and before long was the subject of balladry. More than twenty versions of this ballad have come down to us, all following the same outline of the story. This one is characteristic:

> Four and twenty bonny boys
> Were playing at the ba,

And by it came him sweet Sir Hugh,
  And he playd oer them a'.

He kicked the ba with his right foot,
  And catchd it wi his knee,
And throuch-and-thro the Jew's window
  He gard* the bonny ba flee.

He's doen him to the Jew's castell,
  And walkd it round about;
And there he saw the Jew's daughter,
  At the window looking out.

"Throw down the ba, ye Jew's daughter,
  Throw down the ba to me!"
"Never a bit," says the Jew's daughter,
  "Till up to me come ye."

"How will I come up? How can I come up?
  How can I come to thee?
For as ye did to my auld father,
  The same ye'll do to me."

She's gane till † her father's garden,
  And pu'd an apple red and green;
'Twas a' to wyle him sweet Sir Hugh,
  And to entice him in.

She's led him in through ae dark door,
  And sae has she thro nine;
She's laid him on a dressing-table.‡
  And stickit him like a swine.

And first came out the thick, thick blood,
  And syne§ came out the thin,
And syne came out the bonny heart's blood;
  There was nae mair within.

* caused
† to
‡ a table where food was prepared
§ afterwards

She's rowd* him in a cake o lead,
    Bade him lie still and sleep;
She's thrown him in Our Lady's draw-well,
    Was fifty fathom deep.

When bells were rung, and mass was sung,
    And a' the bairns came hame,
When every lady gat hame her son,
    The Lady Maisry gat nane.

She's taen her mantle her about,
    Her coffer by the hand,
And she's gane out to seek her son,
    And wanderd oer the land.

She's doen her to the Jew's castell,
    Where a' were fast asleep:
"Gin ye be there, my sweet Sir Hugh,
    I pray you to me speak."

She's doen her to the Jew's garden,
    Thought he had been gathering fruit:
"Gin ye be there, my sweet Sir Hugh,
    I pray you to me speak."

She neard Our Lady's deep draw-well,
    Was fifty fathom deep:
"Whareer ye be, my sweet Sir Hugh,
    I pray you to me speak."

"Gae hame, gae hame, my mither dear,
    Prepare my winding sheet,
And at the back o merry Lincoln
    The morn I will you meet."

Now Lady Maisry is gane hame,
    Made him a winding sheet,
And at the back o merry Lincoln
    The dead corpse did her meet.

And a' the bells o merry Lincoln
    Without men's hands were rung,

* rolled

And a' the books o merry Lincoln
   Were read without man's tongue,
And neer was such a burial
   Sin Adam's days begun.[14]

Chaucer lays his version of the story "in Asie, in a greet citee," a fact that has sometimes been made to imply that it exonerates the poet of any ill-will toward the Jews. To hint this is to have read *The Prioresses Tale* with scant attention.

It opens with a brief description of how there was

Amonges Cristen folk, a Jewrye,
Sustened by a lord of that contree
For foule usure and lucre of vilanye,
Hateful to Crist and to his companye;
And thurgh the strete men mighte ryde or wende,
For it was free, and open at either ende.*

The story goes on to tell of a seven-year-old boy, a widow's son, who on his way to school every day would kneel before Our Lady's image and say his *Ave Maria*. At school he was taught to sing the *Alma Redemptoris*; he was too young to know what the Latin meant, but he fell in love with the words and tune till he had got them by heart. All he can learn about the words is, as an elder schoolboy informs him, that they were composed in honor of Christ's mother. When he has learned all the words,

Twyës a day it passed thurgh his throte,
To scoleward and homward whan he wente.

Thus going through the Jewish quarter he was forever singing O *Alma redemptoris*. The murder which is to follow is attributed by Chaucer to Satan:

Our first fo, the serpent Sathanas,
That hath in Jewes herte his waspes nest,
Up swal, and seide, "O Hebraik peple, allas!

* Among the Christian people a Jewish quarter, maintained by a lord of that country for the purposes of foul usury and villainous gain, such as are hateful to Christ and His believers; and through its streets men could ride or walk since it was free and open at both ends.

> Is this to yow a thing that is honest,
> That swich a boy shal walken as him lest
> In your despyt. . . ." *

From that time on the Jews planned the child's murder. They hired one of their number to seize upon the boy in an alley, cut his throat, and throw him in a pit. At this point the Prioress, who is telling the tale, cries:

> O cursed folk of Herodes al newe,
> What may your yvel entente yow availle?
> Mordre wol out, certein, it wol nat faille . . .
> The blood out cryeth on your cursed dede.†

The worried widow goes in search of her son. At last she finds him in the pit.

> This gemme of chastitee, this emeraude,
> And eek of martirdom the ruby bright,
> Ther he with throte corven lay upright,
> He *Alma redemptoris* gan to singe
> So loude, that al the place gan to ringe.‡

Christian folk came to marvel, and quickly sent for the provost. The latter at once ordered the Jews to be bound. The child's body was taken up, he ever singing his song, and carried with pomp to the nearest abbey.

> With torment and with shamful deth echon
> This provost dooth thise Jewes for to sterve
> That of this mordre wiste, and that anon. . . .
> Therfor with wilde hors he dide hem drawe,
> And after that he heng hem by the lawe.§

* Our first enemy, the serpent Satan, who keeps his wasp's nest in the Jewish heart, swelled up and said, "O Hebrew people, alas! Is this a matter of honor to you that such a boy walk as pleases him in your despite?

† O cursed latter-day Herods, what avails your wicked purpose? Murder will out, surely that cannot fail . . . Blood cries out on your accursed deed.

‡ This gem of chastity, this emerald, this bright ruby of martyrdom, where he was lying on his back with his throat cut, began to sing, "O alma redemptoris" so loudly that the whole place began to ring.

§ The provost put to death with torment and shameful end every one of the Jews who knew of the murder, and that at once. . . . Therefore he had them drawn with wild horses, and thereafter had them hanged according to law.

Mass is said for the little corpse; but as they sprinkled holy water on it, the child began to sing "O alma redemptoris" anew. The abbot asks, "O dear child,

> Tel me what is thy cause for to singe,
> Sith that thy throte is cut . . . ?
> "My throte is cut unto my nekke-boon,"
> Seyde this child, "and, as by wey of kinde,
> I sholde have deyed, ye, longe tyme agoon,
> But Jesu Crist, as ye in bokes finde,
> Wil that his glorie laste and be in minde;
> And, for the worship of his moder dere,
> Yet may I singe O *Alma* loude and clere."

The martyred child gives up his ghost at last, and his body is entombed in pure marble. After the conclusion of her story, the Prioress calls upon little Hugh of Lincoln, "also slain by cursed Jews, as is well known, for it happened but a little time ago."

Jews may be pardoned if they feel impervious to the literary excellences of the old ballad or to the artistic finish of Chaucer's tale. Indeed, it is difficult to see how in a world which knows about the ovens of Hitler, any decent Christian can pretend to read either story with pleasure, whatever their esthetic merits. The fantastic imputation of ritual murder to the Jews which this legend celebrates has been the cause or the excuse of too much barbarous inhumanity since. Had Shakespeare been capable of the bigotry Chaucer exhibits in the midst of his piety in *The Prioresses Tale*, there would have been no point to the composition of the present work. As it is, Chaucer seems astonishingly deficient in the fair-mindedness of either his own contemporary, Boccaccio, or Shakespeare's fellow-Elizabethan, the chronicler Holinshed.

As far as Chaucer's version of the story goes, it could not have offended Jews very much—for the simple reason that by the time of its being written there were almost no Jews left in England. On July 18, 1290, Edward I ordered all Jews out of the country before All Saints' Day of that year. Holinshed's account shows how even their expulsion gave new impulse to the rapacity of their persecutors:

> The Jewes [were] banished out of all the kings dominions, and never since could they obteine any privilege to returne hither

againe. All their goods not mooveable were confiscated. . . . A sort of the richest of them, being shipped with their treasure in a mightie tall ship which they had hired, when the same was under saile, and got downe the Thames towards the mouth of the river beyond Quinborowe, the maister mariner bethought him of a wile, and caused his men to cast anchor, and so rode at the same, till the ship by ebbing of the streame remained on the drie sands. The maister herewith entised the Jewes to walke out with him on land for recreation. And at length, when he understood the tide to be comming in, he got him backe to the ship, whither he was drawne up by a cord. The Jewes made not so much hast as he did, bicause they were not ware of the danger. But when they perceived how the matter stood, they cried to him for helpe; howbeit he told them, that they ought to crie rather unto Moses, by whose conduct their fathers passed through the red sea, and therefore, if they would call to him for helpe, he was able inough to helpe them out of those raging flouds, which now came in upon them: they cried indeed, but no succour appeared and so they were swallowed up in water. The maister returned with the ship, and told the king how he had used the matter, and had both thanks and reward, as some have written. But others affirme, (and more truelie as would seeme) that diverse of those mariners, which dealt so wickedlie against the Jewes, were hanged for their wicked practise, and so received a just reward of their fraudulent and mischeevous dealing.

The Jews were not to be re-admitted to England until 1655, during the dictatorship of Cromwell.

There have been many arguments to prove or to deny the existence of Jews in England between 1290 and 1655. It is a fact that in 1232 Henry III had arranged a refuge, The Domus Conversorum, for Jews who converted to Christianity. Between 1232 and 1290 not more than one hundred were housed there, despite the monetary allowance and ecclesiastical backing assured converts. The record shows that from 1331 to 1608 a total of only forty-eight persons was admitted to that institution.[15] It has, however, been maintained that in the sixteenth century, after the expulsion of the Jews from Spain and Portugal, a few Jews filtered into England and there secretly founded a small colony.[16] On the other hand, we are told with equal authority: "In Elizabethan and early Stuart England no unconverted Jews were known to be living." [17] Some modification of such a statement is implicit in the insistence of other historians that when Jews became converted it was only for the purpose of avoiding exile, that secretly they practiced their own religion. It is not important for our purposes to decide among these conflicting claims. Allowing for the existence of some Jews in Elizabethan England, either through secret immigration or under the masquerade of pretended conversion to Christianity, the number must have been insignificant. Officially the Jews were not there. There is perhaps some point to the observation of Holmes concerning their position in Shakespeare's day: "The race had become unfamiliar and exotic"; it was therefore possible "to believe anything of it without any particular ill-feeling." His analogy is with the fashion for peopling early twentieth-century popular novels with sinister Chinese villains, without there having been any real prejudice against the Chinese.[18] The almost total (or actual) absence of Jews from Shakespeare's England may indeed have resulted, as Cardozo has impressively proved,[19] in the word "Jew" being used loosely for anyone outside the pale of accepted respectability—dissenters, foreigners, Christian usurers. This is precisely what happened to the word in Hitler's Germany, e.g., the labeling of the work of the French impressionists, cubists, expressionists, and abstract painters generally, as well as of much modern music and American jazz as "Jewish art." Even today some bigots tend to conclude that Christians of whose dealings they disapprove "must have Jewish blood in them."

Certainly the almost total absence of Jews from England during the period when Elizabethan drama was flourishing would have rendered any "attacks" upon them meaningless, the height of folly and a waste of energy. Who would bother to foment among the public strong feelings of prejudice against a group that was nowhere in evidence?

Only with the reappearance of Jews in England would it have availed a hater of the Jews to arouse antipathy against them. The bigotry then flourished anew. Thus Robert South (d. 1716), noted English divine, in a sermon observed that there is "some peculiar vileness" which is inherent in the Jewish people and which accounts for their having been so widely detested.[20] Mrs. Inchbald, member though she was of the radical circle which included Godwin, Mary Wollstonecraft, Paine, and Blake, could say, "a virtuous miser is as much a wonder . . . as a virtuous Jew." [21] Even such a distinguished Shakespearean scholar as Sir Arthur Quiller-Couch can say about the Jews that "the race has always, from Jacob's time, prospered on usury." [22] In the novels of Evelyn Waugh we meet with the caricatures of Augustus Fagan, Esq., Ph.D., director of a boy's academy (in *Decline and Fall*); Youkoumian, the greasy trader (in *Black Mischief*); and the Jesuit imposter, Father Rothschild (in *Vile Bodies*). It has been said without exaggeration that the Jews are depicted as "cowards and murderers and human lice" in the writings of Wyndham Lewis and Charles Williams, Evelyn Waugh and Graham Greene." [23] D. H. Lawrence and Hilaire Belloc have shown a similar bias. Ezra Pound's hatred of the Jews has been fierce and sweeping; his attitude has in some circles been as fashionable as his verse. Certainly his great admirer, T. S. Eliot, has shot many an imprecation against Jews in his work; witness the portrait of Bleistein, "Chicago Semite Viennese," and the designation of Shylock as "the toad squatting on the window-sill," "the rat beneath the piles." What is sad to report is that this abuse and these sneers are as flat and stereotyped as if they had sprung from some medieval mind. How much in advance of all this is Shakespeare's:

> Hath not a Jew eyes? hath not a Jew hands, organs, dimensions, senses, affections, passions; fed with the same food, hurt with the same weapons, subject to the same diseases, healed by the same means, warmed and cooled by the same winter and summer, as a Christian is? If you prick us, do we not bleed? If you tickle us, do we not laugh? If you poison us, do we not die?
>
> (*The Merchant of Venice*, III, i, 61 seq.)

We are not yet ready to say what Shakespeare meant by Shylock. But this much it is possible to assert now: *The man who could conceive of such a speech for his play was plainly a man who was incapable of bigotry against any race.* Thus much must be conceded even if it could be shown—as it cannot—that fires of hatred for the Jews were raging around Shakespeare.

But let us take an impartial look to see how axiomatic hatred for the Jews may or may not have been in the literature in which they figure before Shakespeare wrote his play.

In medieval drama, the stories taken from the Old Testament naturally presented Jews, and there was no occasion for their appearing in those stories in an unnatural light, as though they belonged outside the human race. Subjects taken from the New Testament, however, frequently pictured the Jews as the tormentors of Jesus. In *The Play of Corpus Christi*, performed in 1415, the cast of characters calls for "4 Jews accusing Christ, . . . 4 Jews persecuting and scourging Jesus, . . . Jews compelling Him to bear the cross," among others. Still, such a cast can hardly be accused of any deliberate departures from the story. But in *The Judgment Day*, Jesus was made to say:

> The Jewes spitte on me spitously;
> Thei spared me nomore than a theffe;

and at the conclusion of the piece, Jews are condemned

> In helle to dwelle withouten ende.

In *The Betraying of Christ*, Judas appeared in the fiery red wig employed in other plays for the character of the Devil; he had a long nose of the same flaming color.[24] In fact, in the mystery plays of York, Coventry, Chester, and Townley, it was apparently usual to outfit Judas as a Jew "with a large nose, red hair, and a red beard." [25]

The Play of the Sacrament, "the earliest English drama extant which has neither allegorical characters nor a plot founded on Biblical narrative or the life of a saint," [26] deals with the supposed desire of Jews to vilify the Host of the communion. In it Jonathas and his fellow-Jews bribe a Christian merchant to steal from the altar of a church the sacred wafer. The Jews convey the holy wafer to the house of Jonathas, where they stab at it and nail it to a wall. The Host bleeds. As Jonathas attempts to take it from the wall, his right hand is torn off from the arm. The wafer is next thrown into boiling oil; the oil turns red and overflows the pot. Next, the wafer is cast into an oven; the oven explodes. Jesus now appears and pleads with his tormentors to stop. Overwhelmed with fear, they beg His forgiveness. Jesus grants them pardon, and the hand of Jonathas is restored to his arm.

In the medieval morality play, *Respublica*, the character of Avaritia (Avarice) among the Seven Deadly Sins was customarily represented as a Jew[27]—no doubt because of the old association of usury with the Jews. Little dignity could have been added to the position of Jews by the growing popularity of the tale of Joseph Cartaphilus,

Jewish shoemaker, the Wandering Jew, a story first told by Roger of Wendover in his *Flores Historiarum* (1228), later by Matthew Paris, and presently by the authors of a number of ballads.

Despite this medieval background of hatred for the Jews, I am convinced by my studies that scholarship has been rather blind in insisting that this attitude remained universally unaltered in the Renaissance. It is pretended that anyone living when Shakespeare lived could not help having inherited that hatred. My own feelings about Shakespeare are that he stood like an Everest above his contemporaries by dint of his unequalled humanity, and that he therefore was capable of any number of sympathies centuries in advance of them. But what I propose to show now is that his contemporaries by no means all shared the cramped bigotry of the medieval mind.

It is an indisputable fact that the humanistic spirit of the new age seems to have enlarged some men's perspective about Jews as human beings. That this was the case is demonstrable in the most celebrated of the writings of one of the fathers of the literary Renaissance, Boccaccio.

There are two stories about Jews in *The Decameron*, the finest of the Italian collections of tales: the second and third *novelle* of the First Day. Neither of them is written with any antagonism toward Jews. On the contrary, the first of these speaks of its Jew as an entirely superior being. (Our quotations are slightly abridged from Frances Winwar's brilliant and spirited translation.*)

> I have heard tell, gracious ladies, of a wealthy merchant who lived in Paris—a fine fellow, loyal and upright, whose name was Jehannot de Chevigny. He carried on an extensive business in cloths and stuffs, and he was a friend, strangely enough, of a very rich Jew called Abraham, a merchant, like himself, and like him, too, an honest and upright man. Observing Abraham's fine qualities, Jehannot began to be very much concerned that the soul of such a splendid fellow should be damned for his mistaken faith, so out of friendship he constantly urged him to forsake the errors of the Jewish creed and embrace Christian verity. . . . At that the Jew would reply he believed no faith but the Jewish to be either good or holy. Besides, he argued, he had been born into it, and in it he wanted to live and die. . . .

* Abridged from The Limited Editions Club edition of *The Decameron* by permission of The George Macy Companies, Inc. and Frances Winwar.

Nevertheless Jehannot was not deterred from returning to the argument. . . . The Jew soon began to take pleasure in Jehannot's arguments. Still, holding firmly to his faith, he would not allow himself to be shaken. The more obdurate he remained, the more insistent grew Jehannot's importunities. Finally, conquered by so continued an attack, the Jew said:

"Now, listen, Jehannot. You insist that I become a Christian. I am willing to do so, but first I want to go to Rome and see the man who, you say, is God's vicar on earth, that I may consider his ways and habits and those of his brother cardinals. If they seem to me such that between them and your arguments I can convince myself your faith is better than mine, as you have gone out of your way to show me,—why, I'll do what I said. If not, I'll keep on being the Jew I am."

Jehannot was exceedingly troubled to hear this, and said to himself: "I've wasted my efforts, which I thought so well-employed, when I imagined I was converting Abraham. If he should go to the court of Rome and see the filthy life of the clergy, far from being converted from Jew to Christian, he would most assuredly turn Jew again were he the most devout Christian in the world!" But turning to Abraham he said: "Now look, my friend, why should you want to go to the trouble and expense of traveling from here to Rome, especially when you consider that for a man of your wealth a trip by land or sea is full of danger?"

. . . "I am sure, Jehannot," answered the Jew, "that everything is as you say. But to make a long story short, if you want me to do what you've asked me so often, I insist upon going on my trip. If not, I wash my hands of the whole matter."

Jehannot saw Abraham was determined. "Well, go and good luck to you," he said, though he was certain Abraham would never become a Christian when he saw the court of Rome. . . .

[At Rome the Jew] began prudently studying the habits of the Pope, the cardinals and other prelates, as well as all the members of the papal court. Between what he himself gathered, for he was a very perceptive man, and what he heard from others, he found that all, from the highest of rank, to the meanest, were shamefully guilty of the sin of lechery. Not only did they indulge in normal lust, but without the least restraint of remorse or shame, even in sodomy, and to such an extent that the influence of whores and minions was of no little importance in currying favor. Various other attributes he found them to possess besides lechery. They were gluttons, swillers, and guzzlers in general, and devoted to their bellies like brute beasts. Investigating further he saw they were all avaricious and greedy for money. Human blood, indeed, Christian and sacred things pertaining to the sacrifice, they used to barter for money, making a bigger business of them and employing more agents than the people of Paris had for their stuffs and merchandise. . . .

These, and many other enormities that were better passed over in silence, offended the Jew, who was a sober and humble man, and thinking he had witnessed enough, he decided to go back to Paris.

When Jehannot heard of his return the last thing he hoped for was that Abraham should have become a Christian. He went to see him, nevertheless, and they greeted each other joyfully. . . . Jehannot asked him what he thought of the Holy Father, the cardinals and others of the papal court.

"I think they are rotten," the Jew readily replied. "God punish the whole brood of them! I tell you—unless I did not see things straight—I found no holiness, no devotion, no good work or example or anything else in a single man of the clergy. On the contrary, lust, gluttony, avarice and worse things, if there could be anything worse—all were in such high favor, I would have taken it for a mill of devilish works, not holy! For all I can judge it seems to me your Shepherd and consequently everyone else with him do their utmost, exercise every care, wit and art at their disposal to ruin the Christian faith entirely and ban it altogether from the world, instead of striving to be its foundation and mainstay. Yet when I notice their aim is not fulfilled, but that your religion grows and becomes more bright and clear, it seems to me very evident that the Holy Spirit is its foundation and support, so it must be the truest and holiest of all faiths. Therefore . . . I tell you frankly that nothing in the world could deter me from becoming a Christian. Come, let's go to the church, then, where I may be baptized. . . ."

Jehannot . . . went with him to the church of Notre Dame in Paris, and . . . raised him from the sacred font and named him Jean. In after-days Jean had himself duly instructed by famous men in all matters pertaining to our faith, which he learned without trouble, and he became a much respected man, renowned for holy living.

This tale invites one to several interesting pieces of speculation concerning *The Merchant of Venice*:

1. In it we perceive that a man of genius, such as Boccaccio was, could be capable of rising above the prejudices of his time. It need not surprise us, therefore, despite all the insistence of some scholars

that Shakespeare was entirely the child of his time, that Shakespeare, a greater genius, should be equally capable of rising above the anti-Semitism of his contemporaries, a couple of centuries later. For Boccaccio's Jew is depicted as a man of unimpeachable decency and integrity.

2. In it, too, we perceive that the author assumes it as possible enough to a solid honest citizen like Jehannot, that he nurture a warm, close friendship with a Jew.

3. We see too that a zealous Christian would look upon it as an act of love to convert a Jew to Christianity. It is his lively concern over the future of his friend's immortal soul which prompts Jehannot's unremitting attempts to convert the Jew.

4. The tale assumes too that there is no need to pretend that Christians own a monopoly on virtue. The whole point of the story turns wittily on the proof that this is far from the case. It is, moreover, the Jew's love of virtue which makes him decide on conversion in very despite of the corruption he has seen in Rome. Certainly, we must conclude, some people—no matter how few—were, centuries before Shakespeare, capable of horizons very close to religious tolerance.

The third story, thanks to *Nathan the Wise,* is now one of the best-known stories in the world. In *The Decameron,* Filomena remarks before beginning this tale that the one just related "reminds me of the scrape a Jew once got into:"

> Saladin, who was so powerful that he rose from an ordinary man to the rank of Sultan of Babylon and won countless victories over Saracen and Christian rulers, found that he had exhausted all his wealth. . . . He felt the need of money, and a lot of it too, and not knowing where he could get it as quickly as he wished, he thought of a rich Jew called Melchizedek who was a moneylender in Alexandria. This usurer, he was certain, had money enough to help him, but he was also aware the man was so miserly that he would never do so of his own free will. Violence Saladin did not care to use. However, urged by his need, and thinking over ways and means of making the Jew serve him, he decided to use a show of force, colored by some plausible reason. Summoning the Jew, he received him cordially, bidding him sit at his side, and then spoke:
> "I have heard from all quarters, sir, how learned you are. . . . I'd be very glad to learn from you which of the three laws you

consider the true one—the Hebrew, the Saracen or the Christian?"

The Jew, who was truly a man of understanding, was only too confident that Saladin was trying to trip him up in some statement, and so have grounds to start a suit against him. He realized he could not praise any one of these three without giving Saladin his pretext. [He therefore told Saladin this story:]

"I've heard tell many times of a rich and powerful man who had among his treasures a rare and valuable ring that he prized above everything else. . . . He decreed, therefore, that whichever of his sons found he had inherited the ring, after his death, should be looked upon as the chosen heir, and be esteemed and respected by the rest, as the head of the family.

"The man to whom the ring was left by his father had the same understanding with his sons. . . . This ring passed from hand to hand many times, until at last it reached a man who had three handsome, virtuous sons, obedient to all his wishes, because of which he loved each one with an equal love. Now the three youths knew the tradition connected with the ring, and as each was anxious for priority over his brothers, he pleaded with his father, who was now of a ripe old age, to leave it to him when he died.

"The worthy man was in a predicament, for he loved the three equally. . . . He decided to satisfy them all. In the utmost secrecy he ordered a skilful goldsmith to make him two other rings, and they were so much like the first that he himself, who had ordered them, scarcely knew which was the original. Then, when his time came to die, he gave each son one of the rings in secret. However, after his death they all wanted to occupy the place of honor and receive the inheritance. . . . Each produced his ring, to prove he was in the right. On examination they were found so similar that the true one could not be detected. Thus the question as to which one was the true heir of the father was unsolved, and remains so to this day.

"And so I say to you, sire, of the three laws given to the three peoples by God the Father. . . . Each race believes it possesses the inheritance and the true law of the Father and fulfils His commandments. But which one it is that is the true possessor still remains a question to be solved, as with the rings."

Saladin had to admit that the Jew had ably extricated himself from the snare laid at his feet. He concluded therefore to speak openly to him about his needs, and find out whether the man was willing to help him. He did as he proposed, confessing what he had secretly hatched in his heart if the man had not answered him so prudently, whereupon the Jew freely gave Saladin all he required.

and Saladin afterwards paid him back in full. Moreover, the Sultan made him many fine gifts and always looked upon him as a friend, keeping him at his court in a high and honorable position.

From this tale too we may draw certain interesting conclusions:

1. Again Boccaccio reveals a broad-mindedness on the subject of religion—a broad-mindedness, indeed, of which many hundreds of thousands even today would be incapable. He sees that it is absurd to delegate moral pre-eminence to one faith at the expense of all the others. If Boccaccio was capable of understanding this much in the fourteenth century, why should not Shakespeare have been equally capable of it in the sixteenth century?

2. The Jew, although assumed by Saladin to be miserly, turns out to be not so at all in the end.

3. Again we find genuine friendship possible between Jew and non-Jew.

4. Melchizedek is depicted without a single one of the traits which scholars for so long have been assuring us are absolutely inevitable in Renaissance portraits of the Jew. Here is a usurer who is not a Judas, not a devil, not a monster, not a ludicrous figure, not an object of ridicule or contempt. If Boccaccio could so conceive his Jew then, why not Shakespeare two centuries and more later?

I do not, of course, pretend by citing these two tales from *The Decameron* that there was a sudden annihilation of bigotry and hatred against the Jews in the Renaissance. But these stories do prove that, with the new spirit of humanism abroad, it became at least possible to write of the Jews without that bigotry or that hatred. This was as true of Elizabethan England as of Renaissance Italy.

Among the earliest theatrical pieces to present a Jew before London playhouse audiences was Robert Wilson's *The Three Ladies of London* (1583), written a number of years before Shakespeare began his career. In this play a Christian is in debt to a Jew, who is the virtuous character of the two.

The Jew, Gerontus by name, lives in Turkey. He has loaned the Italian merchant, Mercadorus, some money; this Mercadorus is a nefarious character who is engaged in bringing English exports to Turkey; he confesses (in language that is presumably an attempt to indicate an Italian dialect) to Lady Lucar:

Shall me say to you Madama dat me have had much business for you in hand,

For send away good commodities out of dis little Countrey England:

Me have nowe sent over Brasse, Copper, Pewter, and many odder ting:

And for dat me shall ha for Gentlewomans fine trifles, that great profite will bring.

When Mercadorus left the country he cheated the Jew out of the money that was owing. The two meet and Gerontus accuses Mercadorus of the cheat:

GERON. But senior Mercadorus tell me, did ye serve me well or no?

That having gotten my money would seeme the countrey to forgoe:

You know I sent you two thousand duckets for three monthes space,

And ere the time came you got an other thousand by flatterie and your smooth face.

So when the time came that I should have receaved my money,

You were not to be found but was fled out of the countrey:

Surely if we that be Jewes should deale so one with an other,

We should not be trusted againe of our owne brother:

But many of you Christians make no conscience to falsifie your fayth and breake your day.

I should have bene paide at the monthes end, and now it is two yeare you have bene away.

Well I am glad you be come againe to Turkey, now I trust I shall receive the interest of you so well as the principall.

MERCA. A good a maister Geronto pray hartly beare a me a little while,

And me shall pay ye all without any deceite or guile. . . .

GERON. Senior Mercadore, I know no reason why, because you have dealt with me so ill,

Sure you did it not for neede, but of set purpose and will: . . .

Well Ile take your faith and troth once more, ile trust to your honesty

In hope that for my long tarying you will deal well with me. . . .

MERCA. Fatta my good friend me tanke you most hartly alway,

Me shall a content your debt within dis two or tree day.

But Mercadorus does not keep his promise. The Jew finds him again:

> GERON.   Senior Mercadore, why doe you not pay mee? thinke you
> I will bee mockt in this sorte?
> This is three times you have flowted mee, it seemes you make
> thereat a sporte.
> Trulie pay me my money, and that even nowe presently,
> Or by mightie Mahomet I sweare, I will forthwith arrest
> yee. . . .
> I have Officers stand watching for you, so that you cannot
> passe by,
> Therefore you were best to pay me, or els in prison you shall lie.
> MERCA.   Arrest me dou skal knave, mary do and if thou dare,
> Me will not pay de one peny, arrest me, doo, me do not care.
> Me will be a Turke, me came hedar for dat cause,
> Darefore me care not for de so much as two strawes.
> GERON.   This is but your wordes, because you would defeate me,
> I cannot thinke you will forsake your faith so lightly.

The Jew is aghast at the idea that a Christian would change his religion just to avoid paying a debt. At the trial, he lessens his plea for what is due him in order to save the Christian from surrendering his faith; he tells the Judge that Mercadorus

> Did borrowe two thousand Duckets of mee, but for a five weeks
> space.
> Then Sir, before the day came, by his flatterie he obtained one
> thousand more,
> And promist mee at two monthes ende I should receive my store:
> But before the time exspired, he was closly fled away,
> So that I never heard of him at least this two yeeres day:
> Till at the last I met with him, and my money did demande,
> Who sware to me at five daies end, he would pay me out of
> hand.
> The five daies came, and three daies more, then one day he
> requested,
> I perceiving that he flouted me, have got him thus arrested:
> And now he comes in Turkish weedes* to defeate me of my
> mony,

* clothes

But I trow he wil not forsake his faith, I deeme he hath more
honestie.

JUDGE. Sir Gerontus you knowe, if any man forsake his faith,
king, countrie, and become a Mahomet,

All debtes are paide, tis lawe of our Realme, and you may not
gainesay it. . . .

Senior Mercadorus is this true that Gerontus doth tell?

MERCA. My Lord Judge, de matter, and de circumstance be true
me know well.

But me will be a Turke, and for dat cause me came heere.

JUDGE. Then it is but a follie to make many wordes. Senior Mercadorus draw neere.

Lay your hand upon this booke, and say after me. . . .

JUDGE & MERCA. Say I Mercadorus, do utterly renounce before
all the world, my dutie to my Prince, my honour to my
parents, and my good wil to my cuntry:

Furthermore I protest and sweare to be true to this country
during life, and thereupon I forsake my Christian faith.

GERON. Stay there most puissant Judge. Senior Mercadorus, consider what you doo,

Pay me the principall, as for the interest, I forgive it you. . . .

MERCA. No point da interest, no point da principall.

GERON. Then pay me the one halfe, if you will not pay me all.

MERCA. No point da halfe, no point denere,* me will be a Turke
I say,

Me be wearie of my Cristes religion, and for dat me come away.

GERON. Well seing it is so, I would be loth to heare the people
say, it was long† of me

Thou forsakest thy faith, wherefore I forgive thee franke and
free:

Protesting before the Judge, and all the world, never to demaund peny nor halfepeny.

MERCA. O Sir Gerontus, me take a your proffer, and tanke you
most hartily.

JUDGE. But Senor Mercadorus, I trow ye will be a Turke for all
this.

MERCA. Senor no, not for all da good in da world, me forsake a
my Crist.

JUDGE. Why then it is as Sir Gerontus saide, you did more for
the greedines of the money. . . .

* a French coin of little value
† because

l

One may judge and speake truth, as appeeres by this,
Jewes seeke to excell in Christianitie, and Christians in Jewisnes.

Here, then, is a pre-Shakespearean play in which the Jew is a generous human being, and the Christian a knave who would change
his religion just to hold on to his ill-gotten money. Obviously, therefore, the Elizabethans were not universally chargeable with bigotry.

In attempting to assess Elizabethan attitudes toward Jews, it is
important to remember a point already adverted to, that the Jews
being virtually unknown in England then, the word "Jew" was frequently used loosely to imply someone outside the pale—in such
cases, at most to mean "non-Christian." This is the meaning in
North's mind when in his *Diall of Princes* (1568) he says:

Let him take heed also that he do not call his servants drunkards,
thieves, villains, Jews, nor other such names of reproach.

This is also what is meant by Lyly in *Euphues* (1578):

Consider thyself that thou art a gentleman, yea, and a Gentile,
and if thou neglect thy calling thou art worse than a Jew.

Worse, that is, than a nonbeliever. This is the sense, too, in which
Falstaff uses the word when he is giving Hal his fabulous account
of the robbery:

PRINCE HENRY.   Speak, sirs, how was it?
GADSHILL.   We four set upon some dozen—
FALSTAFF.   Sixteen, at least, my lord.
GADS.   And bound them.
PETO.   No, no, they were not bound.
FALS.   You rogue, they were bound, every man of them; or I am a
Jew else, an Ebrew Jew.
(*I Henry IV*, II, iv, 192 seq.)

But of course there is no denying that plenty of medieval bigotry
still survived in the literature of the time.

Such, beyond much doubt, must have been the spirit animating a
play called *The Jew*, concerning which Stephen Gosson in *The
Schoole of Abuse* (1579) makes a passing reference; after attacking

the players as corrupters of the public, Gosson exempts from the accusation this play, which was performed at The Bull theater. He tells us that it was a piece which exhibited

the greedinesse of worldly chusers, and bloody mindes of Usurers.

Considerable discussion has been evoked by this brief description. Steevens, in the eighteenth century, felt it "not improbable" that *The Merchant of Venice* was a re-writing of *The Jew*. Skottowe decided from Gosson's few words that the play "combined within its plot the two incidents of the bond and the caskets." And Singer asserted that "it cannot be doubted that Shakespeare, as in other instances, availed himself of this ancient piece." Even Furness, usually so level-headed, was convinced; in 1888 he was saying "Here is a play, in which first, the chief character is a Jew; secondly, in which the choice of the caskets is adumbrated in the 'greedinesse of worldly chusers.'" And he, at the end of a long discussion of possible sources for Shakespeare's play, unequivocally states: "The conclusion, therefore, of the whole subject of the Source of the Plot is, that *The Merchant of Venice* was founded on the play mentioned by Gosson." [28] Naturally, it would have to be conceded that the phrase, "bloody mindes of Usurers," might or might not apply to some lost original of Shylock; but it is the conjunction of that phrase with "the greedinesse of worldly chusers" which seems to have settled the matter for most commentators, who cheerfully follow Furness' lead. Morocco and Arragon, they feel, are Shakespeare's version of the lost play's "worldly chusers." Certainly in no other work extant are the pound of flesh story and the casket story combined.

This is an exceedingly fragile argument on which to have erected the elaborate edifices which are the fabrication of some scholars. I propose later, when discussing the sources of our play, to show that the likelihood is that *The Jew* had nothing at all to do with the casket-story. At this point, let it merely be said—what in the end is all that can be said about the old lost play—that it is a play about whose contents we know absolutely nothing. Why, indeed, should anyone dare assert that in it the Jew of the title could not have been as generous as Gerontus, and some Christian as greedy as Mercadorus?

Robert Greene's *The First Part of the Tragicall Raigne of Selimus,*

Emperour of the Turks (1594), produced in the year of the Lopez execution (though by that time Greene was dead), contains
Abraham, a Jew, who doubtless reminded the audience of Lopez: Abraham poisons Selimus' father to please the son, who refers to
Abraham as "a cunning Jew," well schooled in medicine and prepared to "venture anything for gold."

The Orator (1596) by Lazarus Piot, who is apparently Anthony
Munday writing under a pseudonym, is a collection of one hundred "Discourses"; the ninety-fifth deals with a Jew who wishes to
have a pound of flesh from a Christian in payment of a debt. Of
the connection of this Discourse with Shakespeare's play, we shall
have more to say hereafter. In this place let us merely note some
phrases from the Christian debtor's passage:

> This Jew is content to lose nine hundred crownes to have a pound
> of my flesh, whereby is manifestly seene the antient and cruell
> hate which he beareth not only unto Christians, but unto all others
> which are not of his sect: yea, even unto the Turkes, who over-
> kindly doe suffer such vermine to dwell amongst them.

The last clause reminds us how scarce Jews were in Shakespeare's
England—if indeed there were any living there at all.

We have now arrived at the time of the composition of *The
Merchant of Venice* with one notable exception—the hero of Marlowe's *The Jew of Malta* (c. 1592). I have preferred to consider this,
the most imposing of all pre-Shylock Jews in English drama, out of
his chronological order.

There are a few superficial echoes of Marlowe's play in *The Merchant of Venice,* for which reason Shakespeare has traditionally—
and carelessly—been said to be most indebted to Marlowe's hero for
Shylock. Ward went so far as to say, "The two plays are, so far as
their main subject is concerned, essentially written in the same
spirit.* . . . In both Shakespeare's and Marlowe's play the view in-
culcated is that on the part of a Jew fraud is the sign of his tribe." [29]
This popular view on the subject is as inaccurate concerning Marlowe's intentions as it is concerning Shakespeare's.

Of course, not as much has been written about *The Jew of Malta*
as about *The Merchant of Venice.* But the percentage of irrele-
vancy is as great. One critic has said that Marlowe's play is but "a

* [than which declaration nothing could be further from the truth.]

picture of the popular conceptions of the Jews as it existed in Marlowe's day." [30] Another: Marlowe was "willing to flatter the prejudices" of his fellow-Elizabethans "by attributing almost impossible wickedness to a son of Israel." [31] Another: Marlowe's Jew was "calculated to stir only the worst passions of a listening multitude." [32] To believe this is to miss Marlowe's intent completely. It is true enough that Marlowe was unequal to the broad humanity which is fundamental to Shakespeare—he might, indeed, very well have despised it. But he was, for very different reasons, just as unequal to flattering his contemporaries' prejudices: it is almost impossible to imagine Marlowe flattering anything or anybody.

It is a commonplace to observe that the last three acts of *The Jew of Malta* fail to carry out the brilliant promise of the first two. Marlowe's hero, Barabas, might appear to a casual reader who has no desire to relate the Jew to the rest of Marlowe's work as a monster of cruelty and wickedness. Such a reader would regard Barabas' terrible end as having been deservedly brought upon his head by himself. Viewed thus, independently of Marlowe's total creation, the play could easily enough be interpreted as the product of a kind of medieval hatred for the Jews—and it is the fashion to speak of the play in this way. And, it is inevitably appended, Shakespeare must therefore have been following the lead of Marlowe's bigotry with his portrait of Shylock; if the figure is less barbarous, it is said, the hatred of Jews is no less real in *The Merchant of Venice*. All of which commentary is quite erroneous.

To deem Marlowe remotely interested in playing up to hatred for the Jews is as absurd as to imagine him writing to propound Christian ethics—as though it were his concern to further the traditions of the medieval morality play. There has been for some years, indeed, something like an epidemic among scholars of Elizabethan drama to relate everything of that period to the moralities of the Middle Ages, an epidemic most odious when the seizure is upon the masterpieces of Shakespeare. It would, in many instances, be just as sensible to expect significant light to be thrown upon Shaw's *Pygmalion* by a study of *The Careless Husband* or upon Noel Coward's *Blithe Spirit* by *Ten Nights in a Barroom*.

[A chief exhibit in support of such studies is the fact that in Marlowe's *Doctor Faustus* there is a scene in which the Seven Deadly Sins appear; their presence in the play is interpreted as an Elizabethan residuum of the Middle Ages. But after all, just how piously

do they figure in Marlowe's play? Listen to the speech which is assigned to Gluttony:

> I am gluttony. My parents are al dead, and the divel a peny they
> have left me, but a bare pention, and that is 30 meales a day, and
> ten beavers, a small trifle to suffice nature. O I come of a royall
> parentage. My grandfather was a gammon of bacon, my grand-
> mother a hogs head of Claret-wine. My godfathers were these:
> Peter Pickle-herring, and Martin Martlemas-biefe. O but my god-
> mother she was a jolly gentlewoman, and wel beloved in every good
> towne and Citie. Her name was mistresse Margery March-beere.

There is nothing here that could have repelled the Elizabethan audience as, by Christian standards, the person of Gluttony should. It
is written as though it were a heady excerpt from Rabelais, and in
the same spirit as some favorite Elizabethan songs of the rowdy
variety. At the end of the little scene, Lucifer asks Faustus: "How
dost thou like this?" and Faustus answers: "O this feedes my soule."
In other words, the pageant of the Seven Deadly Sins was, for Marlowe, just another of the colorful spectacles in which the play
abounds.]

To see Marlowe as a belated medievalist is to ignore the contents
of his plays and the facts of his life. From the outrageous splendors
of *Tamburlaine* to the pagan radiance of the first two Sestiads of
Hero and Leander Marlowe's literary career and his life were an intended affront to respectability and standard Christian virtues. All
his heroes lust for a power to which no good Christian dare aspire:
Tamburlaine, for the conquest of the world, "scourging kingdoms
with his conquering sword"; Faustus, for mastery over time, season,
death, and the laws of nature; Barabas, for revenge almost beyond
the reach of human imagination; Edward, for indulgence of such passions as are forbidden.

The hero of *The Jew of Malta* fits in perfectly with the design of
Marlowe's works and deeds: and that design has nothing to do with
Christian piety or Christian detestation of the Jews. The Jew may
strike a modern reader as a monster in his dealings with Christians;
but the man who knows his Marlowe must know that Marlowe's
sympathies were with that monster (just as they had been with his
earlier monster-poet, Tamburlaine) and against the Christians.
Why should one expect anything other from the Marlowe that is

on record? It should be enough to have a look at what Charles Norman has called Marlowe's "Table Talk." There exists one elaborate document which indicates—as everything else about him indicates—that Marlowe's temperament had destined him to an early and violent end.

Within a matter of days of Marlowe's premature death an enemy of his, one Richard Baines (probably an informer), delivered to the authorities "A note Concerning the opinion of on[e] Christopher Marly Concerning his damnable Judgment of Religion, and scorn of Gods word." It is a severe indictment of Marlowe, and would paint him as going out of his way to wound the sensibilities of the righteous. It makes more than likely the possibility that had not Marlowe met his death from the blade of Ingram Frizer's twelve-penny dagger, he might have been brought to it not much later because of his atheistical affronts to the pious. Among Baines's charges against him are these views which Marlowe had announced to the world:

That the Indians and many Authors of antiquity have assuredly writen of above 16 thowsand yeares agone whereas Adam is proved to have lived within 6 thowsand yeares.

He affirmeth that Moyses was but a Jugler & that one Heriot being Sir W Raleighs man Can do more then he.

That the first beginning of Religioun was only to keep men in awe.

That Christ was a bastard and his mother dishonest.

That he was the sonne of a Carpenter, and that if the Jewes among whome he was borne did Crucify him theie best knew him and whence he Came.

That Christ deserved better to dy than Barrabas and that the Jewes made a good Choise, though Barrabas were both a thief and a murtherer.

That all protestantes are Hypocriticall asses.

That if he were to write a new Religion, he would undertake both a more Excellent and Admirable methode and that all the new testament is filthily written.

That the woman of Samaria & her sister were whores & that Christ knew them dishonestly.

That St John the Evangelist was bedfellow to Christ and leaned alwaies in his bosome, that he used him as the sinners of Sodoma.

That all the apostles were fishermen and base fellowes neyther of wit nor worth, that Paull only had wit but he was a timerous fellow in bidding men to be subject to magistrates against his Conscience.

That if Christ would have instituted the sacrament with more Ceremoniall Reverence it would have bin had in more admiration, that it would have bin much better being administred in a Tobacco pipe.

That the Angell Gabriell was baud to the holy ghost, because he brought the salutation to Mary.

That on[e] Ric Cholmley hath Confessed that he was perswaded by Marloe's Reasons to become an Atheist.

Baines went on to affirm that

into every Company he Cometh he perswades men to Atheism willing them not to be afeard of bugbeares and hobgoblins, and utterly scorning both god and his ministers as I Richard Baines will Justify & approve both by mine oth and the testimony of many honest men, and almost al men with whome he hath Conversed any time will testify the same . . . When these thinges shalbe Called in question the witnes shalbe produced.[33]

Allowing for the exaggerations of an enemy, these charges of Baines have the ring of authorship of the man who created *The Jew of Malta*. The Prologue to that play is spoken by Machiavelli, who says, among other things:

> I am Machevill,
> And weight not men, and therefore not mens words . . .
> I count Religion but a childish Toy,
> And hold there is no sinne but Ignorance.

Barabas has his own opinions about Christians, which seem to differ little from Marlowe's:

> Rather had I a Jew be hated thus,
> Then pittied in a Christian poverty:
> For I can see no fruits in all their faith,
> But malice, falshood, and excessive pride . . .
> They say we are a scatter'd Nation:
> I cannot tell, but we have scrambled up
> More wealth by farre then those that brag of faith . . .
> I,* wealthier farre then any Christian.

* Aye

I must confesse we come not to be Kings:
That's not our fault: Alas, our number's few,
And Crownes come either by succession,
Or urg'd by force; and nothing violent,
Oft have I heard tell, can be permanent.
Give us a peacefull rule, make Christians Kings,
That thirst so much for Principality.
I have no charge, nor many children,
But one sole Daughter, whom I hold as deare
As Agamemnon did his Iphigen:
And all I have is hers.

(ll. 152-77)

[It is to be noted that despite sentimental perversions of *The Merchant of Venice*, Shylock nowhere in the play speaks with this kind of affection of Jessica.]

This soliloquy clearly shows that Marlowe's sympathies are with the Jew. Moreover, there is no Christian in the play who is in any way admirable; by and large the Christians are represented throughout as greedy and treacherous.

At the beginning of the work the envoys of the Turkish Emperor arrive at Malta to collect tribute long overdue. They agree to grant the Governor one month in which to raise the money. He at once summons all the Jews in town to him:

GOVERNOR. Hebrewes now come neare.
From the Emperour of Turkey is arriv'd
Great Selim-Calymath, his Highnesse sonne,
To levie of us ten yeares tribute past;
Now then here know that it concerneth us.
BARABAS. Then good my Lord, to keepe your quiet still,
Your Lordship shall doe well to let them have it.

The Governor informs Barabas that the Jews must contribute the entire sum due:

GOVERNOR. For through our sufferance of your hateful lives,
Who stand accursed in the sight of heaven,
These taxes and afflictions are befal'ne,
And therefore thus we have determined;
Reade there the Articles of our decrees.
READER. First, the tribute mony of the Turkes shall all be levyed

amongst the Jewes, and each of them to pay one Halfe of his estate.

BAR.   How, halfe his estate? I hope you meane not mine.

GOV.   Read on.

READ.   Secondly, hee that denies to pay, shal straight become a Christian.

BAR.   How, a Christian? Hum, what's here to doe?

READ.   Lastly, he that denies this, shall absolutely lose all he has. . . .

Three other Jews present are prepared to surrender half their fortune; Barabas upbraids them for their cowardice.

GOV.   Why Barabas wilt thou be christned?

BAR.   No, Governour, I will be no convertite. . . .

GOV.   Sir, halfe is the penalty of our decree,
Either pay that, or we will seize on all.

BAR.   *Corpo di deo*; stay, you shall have halfe,
Let me be us'd but as my brethern are.

GOV.   No, Jew, thou hast denied the Articles,
And now it cannot be recall'd.

BAR.   Will you then steale my goods?
Is theft the ground of your Religion?

(ll. 268-328)

This sounds as though it came from the brain of the man against whom Baines was to lodge his complaint. When Barabas protests against being reduced to beggary, he is told that the fault is with his "inherent sinne" in being a Jew; to which he replies:

What? bring you Scripture to confirm your wrongs?
Preach me not out of my possessions.
Some Jewes are wicked, as all Christians are.

(ll. 343-6)

The Christians continue to be unjust and hypocritical. Barabas suggests that since they have taken everything he owns, they might as well take his life too; to this the Governor answers smugly:

No, Barabas, to staine our hands with blood
Is far from us and our profession.

(ll. 377-8)

Barabas despises his fellow-Jews for preaching patience, and says of them, like a good Marlovian hero:

> See the simplicitie of these base slaves,
> Who for the villaines have no wit themselves,
> Thinke me to be a senseless lumpe of clay
> That will with every water wash to dirt.
> No, Barabas is borne to better chance,
> And fram'd of finer mold then common men.
>
> (ll. 447-53)

The author's bias against Christians continues. Barabas' house is converted to a nunnery; in pursuance of his revenge, he tells his daughter that she must ask to be received as a nun,

> for Religion
> Hides many mischiefes from suspition.
>
> (ll. 519-20)

Mathias, in love with Barabas' daughter, hearing that she is to become a nun, cries:

> Tut, she were fitter for a tale of love
> Then to be tired out with Orizons:
> And better would she farre become a bed
> Embraced in a friendly lovers armes
> Then rise at midnight to a solemne masse.
>
> (ll. 611-15)

The Governor, being offered help against the Turks by a shipload of Spaniards, decides to betray his promise to the Turks and to keep the huge fortune which he seized from the Jews presumably only as tribute-money owing to the Ottoman.

Lodowicke, the Governor's son, falls in love with Barabas' daughter too, and approaches the Jew:

LOD. Barabas, thou know'st I am the Governors sonne.
BAR. I wud you were his father too, Sir, that's all the harm I wish you.* The slave looks like a hogs cheek new sindg'd.
LOD. Whither walk'st thou, Barabas?

* His next remark is obviously an aside.

BAR.   No further. 'Tis a custom held with us,
    That when we speake with Gentiles like to you,
    We turne into the Ayre to purge ourselves.

Lodowicke tries to purchase the favors of his daughter from Barabas; the Jew pretends that he will hand her over as a gift, and explains with withering sarcasm:

          Good Sir,
    Your father has deserv'd it at my hands,
    Who of meere charity and Christian ruth,
    To bring me to religious purity . . .
    Against my will, and whether I would or no,
    Seiz'd all I had, and thrust me out a doores.

                      (ll. 801-39)

Presently Ithimore, the Turkish slave, asks a question typically Marlovian in its juvenility:

    Have not the Nuns fine sport with the Fryars now and then?
                      (l. 1255)

That the sally was not intended as the product of a bigoted Turk is
soon made evident. The daughter dies, a Christian, crying:

          ah gentle Fryar,
    Convert my father that he may be sav'd,
    And witnesse that I dye a Christian. (*Dies.*)
2. FRY.   I,* and a Virgin too; that grieves me most.

                      (ll. 1494-7)

Because of the many crimes he has been committing in revenge of
the wrongs done him, Barabas is approached by "two religious Cater-
pillars," the Friar (quoted above) and a rival friar. It does not take
much to make enemies of these co-religionists. Barabas pretends to
them that there are great sums coming to him from his merchandise
at sea:

BAR.   All this I'le give to some religious house
    So I may be baptiz'd and live therein.
1.   Oh good Barabas, come to our house.

* Aye

2.   Oh no, good Barabas, come to our house.
      And Barabas, you know—
BAR.   I know that I have highly sinn'd.
      You shall convert me. You shall have all my wealth.
1.   Oh Barabas, their Lawes are strict.
BAR.   I know they are, and I will be with you.
1.   They weare no shirts, and they goe bare-foot too.
BAR.   Then 'tis not for me; and I am resolv'd
      You shall confesse me, and have all my goods.
1.   Good Barabas, come to me.
BAR.   You see I answer him, and yet he stayes;
      Bid him away, and goe you home with me.
2.   I'le be with you to night.
BAR.   Come to my house at one a clocke this night.
1.   You heare your answer, and you may be gone.
2.   Why, goe get you away.
1.   I will not goe for thee.
2.   Not? Then I'le make thee, rogue.
1.   How, dost call me rogue?   (*Fight.*)

                                    (ll. 1584-1605)

In the midst of his final villainies, Barabas seems to be giving Marlowe's point of view when he explains:

    And he from whom my most advantage comes,
    Shall be my friend.
    This is the life we Jewes are us'd to lead;
    And reason too, for Christians doe the like.

                                    (ll. 2215-18)

Shylock has little in common with Barabas. But it must be sufficiently clear that Shakespeare's greatest predecessor was no Jew-hater; contempt was an emotion he kept for his Christian characters. Against that contempt and his portraiture of Christians as knaves and traitors nearly all, his sympathies were with his Jew, despite the monstrosity of Barabas' revenge. It is certainly preposterous to see Barabas either as a "buffoon" [34] or as merely "a malevolent Jewish usurer," [35] as he is always being described. On the contrary, with all his excesses and also because of his excesses, he was a typical Marlovian hero, the kind of superman his author admired. In a manner altogether his own, Marlowe is additional proof that hatred for the Jews was by no means universal among the Elizabethan writers.

The truth would seem to be, then, that some of Shakespeare's fellow-authors were bigots, some were not. To complete the picture, let us look at two works of his contemporaries outside the drama.

Thomas Nashe in all his writings might very well be singled out as possibly as typical an Elizabethan popular scribbler as one could find. He has verve, dash, boisterousness to a degree, and, like so many Elizabethans, is capable equally of both extremes of deliberate coarseness and romantic charm. But the level of his understanding is never superior to the general run of his contemporaries; he is as good as any of them, and no better. Nashe's *The Unfortunate Traveller* (1594) is often cited as one of the earliest prototypes of the novel; it contains the account of a long escapade among the Jews of Rome. Its assumptions are sufficiently bigoted; but for the most part Nashe seems less interested in being malicious against the Jews than in using the two whom he introduces in a preposterously unreal narrative, merely to add to the madcap tone of the adventure. Even the revolting extravagance of the details of Zadoch's execution is more the product of a heady misplaced sense of humor than of satire at the victim's expense. The tone of the whole episode is, in short, just what might have been expected of a racy, popular Elizabethan writer with no sense of proportion. And what is of moment to observe is that that tone is totally alien to the tone of *The Merchant of Venice*, which was to appear before the public only a couple of years later. Shakespeare and Nashe were contemporaries, but this episode from *The Unfortunate Traveller* and *The Merchant of Venice*, when placed side by side, could have been separated by centuries. Nothing bespeaks more eloquently the fact that Shakespeare was more than just an Elizabethan: he was Shakespeare.

Nashe's hero, Jack Wilton, has been in search of Diamante, a courtesan of whom he has become enamored:

> Tracing uppe and downe the Cittie to seeke my Curtizan till the Evening began to grow verie well in age, it thus fortuned: the Element, as if it had drunke too much in the afternoone, powrde downe so profoundly, that I was forst to creep like one afraid of the watch close under the pentises, where the cellar doore of a Jewes house called Zadoch (over which in my direct way I did passe) being unbard on the in-side, over head and eares I fell into

it. . . . I cast up myne eyes to see under what Continent I was: and loe, (O destenie,) I saw my Curtizane kissing very lovingly with a prentise. . . .

I was even gathering winde to come uppon her with a full blast of contumelie, when the Jewe (awakde with the noyse of my fall) came hastely busteling downe the staires, and, raysing his other tenaunts, attached both the Curtizane and me for breaking his house, and conspiring with his prentise to rob him.

It was then the law in Rome that if anie man had a fellon falne into his hands . . . by breaking into his house, . . . he might chuse whether he would make him his bond-man, or hang him. Zadoch, (as all Jewes are covetous) . . . went to one Doctor Zacharie, the Popes Phisition, that was a Jew and his Countrey-man likewise, and told him he had the finest bargaine for him that might be. It is not concealed from me (saith he) that the time of your accustomed yearely Anatomie is at hand. . . . The infection is great, and hardly will you get a sound body to deal upon. . . . I have a yong man at home falne to me for my bond-man, of the age of eighteene . . . ; you shall have him for five hundred crownes. Let me see him, quoth Doctor Zacharie. . . . Home he sent for me; pinniond and shackeld I was transported alongst the streete; where passing under Julianaes, the Marques of Mantuaes wives window, that was a lustie Bona Roba, one of the Popes con-cubines, as shee had her casement halfe open, shee lookt out and spide me. At the first sight she was enamoured with my age and beardles face . . . : after me she sent to know what I was, wherein I had offended, and whether I was going? My conducts* resolved them all. Shee having received this answer, with a lustfull colla-chrimation lamenting my Jewish Premunire, that bodie and goods I should light into the hands of such a cursed generation, invented the means of my release.

But first Ile tell you what betided mee after I was brought to Doctor Zacharies. The purblind Doctor put on his spectacles and lookt upon me: and when he had throughly viewd my face, he caused me to be stript naked, to feele and grope whether each lim wer sound & my skin not infected. Then he pierst my arme to see how my blood ran: which assayes and searchings ended, he gave Zadoch his full price and sent him away; then lockt me up in a darke chamber till the day of anatomie. . . .

Miserable is that Mouse that lives in a Phisitions house. . . . Not the verie crums that fall from his table, but Zacharie sweepes together, and of them moulds up a Manna. Of the ashie parings

* conductors

of his bread, he would make conserve of chippings. Out of bones, after the meate was eaten off, hee would alchumize an oyle, that hee sold for a shilling a dram. His snot and spittle a hundred times hee hath put over to his Apothecarie for snow water. Anie spider hee would temper to perfect Mithridate. . . . The licour out of his shooes hee would wring to make a sacred Balsamum against barrennes.

. . . Juliana . . . adventured to send a messenger to Doctor Zachary in hir name, verie boldly to beg mee of him, and if she might not beg me, to buy me. . . . Zacharie Jewishly and churlishlie denied both her sutes. . . . The Pope (I know not whether at her entreatie or no) within two daies after fell sick: Doctor Zacharie was sent for . . . who . . . gave him a gentle comfortive for the stomack. . . . He doubted not but he would be forthwith well. Who should receive thys milde phisicke of him but the concubine Juliana, his utter enemie? she, being not unprovided of strong poyson at that instant, in the Popes outward chamber so mingled it, that when his Grand-sublimity-taster came to relish it, he sunke downe stark dead on the pavement. Herewith the Pope cald Juliana, and askt her what strong concocted broth she had brought him. She kneeled downe on her knees, & said it was such as Zacharie the Jew had delivered her with hys owne hands. . . . The Pope . . . would have had Zacharie and all the Jewes in Rome put to death, but she hung about his knees, and with Crocodile tears desired him the sentence might be lenefied, and they be all but banisht at the most. For Doctor Zacharie, quoth she, . . . hath much Arte, and manie sovereigne simples, oyles . . . in his closet and house that may stand your Mightines in stead, I begge all his goods onely for your Beatitudes preservation and good. This request at the first was sealed with a kisse, and the Popes edict without delaye proclaimed throughout Rome, namely, that all foreskinne clippers, whether male or female . . . should depart and avoid upon pain of hanging, within twentie daies after the date thereof.

Juliana . . . sent her servants to extend upon Zacharies territories, his goods, his mooveables, his chattels, and his servants. . . . Into my chamber they rusht, . . . did . . . seaze upon me, in my cloke they muffeld me, that no man might know me, nor I see which way I was carried. The first ground I toucht after I was out of Zacharyes house was the Countesse Julianas chamber. . . .

Let me dilate a little what Zadoch did with my curtizan, after he sold me to Zacharie. . . . Hee was a Jew, and intrested her like a Jew. Under shadow of enforcing her to tell how much money she had of his prentice so to be trayned to his cellar, hee stript her, and scourged her from top to toe tantara. Day by day he digested his meate with leading her the measures. A diamond Delphinicall drie leachour it was. . . . He had the right agilitie of the lash, there were none of them [i.e., flagelators] could make the corde come aloft with a twange halfe like him.

Marke the ending, marke the ending. The tribe of Juda is adjudged from Rome to bee trudging, they may no longer bee lodged ther. . . . Zacharie came running to Zadochs in sacke cloth and ashes presently after his goods were confiscated, and tolde him how he was served, and what decree was comming out against them all. . . . Zadoch . . . was readie to burst out of his skin . . . ; his eies glared and burnt blew like brimstone and *aqua vitae* set on fire in an egshell, his verie nose lightned glow-wormes, his teeth crasht and grated together. . . . He swore, he curst, and saide, these be they that worship that crucifide God of Nazareth, heres the fruits of their new found Gospell; sulphur and gunpouder carry them all quick to Gehenna. I would spend my soule willingly, to have that triple headed Pope with all his sin-absolved whores and oilegreased priests borne with a blacke *sanctus* on the divells backes in procession to the pit of perdition. . . . If I must be banisht, if those heathen dogs will needs rob me of my goods, I will poyson their springs & conduit heades, whence they receive al their water . . . ; Ile tice all the young children into my house that I can get, and cutting their throates barrell them up in poudring beefe tubbes, and so send them to victuall the Popes gallies. . . .

Zadoch, Zadoch, sayd Doctor Zachery (cutting him off), thou threatnest the aire, whilest we perish here on earth. It is the countesse Juliana, the Marques of Mantuas wife, and no other, that hath complotted our confusion. Aske not how, but insist in my wordes, and assist in revenge.

As how, as how? sayde Zadoch. . . .

[Zachary answered:] Canst thou provide me ere a bond-maide, indued with singular & divine qualified beautie, whom as a present from our synagogue thou mayst commend unto her, desiring her to be good and gracious unto us?

I have, I am for you, quoth Zadoch: Diamante, come forth. . . . How thinke you, master Doctor, will she not serve the turne?

She will, sayde Zacharie; and therefore Ile tell you what charge I would have committed to her. . . . Maide (if thou beest a maide), come hether to me; thou must be sent to the countesse of Mantuaes about a small peece of service, whereby, being now a bond woman, thou shalt purchase freedome and gaine a large dowrie. . . . The pope is farre out of liking with the countesse of Mantua, his concubine, and hath put his trust in me, his phisition, to have her quietly and charitably made away. . . . Thou, if thou beest placd with her as her waiting maid or cup-bearer, maist temper poison with her broth, her meate, her drinke, her oyles, her sirrupes, and never bee bewraid. I will not saie whether the pope hath heard of thee, and thou mayst come to bee his lemman in her place. . . . What, hast thou the heart to go thorough with it or no? Diamante, deliberating wyth her selfe in what hellish servitude she lived with the Jew, & that shee had no likelyhood to be releast of it . . . , resigned her selfe over wholly to be disposed and emploid as seemed best unto them. . . . Presented she was by Zadoch, hir master, to the countesse. . . .

Juliana, liking well the pretie round face of my black browd Diamante, gave the Jew a better countenance than otherwise she would have done, and told him for her owne part she was but a private woman, and could promise nothing confidently of his holines: . . . but what laie in her, either to pacifie or perswade him, they should bee sure off. . . .

His backe turnd, she askt Diamante . . . how shee fell into the hands of that Jew? She answered that she was a Magnificos daughter of Venice, stolne when she was young from her friends, and sold to this Jew for a bond-woman, who (quoth she) hath usde me so jewishly and tyrannously, that for ever I must celebrate the memorie of this daie, wherein I am delivered from his jurisdiction. . . . Madam, your life is sought by these Jews that sue to you. Blush not, nor be troubled in your minde, for with warning I shall arme you against all their intentions. Thus and thus (quoth she) said Doctor Zachery unto me, this poyson he delivered me. . . .

Juliana said little, but . . . vowed though she were her bond-woman to be a mother unto her. The poison she tooke of her, and set it up charely on a shelfe in her closet, thinking . . . when I was consumed and worne to the bones through her abuse, she would give me but a dram too much, and pop mee into a privie. So shee had served some of her paramours ere that. . . .

The foresayd good wife Countesse comes to me; she is no longer a judge but a client. Howe she came, in what manner of attyre, with what immodest and uncomely wordes she courted me, if I should take upon me to inlarge, all modest eares would abhorre me. Some inconvenience she brought me too by her harlot-like behavior, of which inough I can never repent me. . . .

Zacharie, after he had furnisht the wench with the poyson, and given her instructions to goe to the devill, durst not staie one houre for feare of disclosing, but fled to the duke of Burbon, that after sackt Rome. . . . Zadoch was left behind for the hangman. According to his oath, he provided balls of wild fire in a readinesse, and laid traines of gunpouder in a hundred severall places of the citie to blow it up. . . . To the straightest prison in Rome he was dragged, where from top to toe he was clogd with fetters and manacles. Juliana informed the pope of Zacharies and his practise:* Zachary was sought for, but *Non est inventus,*† he was packing long before. Commandement was given, that Zadoch, whom they had under hand and seale of lock and key, should be executed with al the firy torments that could be found out.

Ile make short worke, for I am sure I have wearyed all my readers. To the execution place was he brought, where first and formost he was stript, then on a sharp yron stake fastened in ye ground he had his fundament pitcht, which stake ran up along into the bodie like a spit; under his arme-holes two of lyke sort; a great bon-fire they made round about him, wherewith his flesh roasted, not burned: and ever as with the heate his skinne blistred, the fire was drawen aside, and they basted him with a mixture of Aqua fortis, allum water, and Mercury sublimatum, which smarted to the very soul of him, and searcht him to the marrowe. Then dyd they scourge his backe partes so blistred and basted, with burning whips of red hot wier: his head they nointed over with pitch and tar, and so inflamed it. To his privie members they tied streaming fireworkes: the skinne from the crest of the shoulder, as also from his elbowes, his huckle bones, his knees, his anckles, they pluckt and gnawed off with sparkling pincers: his breast and his belly with seale skins they grated over, which as fast as they grated and rawed, one stood over & laved with smiths syndry water & Aqua vitae: his nailes they halfe raised up, and then under-propt them with sharp prickes, like a Tailers shop window halfe open on a holy daie: every one of his fingers they rent up to the wrist: his toes they brake off by the rootes, and let them still hang by a little skinne. In conclusion, they had a small oyle fire, such as men blow light bubbles of glasse with, and beginning at his feete, they let him lingringly burne up lim by lim, till his heart was consumed, and then he died. Triumph, women, this was the end of the whipping Jew, contrived by a woman, in revenge of two women, her selfe and her maide.

[If only this book had been written by Shakespeare instead of by Nashe! What a lively time the "learned periodicals" would, by this time, have had with it! The year of its publication, 1594, was the year of the execution of Lopez. Given Shakespeare as the author, we can safely predict the "findings" of scholarship:

* plot.
† He didn't turn up.

V. V. Pitmann, Dean of British Shakespearean critics, concludes that Shakespeare, certainly one of the spectators at the Lopez execution, wrote *The Unfortunate Traveller* as a result of that experience. Pitmann's most distinguished former pupil and heir-presumptive to the Deanship, L. Calais Truman, respectfully now points out that there is an entry in the Stationer's Register for 1593 as follows: "xvij^mo die Septembris. John Wolf/Entred for his Copie vnder the andes [i.e., the hands] of the Bishop [i.e., Arch-bishop] of Canterburie and the wardens, A booke intituled the vnfor-tunate travellour. . . . vj^d." Sherry Ffaulkes-Jones, devoted disci-ple of L. Calais Truman, in an article which wins him a pro-fessorship at a large mid-Western university, elaborates upon his master's discovery, and further proves that therefore *The Merchant of Venice* must have been composed in 1593 too, both works with the *impending* execution of Lopez in mind. L. Calais Truman, not to be instructed by a disciple, demonstrates, by a subtle specu-lation on the transmission of the original manuscript, that Pitmann was essentially right, after all: the entry in the Stationer's Register is a manifest forgery, and the date on the title-page of the first edition is a deliberate falsification (ascribable to the printer's connection with the fortunes of Essex) and should read 1595. Ffaulkes-Jones hastens to stand corrected, and moves up the date for both *The Unfortunate Traveller* and *The Merchant of Venice* to that year, both works now clearly and safely allied to the Lopez execution. (Result: a better offer from another university in the East.)

In the meantime Prof. Granrieeb, of Punjabi University, has blandly observed that, after all, the account of Zadoch's execution makes but one paragraph in *The Unfortunate Traveller*. To this L. Calais Truman responds with a new theory: said paragraph is the only one in the entire book from the pen of Shakespeare; what Shake-speare has done here is simply to discard the rest of his book and appropriate an older work of an anonymous scribbler. This idea is welcome to Truman's American colleague, F. F. Lostt, respected chief of his own school of Shakespearean criticism, for it is only new evidence for what he has always maintained: that Shakespeare was neither more nor less than a successful writer of pot-boilers.

By this juncture Ruthven Factualis has already demonstrated that the received accounts of the Lopez execution differ in every detail from the paragraph in question. This provokes Ffaulkes-Jones to go back to his original idea that both this book and *The Merchant of Venice* were influenced by the *impending* execution of Lopez. Icily, L. Calais Truman and others of his school show that the received accounts were all forgeries (connected with the fortunes of Essex) and in no way to be trusted, considering that in the paragraph of *The Unfortunate Traveller* we have Shakespeare's thinly disguised eye-witness account of the actual execution.

All this while other hands are busy in other ways.

The eminent psychoanalyst, Dr. Algernon Smith, sees in our paragraph the expression of Shakespeare's unconscious sadism; for years, before the composition of *The Unfortunate Traveller*, Shakespeare had been smoldering with suppressed resentment against his wife's nagging (his reason for leaving Stratford, of course); at last, in the celebrated paragraph, he found release by causing her to figure as Zadoch (who, note well, is addicted to flagellation); Zadoch-Anne Hathaway has whipped (earlier in the passage) Diamante-Shakespeare. Moreover, this self-identification with the Courtesan opens endless vistas on Shakespeare's sexual nature (see, particularly, the "master-mistress" Sonnet).

Dr. Frederick Rich, Smith's learned colleague, further points out that the author has identified Anne Hathaway with a Jew, i.e., a nonbeliever. Why? Because his marriage having patently been a shotgun one, Shakespeare felt that it was not a "marriage of true minds"—that is, it was not a marriage at all. (See the "second best bed" of Shakespeare's will.)

But since it was Thomas Nashe, not Shakespeare, who wrote *The Unfortunate Traveller*, the author has been spared all this.

This divigation may yet be justified as a service to future scholars. Some day writers of "learned articles" on Shakespeare may conceivably run out of argumentative materials. Should that halcyon day ever arrive, perhaps our footnote may open new perspectives. First prove Shakespeare the author, etc., etc.]

Viewed calmly, the excessively lively episode which has been quoted from *The Unfortunate Traveller* is hardly more flattering to the Pope, Juliana, or Diamante than to the two Jews. Indeed, if one allowed one's humanitarianism to distort Nashe's purposes in the same fashion in which some commentators have distorted Shakespeare's, it would be possible to make a specious argument tending to prove that the account of Zadoch's execution was meant as an indictment of the savage inhumanity of Christians. That would be as false as it would be absurd. Nashe obviously relished writing the account of the execution. But in their setting in the narrative Zadoch and Zachary are as much sinned against as sinning, for no one is admirable. Even the miserliness of Zachary is attributed more to his profession than to his race, as is enforced by the aphorism, "Miserable is that mouse that lives in a physician's house."

The bigotry against Jews exhibited in the story is a mirror of a bigotry that was certainly fashionable in some quarters. But it is also present rather as part of the machinery of a harum-scarum narrative than as a pointed attack on an exiled race. Nothing could be more obvious than the fact that in Nashe's intention Zadoch and Zachary were both comic figures.

What is germane to our inquiry is the question: if Zadoch and Zachary are comic figures, how is it possible to think of Shylock, as has so often been maintained, as a comic figure too? The Jews being exotic to England, there must have been many Englishmen whose attitude toward them was not fixed either in bigotry or decent respect, but wavered between the two extremes. To see how this was eminently possible, let us go to a delightful book which was published more than a dozen years after *The Merchant of Venice*, in 1611, when Shakespeare was nearing the end of his career.

The world has never had a livelier and more insatiably curious traveler than Thomas Coryat. Bibliomaniacs have long cherished his *Coryat's Crudities* (1611), subtitled as "Hastily gobled up in five Moneths travells in France, Savoy, Italy, Rhetia commonly called the Grisons country, Helvetia alias Switzerland, some parts of high Germany and the Netherlands; Newly digested in the hungry aire of Odcombe in the County of Somerset, and now dispersed to the nourishment of the travelling Members of this Kingdome."

Let the insatiable Tom induct you into his book:

> I was imbarked at Dover, about tenne of the clocke in the morning, the fourteenth of may, being Saturday and Whitsun-eve, Anno 1608, and arrived in Calais . . . about five of the clocke in the afternoone, after I had varnished the exterior parts of the ship with the excrementall ebullitions of my tumultuous stomach, as desiring to satiate the gormandizing paunches of the hungry Had-

docks . . . with that wherewith I had superfluously stuffed my selfe at land, having made my rumbling belly their capacious aum-brie.*

From the beginning of his peregrinations nothing escapes his eager eyes. Nothing is too slight to merit recording:

> The fairest cage of birds that I saw in al France, was at the signe of the Ave Maria in Amiens, the workmanship whereof was very curious with gilt wyers. In the same were four Turtle Doves, and many gold Finches, with other birds which are such as our hemp-seede birds in England. . . .
>
> This also I observed in Clermont, in the middest of a streete there was erected a gibbet with the picture of a certaine fellow called Antony Peel, who was painted hanging on a gallowes in the same picture. . . . The reason why his picture was set forth in that manner, was this: That as his picture was there hanged, so should he also if he might be apprehended.

He is particularly avid to see everything connected with the Christian religion: churches, monasteries, nunneries, paintings; and he is never without his comment. On the outskirts of Paris he observes "seven faire Pillars of free stone erected by an equall distance from each other" in honor of St. Denis. The reason for these memorials to the saint is

> that when he walked betwixt Paris (where he was beheaded for the Gospell sake) and a pretty towne four miles from it, which is now called by his name, he rested seven times by the way with his head in his hand, before he came to the towne. A miracle too greate to be true.

In Paris

> many of the streetes are the durtiest, and so consequently the most stinking of all that ever I saw in any citie of my life. . . .

The "French guides otherwise called Postilians" have a diabolical custom:

> Diabolical it may be well called: for whensoever their horses doe a little anger them, they wil say in their fury Allons diable, that is,

* a place for keeping victuals

Go thou divell. Also if they happen to be angry with a stranger upon the way . . . they will say to him le diable t' emporte, that is, The divell take thee. This I know by mine owne experience.

At the Sign of the Three Kings, in Lyons, he met with a French nobleman who had with him "two Turkes that he brought with him out of Turkey." One of these

was a blacke Moore, who was his jester; a mad conceited * fellow, and very merry. He wore no hat at all eyther in his journey . . . or when he rested in any towne, because his naturall haire was exceeding thicke and curled, was so prettily elevated in heigth that it served him alwaies instead of a hat.

Though the temptation is great to quote further from this delectable book, we trust both to have raised a desire to know it more intimately and to have indicated something of Tom's temperament. Let us return to our mutton.

It is when Coryat reaches Italy that he makes his earliest references to the Jews. The first of these would indicate that the fate of Lopez in London was nothing new. Tom records that in Mantua

died the Emperour Carolus Calvus of a fluxe of the belly, or rather with poison (as some thinke) that was given him by a certaine Jewish Physitian called Zedechias, whom he loved very intirely, in the yeare of our Lord 872.

Presently:

The first Jewes that I saw in all Italy were in Padua, where there is a great multitude of them.

Now, Tom is always ready to declare his reactions to what he sees. Considering the universal assumption of scholars that Elizabethan Englishmen (Coryat was born around 1577) were perforce anti-Semitic (and hence, Shakespeare must have, to a degree, been so too), Coryat's failure to make any comment upon either of these observations of his, is surely noteworthy. [Any reader of the *Crudities* can hardly feel that the reference to Zedechias is "dragged in." Certainly it can hardly be thought of as owing to the Lopez

* with a lively imagination

case which had occurred seventeen years before Coryat's book was published (1611).]

Not that Coryat was interested in being generous toward the Jews —as his Venetian experience will shortly demonstrate—but that he was capable of being not particularly rancorous against them. If it was true of him, it must have been true of plenty of other intelligent Englishmen.

At Padua Coryat makes the acquaintance of Paulo Aemylio Musto, "a most excellent Scholler for the three principall languages, Hebrew, Greeke, and Latin." This gentleman

> studied the Hebrew tongue very diligently to the end to discourse with the learned Rabbins of the Jewes . . . and he doth often so earnestly dispute with them, that he hath converted some of them to Christianity, as he himselfe told me.

After Coryat has gone off to Venice, Musto sends him some complimentary verses in Greek with this "merry inscription":

> To the English Gentleman that converteth Jewes, & c., in Venice.

Concerning which, Coryat remarks:

> The history of which my conversion of the Jewes (being rather a disputation with them, then a conversion of them, which I much both desired and endeavoured) I will relate in my observations of Venice.[36]

Venice was probably the prime source of anticipated pleasure with Coryat. [Such is the implication of the "charitable Friend," whose exposition of "The Character of the Famous Odcombian, or rather Polyptopian Thomas the Coryate Traveller, and Gentleman Author of these Quinque-mestriall Crudities," accompanies the book. Coryat, we are told, was "set a going for Venice the fourteenth of May, anno 1608 . . ."[37] This "charitable Friend" was none other than Ben Jonson.] And it is Coryat's experience in that city which makes his book most pertinent to our present study.

He heads this, the longest section of the volume,

> My Observations of the most glorious, peerelesse, and mayden
> Citie of Venice: I call it mayden, because it was never conquered.

The city is a feast to him. He reflects upon the rewards showered
upon Jacobus Sannazarius by the Venetian Senate:

> I would to God my Poeticall friend Mr. Benjamin Johnson were
> so well rewarded for his Poems here in England, seeing he hath
> made many as good verses (in my opinion) as these of Sanna-
> zarius.

He gives a history of the town; describes the houses and their "flat
roofes," the walks between palaces and the water; the terraces;
the sumptuous palaces; the Rialto Bridge; the shops; the "thirteen
ferries, which they commonly call Traghetti"; the gondolas, which
are minutely described. But the boatmen under the Rialto bridge

> are the most vicious and licentious varlets about all the City. For if
> a stranger entereth into one of their Gondolas, and doth not pres-
> ently* tell them whither he will goe, they will incontinently carry
> him of their owne accord to a religious house† forsooth, where his
> plumes shall be well pulled before he commeth forth againe. . . .
> If the passenger commandeth them to carry him to any place where
> his serious and urgent businesse lies, . . . these impious miscre-
> ants will either strive to carry him away, maugre his hart, to some
> irreligious place whether he would not goe, or at the least tempt
> him with their diabolicall perswasions.

After descriptions of the waterways, St. Mark's and its grand piazza,
various churches, libraries, statues, pillars, palaces, walks, paintings,
the town prison, the great Arsenal ("the eighth miracle of the
world"), the ceremony of the Wedding of the Sea, Coryat pauses
to remark:

> I saw but one horse in all Venice during the space of six weekes
> that I made my aboade there, and that was a little bay nagge feed-
> ing in this Church-yard of St. John and Paul, whereat I did not a
> little wonder, because I could not devise what they should doe with
> a horse in such a City where they have no use for him. . . . The

* immediately
† i.e., a bordello

Venetians do use Gondolaes in their streets in steede of horses, I meane their liquid streets, that is, their pleasant channels. So that I now finde by mine owne experience that the speeches of a certaine English Gentleman (with whom I once discoursed before my travels) a man that much vaunted of his observations in Italy, are utterly false. For when I asked him what principall things he observed in Venice, he answered me that he noted but little of the city. Because he rode through it in post. A fiction as grosse and palpable as ever was coyned.

It is not at all malapropos to reflect that Coryat had been as little prepared for the sight of Venetian "streets" as for the sight of Jews. Of them he could have known nothing in England, and whatever thoughts he may have entertained concerning them must have been dependent upon accounts as authentic as that of the acquaintance who had dashed through Venice's canals by horse.

And now, probably for the first time in his life, he meets Jews at close quarters. The passage is not only interesting in itself but also so revealing that we give it *in toto:*

> I was at a place where the whole fraternity of the Jews dwelleth together, which is called the Ghetto, being an Iland: for it is inclosed round about with water. It is thought there are of them in all betwixt five and sixe thousand. They are distinguished and discerned from the Christians by their habites on their heads; for some of them doe weare hats and those redde, onely those Jewes that are borne in the Westerne parts of the world, as in Italy, & c. but the easterne Jewes being otherwise called the Levantine Jewes, which are borne in Hierusalem, Alexandria, Constantinople, & c. weare Turbents upon their heads as the Turkes do: but the difference is this: the Turkes weare white, the Jewes yellow. By that word Turbent I understand a rowle of fine linnen wrapped together upon their heads, which serveth them in stead of hats, whereof many have bin often worne by the Turkes in London. They have divers Synagogues in their Ghetto, at the least seven, where all of them, both men, women and children doe meete together upon their Sabboth, which is Saturday, to the end to doe their devotion, and serve God in their kinde, each company having a several Synagogue. In the midst of the Synagogue they have a round seat made of Wainscot, having eight open spaces therein, at two whereof which are at the sides, they enter into the seate as by dores. The Levite that readeth the law to them, hath before him at the time of

divine service an exceeding long piece of parchment, rowled up upon two woodden handles: in which is written the whole summe and contents of Moyses law in Hebrew: that doth he (being discerned from the lay people onely by wearing of a redde cap, whereas the others doe weare redde hats) pronounce before the congregation not by a sober, distinct, and orderly reading, but by an exceeding loud yaling, undecent* roaring, and as it were a beastly bellowing of it forth. And that after such a confused and hudling manner, that I thinke the hearers can very hardly understand him: sometimes he cries out alone, and sometimes againe some others serving as it were his Clerkes hard withoutet† his seate, do roare with him, but so that his voyce (which he straineth so high as if he sung for a wager) drowneth all the rest. Amongst others that are within the roome with him, one is he that cometh purposely thither from his seat, to the end to reade the law, and pronounce some part of it with him, who when he is gone, another riseth from his seat, and commeth thither to supply his roome. This order they keepe from the beginning of the service to the end. One custome I observed amongst them very irreverent and prophane, that none of them, eyther when they enter the Synagogue, or when they sit downe in their places, or when they goe forth againe, doe any reverence or obeysance, answerable to such a place of the worship of God, eyther by uncovering their heads, kneeling, or any other externall gesture, but boldly dash into the roome with their Hebrew bookes in their handes, and presently sit in their places, without any more adoe; every one of them whatsoever he be, man or childe, weareth a kinde of light yellowish vaile, made of Linsie Woolsie (as I take it) over his shoulders, something worse than our courser Holland, which reacheth a little beneath the middle of their backes. They have a great company of candlestickes in each Synagogue made partly of glasse, and partly of brasse and pewter, which hang square about their Synagogue. For in that forme is their Synagogue built: of their candlestickes I told ‡ above sixty in the same Synagogue.

I observed some fewe of those Jewes especially some of the Levantines to bee such goodly and proper men, that then I said to myselfe our English proverbe: To looke like a Jewe (whereby is meant sometimes a weather beaten warp-faced fellow, sometimes a phrenticke and lunaticke person, sometimes one discontented) is not true. For indeed I noted some of them to be most elegant and

* not charming
† just beyond
‡ counted

sweet featured persons, which gave me occasion the more to lament their religion. For if they were Christians, then could I better apply unto them that excellent verse of the Poet, then I can now.

Gratior est pulchro veniens è corpore virtus.*

In the roome wherein they celebrate their divine service, no women sit, but have a loft or gallery proper to themselves only, where I saw many Jewish women, whereof some were as beautiful as ever I saw, and so gorgeous in their apparel, jewels, chaines of gold, and rings adorned with precious stones, that some of our English Countesses do scarce exceede them, having marvailous long traines like Princesses that are borne up by waiting women serving for the same purpose. An argument to prove that many of the Jewes are very rich. One thing they observe in their service which is utterly condemned by our Saviour Christ, Battologia, that is a very tedious babling, and an often repetition of one thing, which cloied mine eares so much that I could not endure them any longer, having heard them at least an houre; for their service is almost three houres long. They are very religious in two things only, and no more, in that they worship no images, and that they keep their sabboth so strictly, that upon that day they wil neither buy nor sell, nor do any secular, prophane, or irreligious exercise, (I would to God our Christians would imitate the Jewes herein) no not so much as dresse their victuals, which is alwaies done the day before, but dedicate and consecrate themselves wholy to the strict worship of God. Their circumcision they observe as duely as they did any time betwixt Abraham (in whose time it was first instituted) and the incarnation of Christ. For they use to circumcise every male childe when he is eight dayes old, with a stony knife. But I had not the opportunitie to see it. Likewise they keepe many of those ancient feastes that were instituted by Moyses. Amongst the rest the feast of tabernacles is very ceremoniously observed by them. From swines flesh they abstaine as their ancient forefathers were wont to doe, in which the Turkes do imitate them at this day. Truely it is a most lamentable case for a Christian to consider the damnable estate of these miserable Jewes, in that they reject the true Messias and Saviour of their soules, hoping to be saved rather by the observation of those Mosaicall ceremonies, (the date whereof was fully expired at Christ's incarnation) then by the merits of the Saviour of the world, without whom all mankind shall perish. And as pitifull it is to see that fewe of them living in Italy are converted

* Virtue is more pleasing when stemming from a handsome body.

to the Christian religion. For this I understand is the maine impediment to their conversion: All their goodes are confiscated as soone as they embrace Christianity: and this I heard is the reason, because whereas many of them doe raise their fortunes by usury, in so much that they doe not only sheare, but also flea many a poore Christians estate by their griping extortion; it is therefore decreed by the Pope, and other free Princes in whose territories they live, that they shall make a restitution of all their ill gotten goods, and so disclogge their soules and consciences, when they are admitted by holy baptisme into the bosome of Christs Church. Seeing then when their goods are taken from them at their conversion, they are left even naked, and destitute of their meanes of maintenance, there are fewer Jewes converted to Christianity in Italy, than in any country of Christendome. Whereas in Germany, Poland, and other places the Jewes that are converted (which doth often happen, as Emmanuel Tremellius was converted in Germany) do enjoy their estates as they did before.

But now I will make relation of that which I promised in my treatise of Padua, I meane my discourse with the Jewes about their religion. For when as walking in the Court of the Ghetto, I casually met with a certaine learned Jewish Rabbin that spake good Latin, I insinuated my selfe after some fewe termes of complement into conference with him, and asked his opinion of Christ, and why he did not receive him for his Messias; he made me the same answere that the Turke did at Lyons, of whom I have before spoken, that Christ forsooth was a great Prophet, and in that respect as highly to be esteemed as any Prophet amongst the Jewes that ever lived before him; but derogated altogether from his divinitie, and would not acknowledge him for the Messias and Saviour of the world, because he came so contemptibly, and not with that pompe and majesty that beseemed the redeemer of mankind. I replyed that we Christians doe, and will even to the effusion of our vitall bloud confesse him to be the true and onely Messias of the world, seeing he confirmed his Doctrine while hee was here on earth, with such an innumerable multitude of divine miracles, which did most infallibly testifie his divinitie; and that they themselves, who are Christs irreconciliable enemies, could not produce any authority either out of Moyses, the Prophets, or any other autenticke author to strengthen their opinion concerning the temporall kingdome of the Messias, seeing it was foretolde to be spirituall: and told him, that Christ did as a spirituall King reigne over his subjects in conquering their spiritual enemies the flesh, the world, and the divell. Withall I added that the predictions and sacred oracles both of Moyses, and all the holy Prophets of God,

aymed altogether at Christ as their onely mark, in regarde hee was
the full consummation of the law and the Prophets, and I urged a
place of Esay* unto him concerning the name Emanuel, and a vir-
gins conceiving and bearing of a sonne; and at last descended to
the perswasion of him to abandon and renounce his Jewish religion
and to undertake the Christian faith, without the which he should
be eternally damned. He againe replyed that we Christians doe mis-
interpret the Prophets, and very perversly wrest them to our owne
sense, and for his owne part he had confidently resolved to live and
die in his Jewish faith, hoping to be saved by the observations of
Moyses Law. In the end he seemed to be somewhat exasperated
against me, because I sharpely taxed their superstitious ceremonies.
For many of them are such refractary people that they cannot endure to heare any reconciliation to the Church of Christ, in regard
they esteeme him but for a carpenters sonne, and a silly† poore
wretch that once rode upon an Asse, and most unworthy to be
Messias whom they expect to come with most pompous magnificence and imperiall royalty, like a peerelesse Monarch, garded
with many legions of the gallantest Worthies, and most eminent
personages of the whole world, to conquer not onely their old country Judaea and all those opulent and flourishing Kingdomes, which
heretofore belonged to the foure auncient Monarchies (such is
their insupportable pride) but also all the nations generally under
the cope of heaven, and make the King of Guiane, and al other
Princes whatsoever dwelling in the remotest parts of the habitable
world his tributary vassals. Thus hath God justly infatuated their
understandings, and given them the spirit of slumber (as Saint
Paule speaketh out of the Prophet Esay) eyes that they should not
see, and eares that they should not heare unto this day. But to shut
up this narration of my conflict with the Jewish Rabbin, after there
had passed many vehement speeches to and fro betwixt us, it happened that some forty or fifty Jewes more flocked about me, and
some of them beganne very insolently to swagger with me, because
I durst reprehend their religion: Whereupon fearing least they
would have offered me some violence, I withdrewe my selfe by
little and little towards the bridge at the entrance into the Ghetto,
with an intent to flie from them.

[The 1611 title-page of the *Crudities* contains a number of "Emblems" or pictures illustrative of the text. After his encounter in
the Ghetto, Coryat paid an extended but, he tells us, innocent

† innocent
* Isaiah

visit to a courtesan to discover all he could about the operation of her profession in Venice; "I both wished the conversion of the Cortezan that I saw, and did my endevour by perswasive termes to convert her." [38] Emblem F, inspired by both this passage and the one we have quoted on the subject of the gondoliers, shows our hero in a gondola under a window from which a woman is hurling what looks like fruit at him. Emblem G shows him running away from a turbaned, bearded man wielding either a stick or a knife (it is impossible to say which); this picture no doubt refers to Coryat's experience in the Ghetto. The volume itself opens with a series of Couplets by Laurence Whitaker which are intended to explain the Emblems. There are a pair of couplets for Emblem G:

> In vaine here doth Coryate pipe and dispute,
> His wench was, Jewes will not be caught with his flute.
> Or,
> Thy Cortizan clipt thee, ware Tom, I advise thee,
> And fly from the Jewes, lest they circumcise thee.

A second set of verses by Ben Jonson has for Emblem F:

> Religiously here he bids, row from the stewes,
> He will expiate this sinne with converting the Jewes.

and for G:

> And there, while he gives the zealous Bravado,
> A Rabbin confutes him with the Bastinado.[39]

There are also many pages of prefatory commendatory verses, *Panegyricke Verses Upon the Author and His Booke.* Many of them single out the encounter with the courtesan and with the Rabbi as apparently those which impressed Coryat's friends the most. From Robert Phillips':

> Thy danger with the Boore, thy hazard with the Jewes.

From John Strangwayes':

> So that it grew a question whether
> Thy shoes or feete were of more lasting leather.

Which at that time did stand thee in most use,
When as the Jewes would cut off thy prepuce.

From Hugo Holland's ("To Topographicall Typographicall Thomas"): Tom

more prevaild against the 'xcoriate Jewes,
Than Broughton could, or twenty more such Hughs,
And yet but for one petty poore misprision,
He was nigh made one of the Circumcision.

This same friend has another collection of verses in which he says:

Ulysses heard no Syren sing: nor Coryate
The Jew, least his praepuce might prove excoriate.

Robert Richmond's:

The stubborne Jew (if it be true) was by thee catechized

At Venice.
Lionel Cranfield's:

The Author of this worke,
Who saw the French, Dutch, Lombard, Jew, & Turke.

Inigo Jones's opening lines:

Odde is the Combe from whence this Cocke did come,
That crowed in Venice gainst the skinlesse Jewes—

(the first line being a play upon Coryat's birthplace, Odcombe).

Richard Corbet's:

Thou art bred
A terror to all footmen, and all Porters,
And all lay-men that will turne Jewes exhorters.

Peter Alley's:

His dangerous encounter with cruell Jewes.

William Austin finds Coryat's book superior to John Mandeville's book of travels; the latter had nothing to say

> Of jests, mistakings, and misprisions,
> Of pagans, Jewes, and circumcisions.

John Davis refers to the Emblem which shows

> How Coryate from the Jew is Gentilly fleeting,
> Lest if he staid he should be made a Praepuce;
> And so of men, the only womans Refuse.[40]

Obviously the Ghetto episode much impressed Coryat's friends, not only because it forms one of the longest passages in a voluminous book, but possibly also because the Jews must have been a curiosity to Englishmen in those days. It is to be noted that none of these verses is particularly venomous against the Jews; the raillery is good-naturedly aimed at Coryat himself.]

Coryat, though breezy enough in his Elizabethan way, was no Nashe. By contrast to the latter he indicates that a contemporary of Shakespeare's was by no means necessarily rooted in bigotry, even without recourse to the quasi-atheism of Marlowe. We have no right to assume in advance that when Shakespeare created Shylock the portrait must inevitably have been painted with a view to discrediting the Jews.

Marlowe, Nashe, Coryat, none of them really a bigot—how different each is from the other, though all Elizabethans! And how different from all three is Shakespeare, and how immeasurably more modern!

3

Jingler of the Guinea:
The Usurer

O money, money, money.—O. Nash, *Hymn to the Thing That Makes the Wolf Go.*

∷

The jingling of the guinea helps the hurt that Honor feels.—Tennyson, *Locksley Hall.*

∷

Quo mihi fortunam, si non conceditur uti?*—Horace, *Epistles,* I, 5.

∷

"The American nation in the Sixth Ward is a fine People," he says. "They love th' eagle," he says. "On the back iv a dollar."—F. P. Dunne, *Mr. Dooley in Peace and War.*

∷

As to pay, Sir, I beg leave to assure the Congress that as no pecuniary consideration could have tempted me to accept this arduous employment at the expense of my domestic ease and happiness, I do not wish to make any profit from it.—George Washington, *On His Appointment as Commander-in-Chief, June 16, 1775.*

∷

Tho' I owed much, I hope long trust is given,
And truly mean to pay all bills in Heaven.—Epitaph in Barnwell Churchyard, near Cambridge, England.

∷

Ah, take the Cash, and let the Credit go.—E. Fitzgerald, *Rubaiyat,* 13.

∷

Point d'argent, point de Suisse.†—Racine, *Les Plaideurs,* I.

∷

They put money in the bank against a rainy day. But when the rainy day comes and they must draw some of the money out, they nearly die of grief. To see the figures in the bank-book become greater is the pinnacle of human felicity for them; to see them diminish, worse than death.—B. Baergenir, *Hot Nights in Iceland.*

* What is a fortune to me, if it cannot be put to use?
† No money, no Swiss.

Shakespeare, as I understand his play, was far less concerned with the fact that Shylock is a Jew than with the fact that he is a money-lender. It is necessary, therefore, that we know something about the history of usury as well as its position in Elizabethan times.

The Old Testament has a number of things to say about usury which have to a considerable extent conditioned that history.

Bankers in the modern commercial connotation of the term were, of course, undreamt of among the Jews during the earlier period of their post-Egyptian settlement in Palestine. They could not have conceived of the borrowing of money for the purpose of creating capital. The Mosaic Law was obviously framed for a noncommercial people. Its basic text is Deuteronomy xxiii:19-23, which is very specific in:

1. Prohibiting the taking of interest (in any form) for a loan to a fellow-Jew.

2. Requiring prompt payment by the man who has taken an oath to repay.

3. Requiring fulfillment of every obligation voluntarily undertaken.

4. Permitting the taking of interest from a foreigner.

[This permission would seem to be at variance with Leviticus xix:34 as rendered in the King James Version: "The stranger that dwelleth with you shall be unto you as one born among you, and thou shalt love him as thyself, for ye were strangers in the land of Egypt." But the word for "stranger" in Deuteronomy in the Hebrew is *nokhri*, which carries with it the sense of "foreigner," while the word in Leviticus is *ger* which means "dweller." The "American Translation" banishes the spurious paradox by reading instead of "stranger" in Leviticus, "proselyte."]

Exodus xxii:25 forbids taking interest from the poor. Leviticus xxv: 35-37 makes the point that when any Jew becomes so poor that he cannot meet his obligations to another Jew and is reduced to the status of an alien or a serf, he is not to have interest imposed upon him, nor are food and money to be loaned him at interest.

As commerce increased, so must usury have developed too. When Nehemiah was sent to Jerusalem as the Royal Commissioner for Artaxerxes, upon his arrival some of the Jews poured out to him bitter and anguished complaints at losing their property to fellow-Jews because of the famine, and surrendering their sons and daughters as pledges to their wealthier countrymen. Very angry at what he learned, Nehemiah rebuked the nobles and governors for this irreligious exacting of usury from their fellow-Jews (Nehemiah v:7).

There are several other Old Testament passages which stigmatize the taking of interest. Thus, the Psalmist declares that among those who may hope to sojourn in God's tabernacle are the righteous who have never loaned money at interest (Psalms xv:5). The old prohibition is further enforced in Ezekiel xviii:5-9, where among the virtues of the upright man are listed the restoring of the debtor's pledge, the refraining from ever lending money at interest, and the refusal ever to accept interest.

By the time of the composition of the great poem which forms the bulk of Job, the Mosaic prohibition must have been fairly widely ignored. Eliphaz, in attempting to account for Job's afflictions, accuses him of taking pledges from his fellows and of stripping the clothes from the impoverished (xxii:6); Job, on the other hand, ruefully reflects on the wickedness of some who can prosper in spite of the fact that they have taken from the widow her only ox as a pledge (xxiv:3) or have gone so far as to take away as security the offspring of the poor (xxiv:9).

In the New Testament the basic text against the taking of usury is Luke vi:34-35, which asks what merit there can be in lending only to receive, and which bids us do good and lend to our enemies, hoping for nothing in return. [The old Roman law took a very different view of the matter. A creditor could keep his debtor as a slave until the debt was discharged—could even put him to death. Hebraic law permitted temporary bondage for debtors, but specified that such a slave must be freed by the seventh year or the year of the Jubilee (Exodus xxi:2; Leviticus xxv:39, 42; Deuteronomy xv:9).]

It is to be noted that the passage in Deuteronomy xxiii operates both to emphasize the brotherhood of all Hebrews (by forbidding their taking of interest from one another) and to exclude the foreigner from this confraternity (by permitting the taking of interest from him). This doubleness of precept was inevitably a trouble to the medieval moralist; the Church of the Middle Ages prohibited usury under all circumstances; moreover, the Christian ideal of universal brotherhood was in itself a denial of the Mosaic exclusion of the foreigner. There are no foreigners in a New Jerusalem where all are brothers.[1]

The medieval position was further supported by Aristotle's dictum that money was intended only as a medium of exchange; being barren and incapable of being in itself productive, money could not logically command interest for its use:

> The most hated sort of money-making, and with greatest reason, is usury, which makes gain out of money itself, and not from the natural use of it. For money was intended to be used in exchange, but not to increase at interest. And this term usury, which means the birth of money from money, is applied to the breeding of money from money because the offspring resembles the parent. Wherefore of all modes of making money this is the most unnatural.[2]

["In ancient times so much of the lending at interest was associated with cruelty and hardship," says J. S. Nicholson, "that all lending was branded as immoral."[3] In Athens most citizens had been proprietors of small holdings: but by degrees a great number of them were so deeply in debt to the wealthy, that they had degenerated into a dependency close to slavery; it was in this way that, before Solon, the power of the state had fallen into the hands of a small plutocracy. Solon (c. 594 B.C.) therefore canceled all debts involving land or persons as security, made illegal the use of human beings as security, and restricted the pledging of land as security to a share of the debtor's possessions.]

St. Jerome (340-420) declared that the New Testament extended the Mosaic prohibition of usury among brothers to a universal interdiction against the taking of interest. St. Ambrose of Milan (340-397) defined the "foreigner" of the Deuteronomic permission as an enemy of God's chosen; from such, interest might be taken —from the man "whom you rightfully desire to harm, against whom weapons are lawfully carried. Upon him usury is legally imposed. . . . From him exact usury whom it would not be a crime to kill. . . . Where there is the right of war, there also is the right of usury."[4]

The sanction of St. Ambrose made it no sin for Christians to exact interest from the Moslems during the Middle Ages. "It also gave the Jews in Europe *carte blanche*," observes Nelson, "to continue to exact usury from their Christian debtors."[5] It provided as well the authority for elaborate double-dealing on the part of some Christian Italians, Frenchmen, and Catalonians in lending money to the Saracen foe during the Crusades. By the concluding years of the twelfth century Christian moneylenders were so well on the way to outnumbering the Jews that the Church had to re-affirm its stand. The Second Lateran Council (1139) had already "declared the unrepentant usurer condemned by the Old and New Testaments alike, and, therefore, unworthy of . . . Christian burial." [6] William of Auxerre (d. c. 1232) found the prohibition of usury "even more rigorous than the commandment against murder: there is no exception to the law against usury, whereas it is on occasion even meritorious to kill." [7] St. Thomas Aquinas' view was simply stated: "To take usury from any man is simply evil because we ought to treat every man as our neighbor and brother." [8] Finally, Pope Alexander IV issued the *Quod super nonnullis* bull (1258), which made the taking of interest an act of heresy, serious enough to occasion action by the Inquisition. [This position was not changed by the Catholic Church through the eighteenth century. Benedict XIV's encyclical, V*ix pervenit* (1745) branded as the sin of usury the act of accepting more than the amount of the loan advanced, no matter how trifling the sum involved. Only in 1830 did the Church officially permit the taking of moderate interest—with the proviso that the affair be submitted to Papal authority for decision.]

It is not surprising, therefore, that Dante appointed a special place in Hell for the usurers: in the third round of the seventh circle. The poet, on seeing them, is asked to remember the fiat of Genesis, "In the sweat of thy face shalt thou eat bread"; hence from the bounty of Nature and the exercise of Art

> it behoves mankind to gain their life and to advance. But because the usurer holds another way, he contemns Nature in herself, and in her follower,* since upon another thing he sets his hope.

Presently Dante comes upon the usurers sitting on the burning sand beneath the endless fall of flakes of flame:

> Their woe was bursting forth through their eyes; now here, now there they made help with their hands, sometimes against the va-pors,† and sometimes against the hot soil. Not otherwise do the

* i.e. the Arts
† i.e., the falling flakes of flame

dogs in summer, now with muzzle, now with paws, when they are bitten either by fleas, or flies, or gadflies. When I set my eyes on the face of certain of those on whom the grievous fire falls, I did not recognize one of them;* but I perceived that from the neck of each was hanging a pouch, which had a certain color and a certain device.[9]

These devices, the blazons of their families, were basely borne, not upon a shield, but upon their purses. Among the usurers Dante identifies were the Scrovigni family of Padua, and the Gianfigliazzi and Ubriachi families of Florence; singled out for special reference is Giovanni Buiamonte, of Florence too, of whom Benvenuto da Imola said that he "surpassed all others of his time in usury."

Now, moneylending, of course, was an occupation that was necessarily involved with the circulation of money. And of that subject we had better take a brief view. By the beginning of the tenth century, when feudalism is generally conceded to have emerged as the order of society in Western Europe, money had almost ceased to circulate. The Moslems had put an end to Western European trade overseas, and in place of commerce the economy retrogressed to that of an agricultural society. When Western Europeans were themselves growing or making nearly everything that was in requisition, and trade had almost totally declined, there was little need for money.

But with the Crusades (1095-1291) and the consequent revival of trade and growth of industry, money began to reappear as a medium of exchange. The Crusaders found themselves in sudden need of money for the purchase of equipment and supplies. Coins which had been hoarded for centuries began to circulate again; in the thirteen century the gold florin of Florence and the gold ducat of Venice began to displace silver in international exchange.

Rudimentary forms of credit and banking began to develop, the earliest bankers being the Florentines and Lombards. During the Crusades the Templars managed an almost complete monopoly of foreign exchange in the Holy Land. When the banks began to lend money, they were entering the sinful province of usury.

Strictly speaking, anyone who was so un-Aristotelian as to make money breed more money was guilty of the grave sin of usury. The official position of the Church was not altered on that point.

* i.e., they were unworthy of being known

Nevertheless, money was now required for countless purposes. As Europe progressed toward its Renaissance the disparity between Church theory and Christian practice was bound to widen. The re-awakening to the pleasurable calls of terrestrial life meant the need of money to spend on them. Money therefore began to take on an importance such as it had never had before. The proof is that Florentine bankers are on record as having charged as much as 266 per cent interest on loans. For purposes of pleasure, administration, wars, and commercial voyages kings, noblemen, popes and the ecclesiastical hierarchy came to the bankers (i.e., usurers) for money.

Suddenly, even, a millionaire began to appear here and there. Take the case of Jacques Coeur (1395-1456), of Bourges, France. The son of a common artisan, he learned to employ his own wealth to acquire public offices, and public offices to acquire more wealth. He made a fortune by trade with the Moslems in the Near East and by operating ships for pilgrims to the Holy Land. Winning the favor of his king, Charles VII, he financed the last campaigns of the Hundred Years' War. He bought up estates from impoverished noblemen; acquired textile shops and mines; loaned money to half the nobility of France, it is said; paid for the decoration of the cathedral at Bourges; and built himself a palace. But Coeur met with the fate of many another usurer: he had extended himself too far. So many powerful dignitaries were in his debt that it was comparatively easy to concoct a charge against him of poisoning the king's favorite mistress.

Or there is the equally remarkable example of the powerful Fugger family of Augsburg, Bavaria (1450-1600). The foundation of their fortune came from weaving of linen. After buying up mines, the Fuggers became bankers to the Habsburgs and to the Papacy as well. With such patronage they were able to acquire silver, copper, and iron mines in the Tyrol and Hungary. By the mid-sixteenth century the family fortune was fabulous. It was then that they made the mistake of granting too many loans to Philip II of Spain. When he refused to repay, the family was soon forced into bankruptcy (1607).

Excluded by medieval bigotry, as we have seen, from normal intercourse with the brotherhood of Christians as well as from the right to earn a normal living by membership in the trades, the Jews had in numerous cases resorted to moneylending. In the popular mind they were particularly identified with that detested pursuit. (In the coarse mind they still are.) Nevertheless, as respectable historians are all well aware, the Jews—except in Spain until 1492, when they were expelled from the Iberian peninsula— did not play a leading part in banking. The money-making Templars of the Crusades; the French, Italian, and Catalan lenders of money to the Saracens; the Scrovigni, Gianfigliazzi, Ubriachi, and Buiamonte whom Dante placed in Hell for their usury; Jacques Coeur; the Fuggers; the Lombard and Tuscan bankers of whom we have spoken, were all Christian. Indeed, the Wall Street of fourteenth-century Europe was Florence's *Calimala* ("Evil Street"), where the great houses for import and export were operated by leading Tuscan families. Facts, however, have often shown themselves reluctant of acceptance, and to the man in the street "usurer" was synonymous with "Jew."

Certainly a number of Jews were able to thrive on moneylending. They operated without the safeguards or religious interdiction of Christian usurers. The pious Christian who availed himself of their services placed his soul in no jeopardy as a borrower; he might add, moreover, to the masochistic pleasure of considering himself their victim (though it is hard to see how anyone could have been their victim other than voluntarily) the comforting thought that in allowing them to charge him interest he was cooperating in the further damning of the race which had rejected Jesus.

Like Christian usurers, charge interest they did, and frequently at exorbitant rates—though they seldom matched the Florentine 266 per cent. It would be easy to explain why their rates were heavy. The records are copious with instances of deeply indebted princes and noblemen who by decree or simple declaration voided an existing obligation to them—not to speak of the agreed-upon interest. The records are equally eloquent with instances of any excuse's serving for the seizure of Jewish property. Under such conditions, it might be explained, it is not surprising that the Jews would demand all the interest they could get when they could get it. But since no one feels obliged to call Jacques Coeur, the Fuggers, or the Italian bankers to account, or no one, for that matter, feels obliged to explain why banks and loan companies today exact all that the law permits (and, in the case of the loan companies far more than it is the clear intent of the law to permit), it seems superfluous to summon the Jewish usurer to the bar for explanations at this late date. Since through the Jew, the borrowing Christian was able to supply his wants and at the same time keep safely within the precepts of his church—imperiling the soul of no other Christian—he found the Jewish usurer, no matter how much he affected to despise him, indispensable.

In Italy, Jewish pawnbrokers were thriving. They had been invited by the townships to open shop, and had been granted the license to charge as much as 50 per cent interest on loans. Resentment, fanned by the old tales of ritual murder, flared up anew, and again the life and property of Jews were in constant hazard. To counteract their success, however precarious, Rome, despite its official stand on usury, gave its approval to the opening of Christian pawnshops, *monti di pietà*, as they were called; eighty-seven such small banks had been sanctioned in Italy by 1509.

At the same time the attack upon Jewish moneylenders was intensified by the theologians. They argued that the Jews had no right to take interest from Christians, that the Church ought to forbid them to remain in business, that not even the Pope should feel privileged to grant licenses to them, that anyone granting such a license was thereby guilty of mortal sin and was cut off from Mother Church.

There is something very modern about the way this matter was rationalized. Jewish moneylending establishments were regarded as infernal. The Christian pawnshops, on the other hand, had their stout defenders. They argued that the sums accepted in them beyond the amount of the original loan must not be described as interest. Such money was fairly demanded to cover the costs of maintaining the establishment.[10]

It is, of course, now obvious that the line of development of modern industrial society was such as to make the taking of financial profits inevitable, with or without religious sanction. But at the time Shakespeare wrote *The Merchant of Venice* the future and the inevitability of using money to breed money was by no means so clear. The proof of this fact is that as late as the end of the eighteenth century Jeremy Bentham, the so-called Father of Utilitarianism, found it necessary to write a *Defence of Usury*, stating the justification for modern capitalistic society:

> Those who have the resolution to sacrifice the present to the
> future are natural objects of envy to those who have sacrificed the

future to the present. The children who have eaten their cake are the natural enemies of the children who have theirs. . . .

I question whether among all the instances in which a borrower and a lender of money have been brought together on the stage, from the days of Thespis to the present, there ever was one in which the former was not recommended to favour in some shape or other—either to admiration, or to love, or to pity, or to all three—and the other, the man of thrift, consigned to infamy.[11]

As late as 1788, moreover, we see that usury is a term which is still synonymous (in the philosophical realm, at least) with profit-taking.

Indeed, the fourteenth-century reflection of Benvenuto da Imola expressed perfectly the dilemma Western Europe faced for centuries thereafter: "He who practiseth usury goeth to hell, and he who practiseth it not tendeth to destitution." [12]

The credit or blame for finding religious justification for profit-taking, for banishing the Deuteronomic prohibition and the Aristotelian disapproval, for making it possible to be a good Christian and take profits at the same time, belongs to John Calvin (1509-1564). He dismissed the argument that money cannot give birth to money as a merely frivolous one. Isn't money actually more fruitful, he asked, than any other possession one might mention? Then he added ironically, "Certes je confesse ce que les enfans voyent, ascavoir que si vous enfermes largent au coffre il sera sterile." *

The Mosaic ruling against interest, Calvin said, was intended only to encourage brotherhood among the Hebrews; it was not to be understood as a spiritual law to be binding upon Christians. Usury is not forbidden by God as long as no injury is done to a fellow-Christian. But one must not, for example, take interest from the poor. Also, the rate of interest must be within reason. [Nelson's summary of Calvin's importance to the evolution of modern society is precise: "Calvin is the first religious leader to exploit the ambivalence of the Deuteronomic passage in such a fashion as to prove that it was permissible to take usury from one's brother. His exegesis spells the demise of Deuteronomy. He succeeded in legitimizing usury without seeming to impair the vitality either of the universalism or the fraternalism of the Christian ethic. . . . (His words) be-

* Certainly I confess believing, what any child can see, that if you lock up money in a chest, it will then be sterile.

came a Gospel of the modern era. Everyone from the sixteenth to
the nineteenth century who advocated a more liberal usury law
turned to Calvin for support. Even those who would not or could
not mention his name were compelled to speak his words." [13]]

Such ideas could not find instantaneous acceptance in Calvin's
own century, the sixteenth. The battle for Calvinistic theology was
to be waged later. But by 1688 Samuel Pufendorf, great fountain-
head of legal logic, was saying:

> Loans are made these days most commonly . . . that we may
> secure the means to increase our wealth in some notable degree.
> . . . When a man negotiates a loan for this end there is no reason
> why a person should accommodate him gratis.[14]

In sixteenth-century England the law attempted to limit the interest collectable by moneylenders or to abolish the practice altogether. At the time of Henry VIII, 10 per cent was fixed as the
highest rate permitted; to exact more was to invite grave penalties.[15]
Under Edward VI this law was annulled and moneylending forbidden, since "Usurie is by the word of God utterly prohibited as a
vyce most odyous and detestable." [16] Elizabeth, however, restored her
father's edict in 1570,[17] and this was the law of the land when
Shakespeare wrote *The Merchant of Venice*.

But legal limitation or taboos, as the American experiment with
Prohibition illustrated, are likely to be ignored when the need or
the desire is great. And the need and desire for money had become
great in Shakespeare's day. The issues of moneylending and interest
were very much more on the minds of Londoners than how they
ought to feel about the Jews. Draper is almost alone among scholars
(who have largely overlooked the importance of the issue of usury
in *The Merchant of Venice* in their excessive preoccupation with
the matter of Shakespeare's being pro- or anti-Jew) when he remarks: "The question of the moral and legal justification of interest
came close home to every Elizabethan, and was crucial in the transi-
tion from feudal society to modern capitalism. . . . Gold was pour-
ing into Europe from America; prices were rising, and merchants
grew rich, but classes with fixed incomes suffered intensely." [18] The
merchants, of course, needed money for their transactions and were
willing to pay the usurers extravagant rates—as much as 80 per
cent.[19] But the feudal class was not able to keep up with the co-

operation of merchants and moneylenders; their wealth was in land, but their lands no longer supplied them with enough to live on. They were in need of ready money, had to borrow at interest, but found the exorbitant rates undermining to their very basis of living.

There were few or no Jews in England, but there were plenty of thriving usurers. Isaac Disraeli has a fascinating account of one of them who flourished under James I—Hugh, called "the great," Audley, who amassed a vast fortune at the expense of the aristocracy. Audley began with two hundred pounds, and lived "to view his mortgages, his statutes, and his judgments so numerous, that it was observed his papers would have made a good map of England." With one end always in mind, he became a clerk to the Clerk in the Counter, taking "a deep concern in the affairs of his master's clients, and often much more than they were aware of." He was always ready at hand for any gallant in financial trouble, with the money in his purse to provide bail or to compound debts. Landowners or thoughtless heirs fell by great numbers into his nets. "He could at all times out-knave a knave." A certain dishonest draper, for instance, was arrested for a debt of £200; Audley bought up the debt for £40, and then offered to settle with the draper for £50 with this added stipulation: "that the draper should pay within twenty years upon twenty certain days a penny doubled." No arithmetician, the draper eagerly agreed. After twenty months, Audley claimed his doubled pennies—which now had grown into many pounds. "The knave perceived the trick, and preferred paying the forfeiture of his bond for £500, rather than to receive the visitation of all the little generation of compound interest in the last descendant of £2000, which would have closed with the draper's shop."

Audley presently was forming temporary partnerships with the stewards of country gentlemen.

> They underlet estates which they had to manage; and anticipating the owner's necessities, the estates in due time became cheap purchases for Audley and the stewards. He usually contrived to make the wood pay for the land, which he called "making the feathers pay for the goose." Audley was, indeed, ever ready with a wry quip. When a nobleman protested the severity of his exactions with, "Do you not intend to use a conscience?" Audley answered, "Yes, I intend hereafter to use it. We moneyed people must balance accounts: if you do not pay me, you cheat me; but if you do, then I cheat your lordship."

> This usurer, who accumulated over £1,000,000, lived like a Puritan, a life of celibacy, voluntary poverty, and all the mortifications of a primitive Christian.[20]

Although he was born a little too late to serve as Shakespeare's model, this Christian moneylender seems much more of a blood-brother to Shylock than does the stereotype of a Jew.

Though the Jews were banished from England, there were enough non-Jewish usurers in Elizabethan times, and the taking of interest was one of the grim realities of life. Even actors and dramatists were likely to feel no less bitter toward moneylenders than did noblemen or merchants, for they too had constant recourse to the usurer for their needs.[21] This is a fact which ought not be overlooked when estimating the dramatist's intent in composing *The Merchant of Venice*.

The ethical justification of interest-taking was still being argued. Usury remained a sin, but it was, after all, a sin not prohibited by law. Sir Simon d'Ewes called it a "controversial sin"; his father, a contemporary of Shakespeare's, through the taking of interest had been able to acquire a manor, and then lost it to the widow of the man who had sold it to him; old d'Ewes accepted the loss as "a punishment for the usurious loan of money." [22]

Bacon would presently justify usury on the grounds that its suppression would be possible only in a Utopian state. But the old Aristotelian argument was reiterated again and again. For instance, Francis Meres thus firmly restates it:

> Usurie and encrease by gold and silver is unlawful, because against nature: nature hath made them sterill and barren, usurie makes them procreative.

The same idea is inherent in "A Goodly New Ballad," of 1586; among its complaints of contemporary wickedness is:

> Usury weares a velvet coate,
>   by cutting of his brothers throate,
>   which without gaines will not lend a groat,
>   and surely the more is the pittie.[23]

The usurer himself figures consistently as a hated figure in the works of Elizabethan and Stuart men of letters. The reader will observe that the hatred for the moneylender causes him to evolve into a fairly stock figure.

A particularly lively portrait occurs in Nashe's *Pierce Penilesse* (1592). The hero, knowing the want common to poor scholars, draws up a "Supplication to the Divell," with the suggestion that if the Devil were to get rid of some of the misers and usurers around, more gold would be circulating:

> I was informde of late dayes, that a certaine blind Retayler called the Divell, used to lend money upon pawnes, or any thing. . . . But . . . here lies the question; where shal I finde this olde Asse?

Supplication in hand, he searches for him all over London without finding him.

> At length . . . I lighted upon an old stradling Usurer, clad in a damaske cassocke edged with Fox fur, a paire of trunke slops,* sagging down like a Shoomakers wallet, and a shorte thrid-bare gown on his backe, fac't with moatheaten budge,† upon his head he wore a filthy course biggin,‡ and next it a garnish of night-caps, with a sage butten-cap, of the forme of a cow-sheard over spread very orderly: a fat chuffe§ it was I remember, with a gray beard cut short to the stumps, as though it were grimde, and a huge woorme-eaten nose, like a cluster of grapes hanging downe-wards. Of him I demaunded if hee could tell me any tidings of the partie I sought for.[24]

In Rowley's *Search for Money* there is an impressive picture of a usurer. As he descends the stairs "with small interims we might heare on[e] hawking and vomiting his fleame." He opens the door a crack as though it were "a pillory, for even so showed his head forth the dores; but as ill a heade in forme and worse in condition, then ever held a spout of lead in his mouth at the corner of a church; an old moth-eaten cap buttoned under his chinne; his visage like the artificiall Jewe of Maltaes nose."

Joseph Hall in his character of "The Covetous," says of him:

* loose breeches
† lambskin
‡ nightcap
§ avaricious person

He never eats good meale, but on his neighbors trencher. . . .
He lets money, and selles Time for a price; and he will not be im-
portuned either to prevent or defer his day. . . . He breeds of
money to the third generation. . . . He dreames of theeves.

And Thomas Overbury's character of "A Devillish Usurer" (1614)
pillories the usurer in this fashion:

Hee is better read in the Penall Statutes then the Bible. . . .
Hee can bee no mans friend. . . . He puts his money to the un-
naturall Act of generation. . . . The 'Table he keeps is able to
starve twenty tall men; his servants have not their living, but their
dying from him, and thats of Hunger.[25]

These quotations indicate that the figure of the moneylender
was fast becoming a stereotype. And indeed, it has been observed,[26]
in the literature of the period certain conventions are developed for
the depiction of the usurer. These are the most recurrent of the
characteristics with which the writers of the time endow him:

1. Typically he is an old man.
2. He is often the suitor of a young woman (e.g., Chapman's
The Blind Beggar of Alexandria [1596]; Haughton's *Englishmen
for My Money* [1598]).
3. He is always hideous, as we have seen him to be in the portraits drawn by Nashe and Rowley, and is usually described as forever coughing or suffering from the scurvy, the gout, or some equally
unattractive disease. The usurers in Fletcher's *Rule a Wife* (1624)
and Shirley's *The Wedding* (1626) are by exception young, but
they are depicted as extremely repulsive.
4. His nose is always immense, as with the moneylenders of Nashe
and Rowley. Chapman's wears a long false nose as part of his disguise. The moneylender in *Englishmen for My Money* owns a nose
large enough "to shadow Paul's."
5. He wears spectacles (e.g., A *Knacke to Know an Honest Man*
[1596]).
6. At home he starves himself. The moneylender's house in
Lodge's *Wits Miserie* (1596) is described as one wherein "a Rat
could not commit a Rape upon the paring of a moldy cheese, but
he died for it." (We have seen Overbury's comments on the usurer's

table.) He is also the stingiest of hosts to his guests (e.g., *Englishmen for My Money*).

7. He is very hard on his servants. The usurer in Jonson's *The Staple of News* feeds his servants on the leavings of the scraps served his dogs.

8. He dresses miserably, his clothes having usually been acquired from the hangman (e.g., Massinger's *A New Way to Pay Old Debts*; Breton's "An Usurer" in his *The Good and the Badde* [1616]).

9. His robe is, as was the case with Nashe's usurer, trimmed with fur (e.g., Jonson's *The Staple of News*).

10. His ending is a fearful one. The moneylenders of *Jack Drums Entertainment* (1600) and Massinger's *A New Way to Pay Old Debts* finally go mad. Marlowe's Barabas falls into a boiling cauldron. Quarles's usurer in *The Virgin Widow* drinks poison. The moneylender of *A Spectacle for Usurers* (1606) is devoured by rats. But the normal end of the usurer is supposed generally to be at a halter's end (e.g., *Englishmen for My Money*; Beaumont and Fletcher's *The Night Walker*).

Now, as has been intimated earlier, if there is one pastime to which Shakespearean scholars have been addicted it has been their eagerness to foist upon Shakespeare's work the stereotypes of his less gifted contemporaries. Because Shakespeare was undeniably a highly successful dramatist, they would make him out to be no more than a run-of-the-mill writer of popular plays. It is certainly true that the greatest creators of any given age have not always been the greatest successes of their times. It is equally true that the greatest creators of any given age have only rarely, as in the instance of Blake as a poet, been neglected by their contemporaries. And it is also true that there exist instances where the greatest creators of an age have been among the greatest successes of their era. In our own century Joseph Conrad will stand as a lucky example. Shakespeare was another such. His popular success cannot be adduced to prove him a mediocrity.

We have only to examine the list of these stock attributes of the Elizabethan usurer to discover, if we stick close to Shakespeare's play, that Shylock has been equipped with only two of them, and that those two are totally out of the realm of caricature, and are not necessarily such as would rob a man of his dignity. Shylock is, of course, old—though not ancient; and he is hard on his servant,

Launcelot Gobbo. He is not made absurdly to court a young woman or any other woman. There is nothing in *The Merchant of Venice* to indicate that he is hideous, that he is forever coughing, that he suffers from any disgusting habits or disease, that he has a large nose, that he wears spectacles, that he starves himself at home, that he wears fur. We may assume from his eagerness to dine at the expense of his enemies that he would make a grudging host—if, indeed, he ever had guests. But there is no warrant (the traditions of actors and scholars notwithstanding) to think of him as equipped with a ridiculous huge nose, even if it be true that the actor performing Marlowe's Jew, quite possibly only after the author's death, chose to wear one. There is not the slightest reference in the play to anything which would make Shylock a ridiculous figure, a hideous, or a revolting one, and we have not the slightest right to engraft any of these stock characteristics on the play Shakespeare wrote. If, as tradition has it, Shakespeare's favorite actor for his great heroic parts in the tragedies, Burbage, was the original Shylock, then there is all the more reason to reject all these unjustified superimpositions on *The Merchant of Venice* based on our knowledge of what others were doing; we may be sure that Burbage would have presented a dignified, forceful, and attractive Shylock.

As for the bad end waiting for the usurer, Shylock does in truth meet with a crushing defeat, though it is no worse than he merits. But he is not handed over to the ravages of insanity, poison, rats, or a halter. It is interesting that Gratiano, the only truly coarse character in the play, does at the conclusion of the trial make a plea that a halter be substituted for the clemency offered Shylock, but nobody pays any attention to him. One feels that he only embarrasses Bassanio and his friends by his unpleasant gloating over Shylock's reverses.

If I seem to be implying that Shakespeare, despite his great success with the London audiences, could turn his back on literary fashions, I mean precisely that—though it is a premise which professional scholarship has stubbornly refused to grant. (Why, one feels like asking that scholarship, is it so busy with Shakespeare if Shakespeare were no better than any other Elizabethan?) But I do not mean to imply that Shakespeare's originality, though unequalled in the annals of literature, was of the sensational order of *Finnegans Wake* or of *Four Saints in Three Acts*. Clearly, no author is likely to become the most popular writer of his times if he flies in the face of public taste. Shakespeare was of that lucky cast (Conrad was another) which is able to give the general public enough of what is in vogue, without in any way jeopardizing the thing which the creator himself wishes to say. Such writers have something for everybody. Thus, despite the noble dimensions of Conrad's tragic view of life, his incomparable insight into the haunting aspects of nature, and his peculiarly fascinating prose, he managed to be a best-seller while he lived—because the general public, indifferent to such literary appeals, could be sure of finding in his novels and stories an exciting yarn.

Shakespeare, too, knew how to please the most untutored elements of his audience without sacrificing the dignity of his conceptions to their vulgarity. A good instance is the way he presents the three witches in *Macbeth*. For the more simple-minded the witches are endowed with their popular traits: they cause general minor mischief by such acts as the killing of swine, raising storms at sea, visiting sleeplessness upon their victims. But for the larger purposes of *Macbeth* as a great tragedy, the three witches are also awesome figures, taking upon themselves the solemn dignity (and some of the function) of the ancient Greek oracles. Thus, both general public and cultivated audience could admire, each for its own reasons, the play being enacted on the boards.

So, too, Shakespeare in his Shylock gave the general public enough to satisfy the undiscriminating: if they would have their usurer fairly old and mean to his servants, let Shylock be so. If, despite the fact that the Jews were banished from England and that the majority of usurers must have been Christian, the groundlings would persist in thinking of the usurer as a Jew, let Shylock be a Jew. But having to this extent won their attention, Shakespeare would go no further in bending to their fixed ideas. For he had a highly serious and important concept to explore in *The Merchant of Venice*, and it suited his purposes as little to capitalize upon the bigotry of the illiterate as to create yet another caricature of the usurer for them to laugh at. His Shylock was perforce a villain, but he must be also a villain entitled to respect to a degree, a man with his own dignity and perspectives. A lesser figure could have done no justice to the grand idea which was Shakespeare's preoccupation in the play.

That idea required the presence of a usurer. It was doubtless an aesthetic challenge to him that the figure of the moneylender was by no means uncommon to drama. Stonex has listed sixty-nine plays written after 1553 in which a usurer is to be found. [In twenty-six of these the moneylender is either unimportant or else "his usuriousness is incidental, or even doubtful." This leaves an impressive number of plays of the period in which the usurer plays a significant role.]

Before Marlowe's *The Jew of Malta* the moneylender appeared in drama as an abstraction (e.g., Avarice); Marlowe gave his moneylender a name and more dimension. He also introduced a rebellious daughter, who in later plays was to become "almost a *dea ex machina* both in the overthrow of her usurious father, the villain, and the salvation of her prodigal lover, the hero." Such a turn of plot inevitably makes for comedy. The typical situation in this sort of play is this: there is a young spendthrift who is heavily indebted to a usurer; he repairs his impoverished condition by eloping with the moneylender's daughter and carrying away with him everything he can contrive to get hold of. This is not part of Marlowe's play: Barabas' daughter does not elope with anyone, nor is her disobedience responsible for her father's catastrophe. And in Shakespeare's play, though Jessica and Lorenzo do elope and take part of Shylock's money with them, the lover is not in debt to Jessica's father. In order to be in line with the Elizabethan dramatic tradition, as Stonex amusingly observes, Bassanio (not Antonio) should have borrowed the money directly from Shylock, and Bassanio (not Lorenzo) should have eloped with Jessica; and, to make the convention complete, Shylock "might have been one of the unsuccessful suitors for the hand and inheritance of Portia." [27] A play very much in the tradition is Haughton's *Englishmen for My Money*; in it three English spendthrifts are in debt to the usurer; his three daughters, whom he intends to marry off to wealthy merchants, are in love with the three English debtors; the plot deals with the clever foiling of the usurer and his plans, and the elopement of the three English debtors and the three girls; in the end, the usurer repents of his harshness, accepts the three Englishmen as his sons-in-law, and restores their holdings to them.

[Some attempts have been made to interpret the usurer of Elizabethan drama as a re-appearance of the usurer in Latin comedy. But the moneylender of Plautus is, typically, a generous man; the Elizabethan variety is a miser and, as we have seen, usually loathsome and villainous. The presence of the usurer in Elizabethan drama is much more plausibly to be attributed to the very real loathing and hatred with which many Elizabethans had good occasion to regard the usurer in the flesh. We should not forget that to the Londoners of Shakespeare's day the theater offered the most popular of all forms of literary entertainment. They therefore looked to it for some representation of the realities of experience.]

Before leaving the usurer's history, we ought to consider a paradox in *The Merchant of Venice* which has its roots in earlier centuries.

In Shakespeare's play the two antagonists who bitterly oppose each other are a usurer, Shylock, and a merchant-prince, Antonio. The grand theme of the play concerns itself with the totally irreconcilable values of the one and the other. Yet, in theory at least, early Christian dogma could make no distinction between the money-lender and the merchant who became rich on the sale of his commodities. The Aristotelian doctrine that brands as unnatural the breeding of money from money—a doctrine firmly embraced by the medieval Church—implies that no more leniency is due the merchant who makes great profit from his wares than is to be meted out to the man who makes great profit from lending money. The taking of unusual monetary returns in excess of what is given is the principle involved here. Indeed, because this is the principle, it has often been carelessly stated that the doctrine of the medieval Church operated to stifle commercial enterprise.

But economists have proved that by the end of the twelfth century such was in fact not the case. Common sense made it clear by then that there is a difference involved between the accepting of financial rewards for the loan of money and the making of gain in commerce, where there is constant risk of the merchant's investment. In the later Middle Ages, therefore, the emphasis of disapproval began to be placed less and less on the *taking of profits* and more and more on the *source* of profit-taking. By degrees the chief object of attack became the man who openly practised usury. What made the profit-taker subject to the condemnation of the Church "was not the extent of his business or the magnitude of his advances or the purpose of his loans (whether for production or consumption) or the character of his patronage, but it was his visibility, the notoriety of his manifest exercise of infamous usury, and his flamboyance, his avowed accessibility to all." (This was not, however, the view of the civil authorities in the Italian city-states, since they regarded the usurer as a useful member of the commercial community; the city

fathers tended to restrain only those who practised usury secretly
without license.) Thus the usurer and the merchant, originally
identities in early ecclesiastical opposition to the taking of profits,
evolved into two separate and distinct personalities. They became,
as Mr. Nelson has eloquently phrased it, "two disparate figures who
stood at opposite poles: the degraded manifest usurer-pawnbroker,
as often as not a Jew*; and the city father, arbiter of elegance,
patron of the arts, devout philanthropist, the merchant prince. From
Usurer to Merchant Prince. Such miracles of social chemistry are the
harbinger of the modern era." [28]

This is the process by which, by the time Shakespeare was writing
his play, it became possible to conceive of two men, Antonio and
Shylock, both involved in making money, as committed to totally
opposing philosophies of life.

But, it is equally important to remember, big business in the field
of international trade had hardly begun in Shakespeare's day.[29]
Banks, which perform so basic a function in modern commercial
enterprise were then only commencing to figure in large-scale transactions. It was not until 1586, a mere decade before *The Merchant
of Venice* was written, that the Casa di S. Giorgio became the
Bank of Genoa; and it was only the next year that the Banco di
Rialto was founded in Venice. Even then, the early banks were "not
so much places in which money accumulated to be loaned out to
those who needed it as rather places for the safe-keeping of
money." [30] It is significant that the word "bank" in its commercial
sense does not once appear in Shakespeare's works. It was to the
usurer that men had recourse for loans of any kind. He was to
Shakespeare's contemporaries what the banker is to ours.

If then, as has been said, Shakespeare was interested in Shylock
particularly as a usurer, we can follow his thought more closely if
we substitute in our own minds "banker" for "moneylender." It is
the philosophy that emanates from modern bankers that Shakespeare is examining in his portrait of Shylock.

* That is, of course, in countries (like Italy) where Jews were allowed to live.

4

This Bond Is Forfeit:
The Pound-of-Flesh Story

Such is the simplicity of man to hearken after the flesh.—*Love's Labour's Lost*, I, i.

::

Imperat aut servit collecta pecunia cuique.*—Horace, *Epistles*, I, 10.

::

We must all hang together, or assuredly we shall all hang separately.—Franklin, at the Signing of the Declaration of Independence, July 4, 1776.

::

A pound of that same merchant's flesh is thine.
The court awards it, and the law doth give it.—*The Merchant of Venice*, IV, i.

::

My sweet ounce of man's flesh!—*Love's Labour's Lost*, III, i.

::

Take now thy son, thine only son Isaac, whom thou lovest, and get thee into the land of Moriah; and offer him there for a burnt offering upon one of the mountains which I will tell thee of.—*Genesis*, xxii:2.

::

I have never observed that vegetarians, because they do not eat of the flesh, are therefore of milder temperament.—N.D.B. Reinaberg, *Noch Eine "Hamlet."*

The whole fabric of the Antonio-Shylock story (and the source of much misunderstanding of the play) is the bond which Shylock proposes and Antonio willingly signs. These are its terms as the moneylender describes them:

> Go with me to a notary, seal me there
> Your single† bond; and, in a merry sport,

* Gold will be either the master or the slave.
† Simple; or, possibly, "without further conditions," or, "without any other security than your signature."

> If you repay me not on such a day,
> In such a place, such sum or sums as are
> Express'd in the condition, let the forfeit
> Be nominated for an equal* pound
> Of your fair flesh, to be cut off and taken
> In what part of your body pleaseth me.
>
> (I, iii, 145-52)

Bassanio is alarmed at the proposal, and exclaims to Antonio:

> You shall not seal to such a bond for me.
>
> (155)

It is right and human that he recoil from such terms because the loan is being made for him, and he is well aware of Shylock's hatred for Antonio—has, indeed, just been an audience to the hostility between the two. But it is to be noted that Antonio himself feels no revulsion at Shylock's terms, and responds at once:

> Content in faith, I'll seal to such a bond,
> And say there is much kindness in the Jew.
>
> (153-4)

To understand the full force of Antonio's reaction, one should remember that the word "kindness" is normally used by Shakespeare to mean tenderness, affection, love, or humaneness.† Antonio, in short, finds nothing particularly sensational in the idea of staking a pound of his flesh in the signing of the contract. This is all the more remarkable after the contempt with which he has been speaking to the moneylender.

Now, we moderns, despite the fact that the ovens of Hitler and

---

* just (from the Latin *aequus*).

† e.g., If you did wed my sister for her wealth,
  Then for her wealth's sake use her with more kindness.
  (Comedy of Errors, III, ii, 6)

  This is a way to kill a wife with kindness.
  (Taming of the Shrew, IV, i, 211)

  Fare ye well at once: my bosom is full of kindness.
  (Twelfth Night, II, i, 41)

  Lying slave,
  Whom stripes may move, not kindness!
  (The Tempest, I, ii, 345)

the deliberate starvation of millions by Stalin are of our own century, are likely to feel horror at the idea of stipulating for a pound of human flesh as the obligation in a contract. The intent of this chapter, in addition to discovering Shakespeare's actual source for his story, is to make it plain that the Elizabethan audience was likely to have felt no such horror at the proposal.

Human life has not always been held precious. After all, Abraham was quite ready to offer up as a burnt sacrifice his only and well-beloved son, Isaac, at God's behest:

> And they came to the place which God had told him of; and Abraham built the altar there, and laid the wood in order, and bound Isaac his son, and laid him on the altar upon the wood.
> And Abraham stretched forth his hand, and took the knife to slay his son.
>
> (*Genesis*, xxii:9-10)

Whatever emotion the author of this passage expected his reader to experience, we may be sure it was not horror. *Tempora mutantur, nos et mutamur in illis.*

Though not quite. In 1879 a man named Freeman, who lived in Pocasset, Massachusetts, offered up his only child, Edith, as a sacrifice to God. He and his wife were inspired, they said, by Abraham, whose voice called to them to make an offering similar to the one he himself had been prepared to make. They prayed over little Edith, and then plunged a knife into her heart.[1] The accounts do not tell us whether Freeman had a beard.

There is a tale which bears a certain resemblance to the Abraham-Isaac story, told in the *Mahábhárata* (c. 300 B.C.) of the trial of a king, Usmára, who was one of "the best of mankind." To test his uprightness, Indra and Agin assume the guise of a falcon and a pigeon respectively. The pigeon (Agin) is chased by the falcon (Indra), and asks the protection of the king, which he grants. The falcon demands surrender of the pigeon, but the king refuses to give the weaker bird up. The falcon now argues that it is, after all, the law of nature that falcons feed on pigeons. King Usmára offers to give the falcon other food, but this the falcon refuses to accept. The perfect host, Usmára thereupon promises to give the falcon anything else within his power to grant. The falcon asks for the equivalent of the pigeon's weight in King Usmára's flesh. To this demand the king agrees. Scales are brought forth: the pigeon is placed in one of the balances, and Usmára cuts off a piece of his flesh and places it in the other balance. It is not heavy enough. He cuts another piece, finds that it is not enough, cuts another, and another. At length all his flesh has been sheared from his bones, and still the scales are not equal. The king now gets onto the scale himself. Satisfied of his virtue, the gods resume their proper divine shapes. They reveal their identities and assure Usmára that he will be in a state of glory for all eternity. He is transfigured and ascends into heaven.

Though the hero of this pre-Christian story does carve segments of his flesh from his body, and thus does have some affinities with the pound-of-flesh story, we need not look to Asia for the roots of the latter. The origins of the theme are no doubt to be traced to the legal actualities of ancient Roman law as set down in the venerable Twelve Tables—in particular, Table Three. Among the provisions of this third table is that, in the case of debt, the creditor may place the debtor into chains which are not to exceed fifteen pounds, after which he is to produce him on three successive market days before the people, and declare publicly the amount on which the debtor stands condemned. After the third day if the debt has not been paid the creditor may either put the debtor to death or sell him to any stranger beyond the Tiber. Moreover, if there is more than one creditor involved: "After the third market day, his body may be divided. Anyone taking more than his just share shall be held guiltless." [2]

The Twelve Tables are thought to have been drawn up around 454 B.C. One should like to believe that the penalties provided in Table Three were not often exacted. But the fact that schoolboys were expected to memorize the Twelve Tables of their country would seem to indicate that the extravagant severity of Table Three's provisions was intended at least to discourage borrowers—if, indeed, there is any way of discouraging the man congenitally so inclined. The punishment, of course, seems more extraordinary to us than it did to a people whose law granted absolute power of life and death, by these same Tables, to a father over his children.

The Twelve Tables were eventually utterly displaced by the more enlightened Justinian Code. But something of the older asperities must have lingered in men's memories to lend substance to the pound-of-flesh story. Certainly as late as Petronius Arbiter (d. c. 66 A.D.) there survives a remnant of this near-cannibalism. Near the very end of the *Satyricon*, as it has come down to us, Eumolpus declares:

> All those who are going to come into money through my will, with the exception of my freedmen, are to inherit what I leave them on one sole condition: that they cut up my body in small pieces and eat it up in the sight of the assembled people.
>
> Among certain peoples, we know, the law is observed up to this very day that the dead are devoured by their relatives. . . . So I warn all my friends not to deny my stipulation, but to eat up my body as lustily as they have consigned my soul to Hades.

The passage memorializes, at least, recollections of practices not too distant from the stipulation in the bond Shylock proposes to Antonio.

But even without regard to this Roman background, there is little excuse for the shocked judgment of scholars on the subject of Shylock's bond, such as Quiller-Couch's "monstrous and incredible; . . . starkly inhuman," [3] or Ridley's dismissal of it as a fiction "as leaky as a sieve." [4]

Tacitus informs us that the Germans were quite accustomed to offer a nose, an eye, an ear, a foot, or a hand as a forfeit. But more than this, there still exist documents to show that in practice such agreements were indeed made. In Cologne, in 1213, a contract was drawn with the stipulation that the debtor promised to permit himself to be beheaded if he broke his obligation; the agreement was witnessed by a judge and jury. In 1250, one Conrad Blind, of Silesia, agreed to surrender his life if he ever committed "certain transgressions against the Church." [5] There reposes among the state-archives of Genoa a contract drawn up in 1279; according to it, Cerasia, a woman of Sicily, in exchange for being supported by a certain Jacobus agreed to be at his "disposal and command"; if she failed in her obligations, Jacobus was privileged "to cut off her nose, a hand, or a foot"; the document was witnessed by Pietro Bargone, notary of Genoa.[6]

That such contracts were sufficiently common is attested by the many prohibitions on record against the gambling away of an eye, nose, ear, hand, or foot.[7] [It is an historical fact that during the early Middle Ages a master could, at his pleasure, mutilate the body of his serf.[8]]

Here a question might naturally enough be raised. Grant that one might be correct in tracing these (to us) strange provisions to Table Three of the old Roman Twelve Tables, still the old law was intended chiefly to discourage borrowing on the part of those who could not repay, and at its most severe was a punitive measure. How does it happen that such provisions found their way into contracts voluntarily entered?

Our conception of contract is basically an inheritance from Rome; by the thirteenth century Europe was quite familiar with it. *What essentially makes an agreement a contract enforceable at law is a "consideration."** Today, if you wish to make the present of your house to a friend, even though you decline to accept a penny for it, the new deed is likely to read that you have given your property in exchange "for One Dollar and other considerations." The dollar is the consideration necessary to render the document legally binding. The classic definition of a contract is that it is (a) a benefit accruing to the one party or (b) some "detriment" or "loss" which is "given, suffered, or undertaken by the other." The usual stipulation is that some property is given as security; when property is given as security for a debt incurred, says Glanvil, the medieval authority, a legal contract has been set up.[9]

In a legal sense, Antonio's pound of flesh is the property which he offers as his security. For in the case of the bond which he signs for Shylock, *Shylock has refused to accept any financial security or interest; the moneylender pretends that he wishes to make the loan purely as an act of friendship—that, like Antonio when lending to friends, he too wishes to make no profit. Some technical consideration is necessary, however, to be stated in the contract in exchange for the money which he is to hand over. He suggests, therefore, as that consideration something which he intends Antonio to regard as a kind of absurdity, stipulated only to satisfy legal requirements: the pound of flesh.*

It is interesting that, with the exception of a ballad on this subject, there is no instance of the stipulation of a pound of flesh's being proposed in the spirit of jest in all the versions of this story. Shakespeare, as we shall see, introduces the note of the bond's being a "merry" one in the interest of dramatic reasonableness. But that was

---

* *The Catholic Encyclopedia* says of the consideration: "It is a necessary element in a contract, and if it is wanting the contract is null." (New York, 1913) Vol. IV, p. 333.

not traditional, in life or story. We are surely safe in assuming that when the debtor of Cologne, the pious Conrad Blind, or the woman Cerasia signed their contracts, they did not look upon their forfeitures as humorously intended.

Omitting, then, this pretended note of levity, the world of storytelling reveals that there was nothing unique about the terms of Shylock's bond. The old tellers of tales never deemed such terms to be either far-fetched or barbarous.

Antonio, of course, is to presume that Shylock has not the faintest notion of ever demanding the forfeiture in case of Antonio's default:

> If he should break his day, what should I gain
> By the exaction of the forfeiture? . . .
> To buy his favor I extend this friendship.
> If he will take it, so; if not, adieu.

(I, iii, 164 seq.)

However, when Antonio is forced to break his day and he sees that no jest was intended, it never occurs to him that any legal exception could be made to the terms of the bond:

SALARINO.   I am sure the Duke
  Will never grant this forfeiture to hold.
ANTONIO.   The Duke cannot deny the course of law.

(III, iii, 24-6)

Tradition had made such terms seem normal enough to the minds of the Elizabethan audience.

Perhaps the oldest version in fiction of the pound-of-flesh story is to be found in a collection of tales by Johannes de Alta Silva (c. 1200). The story was soon versified in French by Herberz, a *trouvère* (c. 1210). Here the creditor is not yet a Jew, but an ex-serf who has become rich and is filled with hatred for a young knight because the nobleman in a fit of wrath had cut off the serf's foot. The young knight is now in love with a certain lady, much sought after by suitors. Every one of her wooers must pay her 100 marks for spending a night with her; if he succeeds in having his will of her, she will marry him. But thus far all the suitors have failed: beneath the pillow is a magic feather which causes each of them to fall into a deep sleep as soon as he reclines his head. Our young knight has already tried and failed like all the others. In order to make a second attempt he borrows the money from the ex-serf and gives as security the promise of a pound of his flesh should he fail to make good the loan. At his second attempt with the lady he succeeds; accidentally he dislodges the magic feather while turning the pillow. He enjoys the lady. She therefore marries him. But he forgets about his contract with the ex-serf. His creditor, who has not forgotten the loss of his foot, now demands the pound of flesh. The knight's wife, disguised as a knight herself, comes to her husband's rescue. As the forfeit is about to be taken, she warns the ex-serf: let him take care *Qu'il n'en praigne ne plus ne mains* (that he take neither more nor less) than the pound owing to him. The creditor, outwitted, agrees to forgo the forfeiture.

A story in the English *Cursor Mundi* (c. 1290) is quite different in setting and detail. Here for the first time the creditor is a Jew; the tale is laid in the times of the Emperor Constantine, who has sent to the court of his mother, Queen Eline, two Roman messengers, Benciras and Ansiers, to urge her to seek for the True Cross. Queen Eline has in her service a goldsmith who borrows a sum of money from the Jew with the stipulation that if he does not pay back the money by a certain date he is to surrender the weight of the money still owing in his own flesh. The money is not repaid on the date due. The Jew demands the forfeiture at the Queen's court. The two Romans, Benciras and Ansiers, sit as judges in the case. Sharp knife in hand the Jew stands before them; so does the naked goldsmith. Money is offered the Jew in lieu of the goldsmith's flesh. He refuses, assuring the judges that he will exact the worst which the law will allow him. "First I shall put out his eyes, next I shall have the hand he works with, then his tongue, and nose, and so on." The judges certify the legality of the agreement, but add:

> Take then the fless, that grants he,
> Swa that the blod may saved be.

But if a drop of blood is also taken, the Jew is to fall under the doom of the law. The creditor therefore renounces the flesh and curses the judges bitterly. Queen Eline now commands that all the Jew's property be seized; he is also to lose his evil tongue. To save himself from this fate, he offers to reveal where the True Cross is hidden. On condition that he do so he is pardoned.

This version, which has not the closeness to *The Merchant of Venice* plot of the De Alta Silva tale, has nevertheless two new elements which are to be found in Shakespeare's play: the creditor is a Jew; and the judgment is made to hinge upon the shedding of no blood. On the other hand, the desire for the debtor's flesh is motivated in the De Alta Silva story, but is not here. Indeed, in most of the versions of the pound-of-flesh theme, even when the creditor is not a Jew—as very often he is not—no reason is advanced for the cruelty.

A tale in the thirteenth-century collection of tales, the *Gesta Romanorum*, translated into English a century or more later, is clearly an elaboration of the De Alta Silva plot. The lady in this case is the Emperor's daughter; and it is a magic letter, not a feather, which causes the suitors to fall asleep as soon as they get into her bed. Our hero makes two unsuccessful attempts, and, like his fellow-suitors, each time must pay 100 florins. He now goes off to a distant flourishing city of merchants, where among many wise men dwells "Master Virgile the philosopher." In need of money, he attempts to negotiate a loan with a wealthy merchant, not a Jew, and offers his own lands as security. The merchant declines to accept them, and asks instead "that thou make to me a charter of thine own blood" with the condition that if the day of repayment is not met, "it shal be lawful for me to draw away all the flesh of thy body from the bone, with a sharp sword." Once he has committed himself, our hero is naturally a little uncomfortable about his future. He seeks counsel of the philosopher Virgile. Virgile assures him that the contract will stand in law since it was voluntarily entered into. The philosopher also advises him, when next he lies by the side of the Emperor's daughter, to feel about between the coverlet and the sheet of the bed, for there he will find the magic letter which has put him so soundly to sleep. Our hero returns to the palace of the Princess, goes to bed with her, finds the letter, and has his pleasure with her. They are married. But he forgets all about his contract, despite Virgile's warning, until he is two weeks too late. When he recollects his agreement, he hurries, as an honorable knight must, to return to the scene of his contract. He is followed swiftly by his bride, also disguised as a knight. He surrenders to the merchant, who refuses to release him for any amount of money, insisting, "I will have the law . . . for he came to me, and I not to him." Every resource the disguised Princess tries is in vain. Finally, she hits upon her variation of the escape clause: she agrees that the merchant by contract "has power to cut his flesh from the bones, but there is no covenant made of shedding bloode; thereof was nothing spoken." If the merchant should "shed any blood with his shaving of the flesh, for sooth then shall the King have good law upon him." Defeated, the creditor now offers to drop the case if the money he advanced is repaid him. But the Princess announces that he shall "not have one penny." The merchant leaves, the hero returns to his wife's palace. The Princess dons again the knight's garb in which she has disguised herself, and thus reveals to her husband that she has been his savior.

In this version, a new element appears, to be found later in *The Merchant of Venice*. Instead of at once renouncing his claims, the creditor, when he realizes that he cannot have the debtor's flesh, asks for the sum he has advanced, but the judgment is that he must not be paid anything.

There is a Turkish story laid in the time of the Sultan Amurat (1360-1389). Here a Turk lends a Christian 100 ecus; the forfeiture for nonpayment is to be two ounces of the debtor's flesh. The time expires, and the Christian has not paid. Unable to appease the Turkish creditor, Amurat tells him that he must take no more nor less than his two ounces of flesh; if he does, he will be subject to the gravest punishment. At this the Turk willingly extends the time of payment, and presently the Christian refunds the money.[10]

A Persian tale of uncertain date goes this way: There dwells in Syria a poor Mussulman who owns a most beautiful wife, much beloved by a rich Jew, who lives nearby. The Mussulman, intent on a business venture, asks the Jew for a loan of 100 dinars, promising his creditor a share in the gain of his endeavors. Because he loves the man's wife the Jew agrees; but in the bond it is stipulated that the money must be repaid in six months; if the Mussulman fails to meet the day, the creditor is to cut a pound of flesh from wherever it pleases him. The Mussulman agrees to this, receives the money, and sets forth on his business journey. He proves eminently lucky in his dealings, and well before the six months have elapsed sends the money back to the Jew via a trusted messenger. But the Mussulman's family does not give the money to the Jew and uses it instead for family needs. When the Mussulman returns the Jew demands his money *and* the pound of flesh. The first judge ruling on the case decides for the Jew. So does the second. The Cadi of Emessa acts as the third judge; he orders a knife to be brought and commands the Jew to cut neither more nor less than a pound. If more or less than a pound is cut, the Jew must pay with his life. He renounces the forfeiture.[11]

Hunter reports an English ballad called *The Northern Lord*, and says of it that it was reprinted occasionally as late as the nineteenth century. He thus summarizes its story: "A certain lord has two daughters, the one 'brown,' the other 'fair.' A knight who presents himself to the father as a suitor is informed that with the brown he will give as a portion her weight in gold, and that he expects to receive her weight in gold from the person to whom he gives the fair daughter. The knight, of course, selects the beauty, and to raise the money has recourse to a Jew usurer, who supplies him with it, taking his bond for the repayment at a certain day; in case of default the knight is to lose several ounces of his flesh. They marry; in due time a son is born, and time also brings round the day when the money is to be repaid or the forfeit taken. The knight, as the time of repayment drew near, is not prepared with the money, and the lady urges upon him, as the only resource, that they should fly beyond the sea. They go to Germany, where the Emperor, having learned the circumstances under which they had come into his dominions, built for them a 'court,' and showed them great respect, and the rather because they came from Britain, 'That blest land of fame.' Here they lived for some time in great felicity, till a 'Dutch lord,' who was in the Emperor's court, wagered with the knight a ton of gold that he would 'enjoy his lady gay,' and that he would produce a diamond ring from her finger in proof. [This part of the ballad has striking resemblances to the story of Imogen, Posthumus, and Iachimo in *Cymbeline*.] The Dutch lord has recourse to what is the approved stratagem on such occasions; he bribes a waiting-maid of the lady, who steals the ring and gives it to him. When the English knight sees the ring in the stranger's possession he almost swoons; and then, in a state of distraction, flies to his house, and, meeting the lady, who had come to the gate to welcome him, he throws her at once headlong into the moat. So cruel a murder shocks every one, and the knight is brought to trial, convicted, and sentenced to death. While he is awaiting the execution of his sentence, there suddenly appears in the Emperor's court another English knight attired in green, who easily prevails upon the Emperor to grant a second hearing of the case. At this hearing the maid is brought to make full confession of her guilt, and the court become struck with the possibility that the crime of murder may not have been committed, as the evidence went no further than to prove that the lady was thrown into the moat. The life of the knight is saved, and he claims and receives from the Dutch lord the ton of gold which he had justly won. His mind bent on revenge, the Dutch lord sends information to the Jew where his debtor is living. The exasperated Jew instantly repairs to the Emperor, and claims in his court, not the money due him, but the penalty of the bond. While this claim is under consideration, the green knight again appears; mean as the verse is, a short specimen need not be withheld:

> Said the noble knight in green,
> 'Sir, may not your articles be seen?'
> 'Yes, that they may,' replied the Jew,
> 'And I resolve to have my due.'
>
> Lo, then the knight began to read:
> At length he said, 'I find, indeed,
> Nothing but flesh you are to have.'
> Answers the Jew, 'That's all I crave.'
>
> The poor distressed knight was brought:
> The bloody-minded Jew, he thought
> That day to be revenged on him,
> And part his flesh from limb to limb.
>
> The knight in green said, 'Mr. Jew,
> There's nothing else but flesh your due,
> Then see no drop of blood you shed,
> For if you do, off goes your head.' [12]

The green knight turns out, of course, to be the wife who was supposed drowned.

One of the variants of the-pound-of-flesh story, to be found in Anthony Munday's *Zelauto* (1580), has a certain interest because of a vague similarity between the judge's recommendation of mercy to Portia's speech on the same subject, as well as a handful of phrases distantly like some not very significant ones in *The Merchant of Venice*. [The evidence is weak that Shakespeare put the story to much use. Certainly the two plots are quite dissimilar.]

In "the florishing and famous Cittie Verona," at one of its "Accademies so woorthily governed," Rodolfo, of Verona, and Strabino, of Pescara, become bosom friends. Strabino, during his visits at Rodolfo's house, falls in love with his friend's sister, Cornelia. He "although he were her superior: of her was regarded as her farre inferior. He lykes, he looves, he sues, he serves, he runnes, he waytes; she lowres, she frownes, she disdaynes, and utterly rejecteth his company." Despite his ill-treatment, Strabino tells himself: "She is the Saint whome I serve, she is the Goddesse whome I adore." At length he declares his love, and adds, "Thinke you if I would make my choyse, I could not have as good as you, or if my minde had beene so adicted, ere this I could not have beene sped? thinke you all Women are of your minde? or that they will dislyke upon no occasion?" Can it be that she is already betrothed? She tells him she is not, and so leaves him. Now, old Signor Truculento, "an extorting Usurer" who is a Christian, is in love with Cornelia too. He dresses himself in "his Fustian slyppers, and put on his holy day hose, to come a wooing." As a man he was like "an olde Horse in this towne, when he is gnabling on a thystle. This carpet Knight, having pounced himself up in his perfumes, and walking so nice on the ground, that he would scant bruse an Onion," comes to the house of Cornelia's father, Signor Ruscelli, "bringing with him a verie costly Cuppe, wherein was about five hundred Crownes." He offers them as a gift to Ruscelli, who is amazed at "Truculento's lyberalytie, who before would scant bestowe on him selfe a good meales meate for expence of money." Truculento, having been thanked, proceeds to ask for Cornelia's hand. Cornelia's father, who is one who prefers "coyne before courteous civillitie, and rytches before any vertuous action," decides to give her to the Usurer, thinking "if he matched his daughter with him: she would soone send him to Church, and then should she swym in her golden bagges." Cornelia, sent for, makes clear her distaste for the moneylender. Truculento leaves, and Rodolfo and Strabino find Cornelia in the garden greatly upset; she assures them she will never marry the usurer. Cornelia now decides that she loves Strabino, promises to wed him, and grants him a kiss. She has a plan to outwit her father: her brother and Strabino are to go to the usurer, "and there on your credite, take up a great summe of money, as much as you shall thinke good, then go you into La strada di San Paolo, and buy the Jewell which my Father hath long had such great affection to, the which will so win him." They need not worry about the payment of the debt, she concludes, "for that you shall referre unto me." The two young men go to Truculento. Rodolfo pretends to favor his suit, and then speaks up for his friend Strabino, who wishes to borrow four thousand ducats. Strabino offers "his patrimoney, and besydes the best lym of his body." Truculento, complaining of the slackness with which borrowers repay and of the ill-repute of moneylenders once they go to law—"which makes me so lothe to lende"—nevertheless tells Rodolfo that out of love for him he will lend the money, "so that you wyll stande bound unto mee, as straytlie as hee shall." Rodolfo agrees, and the terms of the bond state that if the money is not repaid on the first of next month, "eache of your Lands shall stand to the endamagement, besides the losse of bothe your right eyes." Both young men sign and get the ducats. But now Rodolfo realizes that he is madly in love with Truculento's daughter; so there is a double love-affair to put to rights. The friends buy the jewel and give it to Ruscelli, who is so much delighted that he cries: "Demaund of me what you shall deeme expedient, and I vow to the uttermost to graunt your request." Strabino thereupon asks for Cornelia's hand. Ruscelli at first is unwilling, but Strabino reminds him of his promise. Let Cornelia decide, he suggests, and let us both abide by her decision. To this Ruscelli bends; Cornelia, of course, chooses Strabino, and a date is fixed for the wedding. Next the two friends go to Truculento's house, where Rodolfo discovers to his joy that Brisana, the usurer's daughter, fully returns the passion he feels for her. Telling Truculento that the old man's nuptials are to be celebrated the day after their debt is repaid, he flatters him into granting his permission to wed Brisana. Ruscelli, hearing of the deception, causes the two young couples to marry the very next morning. Truculento learns how he has been duped and vows revenge. The time arrives for discharge of the debt, and Truculento summons Strabino and Rodolfo before the judge. The two young wives tell their husbands not to worry and apparel themselves "all in blacke like a Scholler," and appear before the judge. Truculento accuses the two young men: "They have broken theyr promise, which is open perjurie, and falsyfied theyr faythes, in not restoring the money. Wherefore, that all Gentlemen may be warned by such wylfull offenders, and that God may be glorified in putting them to punishment: I have thus determined. . . . The rendring of the money I doo not accoumpt of, ne wyll I be pleased with twise as much restored: the breach of the Lawe I meane to exact, and to use rygor, where it is so required. The forfayture of theyr Landes, is the one part of the penaltie, the losse of theyr right eyes the whole in-generall, now remembring the wofull estate of theyr solitarie wives . . . I let theyr Landes remayne unto them. . . . I clayme theyr right eyes for falsifying theyr faith: to moove others regard howe they make lyke rechlesse promises. So shall Justice be ministred . . . and myselfe not thought to deale with crueltie." The judge asks everyone involved to swear by the Bible that each will tell only the truth, "whereat they all kissed the booke." Strabino tells his story. "I came unto this Caterpyller," he says, "this aforesayd woorme of the world," because my friend and I needed money. Unfortunately, he continues, circumstances have forced us to go two days beyond the allotted month. We are willing to pay him as much as he wants now. The judge is pleased at this honest reply, and urges Truculento to accept a sum in excess of what he has advanced; "in my opinion you can reasonably require no more." The usurer refuses: "The money is none of mine, ne will I have it, his Landes I respect not, ne care I for them, and now his submission I way not, ne will I ac-cept of it. . . . I plead my privilege . . . and on them bothe I will have Lawe to the uttermost." The judge is astonished that Trucu-lento should have more care for cruelty than "Christian civillitie"; what if God's "fatherly affection, if his mercifull myldnesse, if his righteous regard, dyd not consider the frayltie of your fleshe, your promptnes unto peryll, and your aptnes unto evyll: how mightie were the myserie, which should justly fall upon you? . . . Is this the loove you beare to your brother? Is this the care you have of a Christian? The Turke, whose tyranny is not to be talked of: could but exact to the uttermost of his crueltie. And you a braunche of that blessed body, which bare the burden of our manifolde sinnes: howe can you seeme to deale so sharply with your selfe? seeing you should use to all men: as you would be dealt withall? . . . Let first your right eye be put foorth in theyr presence: and then shall they bothe abide punishment." Truculento declines to make the experiment, and demands his forfeiture. The judge, seeing that the usurer cannot be moved, asks whether any be present to plead for the two young men. Despite Truculento's objections to their be-ing granted attorneys, Brisana speaks up. Suppose, she says, I came to this man to borrow this money, and when I returned to repay on the stipulated day, I found he had left town for a while; he returns a few days later, and spitefully sues me at law. "Am I to be condempned for breaking the Lawe: when the partie him selfe hath deferred the day?" Truculento admits he was not at home on the appointed day, but his "Receyver" was there to take the money. Well then, suggests Brisana, suppose the receiver had been given the money, and "wylfulnesse had allured your servaunt to wandering, and that he departed with the debt he receyved: you returne and finde it styll in your booke, neither marked nor crossed, as if payment had not beene made." Will you then "demaund the debt agayne of me?" Tush, cries Truculento, my servant would have crossed the book before he left my establishment. Well then, she counters, you must admit this much: when the payment is made the bond ought to be handed over to the debtor; but your servant had it not to deliver. Why should I pay unless I got my bond back? Truculento answers, "Noting the receyt in the booke, would have beene sufficient tyll my comming home." At this Cornelia enters the case. Since you are unwilling to listen to reason, she tells Truculento, "Take both their eyes, so shall the matter be ended. But thus much . . . I give you in charge, . . . that no man but your selfe shall execute the deede, ne shall you crave any counsayle of any the standers by. If in pulling foorth their eyes, you diminishe the least quantitie of blood out of their heads, over and besides their only eyes, or spyll one drop in taking them out: before you styrre your foote, you shall stand to the losse of bothe your owne eyes. For that the bande maketh mention of nothing but their eyes, and so if you take more then you should, and lesse then you ought: you shall abide the punishment heere." The judge agrees that this is just. Truculento, confounded, asks for only his money now. The judge decrees that since he refused a most generous offer to begin with, the usurer may have none of it; "the money shall serve to make" the young men amends "for the great wrong" which threatened them. Seeing "no remedy," Truculento "accepted Rodolfo for his lawfull sonne, and put him in possession of all hys lyvinges after his disease.* Thus were they on all partes verie well pleased, and everie one accoumpted him selfe well contented."

It is likely that Shakespeare had read Munday's tale years earlier, and may have unconsciously remembered a detail or two while he was writing his own play. In any case, the indebtedness, if any, was

* decease.

very slight. The story itself, however, is another interesting example of the flowering of the pound-of-flesh story, though here, of course, it is not a merchant, but two university students, who are the creditors, and Truculento is obviously a Christian.

On the Continent there were many analogues of the old pound-of-flesh story.

In the old *Meistergesang* of Kaiser Karls Recht, printed in 1493, there is a story concerning a rich merchant who has left his possessions to his own son. The young man squanders his fortune in but a year, and borrows 1000 guilders from a Jew in order to make a business venture abroad. The condition of the bond is a pound of his flesh. He is successful and returns with plenty of money. But when he calls upon the Jew he does not find him at home. It is three days beyond the appointed day before he catches up with the money-lender. The Jew demands the terms of his bond, but is persuaded to submit the case to the Emperor Charles (who is, possibly, Charlemagne). On the road the young merchant unfortunately falls asleep astride his horse, and accidentally runs over a child and kills it. The child's father follows him, and demands revenge, but he too is prevailed upon to present his case to the Emperor. When they arrive at the Emperor's town, the young merchant is taken into custody and confined to a chamber. Apparently born to misfortune, he falls out of a window. In so doing, he kills an old knight who happened to be sitting below on a bench. The old knight's son comes forth demanding revenge, and even attempts to stab the young merchant, but is prevented from murdering the young fellow by the Jew. The son agrees to wait for the Emperor's decision too. The Emperor now has three cases to rule upon, in all of which the young merchant is the defendant. These are his decisions: as for the bond, the Jew may take his flesh, but he must cut neither more nor less than a pound, on penalty of death; the Jew renounces the forfeit, and makes the young man a present of the money and adds 200 guilders more. As for the father of the child who was run down, the Emperor bids him send the young merchant to the father's wife "that he may beget thee another child." Understandably, the father decides to renounce the opportunity. The old knight's son is told by the Emperor to go up into the chamber and fall out the window and kill the young man in revenge. Afraid for his own skull, the avenger decides not to try the expedient.[13]

Similar anecdotes are common in Persian and Arabic literature during the fourteenth and fifteenth centuries.[14] Sometimes the moneylender is a Jew, sometimes he is not.

In Hamburg, a dozen and a half years after *The Merchant of Venice* was written, according to a Danish account these events are supposed actually to have occurred: In order to procure the money asked for by his prospective father-in-law, so that he may be able to marry Isabella, Andreas, son of a wealthy merchant, borrows a pound of gold from a Jew on condition of surrendering a pound of flesh if he does not pay within seven years. It is twelve years later that the Jew meets Andreas by accident. Isabella, who is thought to be dead by her husband, saves her husband's life by the same admonition concerning the exactness of the weight.[15]

There exist a number of parallel stories, the subject of an interesting study by Nelson and Starr,[16] in which Christ or Our Lady is offered as surety for a loan made by the merchant. These all deal with miraculous intercession of Our Lord or His mother in coming to the rescue of the debtor. While they do not involve the consideration of a pound of flesh, they all deal with a debt owing to a Jewish moneylender. Here the forfeitures are closer to Table Three of the old Roman law, with its provision that the defaulting debtor may be sold by the creditor into slavery. [In the late seventeenth century it was said that "Among the Muscovites, insolvent debtors are first given no mere perfunctory flogging, and then are forced to become slaves of their creditors." [17]]

One of the very oldest of these is a poem by Gautier (thirteenth century). The hero of this story is devoted to the worship of Our Lady, and beneficently expends his fortune on friends and the needy. Having come to the end of his credit, he is compelled to sell everything he owns, and turns to the richest Jew in town. Pretending sympathy for the man's plight because of his known benevolence, the Jew agrees to lend the money. But since the borrower has nothing to offer as security, he gives Christ as his surety. Should he fail to repay the sum at the time agreed, he takes an oath to become "your villein and your serf . . . so that with a ring about my neck you may sell me in the market-place just as any brute beast." This oath is taken in church before both clergy and laymen. The Christian embarks on his voyage overseas. He visits various markets and becomes rich. Unhappily he forgets about his day of repayment until one day before, while he is on the seas. It would take even a bird thirty days to reach the place of reckoning! Placing himself in Christ's hands, he confides the sum owing the Jew to a chest, and throws the chest into the sea. Miraculously the chest travels one thousand leagues overnight. A servant of the Jew, walking along the shore, discovers the chest; master and man convey it to the house. Within is a letter in which the Christian tells of his new wealth. The Jew hides the chest under a bed. When the merchant returns, the Jew demands that he become his slave. The merchant, confident of Christ's care of him, is sure that the chest has come to shore, and challenges the Jew to come with him to church. Before Our Lady the merchant prays, and the icon replies that the Jew has been fully repaid on the appointed day and that the chest is concealed under a bed. Overcome with this miracle, the Jew at once becomes baptized as a Christian.

There is an Arabic version of this story in which the Jew demands better surety than that of Our Lady and Christ, both of whom the merchant offers. The merchant thereupon promises to give his son to the Jew if the debt is not repaid in time. Unable to reach home in time, he places the sum and a letter into a chest, and casts it into the sea. The Jew finds the chest. When the Christian returns, the Jew registers a complaint with the governor. He accepts the Christian's challenge to come to church, witnesses the miracle, and becomes a Christian.[18]

Among these stories in which Christ and Our Lady are mentioned as sureties, one of the most charming is the Byzantine Greek legend of Theodore, Christian shipmaster of Constantinople. The Jew in this legend is depicted as a not ignoble character. Impoverished by shipwreck, Theodore attempts to borrow money, but is refused by his friends. He therefore calls on Abraham, a Jew, who had often suggested their going into partnership together; Theodore had always declined because of the difference in their religion. Abraham now agrees to lend Theodore what he asks for if someone can be found to go surety for him. But none of Theodore's friends is willing, pleading as their excuse that his transaction is with a Jew. He offers the Jew as surety the icon at the Chalkoprateia Chapel, where Theodore makes his devotions. Despite the unsuitability of such a surety, Abraham agrees only because of Theodore's great faith in his God. Abraham fetches 50 pounds of gold, and the transaction is made before the icon. But Theodore's new voyage also ends disastrously: his cargo is lost upon the seas during a storm. He returns to Constantinople, where Abraham does his best to console him in his wretchedness: he lends the merchant another 50 pounds of gold before the icon. This time the ship touches ports hitherto unvisited. In Britain Theodore finds a most profitable market for himself. Before long, in addition to a cargo of tin and lead, he has fifty pounds of gold. How, without returning to Constantinople, is he to send the money to Abraham? Surrendering himself utterly to divine protection, he seals the money in a wooden chest, prays to God to insure its safe arrival, and commits the chest to the sea. That night both Theodore and Abraham dream about the repayment of the loan. Next day Abraham goes down to the harbor with his servant, who finds the chest. When they have it home, Abraham discovers a letter in it from Theodore. The miracle so much impresses him that he decides to become a Christian; when the other members of his household hear the story, they decide to become baptized too. But in order to go more deeply into the affair, on Theodore's return Abraham feigns not to have received the money. Because of his dream Theodore's faith is untouched, and he asks Abraham to repeat his denial before the icon. In the chapel a "lightning-like force" leaps out at Abraham and fells him. When he comes to his senses, he resolves to become baptized before ever entering his house again. Seventy-five members of his household join him in baptism. After he has become Christian, Abraham helps Theodore unload the ship. They find that the tin and lead has been converted to silver. Theodore and his wife take monastic orders. Abraham builds a special chapel for the icon, and eventually becomes a priest.[19]

Having taken a view of the vicissitudes of other merchants and the usurers who had loaned them money, let us come closer now to the possible sources of the pound-of-flesh story as it appears in *The Merchant of Venice*.

In 1585, at least a decade before *The Merchant of Venice*, an arrestingly interesting series of events is recorded as actually having taken place, if we may credit Leti's account in his *The Life of Pope Sixtus* V: "It was reported in Rome that Drake had taken and plundered St. Domingo in Hispaniola, and carried off an immense booty. This account came in a private letter to Peter Secchi, a very considerable merchant in the city, who had large concerns in those parts, which he had insured. Upon receiving this news, he sent for the insurer, Sampson Ceneda, a Jew, and acquainted him with it. The Jew, whose interest it was to have such a report thought false, gave many reasons why it could not possibly be true, and, at last, worked himself into such a passion that he said, 'I'll lay you a pound of my flesh it is a lie.' [Here for the first time it is a Jew whose flesh is offered as forfeit.] Such sort of wagers, it is well known, are often proposed by people of strong passions, to convince others that are incredulous or obstinate. Nothing is more common than to say, 'I'll lay my life on it'; 'I'll forfeit my right hand, if it is not true,' etc. Secchi, who was of a fiery, hot temper, replied, 'If you like it, I'll lay you a thousand crowns against a pound of your flesh that it is true.' The Jew accepted the wager, and articles were immediately executed betwixt them, the substance of which was that if Secchi won, he should himself cut the flesh with a sharp knife from whatever part of the Jew's body he pleased. Unfortunately for the Jew, the truth of the account was soon confirmed; and the Jew was almost distracted when he was informed that Secchi had solemnly sworn he would compel him to the exact performance of his contract, and was determined to cut a pound of flesh from that part of his body which it is not necessary to mention. A report of this transaction was brought to the Pope, who sent for the parties, and being informed of the whole affair, said, 'When contracts are made, it is just they should be fulfilled, as we intend this shall. Take a knife, therefore, Secchi, and cut a pound of flesh from any part you please of the Jew's body. We would advise you, however, to be very careful; for if you cut but a scruple, or a grain, more or less than your due, you shall certainly be hanged; go, and bring thither a knife and a pair of scales, and let it be done in our presence.' The merchant, at these words, began to tremble like an aspen leaf, and throwing himself at his Holiness' feet, with tears in his eyes, protested it was far from his thoughts to insist upon the performance of the contract. And being asked by the Pope what he demanded, answered, 'Nothing, holy father, but your benediction, and that the articles may be torn in pieces.' Then turning to the Jew, he asked him what he had to say and whether he was content. The Jew answered he thought himself extremely happy to come off at so easy a rate, and that he was perfectly content. 'But we are not content,' replied Sixtus, 'nor is there sufficient satisfaction made to our laws; we desire to know what authority you have to lay such wagers. The subjects of princes are the property of the state, and have no right to dispose of their bodies, nor any part of them, without the express consent of their sovereigns.' They were both immediately sent to prison and the governor ordered to proceed against them with the utmost severity of the law, that others might be deterred by their example from laying any more such wagers." The governor was inclined to fine each of them very heavily, but the Pope protested that such a punishment was too lenient. " 'Is it not evident that the Jew has actually sold his life by consenting to have a pound of his flesh cut from his body? Is not this a direct suicide? And is it not likewise true that the merchant is guilty of downright premeditated murder in making a contract with the other?' " Sixtus ended by telling the governor: " 'Let them both be hanged; do you pass sentence on them, and we shall take care of the rest.' " Since Secchi came from a prominent family and the Jew was "one of the leading men of the synagogue," they were both able to offer strong petitions against the sentence. "Sixtus, who did not really design to put them to death, but to deter others from such practises, at last consented to change the sentence into that of the galleys, with liberty to buy off that too by paying each of them 2000 crowns, to be applied to the use of the hospital which he had lately founded." [20]

There is no possibility that Leti's book could have had any influence on the writing of *The Merchant of Venice* since the biography was composed some years after Shakespeare's death. Nor can one be certain that the events Leti describes are historical facts, though some of the personages involved were real contemporaries of Sixtus. It is within the realm of likelihood that the Italian author embroidered upon one of the many old versions of the pound-of-flesh story, this time making the Jew the victim rather than the merchant. On the other hand, Leti's story ends quite differently from the old tales, for adverse judgment is visited upon the heads of both parties to the contract. Moreover, unlike Shylock's bond, the contract between merchant and Jew is affirmed to have been a strictly illegal one.

As for the immediate source of the pound-of-flesh story in *The Merchant of Venice*, there have been three chief claimants: the old lost play of *The Jew*, a contemporary ballad, and a tale by Fiorentino.

Modern scholars, for no very good reasons, have become almost unanimous in the agreement that the play referred to by Gosson in 1579 as *The Jew* "showne at the Bull, . . . representing the greedinesse of worldly chusers, and bloody mindes of Usurers," furnished Shakespeare with most of the materials for *The Merchant of Venice*

(see pp. 43-4). Steevens, Skottowe, Singer, and Furness,[21] were fairly
or completely convinced. The "bloody mindes of Usurers" might
conceivably apply to a prototype of Shylock, though not necessarily
so, since it is a phrase equally applicable to most of the moneylenders we have met in the old tales.

The argument is made to hinge upon the interpretation of "the
greedinesse of worldly chusers," an expression which is taken to refer to originals of Shakespeare's Morocco and Arragon, who have
nothing at all to do with the Shylock-Antonio plot. Hence, scholars
have cheerfully concluded, Shakespeare had ready to hand in the
old play of *The Jew* the materials for both the pound-of-flesh story
and the story of the wooing of Portia. Shakespearean scholars seem
never so happy as when they can deprive Shakespeare of another
vestige of his originality or genius. "Gosson's description," says one
of the Cambridge editors of *The Merchant of Venice*, "may be
taken, even probably, to cover the casket-scenes and Shylock's
bond." [22] The case has presumably been fortified by the observation
that there is a place* in which Shakespeare uses the word "chooser"
in such a way as could be construed to mean "lover." (It is, in point
of fact, the only place in which he uses the word.) And J. Dover
Wilson has attempted to nail down this theory by one of those
"double authorship" flights to which scholarship is subject; he proves
to his own satisfaction that an insignificant passage in *The Merchant of Venice* (a mere six lines, III, iii, 26-31) was written by a
hand earlier than Shakespeare's, and that Shakespeare left this passage as he had found it in the old play of *The Jew*.[23]

The theory is typical of the indifference to the plays themselves,
to which the eagerness of many scholars to make a new "finding"
exposes them. A moment's thought should make it plain that neither Morocco nor Arragon can be accused, in any sense, of demon-
strating "the greedinesse of worldly chusers." Each of them is obviously at least as wealthy as Portia, and certainly of not less rank than
she. Each in his own way is quite honestly desirous of winning Portia herself.

Morocco's reasons for choosing the golden casket do him no
discredit. When he rejects the leaden casket it is because "This
casket threatens," and "A golden mind stoops not to shows of
dross." He rejects the silver casket because, although it promises
the chooser "as much as he deserves," and he concedes that his qual-

* *The Merry Wives of Windsor*, IV, vi, 11.

ities and reputation might entitle him to conclude that he deserves enough,

> yet enough
> May not extend so far as to the lady.

In other words, he admits that, despite his qualities, riches, and title, he may not be quite worthy of Portia. When he does choose the gold casket, it is not at all out of greed. "Who chooseth me shall gain what many men desire," he reads, and exclaims:

> Why, that's the lady! All the world desires her.
> From the four corners of the earth they come
> To kiss this shrine, this mortal-breathing saint.

Moreover, since her picture is to be found in the winning casket, he reflects:

> Is't like that lead contains her?—'Twere damnation
> To think so base a thought. It were too gross
> To rib her cerecloth in the obscure grave.
> Or shall I think in silver she's immur'd,
> Being ten times undervalu'd to tried gold? *
> O sinful thought! never so rich a gem
> Was set in worse than gold.

> (II, vii, 18-55)

No, Morocco's choice of the gold casket is neither a greedy one nor a worldly one. It is based upon a thoroughly decent and romantic veneration for Portia herself.

Arragon, a less attractive figure than Morocco, makes his choice of the silver casket without the slightest motivation of greed. He despises the leaden casket because lead is "base" and is not fair to look at. He rejects the golden casket because he is not interested in obtaining "what many men desire," because by that "many" may be meant

> the fool multitude that choose by show,
> Not learning more than the fond eye doth teach. . . .

---

* The Elizabethan ratio of the value of silver to gold was ten to one.

I will not choose what many men desire,
Because I will not jump* with common spirits
And rank me with the barbarous multitudes.

He chooses the silver casket because it promises that the chooser "shall get as much as he deserves," and he feels that his position and lineage entitle him to expect Portia:

"I will assume desert."

(II, ix, 20-51)

Arragon is vain and arrogant, but he nowhere exhibits any symptoms of greed in his choice.

Hence I argue that there are no grounds for presuming a connection between *The Merchant of Venice* and *The Jew*. All that we know about the latter is Gosson's brief description of it, and that description (the accord of scholarship to the contrary notwithstanding) makes the connection less than likely. The best we can do is forget about the old lost play, since nothing definite or conclusive can be said about it.

Percy in his *Reliques of Ancient English Poetry* reprinted an old ballad, under the following title:

A new song, shewing the crueltie of Gernutus, a Jewe, who lending to a merchant an hundred crownes, would have a pound of his fleshe, because he could not pay him at the time appointed. To the tune of Black and yellow.

The resemblance of the plot as well as a few of the details of this ballad to *The Merchant of Venice* will not escape anyone familiar with Shakespeare's play:

The First Part

In Venice towne not long agoe
    A cruel Jew did dwell,
Which lived all on usurie
    As Italian writers tell.

Gernutus called was the Jew,
    Which never thought to dye,

* agree

Nor never yet did any good
    To them in streets that lie.

His life was like a barrow hogge,
    That liveth many a day,
Yet never once doth any good,
    Until men will him slay.

Or like a filthy heap of dung,
    That lyeth in a whoard
Which never can do any good,
    Till it be spread abroad.

So fares it with the usurer.
    He cannot sleep in rest,
For feare the thiefe will him pursue
    To plucke him from his nest.

His heart doth thinke on many a wile,
    How to deceive the poore;
His mouth is almost ful of mucke,
    Yet still he gapes for more.

His wife must lend a shilling,
    For every weeke a penny,
Yet bring a pledge, that is double worth,
    If that you will have any.

And see, likewise, you keepe your day,
    Or else you loose it all:
This was the living of the wife,
    Her cow she did it call.

Within that citie dwelt that time
    A marchant of great fame,
Which being distressed in his need,
    Unto Gernutus came:

Desiring him to stand his friend
    For twelve month and a day,
To lend him an hundred crownes;
    And he for it would pay

Whatsoever he would demand of him,
   And pledges he should have,
No (quoth the Jew with flearing lookes)
   Sir, aske what you will have.

No penny for the loane of it
   For one yeare you shall pay;
You may doe me as goode a turne,
   Before my dying day.

But we will have a merry jeast
   For to be talked long;
You shall make me a bond, quoth he,
   That shall be large and strong:

And this shall be the forfeyture;
   Of your owne fleshe a pound.
If you agree, make you the bond,
   And here is a hundred crownes.

With right good will! the merchant says:
   And so the bond was made.
When twelve month and a day drew on
   That backe it should be payd,

The marchant's ships were all at sea,
   And money came not in;
Which way to take, or what to doe
   To thinke he doth begin:

And to Gernutus strait he comes
   With cap and bended knee,
And sayde to him, Of curtesie
   I pray you beare with mee.

My day is come, and I have not
   The money for to pay:
And little good the forfeyture
   Will doe you, I dare say.

With all my heart, Gernutus sayd,
   Commaund it to your minde:
In thinges of bigger waight then this
   You shall me ready finde.

He goes his way; the day once past
 Gernutus did not slacke
To get a sergiant presently;
 And clapt him on the backe:*

And layd him into prison strong,
 And sued his bond withall;
And when the judgement day was come,
 For judgement he did call.

The marchants friends came thither fast,
 With many a weeping eye,
For other meanes they could not find,
 For he that day must dye.

The Second Part

Some offered for his hundred crownes
 Five hundred for to pay;
And some a thousand, two or three,
 Yet still he did denay.

And at the last ten thousand crownes
 They offered him to save,
Gernutus sayd, I will no gold,
 My forfeite I will have.

A pound of fleshe is my demand,
 And that shall be my hire,
Then sayd the judge, Yet my good friend,
 Let me of you desire

To take the flesh from such a place,
 As yet you let him live;
Do so, and lo! an hundred crownes
 To thee here will I give.

No: no: quoth he, no: judgment here:
 For this it shall be tride,

* A gesture accompanying the act of arresting the merchant. See Dromio of Syracuse's description of the arresting officer as "A back friend, a shoulder-clapper." (*Comedy of Errors*, IV, ii, 37)

For I will have my pound of fleshe
   From under his right side.

It grieved all the companie
   His crueltie to see
For neither friend nor foe could helpe
   But he must spoyled bee.

The bloudie Jew now ready is
   With whetted blade in hand,
To spyle the bloud of innocent,
   By forfeit of his bond.

And as he was about to strike
   In him the deadly blow:
Stay (quoth the judge) thy crueltie;
   I charge thee to do so.

Sith needs thou wilt thy forfeit have,
   Which is of flesh a pound:
See that you shed no drop of bloud,
   Nor yet the man confound.

For if thou doe, like murderer,
   Thou here shalt hanged be:
Likewise of flesh see that thou cut
   No more than longes to thee;

For if thou take either more or lesse
   To the value of a mite,
Thou shalt be hanged presently
   As is both law and right.

Gernutus now waxt franticke mad,
   And wotes not what to say;
Quoth he at last, Ten thousand crownes,
   I will that he shall pay;

And so I graunt to set him free.
   The judge doth answere make;
You shall not have a penny given;
   Your forfeyture now take.

At the last he doth demaund
    But for to have his owne.
No, quoth the judge, doe as you list
    Thy judgement shall be showne.

Either take your pound of flesh, quoth he,
    Or cancell me your bond.
O cruel judge, then quoth the Jew,
    That doth against me stand!

And so with griping grieved mind
    He biddeth them fare-well,
Then all the people prays'd the Lord,
    That ever this heard tell.

Good people, that do heare this song,
    For trueth I dare well say,
That many a wretch as ill as hee
    Doth live now at this day;

That seeketh nothing but the spoyle
    Of many a wealthey man,
And for to trap the innocent
    Deviseth what they can.

From whome the Lord deliver me,
    And every Christian too,
And send to them like sentence eke
    That meaneth so to do.

Though it has been strongly argued that this ballad must have preceded Shakespeare's play, there is no way of knowing that it really did. Certainly several details are impressively similar to the play. The usurer of the ballad "cannot sleep in rest," and Shylock says:

There is some ill a-brewing towards my rest,
For I did dream of money-bags tonight.

(II, v, 17-18)

When the merchant sees that he will not be able to pay, he reminds the moneylender that "little good the forfeyture/ Will do you."

When Bassanio recoils at the terms of the bond, as proposed by Shylock, the latter responds:

> If he should break his day what should I gain
> By the exaction of the forfeiture?"
>
> (I, iii, 164-5)

Later, Salarino asks Shylock:

> Why, I am sure if he forfeit, thou wilt not take his flesh. What's
> that good for?
>
> (III, i, 53-4)

But perhaps the most striking similarity is the fact that the moneylender proposes the terms, in the first instance, as a "merry jeast." This is the sole case in which we find a parallel to Shylock's description of the bond as being made "in a merry sport" (he again refers to it as "this merry bond")—a point of cardinal dramatic importance to Shakespeare's play.

As inviting as these matters make it to find Shakespeare's source in the ballad, it is just as reasonable to suppose that the ballad was inspired by Shakespeare's play. Moreover, as we shall see, the resemblances of *The Merchant of Venice* to Fiorentino's tale are very much more impressive. There are, too, in the ballad, many details not to be found in the play: e.g., the private life of the usurer is denounced; the moneylender has a wife who also engages in usury; the merchant, foreseeing his inability to repay, asks for clemency; and the moneylender pretends that he will be reasonable. The fourth line of the ballad raises the possibility that its author may have read Fiorentino's tale too; the popular ballads made no great attempt at dramatic depth, and that fact would account for the rather pointless variations made by the balladeer upon the Italian, if he knew it.

Before the vogue set in to identify the source of *The Merchant of Venice* as the lost play, *The Jew*, so sketchily referred to by Gosson, it used to be generally conceded that Shakespeare got his basic plot from a fourteenth-century Italian collection of tales, *Il Pecorone*, (published in 1558) by Giovanni Fiorentino. But no one, to my knowledge, has examined this tale critically enough to establish beyond doubt that this was Shakespeare's actual source, as I am convinced, and hope to demonstrate, that it was. The first story of the fourth day of storytelling in *Il Pecorone* goes as follows:

A Florentine youth, Giannetto (the original of Shakespeare's Bassanio), in accordance with his deceased father's wish, went to Venice to the house of Ansaldo (the original of Shakespeare's Antonio), his godfather and "the richest of all Christian merchants" at that time. Ansaldo welcomed Giannetto with great joy, but grieved to hear of the death of the boy's father "for he helped me win the greater part of what I possess." Since he was childless Ansaldo began at once to treat the young man as his son and heir, ordering all his servants to respect him as such too. He even gave Giannetto "the keys to all his cash," bade him spend money freely on "clothes and shoes" and urged him to develop a circle of friends for himself in Venice.

So, with Ansaldo's complete approval, Giannetto "began to frequent the men of rank in Venice, to exchange visits, to dine and be dined, to get livery for his men-servants, to buy fine steeds, to joust and participate in tournaments, in which he was expert and practiced, and high spirited, and well-bred in all things; and well-skilled in paying honor and courtesy where they were called for, and always according respect to Messer Ansaldo, more than if he had been a hundred times his father."

Before long Giannetto was a favorite with the young nobles and ladies of Venice. Two of his friends, who made a yearly voyage to Alexandria with merchandise, urged Ansaldo to equip a ship for Giannetto so that he might go along with them and see something of the world. Ansaldo was only too willing. He outfitted a fine ship for the young man and "adorned it with banners," informing the master of the ship that he was sending the youth not for gain but, he said, "for his own enjoyment."

The three friends, each in his own vessel, kept company for some days until one morning Giannetto sighted a port which the master informed him belonged to a widow, who had been the ruin of many a man. "She is a beautiful and enchanting lady, and she maintains this law: whoever arrives must sleep with her, and if he possess her must take her for his wife and be lord of the port and all that country. And if does not possess her, he loses all that he owns."

Despite the master's admonitions, Giannetto determined to see this lady. The ship made for port without the knowledge of his friends. In the morning, the widow (the original of Shakespeare's Portia!), hearing of the ship's coming into port, came down to greet Giannetto. After learning who he was and that he knew the stipulations, she feasted him and entertained him the livelong day. At night, she led him to her bed-chamber, where two maids brought wine and dainties. The lady bade him drink since he must be thirsty. Not knowing that the wine was drugged, he drank half a goblet of it, undressed, went to bed, and at once fell asleep.

The lady lay beside him, but by the time he was awake the next morning, she was up and about, and had already ordered that the vessel be emptied of all its fine merchandise. The maids made Giannetto get up, told him of what he had lost, and informed him that he must leave at once. Equipped with a horse and some money by the lady, he left in deep humiliation. Back in Venice, ashamed to see Ansaldo, he went to the house of a friend, to whom he pretended that his ship had capsized on the rocks.

After several days, the friend visited Ansaldo, who was worried about what might have happened to his adopted son. He said, "I cannot find rest and I am not well; so great is the love I bear him." The friend was able to assure Ansaldo that Giannetto was safe and alive, although he had suffered shipwreck. The news was indeed joyful to the older man. He cried, "As long as he is alive, I am content." Ansaldo went to greet his son at the friend's house, was in great joy to see him, and assured him that the loss of the ship did not matter. "Since you have done yourself no harm, I am content."

When Giannetto's friends returned from Alexandria mourning his probable death, they were delighted to find him alive. He told them, too, that his ship had been wrecked on rocks. There was great feasting in his honor, but he could think of nothing but the widow-lady, whom he was determined to win as his wife or else die. Ansaldo, perceiving his son's melancholy, learned from the youth that he was set on making the voyage again. Therefore, when the two friends were ready to sail once more for Alexandria, Ansaldo saw to it that Giannetto had an even better ship with more valuable goods than before.

After a sail of several days, Giannetto again beheld the port which was called "the port of the lady of Belmonte." Again he gave his companions the slip, and entered the port. The next morning the lady "saw the ship's pennants waving in the breeze," and had her recognition of them confirmed by one of her maids, who said, "My

lady, it seems to be the ship of that young man who came here a
year ago." The lady was convinced that Giannetto must love her
deeply, for no other suitor had ever come back after having failed
once. The maid responded, "I've never seen a man more courteous
and gracious than he."

Again Giannetto was banqueted and entertained by the lady. Her
nobles were excited to see him again, for they had all become so delighted with him that they would gladly have had him as their lord.
Again at night the lady conducted him to her bedchamber, again
he was served drugged wine, again he drank and fell asleep, again
the lady lay by his side all night without his awaking. The next
morning she once more caused his ship to be unloaded, and once
more gave him a horse and money and bade him be on his way.

At Venice Giannetto again sought asylum in the house of his
friend and cursed his fate. His friend this time agreed with him, adding that he had ruined Ansaldo, who had once been the wealthiest
of all Christian merchants. The young man at first thought of returning, out of shame, to his native Florence, but at last went to see
his foster-father. Ansaldo was so happy to see him that he made
light of his great losses. The older man had now to sell many of his
possessions to repay the men who had supplied the merchandise lost
with the ship.

On their return from Alexandria, the two merchant-friends heard
anew of a shipwreck and the loss of everything on board. Blaming
themselves for having induced Ansaldo to finance Giannetto's ex-
peditions, they begged Ansaldo to allow them to make a voyage for
his benefit next year. They said, "Therefore do not fear, for while
we have anything, dispose of it as if it were your own." Ansaldo
thanked them but assured them that he had enough for his private
needs.

Giannetto was now inconsolable and told Ansaldo that he would
never have any peace, as he put it, "unless I can regain what I have
lost." When Ansaldo saw that he could not make the young man
content to live on what was left them, he sold everything he had to
outfit another ship. For that purpose, after he had disposed of his
possessions, he still lacked ten thousand ducats. These he borrowed
from a Jew at Mestri, with this agreement "that if he had not paid
back the debt the following June on Saint John's Day, the Jew might
take off a pound of flesh from whatever part of him he wished."
The bond was drawn up in regular form.

The ten thousand ducats went to equip the finest of the three ships which Ansaldo had given Giannetto. The two merchant-friends sailed again too, intending whatever profits they should make to go to Ansaldo. Before their departure, Ansaldo said to his son, reminding him of the bond, that whatever misfortune might occur on sea, "Please come to see me, so that I may see you before I die, and I shall depart contented." Giannetto promised, and sailed away.

Despite their care, Giannetto was able again to evade his friends' watchfulness and make for the port of the lady of Belmonte. Once more the lady recognized the banners, crossed herself, and thought herself again in great luck. His success with the nobles was renewed. Again, after much feasting, Giannetto was led to the bed-chamber. But this time one of the maids, taking pity on him, warned him not to drink the wine that night. When the maids came in with the wine, therefore, Giannetto pretended to drink of it but instead poured it into his bosom. The lady was sure that he would lose his ship again.

To hasten the lady's appearance in bed he began to snore. The lady cried, " 'Splendid!' and quickly disrobed and lay beside Giannetto, who did not lose an instant, but as soon as the lady had come in, turned toward her and embraced her, saying: 'Now I have what I have so long desired!' and with that gave her the peace of holy matrimony, and all night long she did not leave his arms."

Highly pleased, the lady next day summoned her people and announced to them that Giannetto would be their new lord. With considerable magnificence he ruled at Belmonte, never giving a thought to the plight of his benefactor. But one day he was suddenly reminded that it was Saint John's Day, and he remembered Ansaldo, and began to sigh. His lady, seeing that something weighed upon him, would give him no peace until he told her of Ansaldo and the bond, and how this was the day when the sum was due. She urged him to take horse at once and bear with him a hundred thousand ducats. Giannetto set out at once for Venice.

In the meantime, Ansaldo being unable to pay his debt, the Jew had him arrested, and was demanding his pound of flesh. Ansaldo begged only that the Jew wait a few more days in case Giannetto should return. To this delay the Jew agreed, warning, however, that Giannetto or no Giannetto he meant to take the forfeiture. With that Ansaldo was content. Now, many of Ansaldo's fellow-merchants offered to join in paying off the amount, but the Jew refused them since he wished only to be able to boast that he had done to death the greatest of the Christian merchants.

After Giannetto's departure from Belmonte, his wife dressed as a lawyer, and, taking with her two servants, followed him. Giannetto himself went directly to the Jew and offered to pay him as much money as he wanted. The Jew answered that it was too late for money; he would take only the pound of flesh. The case looked hopeless for poor Ansaldo. "Since Venice was held to be a land of strict justice and the Jew had a case that was legal and in public form," there was nothing to do but plead with the Jew. "All the Venetian merchants went to sue to the Jew, but he became harder than ever." The Jew refused first twenty thousand ducats, then thirty thousand, then forty thousand, and finally a hundred thousand from Giannetto, saying, "I wish to act according to my bond."

At this juncture, the lady, robed as a lawyer, arrived at an inn in Venice, and gave out that she was a lawyer who had just finished his studies at Bologna. The landlord told her the predicament in which Ansaldo stood. The lawyer issued a proclamation that anyone with a legal problem might apply to him. Hearing this news, Giannetto proposed to the Jew that they request the lawyer to settle the matter. The Jew agreed.

When they appeared before the lawyer, Giannetto did not recognize his wife because she had used certain herbs to alter her appearance. Examining the bond, the lawyer advised the Jew to accept the hundred thousand ducats and free Ansaldo. But the Jew refused. It was agreed to take the case to court, where the lawyer represented Ansaldo.

In court the lawyer said to the Jew, "Come then! Take a pound of flesh from wherever you wish, and do your deed." The Jew demanded that Ansaldo be stripped naked, and made ready with a razor, and approached his victim. Then the lawyer spoke up: "Be careful what you do. However, if you take more or less than a pound of flesh, I'll see that your head is removed. And I tell you further, if you let fall but the least drop of blood, I'll have you put to death. For your bond makes no mention of the shedding of blood, but says that you must take a pound of flesh, and says neither more nor less. Wherefore, if you are wise you will ponder which way you think you can act best."

Beginning to fear, the Jew, after considerable argument, said,

"Let them give me the hundred thousand ducats and I am content."
The lawyer would grant only the pound of flesh "according to
the bond." The Jew offered to take less, and Giannetto was ready
to give him whatever he asked if Ansaldo might go free. But the
lawyer was adamant. "Give me at least my ten thousand ducats,"
the Jew begged. The lawyer refused to allow him a copper. Realizing himself defeated, the Jew tore up the bond in a rage. Everyone was happy but him. Giannetto joyfully took Ansaldo home.

Then Giannetto went to the inn and offered the lawyer the hundred thousand ducats. The lawyer refused to accept the gift, suggesting that if Giannetto keep the money his lady will think he has
not squandered it. Whereupon Giannetto began to sing the praises
of his wife. "If you will do me so much grace as to come and see
her, you will marvel at the honor she will bestow upon you," he
added. The lawyer professed not to have the time. Since Giannetto
continued to press him to take the money, the lawyer, seeing a ring
on the young man's finger, said, "I should like that ring, and I will
accept no other reward." Giannetto agreed reluctantly, explaining
that "my lady gave it to me, and told me to wear it always for
her love's sake." "Do me a kindness," suddenly remarked the lawyer.
Giannetto assented in advance. Then the lawyer asked him to return
to his lady as soon as possible. For that Giannetto needed no urging.

The lady returned to Belmonte at once, and explained her absence as due to a visit to the baths. At Venice Giannetto banqueted
his friends, gave them many gifts, and left for Belmonte with Ansaldo and a number of companions. On their arrival, "the lady ran
to embrace Messer Ansaldo and feigned being a little angry" with
her husband.

When he was alone with her Giannetto attempted to embrace her,
and asked her to explain her coolness. She pretended to think that
he had been seeing his old sweethearts in Venice. When he protested his innocence, she asked, "Where is the ring I gave you?"
Giannetto swore by his love for God and for her, " 'I gave that ring
to the judge who won the case for us.' Said the lady: 'I swear by the
love I bear to God and you that you gave it to a woman.' " She continued to taunt him with his old mistresses, until he began to weep.

Feeling she had teased him enough, she embraced him laughingly
and showed him the ring, and then told him how she had been the
lawyer who had won the case.

When Giannetto recovered from his astonishment, he began to enjoy the jest immensely. He told all his friends of his wife's great feat, and thereafter he loved her more than ever. As a final gesture, he gave the hand of the maid who had warned him against the wine, to Ansaldo in marriage.

The old story, first told by De Alta Silva, is now in Fiorentino's hands, its most imposing pre-Shakespearean version, equipped with some interesting innovations. Perhaps four of these were the most significant for Shakespeare's purposes:

1. For the first time the merchant borrows the money and signs the bond not to supply his own needs, but to make possible the felicity of the young man he loves so much. This elaboration, besides deepening the dramatic possibilities once the bond is due, also opens up for Shakespeare more complex opportunities for the relationship of the lady to the story.

2. The moneylender, as in some parallel usurer stories but not in the De Alta Silva tale, has become a Jew.

3. The lady disguises herself not as a knight but as a lawyer. This offers Shakespeare the opportunity for writing the most exciting trial scene in drama.

4. The lady reveals her identity to her husband at the end not by donning her disguise again, but through the charming device of the rings. This change makes it possible for Shakespeare to conceive his play not as a melodrama, but as a piece of high comedy.

Fiorentino's substitution of the drugged wine for a magic feather or pillow is an improvement, too; but Shakespeare found the wooing of the lady an unpalatable business in the Italian tale, and sought elsewhere for ideas for the courting of his Portia.

The resemblances between the outline of Fiorentino's story and Shakespeare's plot are too striking to seem accidental. But the actual proof that this was his source is to be found in the details and phraseology. Before we proceed to an examination of them however, let us, in justice to Shakespeare, take note of the great disparities between the Italian tale and the English play.

And the disparities are rather more striking than the resemblances. With the exception of Boccaccio's irritating (to modern taste), Patient Griselda, there is very little attempt in the old tales at characterization. Apart from the fact that the widow of Belmonte has had many unsuccessful wooers, whatever character she has—and that is highly unattractive until she becomes Ansaldo's savior— seems to have much more in common with the enchantresses of medieval lore than with Shakespeare's noble heroine. The cleverness which she exhibits in the first part of the tale, unpleasant as it is, in no way prepares us for the magnanimity and wisdom she exhibits in coming to the rescue of Ansaldo. She becomes suddenly, in fact, another person.

As for the character of Giannetto, what can be said for it? His callous readiness to bankrupt his benefactor goes far beyond what may be excused on the grounds of his being only a thoughtless youth. Even after he has won the lady, it is only accident that puts him in mind of the danger Ansaldo has incurred for his sake. How distant he is from the warm and elegant man Shakespeare created in Bassanio!

Even Ansaldo, whose consistent goodness gives him a reality the others lack, has no dimension. The Jew is but a flat figure who never comes to life; there is no comprehending why he should desire Ansaldo's death—any more than there is in any of the parallel merchant-usurer stories, whether or not the usurer is a Jew. The "motive" advanced in the tale, that he only wished to boast his doing to death the greatest of the Christian merchants, is to modern intelligence silly and beyond belief. How did Shakespeare ever see in him the possibilities for the fascinating figure of Shylock?

Such questions merely make one wonder anew at Shakespeare's inexplicable ability to discover inspiration in material as crude as Fiorentino's (superior as it is to its forerunners). But it is a wonder that recurs whenever one compares any of his plays with its source. How, for example, could he have envisioned the potentialities for his *Othello* in Cinthio's revolting tale, or for his *Hamlet* in the absurd, overtheatrical material available to him? Any one who could answer these questions would probably be writing masterworks of drama himself instead of books about Shakespeare.

Nevertheless, since it could inspire Shakespeare to write one of his richest plays—perhaps the earliest of his flawless masterpieces*—let us be grateful to Fiorentino's tale. That it was his source, we now proceed to prove. And in the proof lies the settling of an old argument: Could Shakespeare have read his Italians in their own tongue?

It is indeed astonishing that no one thus far has troubled to no-

---

* *Romeo and Juliet* is an earlier masterpiece, but a masterpiece with many flaws.

tice how *The Merchant of Venice* contains many echoes of Fiorentino's Italian. A careful consideration of the original has convinced me that a number of expressions in the Italian must have lingered with Shakespeare and become part of the tissue of his own beautiful language in the play. It is to make possible the comparison that I quote the relevant passages in Italian.

Perhaps our simplest way is to follow more or less the order of these expressions as they appear in Fiorentino.

1. When Ansaldo accepts Giannetto as his son and heir, he gives him "the keys to all his cash (*le chiave di tutti i suoi contanti*)." The phrase suggests a locked money-coffer. When Bassanio first broaches his need of money, Antonio assures him:

> My purse, my person, my extremest means
> *Lie all unlock'd to your occasions.*
>
> (I, i, 139)

2. As Giannetto begins to live the life of a wealthy gentleman in Venice he gets "livery for his men-servants (*vestir famigli*)." When Launcelot Gobbo enters Bassanio's service, his new master makes the point that Launcelot is to be given "a livery" (II, ii, 163). It is a matter of which no mention need have been made at all.

3. Ansaldo informs the master of the first ship that the voyage is being undertaken not for gain but for the sake of Giannetto's "own enjoyment (*a suo diletto*)." Salarino reports that when Bassanio took leave of Antonio to sail for Belmont, Antonio urged his friend not to worry or to hurry back

> But stay the very riping of the time

and

> Be merry.
>
> (II, viii, 40, 43)

4. The lady of Belmonte's law stipulates that each unsuccessful suitor "loses all that he owns (*perde tutto ciò ch'egli ha*)." In the source for the casket story, which Shakespeare substituted for this portion of Fiorentino's tale, there was, as we shall see, no penalty

attached to the choice of the wrong vessel. But a penalty is stipulated for all of Portia's unsuccessful suitors: Morocco is told he must

> swear before you choose, if you choose wrong
> Never to speak to lady afterward
> In way of marriage.

> (II, i, 40-2)

The idea is reinforced by Arragon's acknowledging that he has been enjoined by his oath.

> if I fail
> Of the right casket, never in my life
> To woo a maid in way of marriage.

> (II, ix, 11-13)

5. Concerned about the boy's absence, Ansaldo confesses to the friend that "I cannot find rest and I am not well (*io no trovo luogo, e non ho bene*); so great is the love I bear him." Shakespeare has depicted Antonio as suffering from melancholy: the first minutes of the play are given over to his friend's attempts to make him cast it off. Commentators have often observed that this melancholy is not particularly put to any dramatic use. Is it not possible that Shakespeare so conceived Antonio because of his memory of Antonio's prototype, Ansaldo? As for Ansaldo's "so great is the love I bear him (*tanto è l'amore ch' io gli porto*)," as well as his saintly forbearance toward Giannetto, are we not reminded of that love when Salarino says of Antonio's love of Bassanio:

> I think he only loves the world for him.

> (II, viii, 50)

6. The Belmonte of Giannetto's lady becomes the Belmont of Portia.

7. Earlier in the tale, when Ansaldo outfitted Giannetto's first ship, he "adorned it with banners." Now, when Giannetto's second ship is seen in port, the lady comments on "the ship's pennants waving in the breeze (*sventolare le bandiere di questa nave*)." Recollection of this detail may very well have been part of the inspiration for Gratiano's lively comment on Lorenzo's lateness for the appointed elopement:

> How like a younger or a prodigal
> The scarfed * bark puts from her native bay—
> Hugg'd and embraced by the strumpet wind!

> (II, vi, 14-16)

8. One of the lady's maids agrees that it seems the ship "of that young man who came here a year ago (*di quel giovane che ci arrivò, ora fa uno anno*)." Nerissa asks Portia, concerning Bassanio:

> Do you not remember, lady, in your father's time, a Venetian,
>   a scholar and a soldier, that came hither in company of the
>   Marquis of Montferrat?

> (I, ii, 122-6)

9. The maid goes on to say, "I've never seen a man more courteous and gracious than he (*Io non vidi mai il più cortese nè il più grazioso uomo di lui*)." And Nerissa continues:

> He of all the men that ever my foolish eyes look'd upon, was the
>   best deserving a fair lady.

> (I, ii, 129-30)

10. The two friends, after the loss of Giannetto's second ship, say to Ansaldo: "While we have anything, dispose of it as if it were your own (*e mentre che noi abbiamo della roba, fatene come della vostra*)." There is an echo of this in Antonio's response to Bassanio's request for a loan:

> you do me now more wrong
> In making question of my uttermost
> Than if you had made waste of all I have.

> (I, i, 155-7)

11. After losing his second ship, Giannetto is sure he cannot rest "unless I can regain what I have lost (*s' io non racquisto quello ch' io ho perduto*)." In making his request for a loan to Antonio, Bassanio confesses:

> I owe you much, and, like a wilful youth,
> That which I owe is lost.

> (I, i, 146-7)

* adorned with banners.

And, it is to be noted, Giannetto's chief reason for making his third voyage is to retrieve Ansaldo's losses. So, too, Bassanio promises to bring Antonio's newest loan "back again"—and possibly all that he already owes him besides.

12. The terms of the bond which Ansaldo signs are that "if he had not paid back the debt the following June on Saint John's Day, the Jew might take off a pound of flesh from whatever part of him he wished (*una libra di carne d'addosso di qualunque luogo e' volesse*)." Shylock's terms repeat almost the very language:

> If you repay me not on such a day
> In such a place . . . let the forfeit
> Be nominated for an equal pound
> Of your fair flesh, to be cut off and taken
> In what part of your body pleaseth me.
>
> (I, iii, 147-52)

It must be remembered, however, that here Fiorentino's phrasing is fairly traditional.

13. Before Giannetto's third voyage, after signing the bond, Ansaldo says to him, "Please come to see me, so that I may see you before I die, and I shall depart contented (*che ti piaccia venire a verdermi, si ch' io possa vedere te innanzi ch' io moia, e andronne contento*)." Antonio's letter to Bassanio, when the bond has expired, says:

> All debts are cleared between you and I, if I might but see you
> at my death.
>
> (III, ii, 321-3)

14. The lady of Belmonte gives Giannetto a hundred thousand ducats to free Ansaldo; this is ten times the sum owing to the Jew. Portia tells Bassanio,

> You shall have gold
> To pay the petty debt twenty times over.
>
> (III, ii, 309-10)

15. The case looked hopeless for Ansaldo "since Venice was held to be a land of strict justice (*pure considerato Vinegia essere terra*

di ragione)." Portia tells Shylock that if he persists in requiring the letter of the law,

> this strict court of Venice
> Must needs give sentence.
>
> (IV, i, 204-5)

And when Bassanio pleads with her to set aside the law, she answers:

> It must not be. There is no power in Venice
> Can alter a decree established.
>
> (IV, i, 218-9)

16. The Jew refuses Giannetto's offer of even a hundred thousand ducats, saying, "I wish to act according to my bond (*i' vuo' fare quel che dicon le carte mie*)." Before the Duke, Shylock rejects Bassanio's six thousand with:

> I would have my bond!;
>
> (IV, i, 87)

demands of Portia

> The penalty and forfeit of my bond;
>
> (207)

insists

> I stay here on my bond;
>
> (242)

and refuses to have by a surgeon with the defiant

> Is it so nominated in the bond?
>
> (259)

17. At the inn in Venice, Giannetto's wife, dressed as a lawyer, advises the Jew to accept the hundred thousand ducats and free Ansaldo. Portia urges Shylock:

Shylock, there's thrice thy money offer'd thee;

(227)

and again:

Take thrice thy money, bid me tear the bond.

(234)

18. As the lawyer proceeds to judgment, she says to the Jew: "Take a pound of flesh from wherever you wish (*Orsù lievagli una libra di carne dovunque tu vuoi*)." The expression, like the original Italian of the agreement Ansaldo has made (see 12 above) is echoed in Shylock's

> an equal pound
> Of your fair flesh, to be cut off and taken
> In what part of your body pleaseth me.

(I, iii, 150-2)

And Portia, as she comes to the crisis of the trial says to him:

> A pound of that same merchant's flesh is thine.

(IV, i, 300)

19. As the Jew is about to take his pound of flesh, the lawyer warns him: "If you take more or less than a pound of flesh, I'll see that your head is removed. . . . If you let fall but one drop of blood, I'll have you put to death. For your bond makes no mention of the shedding of blood, but says you must take a pound of flesh, and says neither more nor less (*Se tu ne leverai più o meno che una libra, io ti farò levare la testa. . . . Se n' uscirà pure una gocciola di sangue, io ti farò morire; però che le carte tue non fanno menzione di spargimento di sangue, anzi dicono che tu gli debba levare una libra di carne, e non dice nè più nè meno*)." Portia stops Shylock with:

> This bond doth give thee here no jot of blood,
> The words expressly are "a pound of flesh":
> Take then thy bond, take thou thy pound of flesh,
> But in the cutting it, if thou dost shed

One drop of Christian blood, thy lands and goods
Are by the laws of Venice confiscate . . .
Shed thou no blood, nor cut thou less nor more
But just a pound of flesh: if thou tak'st more
Or less than a just pound . . .
Thou diest.

(306-11; 325-7; 332)

20. Realizing himself defeated, the Jew says, "Let them give me a
hundred thousand ducats and I am content (*fatemi dare quei cento
mila ducati e son contento*)." Shylock, checked by Portia, at once
agrees:

I take this offer then,—pay the bond thrice
And let the Christian go.

(318-19)

21. But the lawyer will grant only the pound of flesh "according
to the bond (*come dicono le carte tue*)." Portia will not allow
Bassanio to give Shylock any money, declaring:

He shall have nothing but the penalty;

(321)

and again:

Take thy forfeiture;

(335)

He shall have merely justice and his bond;

(339)

Thou shalt have nothing but the forfeiture.

(343)

23. Giannetto was ready to give the Jew any sum before the
court. Bassanio offers thrice the sum due:

Here is the money.

(319)

24. The Jew pleads, "Give me at least my ten thousand ducats, (*Datemi almeno i miei dieci mila ducati*)" the sum of the original loan. Shylock finally agrees:

> Give me my principal, and let me go;
>
> (336)

and cries again:

> Shall I not have barely my principal?
>
> (342)

25. Giannetto is willing enough to let him have that. So too is Bassanio:

> I have it ready for thee, here it is.
>
> (337)

26. After the trial is over, Giannetto invites the lawyer to his home, "if you will do me so much grace (*Se voi mi volete fare tanta grazia*)." The Duke, it is, who first says to Portia

> Sir, I entreat you home with me to dinner.
>
> (401)

And, after Portia has left in mock-annoyance, Bassanio sends Gratiano after her with the injunction:

>   bring him if thou canst
> Unto Antonio's house.
>
> (453-4)

27. Giannetto tries to press the money due the Jew upon the lawyer as a recompense. So does Bassanio:

> Three thousand ducats due unto the Jew
> We freely cope your courteous pains withal.
>
> (411-12)

28. The "lawyer" decides that she will have the ring on Giannetto's finger: "I should like that ring, and I will accept no other

reward (*Io vuo' questo anello, e non voglio altra danaio nessuno*)."
Portia does likewise with the same sentiments:

> I'll take this ring from you . . .
> I will have nothing else but only this.

(427; 432)

29. Giannetto explains his reluctance to part with the ring:
"My lady gave it to me, and told me to wear it always in love of
her (*la donna mia me lo donò, e dissemi ch' io le portassi sempre
per suo amore*)." When Portia first gives the ring to Bassanio she
says:

> this ring,
> Which when you part from, lose, or give away,
> Let it presage the ruin of your love . . .

(III, ii, 173-5)

And now Bassanio explains to the lawyer:

> Good sir, this ring was given me by my wife,
> And when she put it on, she made me vow
> That I should neither sell, nor give, nor lose it.

(IV, i, 441-3)

30. After accepting Giannetto's ring, the lawyer says, "Do me a
kindness (*Fatemi una grazia*)." Before the business of the ring, Bassanio, trying to force some reward upon the lawyer, says:

> Grant me two things I pray you.

(423)

31. On the arrival of Giannetto and Ansaldo at Belmonte, Giannetto's wife "ran to embrace Messer Ansaldo and feigned to be a
little angry (*corse ad abbracciare messere Ansaldo, e finse esser un
poco crucciata*)" with her husband. Portia is careful to shield Antonio from her feigned anger with Bassanio, and says to him:

> Sir, grieve not you—you are welcome notwithstanding.

(V, i, 239)

32. When Giannetto swears his faithfulness to his wife during his absence in Venice, she asks, "Where is the ring I gave you (*Ov' è l'anello ch' io ti diedi*)?" Portia, when Gratiano tells her that Bassanio too has given his ring away, cries:

> What ring gave you, my lord?
> Not that, I hope, which you receiv'd of me.
>
> (184-5)

33. Giannetto's wife declares: "I swear . . . that you gave it to a woman (*Io ti giuro . . . che tu lo donasti a una femina*)." Portia exclaims:

> I'll die for 't, but some woman had the ring!
>
> (208)

This mass of evidence, it is to be hoped, can outweigh the value of the dubious phrase upon which the whole case for the lost play of *The Jew* has so uneasily rested. It also ought to indicate the great probability that Shakespeare read his Fiorentino in the Italian. The records show no English translation of Fiorentino available to him. But even if there had been one, the resemblances between the original Italian and his play are too striking to be discounted.

5

Shylock Himself

And he that shuts Love out, in turn shall be
Shut out from Love, and on her threshold lie
Howling in outer darkness.—Tennyson, *The Palace of Art.*

: :

A man that studieth revenge, keeps his own wounds green.—
Bacon, *Revenge.*

: :

Malevolus animus abditos dentes habet.*—Syrus, *Maxims.*

: :

I was angry with my foe:
I told it not, my wrath did grow.—Blake, A *Poison Tree.*

: :

Je ne te quitterai point que je ne t'aie vu pendu.†—Molière, *Le
Médecin Malgré Lui.*

: :

Revenge proves its own executioner.—Ford, *The Broken Heart,*
V, ii.

: :

Let him know that hatred without end
Or intermission is between us two.—*Iliad* XV, 270 (Bryant's
translation).

: :

Let me shake thy hand; I never hated thee.—*Antony and Cleopatra,* II, vi.

: :

Odia in longam iaciens, quae reconderet, auctaque promeret.‡—
Tacitus, *Annales* I, 69.

: :

People who have a mastery over the piano tend to play better the
more they practice; but the case with certain amateurs is that the
more they practice the worse they play. This is a perfect metaphor
for the art of living.—E. R. Nargibe, *Tribute to Sam.*

---

* The malevolent soul has hidden teeth.
† I'll not leave you till I've seen you hanged.
‡ Laying aside his resentment, he stores it up only to bring it forth with increased
bitterness.

There are, unhappily, many people who cannot enjoy any work of art without assurance, or, at least, the assertion that it is better than some other work of acknowledged standing. There are no more inane questions than: Which is the best play Ibsen wrote? Is *Vanity Fair* as great as *The Brothers Karamazov?* Is Chopin greater than Schumann? Is Beethoven's Fifth better than the Third? or the Seventh? or the Ninth? Is *The Cherry Orchard* as great as *The Three Sisters?* To be concerned about such matters is to bring in the values of the market place where they have no business to intrude. No doubt the marketer shows good judgment when she weighs the merits of one haddock against those of another; and no doubt, too, the man demonstrates the discretion of genius who can decide in favor of one toothpaste against all the other brands which are equally guaranteed to diminish tooth decay. It is perfectly reasonable to recognize the superiority of a masterwork to a work with undeniable shortcomings: *The Egoist* is beyond denying superior to *Vittoria*, *Madame Bovary* to *Salammbo*, *As You Like It* to *Two Gentlemen of Verona*, *Hamlet* to *Romeo and Juliet*. It is also perfectly normal to *prefer* one masterpiece to another, if one remembers that one's liking does not therefore make it any "better"; I need not apologize that I prefer *The Madonna of the Rocks* to the *Mona Lisa,* the *Venus of Milo* to the *Apollo Belvedere*, the music of Schumann to that of Chopin. It is equally perfectly human and proper to be devoted to a work which is not of first rank and to prefer it to works which are; creators themselves have been known to be partial to their weakest children, as Ibsen preferred above all his successes his greatest failure, *Emperor and Galilean*. I do not ask to be excused that I would rather read Walter Savage Landor than Wordsworth, though I am aware of the stature of the latter.

But when dealing with works which are masterpieces it is a kind of vulgarity to weigh their respective total value. I find it hard to name my "favorite composer,"—almost impossible to name even my favorite three composers. I could not name my favorite Beethoven piano sonatas even if allowed six; I could not name my favorite Shakespeare plays even if limited to as much as a dozen. But if I could name them, it would not occur to me that I was thereby disparaging the greatness of others I did not love as much. Great works take on a complete life of their own, a fullness and a totality independent of everything else under the sun. It is as impossible to set the seal of "the best" or "the greatest" upon that life as it would be to set it upon the life of this or that superior man or woman.

My perspective being understood, I do not hesitate to say that *The Merchant of Venice* is not only the earliest of Shakespeare's flawless masterpieces (it seems to be the work in which he at last came into his own) but also to place it as a peer among his top achievements, *Much Ado, As You Like It, Twelfth Night, I Henry IV, Henry V, Julius Caesar, Hamlet, Othello, Macbeth, Lear, Antony and Cleopatra,* and *Coriolanus.* I should decline to choose, since I know that I could not, which one or which ten of these is "the best."

The Merchant of Venice, like each of Shakespeare's masterpieces, has a richness and magnificence peculiarly its own. It is an endless treasurehouse of good things, spilling over with splendor and beauty. It is also, when understood in its basic meaning, a play of vast and prophetic import.

Yet after the last of the Elizabethan playhouses was shut in 1642 and London was without a public theater for two decades, *The Merchant of Venice* was not performed in the Restoration theaters when they were opened. It lay neglected for a century, though it was not alone in that fate. Not until the season of 1740-41 was it revived, along with *As You Like It* and *Twelfth Night.* By degrees its popularity increased until Hazlitt was able to say of it in 1817 that "this is a play which in spite of the change of manners and prejudices still holds undisputed possession of the stage." [1]

The neoclassicists of the late seventeenth and early eighteenth centuries were not in a position to understand it because of their notion that the serious and the comic must be kept severely apart. Nicholas Rowe (1709) was convinced that Shakespeare had intended *The Merchant of Venice* "tragically." Though conceding that it is "one of the most finish'd of any of Shakespear's" works, he thought that "There appears in it such a deadly Spirit of Revenge, such a savage Fierceness and Fellness, and such a bloody designation of Cruelty and Mischief, as cannot agree either with the Stile or Characters of Comedy." [2] These strictures are better understood when we remember that he had in mind more than four decades of Restoration comedy, all wit and no heart. But he has been by no means the last to believe that to be a comedy a play must be light-headed. Certainly the world has a number of superb comedies written in that spirit—*The Would-Be Gentleman* and *The Importance of Being Earnest,* for example. But the domain of

comedy is a wide one, and there are many fine comedies which contain very serious elements. *Measure for Measure, Tartuffe,* and *Hedda
Gabler* are grim and brilliant comedies. Many superb comedies
work with materials that are nearly tragic in essence, and gain in
dignity for that very reason. The church scene in *Much Ado,* so
much at variance in its dramatic power with the flashing wit of the
verbal duel between Beatrice and Benedick, raises the quality of the
work as a whole. There is nothing light-headed about the human relationships involved in *Twelfth Night, The Winter's Tale,* or *The
Tempest.* The savage ironies of *The Wild Duck* do not weaken its
comic spirit, any more than do the exquisite sensibilities of *The
Three Sisters* or *The Cherry Orchard,* or the forthrightness of *The
Silver Cord.* Almost every play which has come from the hand of
perhaps the most classically graceful and gracious writer of twentieth-century American comedy, S. N. Behrman, has a basic gravity
which, fused with the true comic spirit, lends it a fetching air of
bitter-sweetness and nostalgia.

It would be fair to say that few great comedies venture so precari-
ously near the borderline of tragedy as does *The Merchant of Venice.* But Shakespeare manages with his own secret magic that the
play is triumphantly a comedy—though a serious one, as befits a
play with an important idea.

The twentieth-century writer rarely troubles himself, of course,
with matters like these. He is likely to regard as "merely aesthetic"
the question of what belongs to comedy and what to tragedy. That
is one of the reasons why in the last decades we have had so many
melodramas, and so very very few comedies or tragedies. Ever since
the blight of Naturalism descended upon our authors, aesthetic considerations have been thought abstruse and formulary. As though
honest aesthetic questions ever are! As though Beethoven's sympho-
nies suffer from his constant awareness of what belongs to a symphony and what to a song! In great pieces of creation the aesthetic
consideration so much determines the content and the content the
aesthetic consideration, that the two are inseparable. When we cannot distinguish content from aesthetic consideration and both are
admirable, we are likely to be in the presence of a masterpiece.

The error of the eighteenth century was not the aesthetic questions it raised but the answers it provided to them. Thus, it was not
wrong in asking whether there is not a special language for poetry,
nor was it wrong in deciding that there is. Dante had proved long

ago that there is. And Wordsworth's theory that there is not was going to be shown a grave error by his own example. Nothing in the world can transmute to poetry such lines as

> I hate that Andrew Jones; he'll breed
> His children up to waste and pillage.
> I wish the press-gang or the drum
> With its tantara sound would come,
> And sweep him from the village!

or

> Her beauty made me glad.
> Her eyes were fair, and very fair—

Where the eighteenth century went astray here was its rather absurd ideas as to *what* constitutes the language of poetry. It is ridiculous, not elegant, as it was intended to be, to call a young fish a "speckled youngster"; it is stuffy, not noble, to speak of "The short and simple annals of the poor."

But the eighteenth-century writers were also realists. For all the Graeco-Roman names that appear in their works, they were always writing about their own times, not those of the ancient world. And intolerant realists may easily become entrapped into criteria which are quasi-Naturalistic when the events of a story under consideration are measured against the happenings of everyday contemporary life. Applying such criteria to *The Merchant of Venice*, Rowe said, "The Tale indeed, in that Part relating to the Caskets, and the extravagant and unusual kind of bond given by Antonio, is a little too much remov'd from the Rules of Probability." Scholars today have endorsed that view. Hazelton Spencer says of the play that "its wildly romantic plot has small relevance to life." [3] Poel calls it "illogical." [4] Granville-Barker[5] and Murry[6] agree that it is only a "fairy tale." Ridley charges Shakespeare with playing on his audience "almost a dishonestly clever trick. He takes out of a rag-bag" various odds and ends "such as might be expected to furnish forth a somewhat tawdry scarecrow"; when you read the play, you feel it "has no business to be a success," as it has long been.[7]

We may dispense with Rowe's criticism of the bond; our preceding chapter has demonstrated that the agreement was neither "extravagant" nor "unusual" to the minds of an Elizabethan audience. But his reservations concerning "that Part relating to the Caskets" might give us pause. When indeed has a beautiful, gifted, wealthy, and enchanting girl like Portia ever been wooed and won by a choice among caskets?

Now, Aristotle long ago answered the literary question here involved. "The Poet is not an Historian," he says. What is called for in a story is to present a sequence of events that is made credible. "A sequence of events which, though actually impossible, looks reasonable should be preferred by the poet [i.e., the creator] to what, though really possible, seems incredible." [8] We all know that many actual experiences of life, particularly those which hinge upon unforeseen coincidence or upon accident, become incredible in the telling. Such events, since they have occurred, are clearly possible; since they are incredible in the telling, they are also improbable. The boy who cried, "Wolf!" once too often was telling a possible but improbable story; the wolf was there, and hence his revelation was certainly possible, but he himself had made the event improbable. Here is a possible but improbable story:

> An innocent man, because of the evidence, is convicted of premeditated murder. All appeals to the Governor for a commutation of sentence have failed. On the morning of the scheduled execution, the actual murderer, lying on his death-bed, confesses to the crime and reveals all the facts. Our innocent hero is already strapped to the electric-chair, the executioner has his hand on the lever—when a messenger arrives breathlessly with the information that saves the man's life.

We should have to admit that such things can be. But the story fails to convince us because too much depends upon coincidence, and we cannot believe in it. Again:

> Timothy is a high-minded young man profoundly in love with Millicent, who returns his love in full measure. He has no rivals; his home life is a happy one; he has a bright future before him. One day, as they are out wandering in the fragrant fields, Timothy takes out a knife and stabs Millicent to death.

The newspapers force us to admit that such happenings are possible. But to believe this one at all, we at once decide, forgetting Millicent, "Poor Timothy! He's insane, of course," and begin to probe for the proof of that. Without it, we simply must reject the event as too improbable. (And we prefer never to wonder whether our definition of insanity is not trimmed to account for such events rather than to ask whether such events are really accounted for by the concept of insanity.)

On the other hand, "a sequence of events which, though actually impossible, looks reasonable," can make for the kind of reality with which literature concerns itself. It matters not that there are no ghosts or witches in fact, if the ghosts or witches are made credible (i.e., probable) in a story. It is really irrelevant that such a bond as Antonio signed was not "extravagant" or "unusual" to an Elizabethan; what is at stake here is that Shakespeare made that bond, no matter how unusual it might have been, entirely credible. We are willing to accept any premise to a story, no matter how impossible, as long as the author makes that impossibility thoroughly credible.

An interesting example of how this can be triumphantly carried off will be found in Althea Urn's witty, sophisticated novel, *The Head of Monsieur M* (1961). The premise of the story is that during his honeymoon with his young and inexperienced bride, Henri Malheureusement, a man who bears in his cranium a vast amount of erudition, suddenly and calmly removes his head from his shoulders, just as he would remove a stopper from the neck of a bottle—without any distressing signs of blood or any impairment of his bodily or intellectual powers. The reader quite calmly accepts this untoward occurrence as though it were natural and reasonable enough, because the author has made it entirely credible.

What renders an impossible event probable? Simply this, that the people involved in it behave like real human beings. When Henri removes his head, it is to ease himself of the oppressive weight of all his knowledge; he does it so casually that we are convinced that it is easy for him to do. Had Miss Urn caused his wife, seeing him do it for the first time, to accept the gesture in that same spirit, all credibility would have been sacrificed. The author has Henri's wife react as a human bride should react to such a given occurrence: she is frightened, horrified, puzzled, and fascinated all at once.

It does not matter that in the world of fact it is impossible that Portia's hand should be won by the choice of a casket. The very device is a welcome relief from the clichés of courtship. What *does* matter is that Morocco, Arragon, and Bassanio all react profoundly like human beings to the given necessity of their choosing among three caskets, and that Portia reacts profoundly like a human being while they are making their choice and her destiny hangs in the balance—each according to the dictates of his own powerfully realized personality. This it is which renders the choices real. It would not matter if the bond Antonio signs were in fact unusual: Shakespeare has made it utterly real and normal because of the way everybody behaves in relation to it.

[In short, when Rowe complained that the story of our play is "a little too much remov'd from the Rules of Probability," he was misconstruing his Aristotle. He might have said "Possibility" instead of "Probability" and no one could object that the story is removed from the possibilities of the world of fact. But one would then have to add that the observation is totally beside the business of literary creation.]

The truth of this perspective has been clear to a number of commentators. Sen Gupta observes that in *The Merchant of Venice* we are aware "that the men and women have a deep emotional life." [9] Courthope is strong in his praise of it: "The most completely dramatic of all his plays, certainly the one in which his constructive skill is most evident. . . . Nowhere is the wide grasp of Shakespeare's intellect, or the fine balance of his judgment, more characteristically shown than in his conduct of the action." [10] Such commendation from a critic of superb taste, as Courthope is, could not have been accorded to a work in which even a hint of improbability lurks. Dowden considers it "probably the first of Shakespeare's comedies in which the study of character wholly dominates all other interest." [11] If this is true, a reason for its being so will be found in Courthope's words. Only a play of powerful construction can cause the audience to be totally absorbed in the men and women of the action. A play unsustained by a firm architecture can leave its characters only half-realized, and therefore half-real.

[Characters in a play must reveal themselves chiefly by what they *do*. Their characterization cannot be achieved statically by description or talk, but must be managed dynamically through the action of the drama. The unwillingness to realize this has been responsible for the general flabbiness of recent drama.]

Of course, the chief cause of disapprobation for *The Merchant of Venice* has been a well-meant distortion of Shakespeare's intentions by those who read in it, as Stirling does, "a pretty piece of Jew-baiting." [12] "I do not see," says Spencer, "how a Jew can read *The Merchant of Venice* without pain and indignation." [13] Spencer rejoices in the fact that "in recent years many secondary schools have wisely removed the play" from their courses of study.[14]

Calish accuses Shakespeare of having done "a great wrong" to the Jewish people, not in the portrayal of Shylock, but by associating "the word 'Jew' with the usury, the cruelty, the vindictiveness, and the bloodthirsty vengefulness ascribed to him, by emphasizing at every evil point Shylock's race and religion." [15] That the word "Jew" was associated with usury is a result, as we have seen, not of Shakespeare's deliberate imposition, but of a long precedent, some of it based upon historical fact. That Shakespeare emphasizes "at every evil point Shylock's race and religion" is simply not the fact. Nothing was further from Shakespeare's purposes than to hold up Shylock vindictively as the portrait of a Jew; Shylock, as I have intimated, is the portrait of a moneylender. Calish goes on to declare that no Jew is "vengeful or vindictive," and quotes the Bible to show that Jews are expressly forbidden "to practise cruelty" against even "the beast of the field" (*Exodus* xxiii, 12; *Proverbs* xii, 10) and the birds (*Deuteronomy* xxii, 6),[16] and that therefore Shakespeare was deliberately slandering the Jewish people by making Shylock vindictive and vengeful. This is, unhappily, a very foolish argument. These same Biblical passages hold for Christians too; therefore any portrait of a vindictive or vengeful Christian would have to be held a slander against those of Christian faith. Kittredge has answered this attitude well: "Shakespeare was not attacking the Jewish people when he gave Shylock the villain's role. If so he was attacking the Moors in *Titus Andronicus*, the Spaniards in *Much Ado*, the Italians in *Cymbeline*, the Viennese in *Measure for Measure*, the Danes in *Hamlet*, the Britons in *King Lear*, and the English in *Richard III*." [17]

Quiller-Couch confessed that as a boy he could find no heart in the play at all, and was "chilled" by it; his view as a mature man did not alter much. With the exception of Antonio and Shylock, who is meant to be cruel, he says, every one of the Venetians is either a "waster" or a "rotter" or both—and cold-hearted wasters and rotters at that.[18] This judgment by a Cambridge editor of Shakespeare is a choice misreading of the play.

On the other hand, many have felt that Shakespeare was defending the Jews in his play. Harry Golden goes so far as to see in it "a satire on the Gentile middle class of Venice." Mr. Golden loves his

Shakespeare, and for that one is ready to forgive him his overinterpretation. But he is little short of amazing in his eager distortions to prove his point. Shylock, he is convinced, was intended as the sole sympathetic character in the play. Bassanio's wooing of Portia is purely predatory (herein Golden is at one with Quiller-Couch and many other professional scholars); Golden paraphrases Bassanio's appeal to Antonio for a loan in these words: "Lend me some dough so I can make love to a rich lady who has just inherited a vast fortune"; in his portraiture of Bassanio and Antonio, Shakespeare "was writing an indictment of the hypocrites who vitiated every precept taught them by Christianity." But Golden goes further. Shakespeare has Shylock say: "When you prick us do we not bleed?"; he has Morocco say: "Bring the fairest blond from your northern forests, make the incisions, and you'll find my blood as red as his." Shakespeare's point, according to Golden, is that Morocco, Shylock, and Antonio are all "brothers under the skin." The crowning proof of this is to be found in the Trial Scene. Why should Portia ask, at its opening, "Which is the merchant here and which the Jew?" as though she could not tell at once? [The reason for her question, as we shall see, is really quite simple, much more dramatic, and philosophically far less weighty than the one advanced by Golden.] The reason is, believes Golden, that Shakespeare meant to imply that there were no real differences in character between Antonio and Shylock, that both were made of the same stuff. And by the time the trial is over, this enthusiast observes, the dramatist has left "only Shylock with a shred of dignity."

His love of Shakespeare makes Harry Golden as much a victim of literary strabismus as Shakespeare's detractors. Nevertheless, for all his error and deliberate vulgarity of expression, I respect him more than I do many a seasoned scholar. He is at least wise enough not to believe that Shakespeare was in this play simply writing another potboiler; he at least is sure that Shakespeare had something to say in *The Merchant of Venice*. While many professional scholars are busy diminishing Shakespeare by trying to prove that he was like every other run-of-the-mill Elizabethan, Golden demonstrates anew that a sympathetic reader can discern important matters which scholars tend to believe outside their province. Golden, for all his errors in dates and interpretation, can occasionally hit the nail on the head by saying simply, "Shakespeare was the first writer in seven hundred years who gave the Jew a 'motive.'" Why? Shakespeare did not need to do so, remembers Golden; "certainly his audience didn't expect it." [19] Golden is wrong, of course, in what he believes to be Shylock's motive—Antonio's spitting on him. But my objections to Golden are, after all, of the same order as my objections to eighteenth-century criticism: I approve of the questions he asks; I am merely in total disagreement with his answers.

Before we begin to ask similar questions ourselves, let us see what others have made of Shylock, the chief cause of dissension about the play.

Professional scholars may sneer at the attention I give Harry Golden, who claims no more than to love his Shakespeare. Every Shakespeare-lover who tries to understand him is worthy of more attention than those academic professionals who do not love him, and therefore are unlikely to understand him. The general public has always been Shakespeare's chief audience, not the scholars, for it is for the general public that Shakespeare wrote. But unfortunately the general public's notion of what Shakespeare intended by such characters as Hamlet or Shylock is likely to be formed by the interpretations of actors. Plays are meant to be acted, and under ideal acting conditions—and those conditions are ideal only when actors and directors are gravely concerned with faithfully projecting the dramatist's intentions—a good play can be best understood when acted, not read. Unhappily, when it comes to performances of Shakespeare in our time, nothing is apparently more irrelevant to the minds of directors and actors than the dramatist's intentions. To speak of only the last few years, New Yorkers have seen a *Love's Labour's Lost* made quaint by being given in a Victorian setting, a *Much Ado About Nothing* made quaint by being given in a Latin-American setting, a *Troilus and Cressida* made quaint by being given in an Edwardian setting—though quaintness is a mood foreign to all of Shakespeare's plays. Most recently, *Troilus and Cressida* was made quaint by being given "the scent of magnolia and the gallantry" of an American Civil War setting. [According to Howard Taubman in *The New York Times* for July 24, 1961. He goes on: "When the shooting begins, when cannon are deployed and rifles pop, when soldiers roar across the stage, giving off Rebel yells, the production verges on puerility. It achieves a noisy silliness worthy of Westerns but not of Shakespeare."]

All platitudes to the contrary, Hazlitt makes good sense when he warns that the library may be a better place to study Shakespeare than the theater. Besides the dangers of foolish novelties there is the equal danger of foolish traditions inherited by the acting profession. The stage, says Hazlitt, "is too often filled with traditional common-place conceptions of the part, handed down from sire to son, and suited to the taste of the great vulgar and the small." [20]

Ever since Sir Henry Irving portrayed Shylock as a man greatly sinned against, in 1879, that has been the axiomatic conception of the role. No one seemed more bothered then than he would be bothered now at some unpardonable additions introduced into the play to fortify an actor's or director's, not Shakespeare's, meaning. Only George Bernard Shaw was well aware of what Irving was up to. Despite the universal praise bestowed upon the idol of the age, Shaw said: "Sir Henry Irving has never thought much of the immortal William, and has given him more than one notable lesson—for instance, in *The Merchant of Venice* where he gave us not 'the Jew that Shakespeare drew,' but the one he ought to have drawn if he had been up to the Lyceum mark." Returning to the attack, Shaw said later: "In a true republic of art Sir Henry Irving would ere this have expiated his acting versions on the scaffold. He does not merely cut plays, he disembowels them. . . . A prodigious amount of nonsense has been written about Sir Henry Irving's conception of this, that, and the other Shakespearean character. The truth is that he has never in his life conceived or interpreted the characters of any author except himself." His Shylock was not "a bad Shylock or a good Shylock: he was simply not Shylock at all; and when his own creation came into conflict with Shakespear's, as it did quite openly in the Trial Scene, he simply played in flat contradiction of the lines, and positively acted Shakespear off the stage." [21] These words could be reprinted today with reference to other actors in other roles, almost every time Shakespeare is presented.

Irving made of Shylock "a patriarch of Israel, wronged in his most sacred affections." To increase the distortion, he introduced a scene showing Shylock returning "by light of lantern" to knock "on the door of an empty house." Ellen Terry, his Portia, speaking with the tongue of actors, wrote that "for absolute pathos," she had never seen anything to compare with that scene.[22] What matters it that Shakespeare wrote no such scene, and that its intrusion is in violation of everything he tells us about Shylock's relationship to his daughter? William Winter also paid tribute to that "image of the father convulsed with grief." [23]

To be fair, Irving was actually preceded in his sentimental interpretation of Shylock by an English girl at a performance of the play.
"When I saw this Play at Drury Lane," the poet Heine (d. 1856)
reported, "there stood behind me in the box a pale, fair Briton, who
at the end of the Fourth Act, fell to weeping passionately, several
times exclaiming, 'The poor man is wronged!' It was a face of the
noblest Grecian style, and the eyes were large and black. I have
never been able to forget those large and black eyes that wept for
Shylock! When I think of those tears I have to rank *The Merchant
of Venice* with the Tragedies." It need not be said that despite the
largeness and blackness of her eyes, the pale fair Briton has had less
effect upon stage traditions of Shylock than Irving. But she did succeed in convincing the impressionable German that the play was
tragic.

And tragic it has been held to be by many a critic since. Hudson
said of Shylock that his character is "essentially tragic." [24] If you participate in Shakespeare's own sympathies for him, says Raleigh, you
see Shylock as "a sad and human figure," who makes you deplore
the verdict at the end, so that Portia "seems little better than a
clever trickster." Shylock's "very hatred has in it something of the
nobility of patriotic passion." He is at the end sent off to "insult and
oblivion," and the memory of him gives to the beautiful last act an
"air of heartless frivolity." [25] Unconsciously, Raleigh is echoing Irving's own exposition of his interpretation. He said that he conceived
Shylock as "the type of persecuted race, almost the only gentleman
in the play, and the most ill-used." Encouraged by these words, Packard goes off the deep end on the subject: Shylock may be grasping,
"but what a scrambling after money do we detect among the others,
what eager hunt after heiresses . . . and what a shameful desertion
of a friend by all the Venetian Christian merchants for the sake of
three thousand ducats." Did Bassanio ever return the money which
he borrowed for his fortune-seeking trip? Packard asks. [Bassanio
certainly makes every attempt to do so, and at the earliest possible
moment—with Portia's backing, too. As for the other friends the
play expressly states that they attempt to come to Antonio's rescue,
but Shylock refuses to accept their money once the day of repayment is past.] Lorenzo is nothing more than an infamous burglar,
Packard continues, whereas Shylock loves Jessica "more than ducats
and jewels." Shylock is "distinguished by dignity. He feels and acts
as one of a noble but long oppressed nation." In "intelligence and

culture he is far above the Christians with whom he comes in contact." The proof of these assertions would be far to seek and, I am sure, impossible to find.

Packard unfortunately also makes one of those generalizations to which those who allow themselves to get agitated on the subject of Shylock are prone: Shakespeare's error was in allowing Shylock to "renounce his faith with so little pretence"; Jews are not like that.[26] The simple historical fact is that *some* people of all creeds are like that. It has been said that some few influential Jewish bankers poured money into Hitler's coffers before he came to power, despite his long-avowed intention of exterminating the Jews. And in a movingly authentic study of the Warsaw Ghetto during the Nazi persecutions, *The Wall*, adapted from the novel as a play of the 1960 season in New York, the one wealthy inhabitant of the Jewish quarter renounces his family and his faith in order to survive; his so doing was construed by no one to be a slander against the Jews—since such behavior is certainly within the realm of the possible and the probable.

Calish believes that Shylock speaks "as the representative of his people, voicing the wrongs, the insult, the humiliation" visited upon them. This commentator would place Shylock, "a figure of tragic . . . power . . . by the side of Lear, Hamlet, Othello." [27] Honigman, too, finds the moneylender a spokesman for and an avenger of the Jews' wrongs.[28] Coe is sure that Shakespeare meant to represent Shylock "as the underdog." [29] Even that staunch insister upon Shakespeare's anti-Semitic intentions, E. E. Stoll, finds that Shylock is "given now and then a touch of almost incompatible tenderness." [30] (Here, one fears, Stoll's usual intransigent prosiness of evaluation falls into the opposite extreme only because he seems unaware that Shakespeare [*unlike* many many other Elizabethan dramatists!] does not, with the exception of the early *Titus Andronicus*, deal in monsters.) And Granville-Barker adds another unwarranted sentimental touch by averring that when Launcelot Gobbo leaves his employ to serve Bassanio, Shylock demonstrates that he has "a niggardly liking for the fellow," and "is even hurt a little by his leaving." * [31] Harbage goes further in the way of absurdity by declaring

* These are Shylock's actual words in that scene:
Well, thou shalt see, thy eyes shall be thy judge,
The difference of old Shylock and Bassanio—
. . . Thou shalt not gormandize,

that "Shylock is no miser. . . . The ultimate satisfaction he craves is spiritual; we cannot picture him fondling his gold." [32] As a point of fact that is precisely what we cannot *help* picturing him doing; it is Shakespeare who gives us the cue, when Shylock murmurs:

> I did dream of money-bags tonight.
>
> (II, v, 18)

It is perhaps Goddard who has drawn the sentimental picture of Shylock which is in most ludicrous defiance of the facts of Shakespeare's play. Shylock, he says, is by nature "humane, kindly," and is "the leaden casket with the spiritual gold within." "If ever man was insulted and injured it is Shylock"; he acts "in the exact pattern of his Dostoevskian counterpart. . . . It is as if Shakespeare were confirming Dostoevsky." Shylock as usurer cannot fuse with Shylock as father of his beloved daughter: "they will no more mix than oil and water." These "two Shylocks exist side by side." Thus, too, Shylock, who at first dreams of being accepted as an equal by Antonio when the latter comes to borrow money, suddenly, because of Antonio's storming at him [sic!], "now dreams of shedding the blood of an enemy." At the beginning Shylock "has no idea of literal bloodshed"; does he not say to Tubal concerning Antonio, "were he out of Venice, I can make what merchandise I will"? Apparently Goddard wishes us to understand that this means that the extremest desire Shylock entertains is to have Antonio exiled from Venice! But ah! the sleight-of-hand which selected quotation is capable of! For the full sentence tells us something a little less mild about Shylock's purposes:

As thou hast done with me. . . .
And sleep and snore, and rend apparel out. . . .

Actually poor Launcelot has been so much starved that his ribs are sticking out ("I am famished in his service; you may tell every finger I have with my ribs."— II, ii, 113-14). And when Launcelot leaves the stage, Shylock muses:

The patch [i.e., fool] is kind enough, but a huge feeder;
Snail-slow in profit, and he sleeps by day
More than the wild-cat. Drones hive not with me;
Therefore I part with him, and part with him
To one that I would have him help to waste
His borrowed purse.

(II, v, 1-5; 46-51)

Go, Tubal, fee me an officer. Bespeak him a fortnight before. *I will have the heart of him if he forfeit,* for were he out of Venice, I can make what merchandise I will.

(III, i, 131-4)

Goddard traces the evolution of Shylock's desire for revenge in these steps: At first Shylock intends charging Antonio interest, as is usual with the moneylender. Next he is stung by Antonio's sarcasms. Then he sees his opportunity when Antonio speaks of friends' never lending money to friends at interest. "Here is the chance of chances to humble him (Antonio) by compelling him to do just what he does not want to do, accept a loan . . . on an outward basis of friendship. Such a loan would be heaping coals of fire on his head in the most savage sense. . . . Here would be revenge at its sweetest, in its most exquisite, prolonged, and intellectual form." [33] After that, when Antonio "storms" at him, and only then, does Shylock think of revenge.

A good number of other scholars refuse to believe that Shylock has any nefarious purposes in suggesting a pound of flesh as the forfeit. Walley is of that opinion.[34] And Campbell outlines the attitude of this school of thought by insisting that it is only *after* the bond has been signed that Shylock plots Antonio's death. "To regard him as already scheming to murder" Antonio is to "belittle Shakespeare's artistry." Shakespeare makes it "the subsequent events"—the elopement of Jessica, the merrymaking over his distress—which drives Shylock to seek revenge.[35] Neilson and Hill are of the same opinion: when Shylock's terms are offered in merry sport "there is no real reason to accuse him of diabolical insincerity"; he means what he says when he offers to be friends. What "goads him" later is Jessica's elopement "with a Christian," who is "aided and abetted by Antonio's friends. . . . He is a father terribly wronged." [36]

It is my unpleasant duty to report that despite the authority of some of the names supporting the views of Shylock as a tragic figure, more sinned against than sinning, a wronged father, a feeling man thwarted in his longing for friendship, etc., I am bound to consider those views, in the light of the play Shakespeare wrote, as totally meaningless. In one sentence Mark Van Doren routs all this irrelevance when he justly and powerfully remarks that Shylock's voice "comes rasping into the play like a file; the edge of it not only cuts but tears." [37] That one stroke more accurately depicts Shakespeare's moneylender than all the opinions we have quoted.

But if the sentimental notion of Shylock as the victim of the play is annoying in its blindness to what Shakespeare has actually written, the insensitive conception of him as a comic figure is almost intolerable in its obtuseness.

The chief spokesman for this view has been E. E. Stoll, who in a long and subtle argument filled with learned and copious illustration from other writers, insists that there is absolutely nothing sympathetic about Shylock, and that Shakespeare intended him as the comic butt. Stoll would be very convincing if one did not trouble to re-read the play; his proof is based on the scholarly misconception, a favorite with Stoll, that Shakespeare is never at any time wiser or more farseeing than his fellow-Elizabethans. Shylock is, according to him, an example of Shakespeare's "thoroughly Elizabethan taste for comic villainy." Both Barrett Wendell and Brander Matthews had been of the opinion that the character was taken as comic by the Elizabethan audience, but did not insist that this was Shakespeare's intention.[38] The chief prop for Stoll's argument is that the Restoration thought Shylock comic. Although there were no performances of the play during that period, Thomas Jordan, an actor, published a ballad in 1664 with this description of Shylock:

> His beard was red; his face was made
>   Not much unlike a witches.
> His habit was a Jewish gown
>   That would defend all weather;
> His chin turn'd up, his nose hung down,
>   And both ends met together.[39]

Stoll comments that the Restoration stage was "still swayed by the tradition of Alleyn and Burbage," both of whom have been credited with enacting the role of Shylock in Shakespeare's day. From which Stoll argues that it is "highly probable" that Shakespeare's Shylock wore red hair and beard and a "bottle-nose." [40]

Harbage, with excellent sense, counters to this argument the view that "the expulsion of all qualities except comic ferocity from stage renderings of Shylock must be viewed with double skepticism." The argument from a period earlier than ours is not reliable. "An age nearer the Elizabethan in point of time need not have been nearer it in point of spirit." [41]

This is profoundly true; as regards the neoclassical period and the Elizabethan, it is an understatement. Pepys, most typical of typical Restoration gentlemen thought *Romeo and Juliet* of all plays the "worst that ever I heard in my life," vowed after seeing *A Midsummer Night's Dream* that he would "never see [it] again, for it is the most insipid, ridiculous play that ever I saw in my life," but was delighted with a monstrous perversion of *Macbeth* because of the "variety of dancing and music."

Scholars have only too often come to preposterous conclusions about other Shakespearean plays because of the generally accepted but thoroughly untenable idea that there was a connecting link in the person of Sir William D'Avenant, between the Elizabethan and early Stuart playhouses and the Restoration theaters—despite the lapse of two decades during which the London playhouses were closed. Since D'Avenant knew the theater before the Puritans shut the playhouses, he is conceded to have passed on Shakespeare's intentions to his fellows of the Restoration age. I have answered this assumption elsewhere,[42] and since it is an assumption which has been made the basis for a great deal of nonsense about a number of Shakespeare's plays, I hope I may be pardoned for quoting the pertinent passage:

It is true that one playwright-manager bridged the period from the closing of the theaters in 1642 to the opening of the Restoration playhouses less than two decades later, Sir William D'Avenant. It is also true that D'Avenant was pleased to float the rumor that he was Shakespeare's illegitimate son, in an era when no one seemed to mind branding his mother a harlot to get himself a little extra distinction in the world. Born the son of decent tavern-keepers (the name then was Davenant) whose hostel Shakespeare sometimes visited, he may even have been named for the dramatist —although the name of William is not sufficiently exotic among Englishmen for us to jump at that conclusion. At any rate, D'Avenant was five when Shakespeare retired from the stage, and ten when he died—an age too tender even for a genius (which D'Avenant emphatically was not) to acquire from the master any profound knowledge of Shakespeare's conceptions of his works, even had the latter felt inclined to bestow it on a six-year-old darling of a pigmy size. Moreover, during the Restoration D'Avenant became very much the man of the new age, as his mangling of *Measure for Measure, Much Ado About Nothing, Macbeth,* and *The Tempest* (the last with Dryden's cooperation) abundantly proves. Gosse calls him the 'debaser' of the stage and deems his influence 'wholly deplorable.' [43] It was under his influence that Betterton and his fellow actors of the Restoration took over the French style and that the theater began to be buried under elaborate scenery. Yet, because of his reputed relationship to Shakespeare and the fact that he knew the theater before the Puritan prohibition, it is generally assumed that he passed on Elizabethan tradition to the new age. The Restoration Court, on the other hand, everyone agrees, was notably unreceptive to the Elizabethan style. [And it was the Court which made up the audience for one or the other of the two Restoration theaters, only one of which was ever successful at a given time.] Without setting out to do so, Mr. Hazelton Spencer, in his thoroughly documented study of Restoration adaptations of Shakespeare, *Shakespeare Improved,* makes out a perfect case against the notion of D'Avenant as a sort of belated Elizabethan.

There was no continuity between Shakespeare's age and the age of Charles II in theatrical tradition. Jordan's ballad, therefore, proves absolutely nothing about the way Shakespeare's Shylock was originally presented to the public.

Yet other scholars have hastened to follow Stoll's lead in portraying Shylock as a comic figure, and even twist comic values out of passages that are not in the least comic. Rosenberg says that Shylock is "a bogey," and when he "alludes to his dead wife Leah, the audience is intended to howl him down with laughter." (!!) At his exit line, "I am not well," Rosenberg continues, "the audience is assumed to jeer at his adolescent refusal to take his come-uppance like a man." [44] (Yet Mr. Rosenberg's book is a very thoughtful and honest one as a whole. On the subject of Shylock himself, however, he proves how a scholar can sacrifice his very humanity—without which there is no sense in talking about Shakespeare at all—merely to be consistent with an *a priori* theory.) Stoll had already said, "Shylock's being unwell is received as would be a similar plea from a bully at school, just worsted in a fight." [45]

Spencer believes that Shylock's is "much like the villain's role in Victorian melodrama, who plots, gloats, curses, and ha-ha's his way through to the final scene, when he is exposed, foiled, disgraced, and ridiculed, till he expires, leaves town, or at best slinks off stage with a futile imprecation." He is a "semifarcical villain." [46]

When Shylock says of Antonio that he hates him because he is a Christian and lends out money gratis, it is, says Spivack, as if in our own time "a caricatured villain of a commissar turned to the front seats in order to say of the hero, 'I hate him because he believes in God, and even more because he believes in human liberty and free enterprise.' " [47] Palmer goes still further: "Shylock bidding farewell to his daughter is more truly comic than at any part of the story so far reached." And "there is something grotesque even in his pleading 'If you tickle us, do we not laugh' etc."; Shylock never ceases to be a comic character, "never for an instant." [48] Sen Gupta tries to strike a medium between two views: he sees Shylock as tragic in so far as he hates Antonio, and comic in so far as he is greedy and miserly.[49]

It is hard to believe that the most torpid of readers unencumbered by a "scholarly" theory could possibly come away from his reading of *The Merchant of Venice* with the feeling that Shylock is comic. Whatever the predispositions of the Elizabethan audience, Shakespeare's humanity has shielded his moneylender from that. Indeed, *Shylock is not amusing at any moment of the play.* There is one time in which he figures in a comic scene, his dialogue with Tubal. But there it is Tubal who is comic; Shylock is torn between misery over his lost ducats and exaltation in the prospect of triumphing over Antonio, and the comedy turns upon the way Tubal alternately depresses his friend's spirits and raises them. On the other hand, to insist that Shakespeare has made Shylock a believable human being instead of a caricature, is not thereby to imply that he has sentimentalized him as a man sinned against.

One wonders whether this singularly insensitive view of him as a comic figure does not, in some quarters, proceed from the fact that the *play* is a comedy. We live in a period when true comedies on our stage are almost as rare as true tragedies. There seems to have been in the last decades a total collapse of the concept of comedy, and audiences and directors have had a tendency to equate every comedy with farce. During recent years an off-Broadway theater in New York has given some of the most brilliant performances of Chekov's plays that our times have seen. David Ross, the director, for the first time (in my experience, at any rate) gave the plays as the comedies Chekov intended them to be. When *Uncle Vanya* was so presented, Ross was rightly praised by the drama critics for having understood its spirit and having avoided the heavy-handed pseudo-tragic air with which the plays of Chekov have been always weighed down (even, it would seem, in Chekov's own lifetime, despite his protests to the Moscow theater). The audience, however (to one's great horror), having read in the newspapers that the director had discovered that *Uncle Vanya* is a comedy, came prepared to laugh at everything. They laughed and laughed, drowning lines and upsetting the actors, from curtain to curtain. Yet comedy though *Uncle Vanya* certainly is, there is assuredly nothing to laugh at during the course of the action, nor had Ross directed it as though there were. It seems to be felt nowadays that once a play is labeled "comedy," members of the audience will be found guilty of missing the point if they do not laugh raucously throughout the performance. And so, audiences will greet *The Three Sisters*, when it is correctly performed as a comedy, with the same hoarse roars with which they respond to a slapstick farce of the Marx Brothers. Tennessee Williams' comedy, *Period of Adjustment*, was treated in the same manner, to the utter destruction of the wistful delicacy he purposed.

Directors are guilty of this error too, and sometimes deliberately murder a play by converting comedy into farce. In 1957 *Measure for Measure*, the bitterest comedy Shakespeare ever wrote, was directed for laughs. The savage satire on moral hypocrisy, which is the point of the story of Angelo, Isabella and the Duke, was repressed in favor of a hearty mirth that is not intrinsically there; and the whole tone of the play was debased by emphasizing the stupidities of the clowns (the only revolting clowns in Shakespeare, without whom the play would be the finer), and having those unsavory characters cavort as though they were innocent idiots of the order of Launcelot Gobbo instead of conducting themselves with the grimness suitable to the dregs of humanity. Dutifully the audience laughed and laughed. And all the tense drama and all the sublime poetry in which the play abounds were utterly lost—in favor of an unrewarding and superimposed mood of slapstick. There is very little to laugh at in *Measure for Measure*.

Anouilh, one of the most brilliant of contemporary French dramatists, usually has his comedies victimized on the American stage by this same conviction that comedy is at one with farce. In his plays the delicate air, partaking of both smiles and tears, has been ruthlessly choked in the broad farcical treatment which American direc-

tors have accorded exquisite works like *Mademoiselle Colombe,*
Time Remembered, and *The Waltz of the Toreadors.* Edna Best in
the first and Helen Hayes in the second, moreover, contributed their
share to the ruin of the plays by posturing throughout as though they
were ridiculing the drama itself. I have always been glad that
M. Anouilh has been spared witnessing the fate of his pieces at our
hands.

No, while laughter is natural to many comedies, it is quite foreign
to others. A great comedy need not be basically funny. *The Misan-*
thrope is not funny, except at tangential moments; neither is *Tar-*
tuffe—and the world never had a greater master of laughter than
Molière. Most of the best plays of Ibsen and all the best plays of
Chekov are comedies—but no one of any sensibility will find much
in them to laugh at.

The Comedy of Errors and *The Taming of the Shrew* run over
with merriment; but they do not exhibit Shakespeare's comic art at
its greatest. There is plenty of laughter in *Much Ado, As You Like*
It, and *Twelfth Night*—but there is plenty of gravity too. And there
is much merriment in *The Merchant of Venice:* Portia, Salarino,
Gratiano, Nerissa keep us chuckling and Launcelot Gobbo keeps us
laughing. But there is absolutely no merriment of any kind involved
in Shakespeare's portrait of Shylock.

Shylock, beyond dispute, figures as the villain of our story. He is
not, as some innocently assume, the "merchant" of the title. The
1600 edition of the play has a title-page which makes that plain; it
reads "The most excellent Historie of the *Merchant of Venice.*
With the extreame crueltie of *Shylocke* the Jewe towards the sayd
Merchant, in cutting a just pound of his flesh: and the obtayning of
Portia by the choyse of three chests."

But another school of critics would make Shylock out to be a villain depicted without any mitigating touches of humanity, that is to
say, a villain without any other motive than love of villainy. To see
things thus is to be in the quandary of Launcelot Gobbo—"Thus
when I shun Scylla, your father, I fall into Charybdis, your mother."
(III, v, 13). Spedding and Stoll agree that Shylock is "a cur and a
devil," [50] fiercely thirsting for Christian blood. Fripp finds that
revenge "is part of his religion." [51] Quiller-Couch is sure that Shakespeare meant to make him "a cruel, crafty, villainous Hebrew." [52]
Murry thinks his hatred of Antonio "is represented as deep, irra-

tional and implacable." [53] Spencer believes that Shakespeare "Simply accepts the Jews as a notoriously bad lot," for he "never drew a noble Jew." [54] (It happens to be true that outside of Tubal, he never drew another one!) Frank Harris says that Shakespeare loathed Shylock "more than any character in all his plays." [55] Stirling attempts to have it both ways: Shakespeare, he says, had an ambivalent attitude towards Shylock, partly anti-Semitic and partly sympathetic.[56]

Mark Van Doren again makes sense when he says what is undeniable, that Shylock's creator has not "made the least inch of him lovely." But Shylock is not a monster. "He is a man thrust into a world bound not to endure him." [57] This truth is in accord with the total view I myself entertain regarding Shylock's character, though I am not sure that Van Doren and I come to that particular conclusion with the same thoughts in mind.

I have learned long ago that the only safe way to make one's path securely toward Shakespeare, is to avoid, once one has taken a full view of it, sinking in the morass of Shakespearean commentary (as one is sure to do if one makes a career of refuting it), and to skirt along the edge of it, while walking sure-footedly among the lines Shakespeare himself has written.

What did Shakespeare mean by his play?

C. F. E. Spurgeon has got us in the healthy habit of scrutinizing the imagery of a play when looking for its meaning. The tone of any literary work, so important a part of its meaning, is determined considerably by the imagery it contains. And in the work of any writer who knows what he is about, the tone at the very least must be consonant with what the work is trying to say in its totality.*

Spurgeon notes that in this play there are "most unusual of all with Shakespeare, several detailed glimpses of every day life and experience in a city." [58]

Their presence must have been dictated by Shakespeare's artistic cunning. His meaning in the play, as we shall see, has to do with the world of business—and that is a matter of the town, not the country. He wishes us to feel that we are in a thriving city, and images such as these serve that purpose well:

---

* For an analysis of the leading imagery in *Romeo and Juliet*, *Macbeth*, *A Doll's House*, and several other plays, and the relation of that imagery to the play's meaning, see the present writer's *Playwriting*, pp. 309-26.

1. Salarino compares Antonio's fleet of merchant ships to

> signiors and rich burghers* on the flood [who] . . .
> Do overpeer† the petty traffickers
> That curtsy to them, do them reverence.

(I, i, 10-13)

2. Bassanio, after he has chosen the right casket, evokes the picture of the winner of a wrestling-match. He feels

> Like one of two contending in a prize
> That thinks he hath done well in people's eyes,
> Hearing applause and universal shout,
> Giddy in spirit, still gazing in a doubt
> Whether those peals of praise be his or no.

(III, ii, 142-6)

3. A little later he recreates the picture of the murmuring of a crowd of citizens who have been addressed by the Queen:

> And there is such confusion in my powers
> As after some oration fairly spoke
> By a belov'd prince, there doth appear
> Among the buzzing pleased multitude,
> Where every something, being blent together,
> Turns to a wild of nothing, save of joy,
> Expressed and not expressed.

(III, ii, 179-85)

Clemen has noted that Salarino's lines near the very beginning of the play, when he guesses that Antonio's melancholy may be due to his concern over his ships at sea, "suggest the central theme of the action, which is to keep the audience breathless in the following acts." [59] Had I such ships as yours, Salarino says,

> My wind, cooling my broth,
> Would blow me to an ague when I thought
> What harm a wind too great at sea might do.

* businessmen
† look down upon

I should not see the sandy hourglass run
But I should think of shallows and of flats,*
And see my wealthy Andrew† docked in sand
Vailing‡ her high top lower than her ribs
To kiss her burial. Should I go to church
And see the holy edifice of stone,
And not bethink me straight of dangerous rocks,
Which touching but my gentle vessel's side
Would scatter all her spices on the stream,
Enrobe the roaring waters with my silks—
And, in a word, but even now worth this,
And now worth nothing?

(I, i, 22-36)

The picture evoked is certainly premonitory of the disasters of Antonio at the very time he must repay Shylock.

But all these images, dramatically important as they are, do not make for an approach to the central idea of the play [as do the images of light and darkness in *Romeo and Juliet*, and the images of borrowed clothes and blood in *Macbeth*]. For that it is wise to discover whether there is some ruling image pervading the work. But Spurgeon reports that there is no "continuous symbol" in the play.[60] She, of course, has studied only the figurative images of the plays. There is, however, another technique which can be quite as important and powerful as a continuous symbol, in establishing the tone of a work as a whole. To my knowledge only Mark Van Doren has noted a salient artistic fact about *The Merchant of Venice*; as he has exquisitely expressed it, "The word love lies like a morsel of down in the nest of nearly every speech." [61]

I count 66 lines in which some form of the word *love* appears in *The Merchant of Venice*, whereas I find only 27 in *Measure for Measure* and 20 in *The Tempest*. [It should come as no great surprise to lovers of Shakespeare that among the nouns and verbs probably no word is used more frequently by him than *love*—a revelation highly significant to the over-all meaning of his works. Of course, there are plays in which the word is used more frequently than in *The Merchant of Venice*. I count 159 such lines in *The Two Gentlemen of Verona*, 150 in *Romeo and Juliet*, and 76 in *Troilus*

* sandbanks
† the name of a ship
‡ lowering

and Cressida, but they are, as *The Merchant of Venice* is not, pre-eminently love stories.] It is odd that a play in which the word *love* reappears so often as it does in our play, should impress some with a spirit of fierceness, bloodiness, cruelty, and coldness! Characteristically, while a form of the word *hate* appears 27 times in *Richard III* and 22 in *Coriolanus* (the two plays in which it most frequently is to be found), it occurs but 8 times in *The Merchant of Venice* [and 3 times in *Measure for Measure,* 3 times in *The Tempest,* 9 times in *The Two Gentlemen of Verona,* 18 times in *Romeo and Juliet* (hatred in that play being the background to the love of Romeo and Juliet), and 5 times in *Troilus and Cressida*].

Now, it would be foolish to imply that Shakespeare deliberately inserted some form of the word *love* in so very many places in his play. We have no reason to suppose that for him, of all the world's poets, the imagination directing the creative process was less of a roaring furnace than it was for Blake. The point I am making becomes, indeed, all the stronger if we concede that Shakespeare may have very well been unconscious of the frequency with which the word reappears in his play. If that was the case it is all the more revelatory of what was working in his imagination.

I note further that of these 66 lines in which some form of the word *love* appears, only three are allotted to Shylock. Of these three, one is used in the service of hypocrisy, when he says to Antonio:

> I would be friends with you and have your love;
>
> (I, iii, 139)

and the other two are part of an expression of hatred—once when he is about to dine with Bassanio:

> I am not bid for love; they flatter me:
> But yet I'll go in hate
>
> (II, v, 13-14)

and once when he is defiantly justifying at court his hatred of Antonio:

> Some men love not a gaping pig.
>
> (IV, i, 47)

In the speeches of Antonio, Bassanio, their friends, Jessica, Lorenzo, Portia, and her suitors, however, the word *love* sheds its warm radiance throughout the play.

On the other hand, five of the eight lines in which the word *hate* appears are allotted to Shylock, four times in connection with Antonio:

> I hate him.
>
> (I, iii, 43)

> He hates our sacred nation.
>
> (I, iii, 49)

> So can I give no reason, nor I will not,
> More than a lodg'd hate and a certain loathing
> I bear Antonio.
>
> (IV, i, 59-61)

> Hates any man the thing he would not kill?
>
> (IV, i, 67)

and once in connection with Bassanio:

> I'll go in hate to feed upon
> The prodigal Christian.
>
> (II, v, 14-15)

Once Bassanio uses the word in an attempt to soften Shylock's hatred:

> Every offence is not a hate at first.
>
> (IV, i, 68)

Only once is the word used unconnected with Shylock's state of mind, and then it is by Portia as part of the expression of her love for Bassanio:

> I would not lose you, and you know yourself,
> Hate counsels not in such a quality.*
>
> (III, ii, 5-6)

* fashion

It is significant that once Shylock leaves the scene (IV, i, 400), the word *hate* never again appears in the play.

Before we generalize upon the meaning of all this, it would be well to remember that the Elizabethans were devoted to the Platonic ideal of love. The word *love* was used not only to refer to the relationship between man and woman but also to designate the noblest kind of friendship between man and man. Shakespeare's Sonnets are full of examples in which *love* is equated with *friend* or *friendship*, e.g.,

> Dear my love, you know
> You had a father. Let your son say so.
> (XIII, 13-14)

> Lord of my love, to whom in vassalage
> Thy merit hath my duty strongly knit.
> (XXVI, 1-2)

> For thy sweet love remembered such wealth brings
> That then I scorn to change my state with kings.
> (XXIX, 13-14)

> Let me not to the marriage of true minds
> Admit impediments. Love is not love
> Which alters when it alteration finds.
> (CXVI, 1-3)

It is in this sense that Antonio addresses Bassanio just before the turning-point of the trial:

> Commend me to your honorable wife.
> Tell her the process of Antonio's end,
> Say how I loved you, speak me fair in death,
> And when the tale is told, bid her be judge
> Whether Bassanio had not once a love.
>
> (IV, i, 273-7)

So, too, the word *lover* was often used interchangeably with *friend*: e.g., in the Forum scene of *Julius Caesar*, Brutus opens his address to the citizens with:

Romans, countrymen and lovers!

(III, ii, 13)

In *Coriolanus* old Menenius, seeking to get past the sentinel to Coriolanus, says to him,

> I tell thee, fellow,
> Thy general is my lover.

(V, ii, 13-14)

It is in this sense that Portia uses the word in speaking of the friendship between Antonio and Bassanio to Lorenzo and Jessica:

> this Antonio,
> Being the bosom lover of my lord,
> Must needs be like my lord.

(III, iv, 16-18)

In love and friendship, then, *The Merchant of Venice* luxuriates. Only Shylock, a creature who nourishes but hate, is cut off from these tender and ennobling emotions. And when he disappears from the play in the fourth act, the air is never again tainted with the fumes of hatred.

While the others are joined throughout the drama in the sweet ties of love and friendship, Shylock remains isolated in an enveloping atmosphere that knows neither friendship nor love.

What has made him so? Nothing connected with his being Jewish, nothing connected with his being persecuted or a member of a persecuted race. Shakespeare nowhere implies that what is forbidding, unloving, and unloveable in his character is a result of his being a Jew. [See pp. 178-79; 185 seq.]

His daughter Jessica is proof enough of that. She has "Jewish blood" in her veins, yet is not only capable of great love but also can inspire it. In his love for her Lorenzo has been allotted some of the most beautiful lines of the play to express it. Portia, Bassanio, and their friends treat her with the greatest cordiality and accept her as an equal. It never occurs to anyone to gloat over her deceiving her father or to congratulate her on escaping with some of his ducats and jewels. Nor will it do to explain their kindness to her on the grounds that she has become a Christian.

That such kindness is not, even today, an accepted thing was revealed not so long ago. On January 13, 1961, *The New York Times* featured the following story: A young man who had been born a Jew became converted to the Episcopal faith. "He had been selected as an escort by a girl who was making her debut at the dance, the club's annual Holly Ball," at the Scarsdale Country Club. The mother of the debutante reported that "she had submitted to the appropriate committee at the club the names of her daughter's two escorts for the dance . . . in accordance with the club's regulations." The mother, herself a member of the committee, had been informed by the escort subcommittee "that one of her daughter's choices was unacceptable 'because he is Jewish.' The subcommittee's decision was later confirmed, she said, by the club's board of governors." The affair, by grim coincidence, "was held two days after Christmas." The mother, obviously a woman of character, canceled her daughter's debut in protest. "The youth, who had changed his faith two years ago, was so hurt . . . that he would not go to church to receive holy communion on Christmas Sunday." The Rev. George French Kempsell, Jr. of the Church of St. James the Less was shocked at the affair, and announced that " 'Anyone who has in any way, by word or in thought or in deed, acquiesced with this position of the club is no longer welcome to receive holy communion at this altar—at God's altar—in this parish until such time as he has worked out his own peace with God in his own way.' "

Indeed, far too much has been made of Shylock's being Jewish. Some of the scholars look for his fundamental traits in that fact— in spite of what Shakespeare's play has to say. Shylock's "love of race is as deep as life," says Raleigh,[62] although the evidence is all to the contrary. Schücking lists the "peculiar" Jewish qualities of Shylock: "a keen intellect, a well-controlled though a passionate temperament, . . . a strict adherence to the letter of the law, . . . an insatiable avarice, and an uprightness governed by purely external standards." [63] I should certainly deny that a keen intellect and a well-controlled but passionate temperament are in the monopoly of the Jews, just as I should just as emphatically deny that a strict adherence to the letter of the law, an insatiable avarice, and a purely external morality are not as often found among Christians. Shakespeare, in fact, drew a portrait far more repelling than Shylock's, of a man of strict adherence to the letter of the law and an uprightness governed by purely external standards in the person of the Christian Angelo of *Measure for Measure*.

Doubtless a wrong impression concerning Shylock has been conveyed to moderns because of the frequency with which he is referred to as "the Jew" in the play. He is so called simply because he is not a Venetian. The word *Jew* occurs in 60 lines; the word *Moor* occurs in 55 lines of *Othello* and refers to one of the noblest, purest characters Shakespeare ever drew, a great general revered in the Venetian state. The way it occurs makes it perfectly clear that though Othello is set apart by the word, it is not an insult which is intended; here the word *Moor* is merely a designation signifying that he is not a native Venetian—just as, in the same play, Cassio is set apart from the Venetians by the appellation, "Florentine."

Desdemona never hesitates to use the term for the man she loves entirely,

> So much I challenge that I may profess
> Due to the Moor my lord.
>
> > (I, iii, 189-90)

> That I did love the Moor to live with him . . . ;
>
> > (I, iii, 249)

The Duke obviously uses the term with respect,

> Adieu, brave Moor; use Desdemona well;
>
> > (I, iii, 292)

and the same may be said of the other characters in the play (saving, of course, Iago):

> 'Tis great pity that the noble Moor
> Should hazard such a place as his own second . . . ;
>
> > (II, iii, 143)

> This was her first remembrance from the Moor;
>
> > (III, iii, 291)

> The Moor's abused by some most villainous knave;
>
> > (IV, 2, 139)

And seize upon the fortunes of the Moor,
For they succeed on you.

(V, ii, 366-7)

The same word, indeed, occurs in *The Merchant of Venice*, when
Launcelot Gobbo is revealed to have been up to some lechery on
the side, without any more meaningful connotation:

The Moor is with child by you, Launcelot.

(III, v, 42)

On the other hand, Salerio, who is a foreigner at Belmont, is there
hailed:

What, and my old Venetian friend Salerio!

(III, ii, 222)

In *The Tempest*, Gonzalo is called a "Neapolitan" to distinguish
him from the Milanese (I, ii, 161). And Portia at Belmont certainly
intends no slight when she refers to her suitors as "the Englishman"
and "the Frenchman" (I, ii, 87; 88).

In the 60 lines in which the word *Jew* appears there are only
four in which the word has anything but a sort of national designation. [It may be worthy of note that if Shylock were called *a* Jew
instead of *the* Jew (as he is), it might be possible to say that he
appears as someone typical of his race. But he is always "the
Jew."] It is in this not-meaningful way the term is almost always
used:

Hie thee, gentle Jew.

(I, iii, 178)

To be ruled by my conscience, I should stay with the Jew my
 master.

(II, ii, 24)

Young man, you, I pray you, which is the way to master Jew's?
(II, ii, 35)

I am Launcelot, the Jew's man.

(II, ii, 94)

What sum owes he the Jew?

(III, ii, 299)

Go one, and call the Jew into the court.

(IV, i, 14)

Which is the merchant here, and which the Jew?

(IV, i, 174)

There is no heat or color involved in the term in any of these passages. In the four lines out of the 60 where this is not the case, the word *Jew* is used, in the way we have already said Elizabethans often loosely used it (see pp. 31, 43), to mean any nonbeliever; in this sense its nearest synonym would be "atheist." Launcelot Gobbo uses the word thus three times:

My master is a very Jew.

(II, ii, 112)

I am a Jew, if I serve the Jew any longer.

(119)

[to Jessica] Most beautiful pagan, most sweet Jew!

(II, iii, 10-11)

and Gratiano (the only real anti-Semite in the play) once, in reference to Jessica,

Now, by my hood, a Gentile and no Jew.

(II, vi, 51)

[Since this is Gratiano speaking, it is possible to understand him as meaning to be patronizing here. If so, he is no more condescending than thousands of Jews have been toward Christians.] Of course, Shylock, as "the Jew" is several times spoken of caustically; but in those cases, an adjective is required (e.g., "harsh Jew," "this currish Jew"); the noun itself has no force as an insult, except to the degree that calling anyone "a non-Christian" would be an insult.

Now, in point of fact, Shakespeare has made Shylock not very much of a Jew at all. Every once in a while Shylock does wrap himself in the cloak of his religion, just as many a money-hungry Christian will wrap himself in the folds of Christianity—in both cases only to serve his own irreligious ends. God and the Bible are ever on the tongue of the unscrupulous politician. Men utterly remorseless in their rigid consecration to the doctrine that "Business is business" are often pillars of their church—indeed, find it highly profitable to be so. It is precisely the same with Shylock.

He also does not hesitate to capitalize on the persecutions visited upon his co-religionists—but when he does so, it is craftily, deliberately, with much feigned indignation, and, again for his own particular ends.

In order to apprehend this truth about him fully, it is necessary that we understand *the actual root of his hatred for Antonio*. It *has nothing to do with the difference in their religions, nothing to do with persecution*. Shakespeare could hardly have been at more pains than he has been to reveal what has poisoned Shylock's heart against the merchant. *At least five times during the course of the play Shylock himself*, now consciously, now unconsciously, *explicitly states the source of his hatred*. In his very first soliloquy, he tells us:

> I hate him for he is a Christian,
> But *more* for that in low simplicity
> *He lends out money gratis, and brings down*
> *The rate of usance here with us in Venice.*

(I, iii, 43-6)

As the day of repayment approaches he says in anger to Salanio and Salarino:

> A bankrupt, a prodigal, who dare scarce show his head on the Rialto; a beggar, that was us'd to come so smug* upon the mart; let him look to his bond. *He was wont to call me usurer*; let him look to his bond. *He was wont to lend money for a Christian courtesy*; let him look to his bond.

(III, i, 46-50)

and a minute later:

---

* well-dressed

He hath . . . hindered me* half a million.

(55-6)

and soon to Tubal:

> Go, Tubal, fee me an officer; bespeak him a fortnight before.
> I will have the heart of him, if he forfeit; for, *were he out of*
> *Venice, I can make what merchandise I will.*

(131-4)

After that, when Antonio has been taken into custody, Shylock says
to Salarino and the Gaoler, sneeringly:

> Gaoler, look to him; tell not me of mercy.
> *This is the fool that lent out money gratis!*

(III, iii, 1-2)

Moreover, Antonio knows perfectly well, however Shylock may have
pretended otherwise, the reason for Shylock's hatred:

> his reason well I know:
> *I oft deliver'd from his forfeitures*
> *Many that have at times made moan to me;*
> Therefore he hates me.

(21-4)

Of course Shylock throws up a lot of dust in masking this basis
for his fury against Antonio: it is only in the apartness of a
soliloquy or in the confidence to an associate or in the uncensored
outpouring of wrath that he allows himself to speak out the clear
truth. But, as we shall soon see, even while he is attempting to
cover the truth, it pierces through his pretences.

It is this hatred of Antonio for jeopardizing his profits from
moneylending—the hatred of a banker for a man whose generosity
is causing business to diminish—which constitutes Shylock's function in the dramatic representation of Shakespeare's ruling idea
in the play.

Money, as we have seen, was in Shakespeare's day not the all-
determining factor it has become since the growth of industrial
society. That it was becoming increasingly important was clear
* kept me from making

enough. Shakespeare seems to have been asking, But what is its future to be?

He did not have the kind of naïveté we have encountered since that era to suggest, as did Rousseau or Carlyle, that in search of felicity we turn back the hands of the clock to an earlier epoch. He was not so simple-minded, either, as to look upon money as inevitably an evil.

He saw that money, when used properly as a means to an end, can make life more beautiful and gracious, can enrich human relationships—not poison them—if it is remembered that money is meant to spend, not hoard. Thus, Antonio is a merchant. Historically, merchant and usurer were as one under the interdiction of the Church. But commerce inevitably began to expand its operations, and the new question became not one of the *taking* of profits, but the *use* to which profits were put. As a merchant, Antonio may be expected to profit from the sale of his commodities, and naturally must re-invest some of his gains for the purchase of other commodities. But he does not think of the accumulation of money as an end in itself. His desire for money is not to see gold added to gold, but to employ it for the enrichment of his life. When his friends are in need, he lends them money freely— that is what friends are for, according to his philosophy—and he is horrified at the very idea of profiting from their necessity. When Bassanio shyly approaches him for another loan, he is upset at his friend's embarrassment:

> out of doubt you do me now more wrong
> In making question of my uttermost
> Than if you made waste of all I have.
> Then do but say to me what I should do
> That in your knowledge may by me be done,
> And I am prest unto it.

(I, i, 155-60)

The people in Antonio's circle know how to love—that is, how to live. No friend is reduced to the humiliation of begging. When one approaches another for a favor, he is not first asked cautiously, "What is it?":

GRATIANO. Signior Bassanio!
BASSANIO.   Gratiano?

GRATIANO.   I have a suit to you.
BASSANIO.   You have obtained it.

(II, iii, 185-6)

The values of the stock exchange have not yet invaded personal relationships. Nor need they have ever. When I ask my friend, "Will you do me a favor?" I expect him to assume that I am not about to ask him to sacrifice his life for me, and therefore if he answer, "What is it?" I shall tell him, "Never mind." What I look for is such an answer as Bassanio's.

This understanding that friendship and compassion are the very sources of the good life is part of Portia's deep wisdom too. Immediately after the man of her choice has chosen the right casket, the letter from Antonio arrives telling of his quandary:

PORTIA.   What sum owes he the Jew?
BASSANIO.   For me, three thousand ducats.
PORTIA.   What, no more?
  Pay him six thousand, and deface the bond—
  Double six thousand, and then treble that,
  Before a friend of this description
  Shall lose a hair through Bassanio's fault.

(III, iii, 300-5)

This is the line she pursues in court, urging upon Shylock several times the amount due him. And it is to be remembered that the money she wishes him to accept is hers.

In qualification of this fact I have been reminded by a number of people that, after all, Portia is very wealthy. But the experience of industrial society is that those who are wealthiest are often least prepared to part with money—except for purposes of income-tax reduction. That is perhaps natural. The poor and the nearly poor are too well acquainted with poverty to be afraid of it. It is not the men with the prospect of bread-lines but the men whose income is decreased by a couple of thousand dollars a year, who in a financial depression walk out of sixteenth-storey windows. To the very rich today poverty means the end of everything; the poor know that somehow or other they can survive. Some years ago, the New York taxi-drivers were canvassed for their experience in receiving tips; they were unanimous in agreeing that the most miserable tips came from their wealthier passengers; it was the man

who works for his living, out for a Saturday night with his girl,
who gave the really lavish tips. No, by modern standards, it is
perhaps all the more remarkable that Portia, having so much, should
be so willing to part with it.

But, the point is, the world was not yet in Shakespeare's day
what it has become. And it was because of a certain concern for
what it might become that he wrote *The Merchant of Venice*.

Shylock, on the other hand, looks upon money only as an end
in itself.

> Fast bind, fast find,
> A proverb never stale in thrifty mind.

(II, v, 54-5)

Keep the ducats safe under lock and key is his credo. It is perhaps
both ironic and eloquent of the direction industrial society has
taken that his favorite motto might have later appeared virtuously
in *Poor Richard's Almanack*. He has no use for the code of *noblesse
oblige* by which the others in the play choose to live. From his
point of view they might very well seem to have adopted the
values of an outmoded feudal order, in which a man owed something to the world in the way of compassion and kindness just because of his exalted social position. For him the values of the future:
ruthless, cut-throat competition.

Whether or not he had any liking for the arts, the nobleman
felt it owing to his lineage to support painters, musicians, and poets.
It was a debt he felt his position conferred upon him. The merchants
were sons of the new order. But in the Renaissance they understood, many of them, that in the world that was passing was something worth salvaging: the sense of duty to society that a man of
eminent position ought to feel. And as we all know, the Renaissance
merchants vied with one another in patronizing the arts. Much
of the world's greatest painting, music, and sculpture would have
been impossible of achievement without their support. Today if
merchants feel inclined to support anything it is likely to be musical
comedies! The creative artist has been forced to become a merchant too, vulgarizing what he wishes to communicate because of
the pressures of cut-throat competition to which he himself is subject. Once a poet or composer of music had to please only a patron
—sometimes a man of great taste. (Haydn fared not badly with his

Count Esterhazy!) Today let him find a publisher if he can! The publisher will only tell him, "Who buys poetry?" or "How many copies of your composition do you suppose I can sell?"

So, too, your Renaissance merchant often enough felt called upon to prove by his capacities for friendship and generosity that, eager to make profits from his merchandise as he was, he was not going to be cheated of the richness of human relationships which had been within the scope of the old feudal life.

We can readily enough imagine Antonio, Bassanio, or Portia acting as a liberal patron of the arts. Portia, in point of fact, has her own company of musicians, who play for us in the last act. But who can think of Shylock as expending a copper on such delights? It is plain that he thinks their mode of living ridiculous. It is to him mere idiocy ("low simplicity") in Antonio to lend money gratis (1, iii, 44); to Antonio's face he sneers, "This is the fool that lent out money gratis" (III, iii, 2).

These are the forces at work in *The Merchant of Venice*: the bountiful grace and liberality of Antonio, Bassanio, Portia, and their friends, who are determined that money shall be a prop to those enrichments of life, not the death of them; and the suppression of all grace and liberality on the part of Shylock, who is convinced that money by itself is the only measurement of joy in life.

Interestingly enough, these are the same forces which are at work in Chekov's exquisite *The Cherry Orchard*: the grace and liberality of Mme Ranevsky and the ruthless march of material progress as exhibited in the stand of Lopakhin. But it is three centuries later: the die has been cast. And so the tones of the two masterpieces are diametrically opposed. Shakespeare is full of hope that as the world becomes richer, personal relationships shall become richer too. His eyes are bright with the vision of a future of Bassanios, Portias, and Antonios. But by Chekov's time, Shylock has won out. So Chekov writes with a delicate sadness for the change that has come over the world. He sees the silliness and, yes, the shams of Mme Ranevsky's aristocratic world; he knows that the law of change has decreed that they must pass, and he is glad enough to have them go. But he also sees the aristocratic grace and the charm which are about to pass from life too, the kindness and compassion, and at their passing he feels an aching nostalgia. Why is it needful, he seems to ask, that the ax which cuts down the follies of the past to make way for a better world materially, must needs destroy all in the past that was beautiful and lovely too? To be better must the future be also so unlovable?

But Shakespeare could not know that the world would choose, of the two paths open to it, the one in which money became the destroyer of love and friendship. Only Shylock, in his play, prefers that road. Shylock is isolated from love and friendship, and insulated against them, because he has nothing of himself to spare for them. Whatever affections he owns are expended upon the accumulation of money and the making of money from money. He bullies his daughter and starves his servant. Shakespeare, never the creator to put the case weakly, makes this greed for money all the more deplorable in that Shylock is a man of no mediocre qualities. He has dignity, strength, purposefulness, tenacity, courage, an excellent mind, a cuttingly wry sense of humor. It is a great injustice to the man Shakespeare has depicted to imagine him "servile and repulsive," [63] "fawning" [64] or "sneaking and underhanded" [65]—as many commentators and actors have depicted him. It is an equally grave injustice to him to conceive him, as so many others have done, as suffering from racial persecution. He is too strong-minded, too conscious of personal dignity for that. It is he who looks down upon the Christians, not they on him. He stands on too much of an eminence to feel persecuted, and he who does not feel persecuted, is not persecuted. Shakespeare has so presented him that we are bound to feel the great waste that such a man, framed for noble ends, should be debased by his ruling greed. Without the disease of greed, it is easy to imagine Shylock as walking like a king among men. But this one, terrible obsession channels all his best traits into the service of villainy. And for that he comes to grief in the end. The gods are just, Shakespeare always feels, and of our vices make instruments to plague us.

I am aware that to assert so unconventional an interpretation of Shylock entitles me to no more credence than is to be accorded the time-honored views of him as a pathetic, comic, or conventionally villainous Hebrew, without the proof. The proof is in the play.

Shylock appears in but five scenes of *The Merchant of Venice*. Let us trace what Shakespeare shows us of him, step by step, from the beginning. One of the chief causes of confusion concerning his character comes from the failure of commentators to consider Shylock's speeches in the order in which they occur. If I commence by seizing upon the "Many a time and oft" and "Hath not a Jew

eyes?" passages (I, iii, 107 and III, i, 61), I might convincingly
enough make out Shylock to be a tragic representative of his race.
On the other hand, if I choose to commence with Gratiano's slurs in
the trial scene (IV, i, 364; 379, 398), I might convincingly enough
make out Shakespeare's purposes to be anti-Semitic. But if I honestly
wish to discover Shakespeare's intentions, I will begin with no
preconceptions concerning Shylock's character, and start gauging
him from the moment we first meet him in the play. If we are to
understand him, we must be patient; we shall be wise to take the
advice of the King in *Alice's Adventures in Wonderland*: "Begin at
the beginning and go on till you come to the end: then stop."

We first meet Shylock in I, iii. [His name has been said, variously,
to be a transliteration of Shalach or Shelach (*Genesis* X, 24),
"cormorant," or of Shiloh, the sanctuary of Jehovah. The former
seems likely since in the next chapter we meet with the origin of
Jessica's name, Iscah or Jeska, "she who looks out." Tubal and Chus
are found in these Biblical passages too.] Bassanio has already
broached the subject of the loan. From the very outset we see the
moneylender standing firm and as unyielding as solid rock. Bassanio
is edgy, Shylock absolutely noncommittal: he may lend the money
and then again he may not. In these lines which open the scene, it
is Shylock who is in control of the situation:

SHYLOCK.   Three thousand ducats. Well.
BASSANIO. Ay, sir, for three months.
SHYLOCK.   For three months. Well.
BASSANIO. For the which, as I told you, Antonio shall be bound.
SHYLOCK.   Antonio shall become bound. Well.
BASSANIO. May you stead me? Will you pleasure me? Shall I
           know your answer?
SHYLOCK.   Three thousand ducats for three months, and Antonio
           bound.

Shakespeare, as ever, is remarkable in his ability to cause us to hear
the very tone in which his characters speak: the calm, deliberately
unemotional voice of Shylock, giving not the slightest intimation
of his intentions, and the nervous, high-strung anxiety of Bassanio.
Nor does Shylock do anything to make Bassanio more comfortable:
he is enjoying too much keeping him dangling:

BASSANIO.   Your answer to that.
SHYLOCK.   Antonio is a good man.

There is something in his voice so arrogant that Bassanio hotly demands:

> Have you heard any imputation to the contrary?

To which Shylock rejoins, with the loftiness of an adult quieting a child:

> Ho, no, no, no, no! My meaning in saying he is a good man is
>   to have you understand me that he is sufficient.

And then he begins to enumerate the risks, with the precision and carefulness of the man who is used to counting every penny— the risks of ships, seas, human fallibility, pirates, winds, rocks; and ends, once more without in any way hinting that he will oblige:

> The man is, notwithstanding, sufficient. Three thousand ducats;
>   I think I *may* take his bond.

That he deliberately stresses the "may" to embarrass Bassanio further is proved by the latter's next line:

> Be assured you may.

Which only calls forth a further piece of haughtiness from Shylock:

> I *will* be assured I may, and that I may be assured, I will bethink
>   me.

In other words, Don't try to rush me; I mean to think this over.

We have progressed only 30 lines from his first appearance, and it is already too late for us ever to expect a cringing, fawning, imposed-upon Shylock. Whatever we hear him say later, we are bound to interpret in terms of the Shylock we already know.

It is now that Bassanio invites him to meet Antonio over dinner, and that he replies haughtily in words that have been so much and so blindly overinterpreted: he will not go to smell pork.

> I will buy with you, sell with you, talk with you, walk with you,
>   and so following; but I will not eat with you, drink with you,
>   nor pray with you.

These certainly sound like the words of a pious Jew. But how seriously are we to take them? Presently we shall learn that he does indeed go to eat and drink with the Christians, and for reasons which do him no credit. Since he has no intention of refusing the invitation, how are we to take his words? In the same spirit as everything else he has thus far said: to make Bassanio uncomfortable.

Antonio now appears, and while Bassanio is greeting him, Shylock has his first soliloquy.

[Shakespeare's predecessors had used the soliloquy either to inform the audience of certain facts and situations, or for only the crudest kind of self-revelation by a character (akin to the silly confidences made in mid-Victorian melodramas by the villains to the audience, while they twirled their mustaches). But Shakespeare found a new use for the soliloquy. As we listen to one of his characters thinking aloud, he invites us to inspect the working of the man's soul. Often, as later in Browning's dramatic monologues, while we hear the character attempting to rationalize or justify his conduct, we understand him better than he is able to understand himself.[66]]

This is particularly true of Shylock's first soliloquy. Indeed, I believe that it is the earliest example of Shakespeare's putting the soliloquy to this exciting dramatic use.

Here Shylock expresses his burning hatred for Antonio for the first time. He would like to pretend to himself that that hatred is based upon lofty, religious grounds. But the truth will out in spite of him:

> I hate him for he is a Christian,
> But *more for that in low simplicity*
> *He lends out money gratis and brings down*
> *The rate of usance here with us in Venice.*
> If I can catch him once upon the hip,
> I will feed fat the ancient grudge I bear him.

[How, after these words, is it possible to construe, as some critics have amiably done, the bond later proposed as really offered in the spirit of friendship?]

He hates our sacred nation, and he rails
Even there where merchants most do congregate,
On me, *my bargains, and my well-won thrift,*
Which he calls interest. Cursed be my tribe
If I forgive him!

I have italicized the pertinent passages to show that underneath all his pretenses to himself, it is only Antonio's disdain of interest which rankles. Shakespeare is here, as always, fascinating in his psychological presentation. [Surely one of the chief reasons why Shakespeare is so universally admired. But some scholars will not tolerate that. E. E. Stoll: "It is poetically, dramatically, not psychologically, that the characters are meant to interest us." [67] This is again a run-of-the-mill Shakespeare. In a few moments we shall have occasion to remark that in a play we must understand what the characters *are* chiefly by what they *do*. But it is surely absurd to deny that the characters are supposed to hold any psychological interest for the audience. What they *do* gives the psychological key to what they *are*. In a great play what they *are* is certainly, in the end, more important to the audience than the story in which they figure. An offshoot of that doggedly dehumanized sort of scholarship is the frequently heard argument that the characters in a play ought never to be discussed as though they were live figures. Palmer: "Critics and editors insist on viewing every character . . . in the broad light of common day: . . . each character is submitted to everyday tests of moral worth and social decorum." And Palmer believes this a literary crime.[68] But why should we not do precisely what he forbids? If literature worthy of the name is, as it should be, an imitation of human beings in their interrelationships, to what other criteria are we to submit their character traits if not to those of life itself? It is a gross error to lose sight of the play as the author has written it; but it is equally in error to insist that the characters in that play need not be life-like. For what other purpose is literature created? I have found it useful even to ask college students, "How would Beatrice behave in Desdemona's situation?" "How Portia in Ophelia's?" The validity of such questions is proved by the readiness with which they can be answered.]

See how Shylock twists and turns, trying to posture to himself as indignant on grounds purely impersonal and larger. Antonio, according to him, hates the Jews. How does he show it? Not by railing against them but by railing against Shylock. What does he rail against Shylock for? His religion? No. For his taking of exorbitant interest—and, at that, *where other merchants can hear.* All this Shylock chooses to construe as an insult to all the Jews, and on those grounds he vows vengeance. But, for all that, the real basis for his fury has revealed itself. A perfect example of an all-too-human self-justification.

It is part of Shakespeare's profundity that Shylock should not accurately know himself. What miser ever faced the truth about himself, or failed to call his penuriousness by some better-sounding name like thrift or self-restraint? That is why the greed of a Jonsonian miser is not really credible, and Shylock's is. This inability to face what he really is will make itself dramatically vocal when we meet him for the last time, in the trial scene.

Now Shylock forces Bassanio to press him again for an answer, pretends still to be mulling over the loan, and then feigns seeing Antonio for the first time—Ah, how do you do? We were just talking about you. ("Your worship was the last man in our mouths.") Still the condescending Shylock.

Up to this point in the play Antonio, when we have met him, has had nothing to say about Shylock. It is in this scene that we are first given to know how he feels about the moneylender. He speaks to him coldly; this is merely a business matter, and he is quite prepared to pay the interest he disapproves of, since Shylock, of course, will ask for it. His voice is neither friendly nor hostile; Shylock, in responding, lines his words with irony:

> ANTONIO.   Shylock, albeit I neither lend nor borrow
>   By taking nor by giving of excess,
>   Yet to supply the ripe wants of my friend,
>   I'll break a custom. (*to Bass.*) Is he yet possess'd
>   How much ye would?
> SHYLOCK.   Ay, ay, three thousand ducats.
> ANTONIO.   And for three months.
> SHYLOCK.   I had forgot; three months; you told me so.

But he still refuses to indicate whether or not he will lend the money. Moreover, this is too good an opportunity to miss. I thought, says he, you make it a practice never to ask or give interest on a loan? I never do, Antonio replies.

Now that he has Antonio at a disadvantage, Shylock cannot let slip the occasion to justify the taking of interest. By citing the enterprise of Jacob while serving Laban, he attempts to confute the Aristotelian argument that money, being inanimate, is put to unnatural uses when it is employed only to multiply itself. Again Shylock demonstrates the characteristic precision of his mind: This Jacob was the third in line from Abraham—let's see, wasn't he? Yes, he was the third. Antonio, knowing his man, cuts in: Did Jacob take interest? Shylock does not like such a forthright question:

> No, not take interest, not, as you would say,
> Directly interest.

But Jacob was not above a little trickery to insure his own welfare; it was a way to profit, and profit is a blessing when it isn't stolen. Antonio blasts through the sophistry: was the Scriptural passage written to justify the taking of interest,

> Or is your gold and silver ewes and rams?

Shylock answers him and Aristotle wryly:

> I cannot tell; I make it breed as fast.

Antonio seems well aware that Shylock is a religious hypocrite; in disgust he observes that the Devil knows how to cite Scripture for his purpose:

> O, what a goodly outside falsehood hath!

Unperturbed, Shylock goes back to considering the loan. No hint from him whether it is to be granted. No, not yet—let them wait. Thus, Antonio is compelled to ask again: Will you lend this money? It is here that Shylock delivers one of his celebrated speeches. It is odd that despite its fame, it has never been seen to reveal Shakespeare's psychological cunning.

Shylock has intimated nothing of his intentions concerning the ducats asked for. First he must make Antonio—him who condemns interest—smart, now that he comes asking for a loan. So, for the hated one's benefit, Shylock cloaks himself in the dignity of race.

But again, in despite of himself, he reveals that he is not complaining of persecution, only justifying his taking of interest. Many a time and oft Antonio has berated him on the Rialto (where merchants most do congregate!)—about what? His religion? No:

> About my moneys and my usances.

But this Shylock deliberately confuses as though it were an insult to all Jews:

> Still have I borne it with a patient shrug,
> For sufferance is the badge of all our tribe.

We may well imagine that Antonio, no fool, is experiencing a queasiness at this smug sanctimoniousness. Shylock, thoroughly enjoying himself at the others' discomfort, now accuses Antonio of having spat upon his "Jewish" gaberdine. For what? His religion? No, despite his intention of capitalizing on the persecution of the Jews, Shylock finds himself saying:

> And all for use of that which is mine own.

It is the need of justifying his greed which rankles in him. And having a first-rate intelligence and great powers of expression, he hurls at his enemy one of the loftiest pieces of sarcasm ever penned:

> Well, then, it now appears you need my help.
> Go to, then! You come to me, and you say,
> "Shylock, we would have moneys;" you say so—
> You, that did void your rheum upon my beard
> And foot me as you spurn a stranger cur
> Over your threshold; moneys is your suit.
> What should I say to you? Should I not say,
> "Hath a dog money? Is it possible
> A cur can lend three thousand ducats?" Or
> Shall I bend low and in a bondman's key,
> With bated breath and whispering humbleness,
> Say this:
> "Fair sir, you spat on me on Wednesday last;
> You spurn'd me such a day; another time

You call'd me dog; and for these courtesies
I'll lend you thus much moneys."?

The indignation is superb, and it is a callous audience that will fail to be overwhelmed by it. But coming after what has preceded it, it can have but one purpose in Shylock's mind. He has been doing his best to make Bassanio and Antonio squirm. This speech is his crowning effort to humiliate them.

But at this point we have a difficulty. He has charged Antonio with spitting upon him because of his taking interest. Scholars have hastened to ascribe to that contemptuous and contemptible behavior of Antonio the cause of Shylock's hatred. Yet, when we shall presently consider Antonio's character traits, we shall find nothing in his behavior which could possibly be consonant with such conduct. He is at every point a gentle, mild, loving, and modest man. Nowhere up to the very trial scene (Act IV) does he ever say a single thing that is vaguely anti-Semitic about Shylock—not even after he has been taken into custody and his life is in peril. It will not do to say that Antonio's spitting upon Shylock would in that age have been no blot upon his character. That explanation would do very well for a rather vulgar man like Gratiano. Shakespeare proves himself in the play totally alien to bigotry: why should he not have made his hero above it?

In every play there are things said, things thought, and things done. Of these the most important are the things done. ("The primary objects of artistic imitation are human beings in action, men, performing or doing something."—Aristotle).[69] . . . The very word *drama* comes from the Greek verb *dran, to do* or *to act.* Hence, to understand a play we must focus our attention primarily on the things done during the course of the plot. Things thought and said must be interpreted according to the light thrown upon them by the action of the play.

Further, in a drama of even the feeblest pyschological insight our interpretation of the things said is subject to what is actually being thought. . . . Our comprehension of a play begins with the transactions of the plot; with them in mind we pierce through the words spoken to what the characters are actually thinking, for without the action we should not know how to understand the words. For instance, when Iago says to Othello: "My lord, you know I love you" (III, iii, 117), we are not to interpret the words on their face value, we are not to believe that Iago's bosom overflows with welling affection for Othello or to prepare ourselves for deeds of kindliness and generosity. Rather, since this is a play, we first recollect that Iago is at the moment busy destroying Othello (the action), and next realize (since this is a play of psychological depth) that he speaks these words only because he is gloating over his growing success in winning power over the Moor. Thus, when we analyze a drama, we must first place emphasis on the things being done, next, the thing being thought, and—in view of these —last, the thing being said.[70]

Of the world's dramatists, no one believed more firmly than Shakespeare in having characters reveal themselves by what they *do*. For instance, in the scene we have been examining, the salient fact about Shylock is that he has kept Antonio and Bassanio in suspense, has done all he could to aggravate their embarrassment in having to come to him for a loan, and has refused to alleviate their discomfort by even a hint that he might lend the money. This, as far as we have progressed in it, is the basic action of the scene. Now Shylock has *said* that Antonio has spit upon him. But if we were asked to believe that this is the truth, it would be Shakespeare's practice to show us Antonio *conducting himself* elsewhere in the play *in a manner consistent with such an act.*

As an analogy: In order to justify his knavery to himself, Iago pretends to believe that Othello has been sleeping with Emilia, Iago's wife. [The "unscholarly" lover of Shakespeare will perhaps be astonished to learn that because Iago *says* this, many scholars believe him, and proceed to discuss Iago's "motives" as though Othello's having cuckolded him were an established fact!] If Shakespeare wished us to entertain even the possibility that such a state of affairs existed, it would have been his practice to show onstage this relationship between Othello and Emilia. In that play such a liaison would constitute too powerful an excuse for Iago to be left even in question by the dramatist. As it is, in the play Shakespeare wrote Othello is hardly aware of Emilia's existence, and she is in considerable awe of him.

Now, since we nowhere see Antonio behaving in a way that would make it possible for us to think of him as spitting on anyone, is it not possible that Shylock is making the charge against him—just as Iago makes his charge against Othello—without really believing a word of it, only to erect a false justification for himself, and, most of all, because he gauges that Antonio's pride will not permit the merchant to defend himself?

If, for the sake of argument, we grant that this is indeed the case—if Antonio is aware of what Shylock is up to, trying further to annoy him—should we expect Antonio to deny hotly, "When did I ever spit on you?" If your enemy approached you and accused you of committing incest with your sister, and you were, moreover, an only child, would you be behaving with any dignity to exclaim, outraged, "Why I haven't got a sister!" Would it not be more consonant with manly pride to answer coolly, "With which sister do you mean?"

It is in a similar spirit that I understand Antonio's making response to the charge. At the moment he is revolted at Shylock's attempts to ennoble the taking of interest; he is disgusted at being kept dangling—after all, he and Bassanio have not come to ask a favor but to engage in a distasteful commercial transaction. We may be sure that if this loan were for his own needs, not his friend's, he would have turned on his heel before this. Instead, he masters his ire, and answers coldly and with unconcealed contempt for Shylock's brazen hypocrisy: Very well, I'll do the same things all over again; for we are not talking as friends; we ask for a loan at your usual rates; when did a friend ever ask interest for a loan?

> I am as like to call thee so again,
> To spit on thee again, to spurn thee too.
> If thou wilt lend this money, lend it not
> As to thy friends; for *when did friendship take*
> *A breed* for† barren metal of his friend?*

There is no point, Antonio is implying, in your talking to me as though we were meeting as intimates. Your attitude toward taking interest makes this purely a matter of business: let's keep it on that level.

> But lend it rather to thine enemy,
> Who, if he break, thou mayst with better face
> Exact the penalty.

* increase
† for the use of

Shylock is satisfied that he has pushed Antonio to the limits of annoyance, and so his tone swiftly changes: But why do you take on so? I'm perfectly willing to be your friend, lend you the money, and not take a cent of interest. My offer is kind. (Up to this moment he has made no offer!)

Bassanio who, though silent, has necessarily been more upset by the talk than Antonio could be, since he is the cause of it all, with relief cries, "This were kindness."

And now Shakespeare comes to the knottiest problem in the plot he has inherited from Fiorentino. Stipulating for the illusion of flesh-and-blood reality in his plays, how was he to make it credible that Antonio would sign a bond which places his life in jeopardy? His solution was brilliant. Some sort of consideration will be necessary to make the contract legal. Shylock refuses any financial security, since he is acting as a friend. Well then, let us mention as the consideration something absolutely absurd, just to show my complete confidence in your word. Let us make it something as ludicrous as, say, a pound of your flesh. What is important in this speech is that the bond is framed "in a merry sport," as he puts it. [The whole effect has been ruined by fawning, sniveling Shylocks I have seen— precursors of Uriah Heep—when they approach close to Antonio at "an equal pound/Of your fair flesh" and with a gesture seem to be cutting it off in anticipation of the event! That should be enough to scare off anyone from signing the bond!]

Innocently Antonio accepts the terms as framed in a merry sport, and is ready to believe that Shylock desires to be friendly. He considers the offer very decent of Shylock ("there is much kindness in the Jew"). Naturally, Bassanio, oversensitive because of his role in this affair, expresses alarm. But Antonio reassures him: No need for alarm; my ships come back laden a good month before the money is due. Shylock, gleeful at the success of his ruse, feigns shock at Bassanio's suspicions in a tone which is anything but humble: What creatures these Christians are, who judge others by their own unfeeling ways! Tell me, what should I do with a pound of his flesh, if I seriously hoped to have it? (With mixed insolence and ever-present greed) he says further: a pound of man's flesh

> Is not so estimable, *profitable* neither,
> As flesh of muttons, beefs, or goats.

I'm willing to act like his friend: let him take the offer or leave it. But in all fairness, don't do me the injustice of ascribing sordid motives to what I am willing to do generously.

Antonio is unworried, and Shylock once more emphasizes that this is to be a "merry bond." Antonio's farewell acknowledges that Shylock's behavior is princely:

> Hie thee, gentle* Jew.

Before we meet Shylock again, we learn interesting things about him. His household is a joyless one, and he wishes it to be so. Launcelot Gobbo, his poor idiot of a servant, is becoming skin and bones from starvation. This amiable halfwit is the only companion Shylock's daughter is permitted to have; at the prospect of his leaving Shylock's employ she is unhappy:

> I am sorry thou wilt leave my father so.
> *Our house is hell,* and thou, a merry devil,
> Didst rob it of some taste of tediousness.
>
> (II, iii, 1-3)

That she does not exaggerate will be evident enough in a scene which shortly follows. But apparently the little pleasure she can have in talking to Launcelot must be snatched in secret too. She cuts short their conversation with:

> And so farewell. I would not have my father
> See me in talk with thee.
>
> (8-9)

In a handful of lines Shakespeare has vividly sketched the gloomy and prisonlike atmosphere of Shylock's home.

Jessica turns out to be something less than an ideal daughter, satisfactory as she is in her devotion to Lorenzo. But there is no reason why she should love her father. It is clear from the outset that she has never known tenderness or love from him.

---

* The usual connotation of "gentle," a word used by his contemporaries to describe Shakespeare himself, was "well-born," "civilized."

When one considers how careful Shakespeare has been to make this relationship clear, the sentimental vagaries of commentators are truly astounding. They build up the notion of a Shylock who, after lavishing affection on his daughter, is treacherously betrayed by her. They tell us that Jessica "is bad and disloyal, unfilial, a thief, frivolous, greedy, without any more conscience than a cat and without even a cat's redeeming love of home. Quite without heart, on worse than an animal instinct—pilfering to be carnal—she betrays her father." [71] "Shylock as well as Lear has reason to know 'how sharper than a serpent's tooth it is to have a thankless child.'" [72] She was a "pert, disobedient hussy"; "her conduct I regard as in a high degree reprehensible; and those who have the care of families must, I think, feel as I do. [Those who have the care of families had better expend some affection and understanding on their daughters, unless they wish to be treated by them as Shylock is treated by Jessica!] She was a worthless minx, and I have no good word to say of her. . . . Why should she, a maiden of Israel, leave her poor old father, Shylock, alone in the midst of his Christian enemies?" [73] [Her poor old father Shylock, in Shakespeare's play, at least, *is* the enemy threatening the life of Antonio and the peace of mind of Bassanio and Portia.] Her father "is intolerably wronged by Jessica." [74] Margaret Webster sums up this groundless school of thought, by blandly asserting that Shylock loves his daughter, "though Heaven knows why, for she is a little baggage." [75]

Apparently only Graham has noticed that "there is not one line in the entire play in which Shylock directly expresses affection for his daughter." [76] That is indeed the truth, and we have no right to ascribe to Shylock tender emotions which Shakespeare has not endowed him with. [Packard, who grants that Shylock may be a man of "ungentle feeling," takes that as a demonstration "that there is a side of Jewish life that Shakespeare never knew—the domestic." (Shakespeare probably never crossed the English Channel: where was he to have studied Jewish life, domestic or public?) All Jews, Packard insists, are gentle with their children; all Jewish children are devoted to their parents. "Jewish life presents a beautiful picture. Seated about the fire at eventide, the father and husband opens unto his own the burdensome history of the day. The Torah, from which he draws his consolation, is ever at his side. . . . Temperate, patient, gentle, regular in habits, how could the home life of the Jew be otherwise than pleasant?" Shylock's home is not really a

Jewish home.[77] It is doubtless futile to argue with anyone who sees his own people in so beatific a light. But just as I deny that Jews are characterized by miserliness, so do I deny that they tend more than others to gentleness and affection. Jews who have children are surely like other people who have children: probably, a minority of them love their children with tenderness and intelligence; probably, a minority of them love their children not at all; probably, a majority of them love their children with indulgence and without intelligence—like other human beings. Some of them will reap love for love lavished; some of them will reap hate for love lavished; some of them will reap indifference for indifference; and some of them will quite unjustifiably reap love for indifference—these being the human averages of children's affections. It is too late in the day to insist that all parents (of whatever people) know how to love. It may also be hoped that there are some Jewish fathers rather better than Packard's roseate picture of them—some who will spare their families the opening of the burdensome history of the day, and report only its felicities.] Though somewhat overstating the case, Murry is nearer the fact than most critics when he says of Jessica that she is "a princess held captive by an ogre." [78]

The next time we meet Shylock (II, v) he is before his house. He assures poor Launcelot, him whose ribs are showing from hunger, that he will not be able to gobble up everything in sight at Bassanio's, as he has done at Shylock's household. (In Shylock's diseased mind every scrap of bread is begrudged his servant.) Shylock is about to go to Bassanio's for dinner. The very invitation shows that Antonio and Bassanio are ready to accept his proffered friendship. And Shylock means to go, despite his earlier high-sounding talk about not eating with Christians. His reason for going? The more he eats of Bassanio's feast, the less Bassanio will have. ("I'll go in hate to feed upon the prodigal Christian.") How well Shakespeare understood every aberration of human nature! Though extreme, Shylock's point of view is of one piece with his embracing the philosophy of cutthroat competition: the less others have, the richer he himself can feel.

But he has a premonition of something unpleasant in the stars: he dreamt last night of money-bags, and is "right loath to go." Launcelot, appropriating the lofty airs that he feels are owing to his new uniform, says grandly, misusing "reproach" for "approach":

> I beseech you, sir, go. My young master doth expect your re-
> proach.

Shylock seizes upon the malapropism, and retorts with concentrated malice masked as wry humor:

> So do I his.

This quibble is like a sword-thrust: it should be enough to raise goose flesh. It means only one thing: Shylock has every intention of collecting the pound of flesh, and has a plan for making sure he will have it.

Now foolish Launcelot emits what is meant to be a hint to Jessica, but might easily have prevented her intended elopement if Shylock had had any notion of it: there's going to be a masque tonight. At the very mention of purposed merriment, Shylock's hatred of all that is delightful and gay is aroused:

> What, are there masques? Hear you me, Jessica.
> Lock up my doors; and when you hear the drum
> And the vile squealing of the wry-neck'd fife,*
> Clamber not you up to the casements then,
> Nor thrust your head into the public street
> To gaze on Christian fools with varnish'd faces,
> But stop my house's ears, I mean my casements.
> Let not the sound of shallow foppery enter
> My sober house.

He has no use for music. He does not want even the echo of it to penetrate his house. Obviously Shakespeare will later mean us to take quite seriously Lorenzo's dictum:

> The man that hath no music in himself,
> Nor is not mov'd with concord of sweet sounds,
> Is fit for treasons, stratagems, and spoils. . . .
> Let no such man be trusted.
>
> (V, i, 83-8)

It certainly applies to Shylock. And luckless Jessica! She is not to dare watch the fun in the streets by looking out the window or even

* fifer

from behind it. Her eyes and ears are to be sealed against the most innocent pleasure. Small wonder that she will leave her father's house without regret.

Launcelot goes off, and Shylock reflects that he is glad to be rid of such a huge feeder (poor, starved Launcelot!); he is, moreover, delighted to think of how he will now help to waste Bassanio's substance. Then, before he himself departs, he threatens Jessica: she had better obey every article of his commands:

> Perhaps I will return immediately.

Clearly her life under her father's roof is an endless series of commands and warnings against disobedience—not the sort of existence to evoke love or even duty.

This scene demonstrates how far from the point those stray who insist that it is only Jessica's elopement which turns a benevolent Shylock into a hating one. She has not yet eloped, and we have seen him full of malevolence against Bassanio and Antonio, most of all in that blood-chilling "So do I his."

Irving, as we have already related, interpolated a scene in which Shylock is seen returning amidst the revelry of the masques, lantern in hand, knocking in vain at the door of his empty house for a beloved daughter who has wantonly deserted him. Shakespeare surely had enough imagination to write such a scene, if it had been to his purpose. He was careful not to write it, for the very simple reason that we are not to feel particularly sorry for Shylock when Jessica takes wing—rather, to feel relief that she has escaped from prison. Neverthless, Quiller-Couch, Cambridge editor of Shakespeare, can speak of Shylock's returning "from a gay abhorrent banquet to knock on his empty and emptied house." [79] (That "emptied" is a rather deliberate exaggeration.)

Before we meet Shylock again (in Shakespeare's version), the elopement has taken place. I suspect that neither the dramatist nor his audience understood her taking money and jewels with her to be conduct as heinous as modern interpreters have construed it. Her life with Shylock has been a stunted one; what she has appropriated has not left him impoverished. Even today Europeans generally expect that when a girl of means is married, her father will provide a suitable dowry. It is more than likely that we were intended to feel that Jessica has done little more than take with her the marriage-portion that ought to have been hers. (In the probable source for the Jessica-Lorenzo story, we shall see, the girl in that tale also helps herself to her father's possessions when she elopes.)

After the elopement we hear Salarino and Salanio discussing the effects of it upon Shylock. Their picture of his running through the streets shrieking

> My daughter! O my ducats! O my daughter!
> Fled with a Christian! O my Christian ducats!
> Justice! the law! my ducats, and my daughter!
> A sealed bag, two sealed bags of ducats,
> Of double ducats, stolen from me by my daughter!
> And jewels, two stones, two rich and precious stones,
> Stolen by my daughter! Justice! find the girl;
> She hath the stones upon her, and the ducats.

is deliberately grotesque. But it has some of the ring of truth in it too. The emphasis upon the ducats and the stones sounds like the Shylock we know. Likewise does his wish, not so much to have his daughter back for herself, but to find her so that he can retrieve his ducats and his jewels.

In the scene in which we next meet Shylock (III, i), there is more talk of ships wrecked at sea and the possibility that they could be Antonio's (the talk began in II, viii, 25-32). Shylock comes in, and he is in a terrible rage:

> You knew, none so well, none so well as you, of my daughter's
> flight,

he storms at Salanio and Salarino. The latter tries to moderate Shylock's fury: Shylock must have been aware that Jessica was of an age to think of marriage. But he will not be mollified:

> My own flesh and blood to rebel!

Salarino denies that Jessica is a replica of her father, and does so in language that exonerates him from any charge of anti-Semitism:

> There is more difference between thy flesh and hers than be-
> tween jet and ivory; more between your bloods than there is
> between red wine and rhenish.

He changes the subject to ask whether Shylock has heard anything
of Antonio's ships. The question but adds fuel to Shylock's passion:

> There I have another bad match. A bankrupt, a prodigal, who
> dare scarce show his head on the Rialto; a beggar, that was
> us'd to come so smug upon the mart; let him look to his
> bond. . . . He was wont to lend money for a Christian cour-
> tesy; let him look to his bond.

In wine and in wrath the truth will out. Shylock's list of Antonio's
offenses this time significantly omits any reference to spitting on
Jewish gaberdines or to insults against the Jews. No, in his fury it
does not occur to him to mask the real sources of his fury: Antonio's elegant appearance, Antonio's wasting of money, Antonio's
lending money without interest. These are the crimes for which he
hates the merchant.

When Salarino asks of what use the forfeiture could be to Shylock, Shylock responds in a way that again is a tribute to Shakespeare's psychological insight. Now that he has been called on to
state his grievances, Shylock once more tries to pass off the reasons
for his thirst for revenge as better than they are. But, in spite of
his tone of injured innocence, he reveals that it is only matters of
money which cause his hatred:

> He hath disgrac'd me, and *hind'red me half a million*; laugh'd
> at *my losses*, mock'd at *my gains*, scorn'd my nation, thwarted
> *my bargains* . . .

The reference to his "nation" is almost parenthetical—as though he
had thought of something that must be slipped in to justify the rest.
Again, despite himself, Shylock makes it plain that the only thing
Antonio has done to injure him has been to lend out money gratis.

From the indictment he soars into one of the most movingly written orations ever penned:

> And what's his reason? I am a Jew. Hath not a Jew eyes? Hath
> not a Jew hands, organs, dimensions, senses, affections, pas-
> sions; fed with the same food, hurt with the same weapons,
> subject to the same diseases, healed by the same means,
> warmed and cooled by the same winter and summer, as a

> Christian is? If you prick us, do we not bleed? If you tickle us,
> do we not laugh? If you poison us, do we not die? And if you
> wrong us, shall we not revenge? If we are like you in the rest,
> we will resemble you in that. If a Jew wrong a Christian,
> what is his humility? Revenge. If a Christian wrong a Jew,
> what should his sufferance be by Christian example? Why,
> revenge. The villainy you teach me, I will execute, and it
> shall go hard but I will better the instruction.

As we have already said, the author who composed these lines must
of necessity have stood far above all possibility of nurturing anti-
Semitic feelings—else how could he have conceived the passage? It
is noble, manly, superbly convincing. But when we have recovered
from the power of its appeal (which Shylock fully intended to be
powerful) and ask ourselves why Shylock has said all this and why
just now, we are forced to realize that it is all an elaborate piece of
self-justification for villainy intended. His accusations of injustices
visited upon the Jews by Christians in general are meant by implication to apply to Antonio in particular, even though we have not
seen Antonio wronging anyone or revenging himself on anyone.
By the very force of his eloquence Shylock is convincing himself
(and has convinced many critics!) that he proposes to take reprisals
for the persecutions of his people.

Antonio's friends leave, Tubal comes in, and we are witnesses to
a wonderfully written scene. Tubal has just arrived from Genoa; he
has often heard of Jessica but did not encounter her. Shakespeare
now fortifies our previous knowledge of Shylock's inner drive. Shylock is talking to an intimate (we cannot think of his having a true
friend, nor does Tubal behave like one), and he speaks without
pretense:

> Why, there, there, there, there! A diamond gone, cost me two
> thousand ducats in Frankfort! *The curse never fell upon our*
> *nation till now. I never felt it till now.*

At last the whole truth. Shylock has never felt hurt before. But any
wrong to him is a wrong to all Jews. What are the injustices meted
out to his co-religionists compared with the loss of two thousand
ducats by him? He goes on, and his diseased passion for accumulation vents itself with increasing violence:

Two thousand ducats in that; and other precious, precious
jewels. *I would my daughter were dead at my foot, and the
jewels in her ear! Would she were hears'd at my foot, and the
ducats in her coffin!*

These shocking sentiments are scarcely in harmony with the long-
suffering and loving paterfamilias of the sentimental school of critics.
They are among the most horrifying sentences in literature. Confronted with them even the critic who finds Shylock *molto simpatico*
would be compelled to admit that it is not that he loved Jessica less
but loves his ducats more. And he continues to lament his losses
—though surely the bulk of his vast hoard has remained untouched:

No news of them? Why so? *And I know not what's spent in the
search. Why, thou loss upon loss! the thief gone with so
much, and so much to find the thief.* . . .

Not a word about missing his beloved daughter, but much on the
subject of missing his ducats. And why is it, he cries, that I am the
only man to have all this misfortune? Tubal raises his spirits by beginning to say that he has heard in Genoa of Antonio's ill luck.
Eagerly Shylock demands to know more. Yes, Tubal says, Antonio
is said to have lost a fleet coming from Tripolis. "I thank God, I
thank God!" Shylock cries with exaltation. He laughs with delight:

Good news, good news! Ha, ha! Here in Genoa!

[Here occurs what is perhaps the only crucial phrase in the play to
be disputed. The original editions all have "Here in Genoa." But
Rowe, remembering that the scene was in V*enice*, thought "here" a
typographical error for "where." Most editions have followed his
emendation, and read, "Where? In Genoa?" Furness, however, points
out that "Here in Genoa," may very well mean "Here in Italy." As
he explains it, Shylock is laughing aloud "at the thought that the
loss which is reported as fallen on Anthonio has happened, not far
off, in England, but is known 'here' in Italy, 'in Genoa.'" [80] I am
not only fully in accord with Furness' interpretation; I also believe
that the word "here" means more than he thinks, as the ensuing
discussion indicates. Brown would emend the word to "heard," so
that the line would read "heard in Genoa!" [81] If emendation is

necessary I much prefer this suggestion, which is in consonance
with my interpretation of the line.]

That last brief phrase for what it implies should make us pause to
consider one aspect of the plot about which few commentators have
troubled their heads.

Unless we are willing to conceive that Shylock originally suggested taking a pound of Antonio's flesh purely as a gesture of
friendship—an interpretation in violence with his first soliloquy and
everything he had been thinking before Jessica ever eloped—we
must surely feel that a man of his particular purposefulness would
never have stipulated for such terms if he had merely hoped or had
left it to chance to bring Antonio within his power. At the time the
bond was signed, there was not even a wisp of doubt that Antonio
could comfortably repay the money long before it was due. I have
already remarked that there is something terribly ominous about
Shylock's turning Launcelot's malapropism, "My young master doth
expect your reproach," with a wry, "So do I his" (see page 200). Nobody ever depended less than Shakespeare upon accident for dramatic effect. His leading characters are always people either of strong
will or wilfullness; and his strongest strokes as a storyteller are always closely related to character-traits of the persons involved, not to
external, accidental influences. [Even Morocco and Arragon make a
choice of the wrong caskets and Bassanio of the right one, because
of their own temperaments.] It would be most unlike Shakespearean practice that Shylock, once he has proposed a contract with
such terms in it, win power of death over Antonio through the operation of fate.

At the end of the play (V, i, 276-77) it turns out that Antonio's
ships have come safely to port richly laden, after all. What has happened to Antonio, then, in the interval between his signing of the
bond and Shylock's bringing him to trial?

Obviously, it chanced that nearly all of Antonio's ready money,
at the time Bassanio asked for a loan, was invested in his ventures
abroad, else there had been no need of borrowing the money from
Shylock. What could Shylock do, under these circumstances, to insure his collecting the forfeiture? Only one thing: ruin Antonio's
credit. In II, viii, Salarino reported talking with a Frenchman, who
had told him of an Italian ship wrecked in the English Channel.
Shylock has seized upon this piece of gossip, attributed the loss to
Antonio, and broadened it to include the rest of Antonio's ships.

[I am indebted for the basis of my interpretation of this part of the story to these intelligent words of Hudson: Shylock looks forward to

> the bankruptcy of Antonio. This would seem to infer that Shylock has some hand in getting up the reports of Antonio's "losses at sea"; which reports, at least some of them, turn out false in the end. Further than this, the Poet leaves us in the dark as to how those reports grew into being or gained belief. Did he mean to have it understood that the Jew exercised his cunning and malice in plotting and preparing them? It appears, at all events, that Shylock knew they were coming before they came. . . . He would hardly grasp so eagerly at a bare possibility of revenge, without using means to turn it into something more. This would mark him with much deeper lines of guilt. Why, then, did not Shakespeare bring the matter forward more prominently? Perhaps it was because the doing so would have made Shylock appear too deep a criminal for the degree of interest which his part was meant to carry in the play. In other words, the health of the drama as a work of *comic* art required his criminality to be kept in the background. He comes very near overshadowing the other characters too much, as it is.[82]]

Shylock, it is plain, has the means to spread such rumors abroad. (We have just learned that his agents have been trying to track down Jessica and his ducats abroad.) To be most effective, such rumors had better come from distant places—England or France, for instance. I therefore take his exulting cry, "Good news, good news! Ha, ha! Here [or, as Mr. Brown prefers, "heard"] in Genoa!" to mean, "So at last! These rumors have at last reached Italy, near home!"

To continue with the scene: Tubal, apparently unable to allow Shylock his moment of joy, cuts in with the information that

> Your daughter spent in Genoa, as I heard, in one night four-score ducats.

The very thought of which brings Shylock back to his misery over his losses:

> *Thou stick'st a dagger in me, I shall never see my gold again.*
> *Fourscore ducats at a sitting! Fourscore ducats!*

This amusingly inscrutable Tubal continues to play on Shylock as on an instrument: Antonio, he learns from the creditors, is sure to become bankrupt. Once more Shylock rejoices: he is very glad of it; he will plague and torture Antonio. Once more Tubal turns aside Shylock's pleasure:

> One of them showed me a ring that he had of your daughter
> for a monkey.

Shakespeare does not deal in monsters, and he here gives Shylock the one softening touch allotted him in the whole play:

> It was my turquoise; I had it of Leah when I was a bachelor. I
> would not have given it for a wilderness of monkeys.

It is a wonderfully simple human touch, and it reminds us that Shylock, before he gave in to his passion for accumulating money, was once a human being too. Tubal goes back to Antonio's losses, and Shylock eagerly looks forward to his pound of flesh: to be sure of it he arranges a fortnight in advance that an officer arrest Antonio on the day the bond is due.

In the next scene (III, ii) we are in Belmont, and rejoice to watch Bassanio's choosing the right casket. But he and Portia have barely time to revel in the happy fulfillment of their wishes when news comes from Venice that Antonio's ships have been lost and his credit has been ruined. His friends have managed to get together the money owing, but Shylock refuses to accept it, now that the day of repayment is past. Twenty merchants, the Duke of Venice, and leading citizens have pleaded with him in vain; Shylock refuses to accept anything but his pound of flesh. No one can drive him from his malicious stand that he will have only the forfeiture —which he calls demanding justice (275-86).

It takes a little time to get a large sum of money together. No one has seriously expected that Shylock would insist upon the terms of the bond. On but one day after the contract's expiration, we are to suppose, Antonio's friends have approached Shylock with the money, and he has refused them on the technicality of the date. No one, naturally, was prepared that he take such a position, particularly when he is notorious for his love of gold. But Jessica tells the others that she has often heard her father say

That he would rather have Antonio's flesh
Than twenty times the value of the sum
That he did owe him.

(289-91)

(We do not like Jessica for saying this. On the other hand, we should like her less if she approved of her father's murderous intentions; she has chosen to be human rather than dutiful.)

In the next scene (III, iii) we are back in a street of Venice. Antonio, in the custody of the Gaoler, and Salarino are pleading with Shylock to be merciful. But he will allow them to speak hardly a syllable. He is absolutely intransigent. Now that he has Antonio completely in his power, now would be the time, if there were any truth in his allegations that he has endured indignities at Antonio's hands, to speak them out. With what crushing force could he now hurl at Antonio that business of spitting upon him and kicking him out of doors—if that had been the truth. But it was not the truth; he seems even to have forgotten his inventions. In his adamantine sense of power he does not try to conceal his motives as other than they are:

Gaoler, look to him; tell not me of mercy,
This is the fool that lent out money gratis!

After a few words of scornful abuse, he leaves. Antonio is well aware that Shylock hates him only because he has often rescued people who were in debt to Shylock. He is also fairly convinced that the bond is legally unassailable.

We come now to the great scene of the play, the Trial Scene (IV, i), the last in which Shylock appears. Before Shylock's entry, the point is made again that the Duke has done all he could to urge Shylock to accept the sum of money he advanced and renounce the forfeiture, but without success. The Duke now realizes that the moneylender is

A stony adversary, an inhuman wretch
Uncapable of pity, void and empty
From any dram of mercy.

Shylock comes into court, and the Duke goes out of his way to speak gently and without animosity to him, in the hope of softening his cruelty. We all really believe, he says, that you are only pretending to claim the forfeiture so that at the last minute your mercy and pity will appear all the greater; we expect you not only to renounce the stipulation but also to overlook a portion of the sum due you, considering Antonio's losses; surely you will not behave as only Turks and Tartars do; we all expect a civilized answer to what I ask. But the Duke has underestimated his man. Shylock is like rock, and challenges the city to deny its legal processes.

> You'll ask me why I rather choose to have
> A weight of carrion flesh than to receive
> Three thousand ducats.

This sounds like a prologue (an arrogant and insulting one, to be sure) to a rehearsal of wrongs suffered as Antonio's victim. Now is the time, if ever there was time, for him to justify what he wishes to do, to tell the whole world of his injuries and persecutions. What a triumphant moment for him to do himself justice! But he has nothing to say of the old charges of anti-Semitism. He has nothing to say because they were false.

Moreover, no one has asked him why he chooses a pound of flesh rather than accept three thousand ducats. It is his own intelligence which makes him realize the enormity of his choice in the world's eyes. Perhaps this is the first time he has asked himself the question. Well, and what is his explanation? He has none.

> I'll not answer that;
> But say it is my humour. Is it answer'd?
> What if my house be troubled with a rat
> And I be pleas'd to give ten thousand ducats
> To have it ban'd? What, are you answer'd yet?

His insolence to the Duke would be astonishing in anyone other than this proud, strong, powerful man, who has never in his life known what it is to fawn or cringe. There is not even a hint of respect for the Duke's authority in what he says, as he continues: Some men can't stand roasted pig, some can't tolerate cats, some can't listen to the sound of bagpipes without becoming ill,

> *So can I give no reason, nor I will not,*
> More than a lodg'd hate and a certain loathing
> I bear Antonio, that I follow thus
> A losing suit against him. Are you answer'd?

His last line adds sarcasm to his insolence. But again, despite himself, Shylock declares the truth: he can give no reason and therefore will give no reason for wishing to kill Antonio.

Now, it might be asked: If indeed Shylock has so overpowering a greed for money as has been thus far depicted, why has he not accepted the offer of Antonio's friends to pay him a liberal amount in addition to the money he has loaned the merchant? Why will he refuse Portia's offer of thrice the amount of the loan? Why would he rather have, as Jessica has reported, Antonio's flesh than "twenty times" the sum?

The answer to these questions lies in the very nature of hate. The genesis of Shylock's hatred for Antonio was money. But hate is a cancer that grows and feeds on a man until it devours all of him. When hate becomes an obsession, its origin becomes forgotten, and only the hate itself becomes real. William Blake's *A Poison Tree* is a magnificent poetic exposition of the life-history of a hatred:

> I was angry with my friend:
> I told my wrath, my wrath did end.
> I was angry with my foe:
> I told it not, my wrath did grow.
>
> And I watered it in fears
> Night and morning with my tears,
> And I sunnèd it with smiles
> And with soft deceitful wiles.
>
> And it grew both day and night,
> Till it bore an apple bright,
> And my foe beheld it shine,
> And he knew that it was mine,
>
> And into my garden stole
> When the night had veiled the pole;
> In the morning, glad, I see
> My foe outstretched beneath the tree.

The hater has become a murderer, and his hate has destroyed both the man he hates and himself.

Iago is in a situation parallel to Shylock's. All through *Othello* he is full of reasons for his unremitting hatred of the Moor. When in the last scene, after all the facts have been made known, Othello says:

> Will you, I pray, demand that demidevil
> Why he hath thus ensnared my soul and body?

Iago now has the opportunity, if he has been wronged, at least to explain his terrible vengeance: he can speak of his (pretended) convictions that Othello has slept with Emilia, of his having been unfairly superseded by Cassio, etc. But no. He has the brains to realize that there is nothing he can say to account for his monstrous villainy. Moreover, he is unable, now that he is forced to confront it, to understand his hate himself. And so, he too replies that he can give no reason and therefore will give no reason for his villainy:

> Demand me nothing. What you know, you know.
> From this time forth I never will speak word.
>
> (V, ii, 301-4)

These are, indeed, the last words he speaks in the play: he is probably as bewildered as everyone else at his conduct, and he is left to contemplate what is to him probably an insolvable puzzle.

Thus, too, Shylock, eaten up with hate, can really give no reason for desiring Antonio's death. This cancerous hatred, nourished by greed, is all that is left of him.

And here we shall leave Shylock for the moment. Presently he, creature of cold hate and greed, bolstering that hate and greed with a demand for the strict letter of the law, will have to confront his great opponent, Portia, the personification of all he despises in life— generosity, warmth, compassion, and love—Portia, with whom mercy is to be preferred far above mere justice.

In Shakespeare's play generosity, compassion, love, and mercy will triumph, as Shakespeare was convinced that they could and should triumph in life.

They could have triumphed, no doubt. Money need not have

poisoned the wellsprings of human existence if Christ's teachings had meant anything to Christians.

Alas! in the course of time it is not Portia and Shakespeare, but Shylock who has won out. Nowadays if a man, pillar of his church, synagogue, or mosque, lends his brother a hundred dollars, he will probably expect him to pay him six per cent interest. "Why shouldn't he pay it to me?" he will say in self-justification, "since he will have to pay as much if he goes to a bank? Business is business."

Yes, most of the world has adopted Shylock's philosophy, which is the philosophy of banks. No one expects compassion from a bank.

6

Who Chooseth Me Must Give and Hazard All He Hath: The Lovers

To friendship every burden's light.—Gay, *The Hare with Many Friends*.

: :

There is no fear in love; but perfect love casteth out fear.—*1. John* iv:18

: :

Such is the power of that sweet passion,
That it all sordid baseness doth expel,
And the refined mind doth newly fashion
Unto a fairer form, which now doth dwell
In his high thought, that would itself excel.—Spenser, *Hymn*.

: :

Cras amet qui nunquam amavit,
Quique amavit cras amet.*—*Pervigilium Veneris*.

: :

Madam, I have been looking for a person who disliked gravy **all** my life; let us swear eternal friendship.—S. Smith.

: :

L'amour est un égoîsme à deux.†—Antoine de Salle.

: :

Wenn ich dich lieb habe, was geht's dich an?‡—Goethe, *Wilhelm Meister*, IV, 9.

: :

Love's life's reward, rewarded in rewarding.—P. Fletcher.

: :

Amor ch' a nullo amato amar perdona.§—Dante, *Inferno*, V.

: :

---

* Tomorrow there shall be love for the loveless; for the lover tomorrow there shall be love.
† Love is an egoism of two.
‡ If I love you, what business is that of yours?
§ Love, which requires that love must always be returned.

Omnia vincit amor.*—Virgil, *Aeneid*, X.

: :

I have a friend: I am rich.—Granrieeb, *Punjabi Table-Talk.*

The conflict of values in *The Merchant of Venice*, then, is between the greed and hate of Shylock and the generosity and love of the other characters. The catalyst which causes the workings of these values is money—more particularly, the way in which money is used. We now know the man who embodies greed and hate. Let us become acquainted with those who can love and be generous.

In order not to establish *a priori* ideas about them, let us take them in the order of their appearance.

The first among the principal characters to appear is Antonio, the merchant of the title. [Ridley says, "The very title is a fraud, for Antonio is neither a considerable character nor an interesting one." [1] This is a curious error for an editor of Shakespeare's plays. *Julius Caesar*, both parts of *Henry IV*, and *Cymbeline* derive their titles from men who are not the central characters in those works: yet the title in each case is justified because the action of the play derives from the very existence of these men—the Brutus-Cassius conspiracy, the revolt of Hotspur, etc.] The opening line of the play tells us that he suffers from a species of melancholy:

> In sooth, I know not why I am so sad.
> It wearies me; you say it wearies you;
> But how I caught it, found it, or came by it,
> What stuff 'tis made of, whereof it is born,
> I am to learn.

One would think that this is explicit enough, yet commentators have made a considerable to-do on the reason for his "sadness." (It must be remembered that in Elizabethan usage *sad* means "serious," and *sadness*, "seriousness"; the words have no connotation of sorrow.) Chambers and others have remarked that "his melancholy is inexplicable unless we regard it as produced by Bassanio's forthcoming marriage." [2] Such an explanation is absurd: his melancholy antedates the commencement of the play; and even when Bassanio will broach the subject of his suit there is no guarantee that Bassanio

* Love conquers all.

will choose the right casket. J. D. Wilson, who is devoted to the idea that Shakespeare's texts must be tampered with, accounts for the un-explained nature of Antonio's melancholy by asserting that Shakespeare had originally written passages that would have explained it, but that these passages were later cut out.[3]

["We have here a dramatic motive deliberately suppressed at the time of a revision, and the broken line 'I am to learne' shows us where one of the 'cuts' involved in this suppression took place," says Mr. Wilson, who has for more than a generation been revered by most Shakespearean scholars as perhaps the outstanding editor and commentator on Shakespeare—a veneration I have not shared. Elsewhere I have shown how he has introduced spurious stage-directions and twisted the normal meanings of words to support his own (and, I believe, unwarranted) interpretation of *Hamlet*.[4] But this large deduction made concerning a "broken line"—i.e., that it implies a cut in the text—is little less than amazing on the part of a scholar who has edited so many of Shakespeare's plays. Can it be that he has never noticed how frequently these "broken lines" appear in Shakespeare? Take *Othello* for an example (any play would do as well).

In the very first scene Iago, accusing the Moor of injustice to him, says,

> But he, as loving his own pride and purposes,
> Evades them, with a bombast circumstance
> Horribly stuffed with epithets of war.
> *And in conclusion,*
> Nonsuits my mediators, for, "Certes," says he,
> "I have already chose my officer."
> *And what was he?*
> Forsooth a great arithmetician. . . .

$$(I, i, 12\text{-}19)$$

In answer to Roderigo's question as to why he remains in Othello's service, Iago says,

> *Oh, sir, content you,*
> I follow him to serve my turn upon him.

$$(41)$$

Presently Roderigo shouts to Brabantio to wake up,

> Look to your house, your daughter and your bags!
> *Thieves! Thieves!*

(80-1)

Brabantio appears at the window to ask,

> What is the reason of this terrible summons?
> *What is the matter there?*

(82-3)

Roderigo asks whether Brabantio knows his voice; Brabantio replies,

> *Not I. What are you?*

(93)

When Brabantio descends into the street, he asks Roderigo whether he thinks Othello and Desdemona have married; Roderigo answers:

> *Truly, I think they are.*

(169)

There is no need of further demonstration that Shakespeare frequently uses an incomplete line of verse. We have cited seven examples in one brief scene. It will be noted that each of these lines is an emphatic one—and there we may have his reason. The case of Antonio's "I am to learn" is a similar one. The unfinished pentameter allows the actor to pause and ruminate on the possible reasons for a melancholy he himself does not understand.]

Griffith ascribes the feeling to "the forebodings or presentiments of evil." [5] Furness quotes Ulrici as saying, "it is the contrast between the real and the ideal, and the power of deceptive appearances, which have robbed Anthonio of his gayety; he feels that 'his foreboding mind will one day fall between the extremes of this contrast' "—to which piece of Germanic profundity, Furness understandably appends, "which I do not understand." [6] Gervinus thinks Antonio has "the malady of the rich, who have been agitated and tried by nothing." [7] Elze goes further: "His wealth has blunted his feelings and made him effeminate." [8] Heine, possibly because of the overpowering impression made upon him by that classic-featured fair Briton of the large eyes (see page 158), truly goes to extremes:

"Antonio is a poor-spirited creature, with the heart of a worm, whose flesh is really worth nothing else but to bait fish withal." [9] Ridley introduces the abnormal with his explanation that Antonio nurtures "an enfeebling infatuation for Bassanio." [10] I find good sense on this speech only in the words of Spencer and Van Doren. Spencer says: "He says he is sad because he is sad; it is idle to invent external reasons." [11] And Van Doren with a poet's vision remarks that Antonio "is abstracted and sad for no reason that he knows"; for the tone of the play, this melancholy "must remain a grace, . . . a beautiful sadness of that sort which it is the highest pleasure not to explore." [12]

It is odd that so many commentators should not be aware that many human beings experience just such fits of "sadness." The poet Verlaine has written some celebrated verses in exploitation of just such a mood:

> Tears fall within my heart,
> As rain upon the town:
> Whence doth this languor start,
> Possessing all mine heart? . . .
>
> Tears that have no reason
> Fall in my sorry heart:
> What! was there no treason?
> This grief hath no reason.
>
> Nay! the more desolate,
> Because, I know not why,
> (Neither for love nor hate)
> My heart is desolate.
>
> (Translation by Ernest Dowson)

Neither for love nor hate. So it is with Antonio. His friends, Salanio and Salarino try to cheer him, and suggest that it is his ventures abroad which make him so sober-minded. Not at all, he assures them. Well, then, he must be in love. To that Antonio can reply only with an amused "Fie, fie!"

In their attempts to lighten his mood, his friends show their devotion to him. Pretending to believe that it is the thought of his ships which weighs upon Antonio, Salarino is very droll. Were he in Antonio's place, when cooling his broth, he should think at once of what winds at sea could do; when seeing an hour-glass, he would be reminded of the perils of sandy shallows; when going to church, he would be forced by the stones of the edifice to think of perilous rocks. Antonio denying that commerce or love is the cause of his somberness, Salarino tactfully suggests: you are sad then only because you are not merry; would it not be just as easy to be merry because you are not sad?

This pleasant company is joined by Gratiano, Lorenzo, and Bassanio. Lorenzo is a man of few words, but later under the impetus of love he will deliver some of the most exquisite lines in the play. Gratiano is something of a chatterbox who, nevertheless, on occasion can talk sense. He begins at once to warn Antonio not to think so much about the way the world wags ("You have too much respect [i.e., you expend too much thought] upon the world"). But Antonio is used to living with his sober thoughts:

> I hold the world but as the world, Gratiano,
> A stage where every man must play a part,
> And mine a sad one.

(Clemen notes that the imagery in these lines will fill the audience "with a certain degree of tense expectation." [13]) As a close friend Gratiano proceeds to administer to Antonio a good dressing down. He, for one, would rather have his wrinkles come from laughter than from care. Why should a warm-blooded man behave like a funeral monument carved in alabaster? Many people make a point of being silent only because they wish to be thought profound, whereas if they did speak they would prove themselves idiots. All this is said in merriment and instigated by affection. As the others go out to leave Antonio alone with Bassanio, we reflect on how rich Antonio is in possessing such friends.

[Nevertheless, Quiller-Couch: Antonio is one of those men who prefer to keep "company with their moral and intellectual inferiors." While Antonio's speeches reveal intelligence, his intellectual powers are not particularly emphasized (as are Hamlet's, for instance); the plot of the play does not require that that side of his equipment be brought to the fore. Nor is any of his friends demonstrably his intellectual inferior—though Gratiano's bigotry renders him inferior to the rest. Bassanio, in his choice of the caskets, exhibits a nice perception of the distinctions that must be made between appearances and reality.]

We are now privileged to listen to a scene of considerable beauty and delicacy of presentation.

Bassanio and Antonio are bosom friends. The plot would require them to be so, for only such a friendship could make conceivable the agreement to such a bond as Antonio is to sign. In these wicked post-Freudian times, the noble institution of friendship is in decay. Every great friendship of literature has been subject to the attack of nauseating interpretations: David and Jonathan, Hamlet and Horatio, for example. If one man hates another that is now considered perfectly normal, but if he feels great affection for another he had better run quickly to see a psychoanalyst. Years ago *The New Yorker* printed an excellent quip: things have come to such a sorry pass that two men dare not go off together for a weekend in the country without taking along a girl. So, O'Connor finds that Bassanio has a "peculiar, half-loverlike relationship with Antonio." [14] Things being as they are these days, I feel that Spalding was ill-advised to employ archaisms (if indeed that is all he was doing) when he says, "In love and in debt, Bassanio can fulfill his desires only by approaching his lover Antonio; his argosies at sea, Antonio can assist his beloved only by approaching the Jew." [15] The day may not be distant in which no man will risk having a dear friend lest he be counted abnormal.

Many critics who have not sullied the love Antonio holds for Bassanio, have been disgusted with Bassanio, considering him unworthy of his friend's kindness and affection. "Bassanio is a downright fortune-hunter," Heine declares[16]; Harbage agrees.[17] He is "a fortune-hunter," says Sewell, "who borrows money from his friend and allows him to sign a fatal bond"; "commercial society applauds his determination to get rid of his debts and aristocratic society has never condemned a gentleman for entering into matrimony to mend his fortunes. Gallant society . . . is prepared to condone his 'wilfull youth' since the sowing of wild oats is a guarantee against worse disorder." Bassanio belongs to a society which dictates that "he must go to Belmont with his baggage full of presents, even though he has to borrow the money to pay for them." [18] (This middle-class interpretation, with its love of thrift and disapproval of mutual generosity, would have satisfied Shylock!) What Bassanio actually proposes to Antonio, according to Goddard, is this: "Lend

me a little money to make love to a lady who has inherited a fortune." [19] Harry Golden almost repeats the same words: "Lend me
some dough so I can make love to a rich lady who has just inherited
a vast fortune." [20] Quiller-Couch pronounces this judgment on him:
his reasons for wishing to marry Portia are "dishonouring to Bassanio." [21] Jastrow goes to the extreme of caricaturing Antonio and
depicting his virtues as mere affectations, his friends shabby parasites.[22] Ridley frankly despises Bassanio, whom he finds competing
with Claudio (of *Much Ado*) and Bertram (of *All's Well That Ends
Well*) "for the distinction of being the poorest specimen of a man
among Shakespeare's comedy heroes." "Bassanio is dishonest"; he
trades on Antonio's generosity but withholds the truth. "He knows
perfectly well that no amount of fine clothes and retinue and display can advance his cause one iota, since they can hardly stimulate
his brains or his instinct to the choice of the right casket. . . .
What is almost worse, he gives not the least indication of anything
that can be called love for Portia. . . . He is just the mercenary
adventurer, trying to repair his fortunes." [23]

Some of these judgments read like the depiction of a villain in a
Horatio Alger novel. All of them I believe to be a complete distortion, wilful or blind, of the play Shakespeare has written. Let us listen to it.

From the moment Bassanio begins to speak earnestly to Antonio,
broaching his present need, his language is arresting for what it dis-
closes of his quality as a human being. No man in Shakespeare, with
the possible exception of Othello, speaks with more unfailing elegance than he—a real elegance which is at the opposite pole from
pomposity—an elegance which is innate and unconscious. Every
time he opens his lips pearls drop from them. The miraculous thing
about the way Shakespeare has managed this, is that this elegance,
this patrician quality of the mind, is united (as it seems so rarely
to be in life) with a manliness, an unaggressive virility of a kind to
which the twentieth century is becoming totally a stranger. The
only person in the play to match this inner elegance is Portia, which
is, of course, as it should be.

It is Antonio who commences the subject of Bassanio's suit. Bassanio responds by first acknowledging his own extravagance:

>'Tis not unknown to you, Antonio,
>How much I have disabled mine estate

By something showing a more swelling port
Than my faint means would grant continuance.

With the triumph of middle-class industrial values thrift has come
to be considered a virtue next to godliness, if not higher. Though
some Scottish critics and others of no less strict propriety have
damned Bassanio for living beyond his means, as he cheerfully admits
he does, if squandering money be a vice it is certainly the most amiable of vices. But it is not having to trim his sails that Bassanio minds:

> Nor do I now make moan to be abridg'd
> From such a noble rate; but my chief care
> Is to come fairly off from the great debts
> Wherein my time something too prodigal
> Hath left me gag'd. To you, Antonio,
> I owe the most, in money and in love,
> And from your love I have a warranty
> To unburden all my plots* and purposes
> How to get clear of all the debts I owe.

(If anyone has a pair of ears, he cannot anticipate anything base
from a man the music of whose natural expression has such manly
elegance.)

Antonio wishes to know what he can do; if it is a demand as honorable as Bassanio himself always† is, he will do all in his power to
fulfill it.

Bassanio is, of course, embarrassed to have to ask for another
loan, and I know nothing in poetry more fetching than his shy
prologue to the request. When I was a boy, he says, and playing at
archery, when I lost an arrow I was sometimes able to retrieve it by
discharging another arrow in the same direction,

> and by adventuring both
> I oft found both. I urge this childhood proof,
> Because what follows *is* pure innocence.‡
> I owe you much, and, like a wilful youth,

* plans
† "still" = always
‡ childishness

That which I owe is lost; but if you please
To* shoot another arrow that self way
Which you did shoot the first, I do not doubt,
As I will watch the aim, or† to find both
Or bring your latter hazard ‡ back again
And thankfully rest debtor for the first.

[This passage, which I find irresistibly engaging, is not so to Quiller-Couch. He criticizes it as "mighty poor poetry. For poetry, like honest men, looks things in the face and does not ransack its wardrobe to clothe what is naturally unpoetical." Shakespeare is here unconvincing. As for Bassanio's charming image drawn from archery, Quiller-Couch calls it mere "windy nonsense." [24] If this criticism is just, how sad for Shakespeare! I have counted at least twenty-eight such images in his works.]

Antonio is touched—as who ought not be?—by Bassanio's charming prelude. [Quiller-Couch: Bassanio's speech is rather too much for Antonio, whose "gentle impatience throughout the scene is well worth noting." (I cannot find it.) It is almost unbearable, says Quiller-Couch, that Antonio should be lectured to this way by Bassanio on the subject of money.[25]] You know me too well, he says affectionately, to beat about the bush this way, and you wrong me more in doubting that I will do all I can for you than if you threw away all I possess,

Then do but say to me what I should do
That in your knowledge may by me be done,
And I am prest unto it; therefore, speak.

Assured of his friend's sympathies, Bassanio comes to the point. He begins:

* I should like to insert a dash before "shoot" because I have never been able to read the line without hearing Bassanio pause in shyness for a moment before finishing the phrase.
† "or . . . or" = either . . . or.
‡ I note that *hazard* is a key word in the wooing of Portia. The man who is to win her must be prepared to hazard everything he has. Bassanio is a man accustomed to taking hazards. It is another consummate artistic stroke, I believe, that Shakespeare should have him unconsciously forecast his destiny by employing the word here.

In Belmont is a lady richly left. . . .

Poor Bassanio! How he has paid for his modesty at the hands of the critics! That opening line has caused most of them to credit him with only the most mercenary motives. Yet, put yourself in his place, remembering his refinement of mind. He is encumbered by the knowledge of his own prodigality and present indebtedness as he asks for the loan from his best friend: would it be decent for him to begin with a rhapsody on his love for Portia? His very elegance militates against his wearing his heart on his sleeve, or making public declarations of his deepest feelings. Shakespeare makes the point in both *Romeo and Juliet* and *Much Ado* that those who love most profoundly do not always tell the world about it. When the lovers lie dead at the end nobody but his confessor and his servant knows that Romeo has even met Juliet, nobody but her confessor and her nurse knows that Juliet has even met Romeo. As for Beatrice and Benedick, up to the very last scene they have so well concealed their love that their friends imagine they have always despised each other.

From Bassanio's point of view, when he is asking for the loan, *it is not his love for Portia which is important to state to his friend, but the assurance that there is good reason to promise return of the loan.* Hence that opening line. As he goes on to speak of Portia, note well, he has nothing more to say about her riches. His tribute to her, which begins in the very next line, is exalted without being offensively rhapsodic, and leaves no doubt in the mind of the unbiased reader that it is Portia he loves, not her money:

> And she is fair and, fairer than that word,
> Of wondrous virtues. Sometimes from her eyes
> I did receive fair speechless messages.
> Her name is Portia, nothing undervalu'd
> To Cato's daughter, Brutus' Portia.
> Nor is the wide world ignorant of her worth,
> For the four winds blow in from every coast
> Renowned suitors; and her sunny locks
> Hang on her temples like a golden fleece,
> Which makes her seat of Belmont Colchis' strand,
> And many Jasons come in quest of her.

It is her qualities and her beauty which bring suitors from the four corners of the globe, not her money. When she and Bassanio met it was, as ever in Shakespeare, love at first sight. Like all generous people, Bassanio is used to living intuitively, and his intuitions assure him that since they love each other, he cannot fail winning her. And so, he concludes:

> O my Antonio, had I but the means
> To hold a rival* place with one of them,
> I have a mind presages me such thrift,
> That I should questionless be fortunate!

To accuse him of merely wishing to put on a "display" when he comes a-courting, as does Ridley,[26] is strangely unimaginative. He knows that her "renowned suitors" are bound to come in princely style, bearing gifts, and, understandably, he does not wish to appear like a beggar in their midst. This is a simple matter of pride. That he has already made no pretenses to Portia of being any richer than he is, Shakespeare makes quite explicit, for in his first scene with her he says:

> Gentle lady,
> When I did first impart my love to you,
> I freely told you, all the wealth I had
> Ran in my veins.

> (III, ii, 255-8)

Quiller-Couch, who equally detests this most charming young man, denies him the right of his intuitions: "Why should this fortune-hunter count" on being fortunate when "he knows perfectly well, but does not choose to confide" in Antonio that "all depends on his choosing the right one of three caskets—a two to one chance against him?"[27] Ridley seconds the judgment by reminding us that all of Bassanio's "fine clothes and retinue and display . . . can hardly stimulate his brains or his instinct to the choice of the right casket."[28] If it is necessary to extrude this blast of prose from the refined air of poetry into which it so unceremoniously thrusts itself: it is not that wearing the clothes and bearing the company and gifts suitable to a wooer of Portia will direct Bassanio to the

* rival = equal

right casket. It is that without these appurtenances to his rank Bassanio would not go to Belmont to make a choice at all. In the generous-minded circle in which he lives it is perfectly normal to give handsome gifts to those one loves. In a world molded by Shylock's precepts, the newer virtue is to give only the most trifling gifts—"to avoid embarrassing" the recipient, the phrase goes—or even to avoid that risk by giving no gifts at all. It is certainly a more economical rationale for friendship!

But it is not Antonio's. He happens at the moment to have no ready cash, and so at once tells Bassanio to arrange for a loan wherever it is to be procured.

I have dwelt at this length upon the scene between the two friends not only because it is here that Shakespeare has laid the foundations for their characters and their affection, but also because criticism has outrageously perverted the quite beautiful figure Bassanio cuts in Shakespeare's play. Spurgeon has observed that Bassanio is allotted "the greatest number of images" in the play, and that Portia "runs him very close." [29] Whether consciously or unconsciously so managed by the dramatist, was not this Shakespeare's subtle way not only of making us feel a strong affinity between the two but also of indicating how much charmed he himself was by Bassanio?

We come now to Portia, in the second scene. For her Shakespeare felt it was necessary to develop materials not to be found in the tale told by Fiorentino.

In the old versions of the story, the loan stipulating the forfeiture of a pound of flesh was contracted to make possible the wooing of a lady. Her method of finding a husband would have seemed, at the least, too indelicate to Shakespeare for a heroine of his. A girl who admitted a succession of suitors to her bed only to eliminate all but the one who could resist the somniferous effects of a magic feather or letter, or a cup of drugged wine—how could he have anything to do with such a one? How could he make such unsavory behavior consistent with the noble role she would have to play, once she came to her husband's rescue? Fiorentino perhaps compounded a little with the odiousness of her conduct by converting the lady of Belmonte to a widow, possibly with the idea that in a widow her methods would appear less shocking. But Shakespeare must have felt that that part of his plot would have to be radically changed.

For this alteration he hit upon a theme old in folklore: the winning of the prize by a choice among three alternatives—in this case, three caskets.

In the ninth century a Greek monk, Joannes Damascenus, wrote such a story. It tells of a king who, much to the disgust of his courtiers, engages in a conversation with two wretchedly garbed men. To teach his nobles a lesson he orders the making of four caskets: two containing rotted bones are covered with gold; two containing valuable jewels are covered with pitch. He then demands that his noblemen choose among the chests. They choose the gold caskets. The king informs them that he was certain in advance of their choice, and reveals the precious contents of the ill-seeming caskets. He tells them that they have learned to look only with "the eyes of sense," not "with the eyes of the mind."

The tale was repeated, with variations, by a number of writers, among them Gower and Boccaccio. The version nearest Shakespeare's, and one which it seems more than likely he read, is in an English translation of the *Gesta Romanorum*, first made in 1577 and "bettered" by the translator, Richard Robinson, in 1595—that is, shortly before Shakespeare began *The Merchant of Venice*. This is the gist of Robinson's second version:

The King of Ampluy, learning that the Emperor of Rome had been presented a son by the Empress, thought: I have warred against the Emperor all the days of my life; now he has a son who will avenge all the wrongs I've committed against his father, once he comes of age; I'd better arrange peace with the Emperor now. Realizing the offer was made out of fear, the Emperor demanded security and tribute. The King of Ampluy therefore suggested a marriage between his daughter and the Emperor's son. The Emperor was pleased at the proposal, and replied that if the daughter were truly a virgin, he consented. The king reassured him on that point, and the agreement was signed.

The King of Ampluy fitted out a ship for his daughter, and sent along with her many knights and ladies, and a store of riches. But en route to Rome, a terrible storm arose; the ship broke upon a rock, and everyone was drowned except the Princess. She, carried along by the waves, was devoured by a whale. When she found herself in the whale's belly, she took a knife and wounded the whale in many places. The whale, feeling himself injured, began to swim toward land.

Now, a certain earl named Pyrris, walking by the shore, observed the whale coming toward him. He gathered strong men and they caught the animal, and began to wound him anew. At this the Princess within begged for mercy and compassion, adding that she was a king's daughter and had been a true virgin from the hour of her birth. When Pyrris heard this he was filled with wonder. Opening the side of the whale, he extracted the true virgin, who told him her entire story. Learning that she was destined for the Emperor's son, he sent messengers to the Emperor informing him that the king's daughter was safe.

The Emperor was glad when she arrived at court, saying "A* good Mayde for the love of my sonne thou has suffered much woe, neverthelesse if thou be worthy to be his wife soone shal I prove." He thereupon caused to be brought forth three vessels.

"The first was made of pure Gold well besette with precious stones without and within, full of dead mens bones, and thereupon was engraven this posey†: *Who so chooseth me shall finde that‡ he deserveth.* The second vessell was made of fyne silver, fylled with earth and wormes, and the superscription was thus: *Who so chooseth me shall finde that his nature desireth.* The third vessell was made of Lead, full within of precious stones, and thereupon was insculpt§ this posey: *Who so chooseth mee, shall finde that God hath disposed for him.*"

First praying to God for help, the Princess looked over the three vessels. She rejected the gold one, saying, "Though this vessel be

---

* Ah.
† motto.
‡ that which.
§ The earlier translation reads: "and with oute was sette this scripture." In Shakespeare's play, Morocco while examining the caskets says:

> They have in England
> A coin that bears the figure of an angel
> Stamp'd in gold, but that's insculp'd upon.

(II, vii, 55-7)

Since this is the only instance in Shakespeare's works of the use of "insculp," it would appear that it was the 1595 translation which Shakespeare knew. Moreover, in the earlier translation the inscriptions on the caskets read, "Thei that chese me," and "Thei that chesithe me"; whereas the "Who so chooseth me" of the later translation is close to Shakespeare's "Who chooseth me" (II, vii, 5, 7, 9). Which, by the way, makes a date earlier than 1596 for the play fairly impossible. There goes the Lopez theory!

full precious and made of pure gold, neverthelesse know not I what is within." As for the silver vessel, which promised "that his nature desireth," she rejected that one too, reflecting "If I choose this vessell, what is within I know not, but well I wot there shall I finde that [na]ture desireth, & my nature desireth the lust of the flesh." When she beheld the third vessel and read its superscription, she thought, "This vessell is not passing* riche, ne thorowly precious, neverthelesse the superscription saith, who so chooseth mee, shall finde that God hath disposed, & without doubt God never disposed any harme, therefore as now I will choose this vessell, by the leave of God."

The Emperor was delighted with her wisdom, and "ordained a marriage, and wedded them together with great solempnitie, & much honour, and so continued to theyr lives ende."

The "Morall" of this tale informs us that by the gold vessel "we shall understand some worldly men, both mightie men & riche, which outwardly shine as golde in riches and pomps of this world. Neverthelesse within they be full of dead mennes bones, that is to saye, the workes that they have wrought in this world bene dead in the sight of god thorough deadly sin. . . . And such men be like toumbes that be white and roially painted and arayed without and covered with cloth of gold and silke, but within there is nothing but dry bones." †

By the second vessel, of silver, we are to understand "some Justices & wise men of this world which shine in faire speach but within they be full of wormes and earth."

By the third vessel, of lead, we are to understand "a simple life and a poore, which the chosen men choose, that they may be wedded to our blessed Lorde Jesu Christ by humilitie and obeysance, and such men beare with them precious stones, that is to saye, faith and hir fruitfull workes, pleasinge to God."

From this moral tale Shakespeare took the hint of the three caskets.

There was possibly another incentive for his discarding everything connected with the proclivities of the Fiorentino heroine and her

---

* surpassingly
† The scroll within the gold casket in *The Merchant of Venice* reads:

Gilded tombs do worms infold.

(II, vii, 69)

forebears for a variety of bedfellows. In that part of the old story which deals with the suing for the lady's hand there was implied a kind of contract too: the unlucky wooer had to agree in advance to forfeit a sum of money or (as in Fiorentino) his ship and all its precious cargo. Shakespeare's powerful sense of dramatic structure must have sensed the value of the theme of contract and forfeiture's being echoed in his subplot. But it would be imperative that the suitor for the hand of Portia, who refuses to look on money as an end in itself, should have to agree in his contract to some kind of forfeit more important to the values prevailing at Belmont than money or material possessions. Of course, some kind of consideration was called for in this agreement: it would hardly be acceptable that anyone under the sun, having nothing better to do, should be able to have a fling at trying to win Portia. Some penalty must be demanded of the loser; and for the purposes of this play, not a financial one. The prospective chooser, Shakespeare decided, is told: you must

> swear before you choose, if you choose wrong
> Never to speak to lady afterward
> In way of marriage.
>
> (II, i, 40-42)

With such an oath required of him a gentleman would think twice before choosing, as he should with such a prize as Portia to be won. Then, as a practical measure, Shakespeare adds two other stipulations: the suitor, before he chooses, must also swear that if he fails he will never reveal to anyone else which casket he has chosen; and he must leave Belmont at once (III, i, 10-16).

Portia is one of Shakespeare's most enchanting heroines. She was a great favorite of Mrs. Jameson among the heroines of Shakespeare's comedies; "as women and individuals, as breathing realities, clothed in flesh and blood, I believe we must assign the first rank to Portia, as uniting in herself in a more eminent degree than the others, all the noblest and most lovable qualities that ever met together in woman. . . . She is individualized by . . . her high mental powers, her enthusiasm of temperament, her decision of purpose, and her buoyancy of spirit. . . . There is a commanding grace, a high-bred, airy elegance, a spirit of magnificence in all that she says and does." [30]

Mrs. Kemble chose Portia as "my ideal of a perfect woman . . . Laughter-loving, light-hearted, true-hearted, deep-hearted woman, full of keen perception, of active efficiency, of wisdom prompted by love, of tenderest unselfishness, of generous magnanimity." [31] Women are rarely remarkable for their appreciation of members of their own sex (I have never heard one who had a good word to say for that bewitching little devil, Becky Sharp), but these two ladies are to be commended for saying little less, despite their enthusiasm, than the truth about Portia.

Hazlitt, however, did not like her very much, and accused her of a certain amount of "affectation and pedantry." [32] Ridley goes further and calls her "the least lovable" of the heroines; "our hearts never warm towards her. . . . She is a trifle colorless." [33] Palmer cannot think of her as real, and declares her "first to last . . . as legendary a figure as Shylock" [34]—the last phrase of which criticism condemns the whole.

I, for one, find it impossible to choose among Shakespeare's women. Juliet, Portia, Beatrice, Viola, Desdemona, Isabella, Cordelia, Cleopatra, Imogen—what a gallery of irresistible women! One of the most amazing things about Shakespeare's modernity is that two centuries before Mary Wollstonecraft was hinting that women have souls and minds that deserve as much respect as men's, Shakespeare was calmly assuming that this was the case. In the great comedies it is always a girl who is the focus of interest, and she is always rather the superior of any man in the play. Though she gets the man she wants in the end, we always feel that he is not quite good enough for her. Even Benedick is not quite up to Beatrice, as brilliant as he is—but that may be because he is compelled to be a gentleman and no woman need be a lady in such a duel as they continue to have. All the wonderful women of the world seem to find their counterparts somewhere in Shakespeare's collection. For the connoisseur of his plays, however, there is one danger: these girls of Shakespeare's are so enchanting, so bewitchingly feminine, all of them, that the lover of Shakespeare is likely to expect too much of the women he can meet in the world.

Another astonishing thing about Shakespeare's heroines is that though they are all beautiful, of high spirits, intelligent, compassionate, womanly, each one of them has been so well individualized that she is herself only, and like no one else.

Let us observe our Portia from the beginning. Her opening scene is the only one in which we find her low-spirited. Her first words are:

> By my troth, Nerissa, my little body is aweary of this great world.

Rather short-sightedly Fripp, on the basis of this, calls her a "melancholy young lady." [35] The most fun-loving girl in the world—and Portia is fun-loving—may have her depressed moments for causes. And Portia, when we first meet her, has her cause which, before the scene is over will be clear enough: Here are all these suitors coming to woo her, and why, oh why, does not Bassanio come before it may be too late? Nerissa, who has more than a notion as to the grounds of this unwonted melancholy, reminds her that she has very little to complain about: but perhaps Portia has *too much* to be happy about? Those who have too much come sooner by white hairs; those who have just enough live longer. To which Portia responds, thoughtfully: Good judgments and well expressed!

At once, thus, she reveals her leading trait: she is, like Hamlet, for all her vivacity, a thoughtful human being with a highly philosophical turn of mind. Throughout the play we find her reflecting upon what is being said and done around her. For this reason, we are not at all surprised that she should later assume the responsibilities of a judge and be prepared to decide upon a most difficult case.

Nerissa counters with the suggestion that her "good sentences" would be better if anyone followed them. And here we are given a penetrating glance at the humanity of Portia's philosophy:

> If to do were as easy as to know what were good to do, chapels
> had been churches and poor men's cottages princes' palaces.
> . . . I can easier teach twenty what were good to be done,
> than to be one of the twenty to follow mine own teaching.

Her awareness of her own fallibility endears her to us. She can be compassionate toward others because she knows herself to be only too human.

Now she comes closer to the cause of her present discontent, and complains that her father's will gives her no freedom to choose the man she is to wed. To divert her, Nerissa suggests that she give her opinion on the suitors that have already come. (I hear Nerissa slyly accenting that "already.") As Portia thinks of her unwelcome wooers her normally high spirits return. The Neapolitan prince is really a colt (a skittish young fellow), who can talk of nothing but his horse and boasts of shoeing him himself. Prenatal influence?

I am much afeard my lady his mother played false with a smith.

(In Shakespeare's day, a charming girl lost no dignity by telling a racy story or indulging in a spicy witticism, if it was well phrased; she was not expected, like her later Victorian sister, to listen through keyholes and faint in public at them.) The Palatine Count is too serious; he frowns at everything and is amused by nothing—what will he be like when he is older, being such a heavy bore when he's still young? The French lord? Portia pauses, knowing it is a little wicked to laugh at others; but the recollection of the follies of that Frenchman is too much to restrain her satire. The French lord has all the vices of the other two; marrying him would be like marrying twenty husbands. The young English baron is a proper enough man, despite the excessive modishness of his attire and manners, but he speaks not a word of any language except English and speaking with him must be done in pantomime. The Scot lord won't do either. And as for the young German! He's intolerable when sober, and a mere beast when drunk, which he is most of the time. To make sure he chooses one of the wrong caskets, we had better put a glass of wine on it, she concludes; I'll do anything rather than be married to a sponge.

[Poor Portia is not allowed to have any fun by Goddard, who says that she "is the darling of a sophisticated society which has nurtured in her anything but unself-consciousness. . . . She mocks half a dozen of her suitors unmercifully (!). . . . It never seems to occur to her that any man who could would not choose her. (She nowhere says anything like this; but if she did think this, why shouldn't she? What man in his right mind would not choose her?) Yet it is not easy to imagine Hamlet choosing her, or Othello, or Coriolanus." [36] I find nothing easier to imagine than Hamlet's choosing her; what a lively time the two of them would have passing the world in review with their merry but compassionate tongues! As for Othello, he could not fail to respect Portia's dignity and love her for it. Coriolanus I cannot imagine choosing anyone; I never could understand how he managed to win any woman. Of course the woman he did win is more of a wraith than a creature of flesh-and-blood. However, it happens that not Hamlet, nor Othello, nor Coriolanus was given the opportunity by Shakespeare to choose Portia. Bassanio was.

Sewell: "The suitors whom Portia would reject, are so rejected because they fall short of social approbation." Bassanio, however, "is altogether acceptable." Among other things in his favor is that he came once before to Belmont in the company of a marquis.[37] This is an excellent example of typical scholarly card-stacking. After all, the Neapolitan is a prince, the Palatine is a count, the Frenchman is a lord, the Englishman is a baron, the Scot is a lord, and the German is the nephew of the Duke of Saxony—whereas Bassanio, though a gentleman, is only a soldier and a scholar!

Stauffer, always a pleasure to read, says with real understanding: Portia "has a comprehensive and balanced spirit." Though she is "practical" and "self-critical . . . she feels the overmastering power of love." [38]—all of which is true of Shakespeare's heroine.]

Luckily these princely wooers of Portia are unwilling to risk taking the oath required, and are about to quit Belmont.

> I am glad *this* parcel of wooers are so reasonable, for there is
> not one among them but I dote on his very absence.

But she sighs just the same. (Oh, Bassanio, Bassanio, why don't you come?) Nerissa, guessing her thoughts, teases her:

> Do you not remember, lady, in your father's time, a
> Venetian—?

Does she remember that Venetian? Portia's heart begins to flutter, and she cries:

> Yes, yes, it was Bassanio—

and then with feminine deviousness, adds in confusion:

> as I think, he was so call'd.

(Lovely touch!) Nerissa, her eyes sparkling, continues knowingly:

> *True,* madam. He, of all the men that ever my foolish eyes
> look'd upon, was the best deserving a fair lady.

Her attempted subterfuge unmasked, Portia atones by being honest:

> I remember him well, and I remember him worthy of thy praise.

In the meantime, Nerissa has told us something else about Bassanio; he is "a scholar and a soldier." No wonder he has no money!

The next scene (I, iii) in which Antonio agrees to Shylock's bond we have already examined (see pp. 186-97).

Next (II, i) we meet the Prince of Morocco, who has come to take his place among Portia's wooers. Here we may catch a hint of Shakespeare's own intellectual convictions. Morocco and Arragon will each choose the wrong casket, but Shakespeare has made the Moor far superior to the Spaniard, despite his color. Morocco thinks rather well of himself, but better of Portia; when he will choose "the contrary casket," we shall feel even a little sorry for him. His reasons for his choice will be such as do him no dishonor. Arragon, on the other hand, though white, is unbearably arrogant, almost offensively so, and his conceit is both amusing and irritating. When he will choose the wrong casket it will be for reasons which make us rejoice at his failure.

I believe that no one has remarked that the Prince of Morocco is probably the earliest example in Elizabethan drama of a Moor who is not villainous. Shakespeare himself, during his apprenticeship, had followed the fashion by creating a horror of a Moor in his dreadful piece of blood-and-thunder, *Titus Andronicus,* one of the worst plays ever written. (I never mind saying that about Shakespeare, since he eventually came to write so many of the world's best plays.) This Moor has dignity, and despite his pride, a certain amount of modesty and great courtesy. Later Shakespeare was to create the purest of all his male characters, and one of the very noblest, in the person of another Moor, Othello. Since these creations were not at all in the stream of Elizabethan prejudice and fashion, it is all the more conceivable that his Shylock should not be.

In our scene, Morocco with dignity defends the sincerity of his love for Portia and his reputation as a warrior, against the disadvantages he might be expected to feel because of the color of his skin,

The shadowed livery of the burnish'd sun.

He goes on to say proudly,

> I would not change this hue,
> Except to steal your thoughts, my gentle queen.

Portia, obviously touched, though hoping he will lose, answers with characteristic gentility: I am not free, she says, to choose myself because of my father's will, but if I were free to choose,

> Yourself, renowned Prince, then stood as fair
> As any comer I have look'd on *yet*
> For my affection.

In her private thoughts this is not saying much, for we know what she thinks of those other suitors. Nevertheless, her kind words put him, as they are intended to do, at his ease. Now he pauses to reflect on how much easier it would be to do some daring deed to win her, than to leave it to the chances of a lottery—

> so may I, blind fortune leading me,
> Miss that which one unworthier may attain,
> And die with grieving.

Hoping that further thought might dissuade him from entering the lists, Portia reminds him of the stern terms of the choice: if he loses he must die unmarried. "Therefore be advis'd." But he is determined to try. His love for her is beyond question.

After a scene (II, ii) in which famished Launcelot Gobbo decides to leave Shylock's employ, and procures a position with Bassanio, we meet Jessica (II, iii). We have already commented on her relationship to her father (see pages 197-98). She takes her leave of Launcelot, giving him a letter to deliver to Lorenzo. She is ashamed to be her father's child for,

> although I am a daughter to his blood,
> I am not to his manners.

Though the Jessica-Lorenzo story bears some faint resemblance to the roles played by Brisana and Rodolfo in Munday's *Zelauto*, which we have already quoted (see pp. 108-13), Shakespeare seems to have been actually indebted to a novella in the Italian collection of tales, Masuccio's *Il Novellino*. The following pages are an abridgement of W. G. Waters' nineteenth-century translation of the fourteenth tale:

At this time there chanced to be in Naples a certain cavalier of the city of Messina, called by name Giufreddi Saccano. . . . One day, when, according to his habit, he was making a round of the city on horseback, he happened to espy at a window a very lovely damsel, the daughter of an old man, a merchant, whose name at this moment I cannot rightly call to mind. Now, as he was beyond all measure delighted with her appearance, he found himself straightway inflamed with a violent passion for her, and, as the kindly fortune of them both willed it, the young girl, whose name was Carmosina, perceived in her heart that she found favour in the eyes of this gentleman. Although she had never before known what manner of thing love might be, and had scarcely ever set eyes on a man, the affair came to a strange issue. . . .

He discovered who her father was, and learned besides that he was an old man inordinately jealous and avaricious. . . . Furthermore he ascertained that the miser, in order to escape the prayers of suitors to bestow his only daughter in marriage, was accustomed to keep her always closely shut up in the house. . . .

[Giufreddi] contrived to contract a close and intimate friendship with the damsel's father, . . . purchasing very often from the old man divers wares at a monstrous price, for which things he had no need whatever. . . . Seeing that the old merchant drew very great advantage from his traffic with the cavalier and his friends, he let grow up between himself and the young man so close a friendship and intimacy that all those who knew him were mightily astonished. . . .

[The cavalier, at last, feigned to the old merchant that it was necessary for him to return home at his father's bidding. He asked the miser to hold some of his possessions for him until his return; he was particularly concerned about a certain female slave of his, whom he was unwilling to sell because of her goodness. But he found himself short of thirty ducats for his journey, and could not think of bothering his friends about so trifling a sum. He therefore was going to ask the old merchant to accept the slave as a security

for the loan. The greedy old miser eagerly promised to accommo-
date him.]

[Giufreddi], having mounted his horse . . . , made his way
along the street in which was the lodging of his lady-love; . . . he
espied by chance the form of the damsel partially revealed at the
casement of her chamber. . . . She cast down upon him a sweet
and piteous glance; whereupon he, looking cautiously around and
observing no one in the neighborhood, and conscious that he had
no time to spare for the making of long speeches, said to her:
"My Carmosina, be comforted, forasmuch as I have at last found
a means by which I shall be able to deliver you from your prison."
And having spoken he went his way. . . .

The cavalier, when he had returned to his house, called his slave
into his presence and said, "My good Anna, the business which we
discussed and arranged is already set in order." . . . The cavalier
caused her to rehearse several times afresh the concerted plan of
their subtle stratagem. . . .

[A few days later Giufreddi came to see the old merchant to take
his leave of him and to get the thirty ducats. The old man, who
had begun to fear that the cavalier had forgotten their agreement,
was delighted. He handed over the money, and sent for the slave,
who brought with her certain small valuable objects belonging to
Giufreddi. The cavalier that night, in the company of the old
man, went to the seashore to embark for Messina. He took farewell
of his friends. But when only a short distance out, he asked for a
small boat, and in this had himself conveyed to Procida, an island
lying between Ischia and the mainland. There he lodged with a
certain friend of his for three days. On the night of the third day
he returned secretly to Naples, where he went to stay with friends
at a house close to that of the old merchant. In the meantime the
female slave had become an intimate of Carmosina, to whom she
laid bare the plot her young master had evolved. She told the damsel:] "My master and his servant and certain other companions of
his are now concealed in the house next door to us." . . . When
the young girl heard how short was the time before her flight, she
gave the slave a thousand kisses, and told her that she possessed
nothing of her own, either great or small, which she could take
away with her, but that she had made up her mind to abstract
from the store of her avaricious old father a much greater sum of
money than anyone could have reckoned sufficient for her dowry.

When they had brought the matter to this conclusion, and when
the midnight hour had come, and the old man and everyone else
in the house were fast asleep, Carmosina and the slave broke open
a chest and took therefrom jewels and money of a value exceeding

one thousand five hundred ducats, and, having bestowed these safely away, they silently crossed over the courtyard and came to the spot where the cavalier was awaiting them. He, with the greatest joy, took the young girl in his arms and covered her lips with ardent kisses. . . . The whole company set out on their way, and took the road which led to the seashore. . . . They found their bark ready armed and fully equipped for a swift passage, and ready to cast off at a moment's notice. Whereupon they all went on board the same, and . . . found themselves at Ischia before many hours had elapsed. Then the cavalier and all those accompanying him presented themselves before the lord of that place, who chanced to be a particular friend of Messer Giuffredi. . . . From this gentleman they all received most kindly and hospitable reception. . . .

In the meantime the old father, when the daylight came, first found that neither his daughter nor the slave . . . were in the house, and then became aware that he had been robbed of his money and his jewels to boot, and for the last-named loss he felt no less grief than for the first; indeed, how sore were his tears and lamentations each one may judge for himself.

The following resemblances between Carmosina and Jessica are striking:

1. Her father is inordinately avaricious.

2. He keeps her closely shut up in the house. (We may well suppose that Jessica, like Carmosina never had a chance to see or converse with her lover except by leaning out of the casement when her father was not at home.)

3. She takes with her in her flight money and jewels, in lieu of a dowry.

4. Her escape is as from a prison.

5. When she is gone her father laments the loss of his money and jewels more than the loss of his daughter. In other words, in the instance of this tale Shakespeare kept the relationship of father and daughter pretty much as he found it. Inevitably so, since it accommodates itself perfectly to the portrait of his own Shylock.

Masuccio's own reflections on his story will reinforce what I have had to say about the relationship of Jessica and Shylock:

The fortunate ending which I have let ensue to the story I have just completed will, I make little doubt, give cause to many of those who may read the same to hold up for approbation with unbounded praises the great foresight and sagacity of the young girl, who, marking how she was thus kept in this wretched plight and held to be meaner than the meanest hireling, contrived to procure for herself so seemly and valiant a lover; and, besides this, to obtain out of the hoard of her miserly old father a greater sum of money than would have been given to her as a dower, becoming in the end the wife of her lover with honour and happiness. . . . The things above written . . . may be laid less to her charge than to that of Love, who awakened her slumbering wits and thereby taught her how to bring to an issue with the greatest courage those lessons which he himself had taught her. . . . Furthermore I am persuaded that it is a fact to be controverted by no one that the inordinate suspicion combined with the senile avarice of the old merchant were the real causes of the flout that was put upon him, and of the heavy loss which accompanied it.

In this part of his play Shakespeare was more influenced by his source in his conception of the relationship of the characters involved than in any other part of his story. Naturally, he discarded everything which did not fit into the design of his version of the pound-of-flesh story.

In the next scene of *The Merchant of Venice* (II, iv), preparations are made for the elopement of the lovers, and Lorenzo is handed a letter from Jessica by Launcelot. At the sight of her handwriting, Lorenzo breaks forth into a lyric tenderness that leaves no doubt of the sincerity of his love:

> I know the hand; in faith, 'tis a fair hand,
> And whiter than the paper it writ on
> Is the fair hand that writ.

And presently:

> If e'er the Jew her father come to heaven,
> It will be for his gentle daughter's sake.

The following scene (II, v), in which Shylock orders his daughter to lock the doors and not to dare look out the window at the merriment of the masques, we have already examined.

In the next scene (II, vi) the elopement takes place. Jessica stands on the balcony. There is a delightful little touch here. Although everything has been arranged, Jessica, with characteristic feminine coyness will not descend until her lover speaks the right reassuring words of love. With the exception of Miranda, who, having seen only her father and Caliban since infancy, knows nothing about coquetry, all of Shakespeare's girls, no matter how close they push their lovers to the door of matrimony, insist on this reassurance from them before taking the last step*:

> JESSICA.   Who are you? Tell me, for more certainty,
>   Albeit I'll swear that I do know your tongue.
> LORENZO.   Lorenzo, and thy love.
> JESSICA.   Lorenzo, certain, and my love indeed,
>   For who love I so much? And now who knows
>   But you, Lorenzo, whether I am yours?
> LORENZO.   Heaven and thy thoughts are witness that thou art.

Assured by his words, she joins him.

[It is not to be imagined that Lorenzo has been spared a drubbing by the critics. Heine brands him as "an accomplice in a most infamous burglary, and under Prussian law he would have been condemned to fifteen years in the penitentiary." [39] Quiller-Couch: "One of the most heartless fribblers on the list of Antonio's friends, which is to say much." [40] (Yet *Shakespeare's* Lorenzo is the man who declares that the man who has no music in his soul is fit for treason and unworthy of any trust!) Golden: He and his friends "induced"

---

* e.g. Juliet in the balcony scene:

> JULIET.   Three words, dear Romeo, and good night indeed.
>   If that thy bent of love be honorable,
>   Thy purpose marriage, send me word tomorrow
>   By one that I'll procure to come to thee,
>   Where and what time thou wilt perform the rite,
>   And all my fortunes at thy foot I'll lay,
>   And follow thee my lord throughout the world.
> NURSE.   (*Within*) Madam!
> JULIET.   I come, anon.—But if thou mean'st not well,
>   I do beseech thee—
> NURSE.   (*Within*) Madam!
> JULIET.   By and by, I come—
>   To cease thy suit, and leave me to my grief.
>   Tomorrow will I send.
> ROMEO.   So thrive my soul—!
> JULIET.   A thousand times good night! (*Exit*)

(II, ii, 142 seq.)

Jessica "not only to desert her widowed father (soft violins here!) but to rob him." [41] (There is not a line in substantiation of the last charge in the entire play; there was nothing like it, either, in Masuccio's story; the young ladies, one a Christian, one a Jewess, in both cases were the originators of the idea themselves.)]

A few more words on the subject of Jessica's taking the money and jewels with her. As we have said, in both Masuccio and Shakespeare, the sentiment is that the girl was appropriating her dowry as she fled into the welcome arms of matrimony. But beyond that, when it comes to these peculations recounted in story, are we not expected to be lenient toward them when the absconder is a character with whom we sympathize? Even the Bible is not without such examples. Thus we read that when Jacob at last fled from Laban with his wives and family:

> Rachel had stolen the images that were her fathers,

and that later when Laban caught up with them and upbraided Jacob for the theft, Jacob said:

> With whomsoever thou findest thy gods, let him not live . . . For Jacob knew not that Rachel had stolen them.

They searched all the tents until they came to Rachel's:

> Now Rachel had taken the images and put them in the camel's furniture, and sat upon them. And Laban searched all the tent and found them not. And she said to her father, Let it not displease my lord that I cannot rise up before thee; for the custom of women is upon me. And he searched, but found not the images.
>
> (*Genesis:* XXXI, 19-35)

We read further that when the chosen people were about to flee Egypt they were ordered to rob their neighbors by the Lord:

> Let every man borrow of his neighbor, and every woman of her neighbor, jewels of silver and jewels of gold. . . . And the children of Israel did according to the word of Moses; and they borrowed of the Egyptians jewels of silver, and jewels of gold, and raiment.
>
> (*Exodus:* II, 12, 35)

To return to our play. We are again back in Belmont (II, vii) to witness the first of the three casket scenes. Speaking like an English Boileau, Ridley considers all three totally irrelevant to the plot.[42] Since the wooing of Portia is the subplot of the play, the scenes are anything but irrelevant. They serve, moreover, the valuable dramatic function of enabling Shakespeare to move back and forth between Venice and Belmont, so that we sense time elapsing as the day of reckoning approaches. Goddard, on the other hand, objects to the inscription on the winning casket because it calls for sacrifice: "there is nothing to indicate that life has ever called on her [Portia] to sacrifice even a small part of what she has." [43] To answer this it would be enough to remind Goddard that Shakespeare was not writing a Dostoievskian novel, but a play of but a few hours' duration. His observation is also a choice piece of wilful scholarly strabismus. As soon as Portia hears of Antonio's difficulties, she will offer from her coffers all the money that can be asked to set him free.

Morocco acquits himself with dignity in our scene, though Parrott calls him "a braggart" [44] (a term that might better be applied to Arragon), Ridley finds him "otiose," [45] and Craig says mysteriously that he represents "mere sensual love." [46] I can only say that I find no syllable in the play to justify any of these judgments.

To my knowledge no one has commented upon Shakespeare's psychological subtlety in the casket scenes.

When this one opens, Portia is naturally tense. Shakespeare has managed her first speech so that it contains not an emotional overtone: she is brief because she wants to give Morocco no hint that might help him:

> Go draw aside the curtains and discover
> The several caskets to this noble prince.
> Now make your choice.

He reads the inscriptions on the gold and silver caskets, but before he even examines the third, he has unconsciously chosen against it:

> This third, *dull* lead . . .

At this Portia begins to breathe again. When he now asks

How shall I know if I do choose the right?

there is a touch of mild derision in her answer:

> The one of them contains my picture, Prince:
> If you choose that, *then* I am yours withal.

She already knows that he has rejected the lucky casket!

Being human, Morocco has no trouble finding a good reason for refusing the casket he doesn't like; the reason is in itself not a discreditable one:

> "Who chooseth me must give and hazard all he hath."
> Must give: for what? For lead? Hazard for lead?
> This casket threatens.

And now, although he himself does not know it, he reveals that he has already chosen:

> A *golden* mind stoops not to shows of dross.

(Subtle Shakespeare!) He next considers the silver casket, which promises the chooser as much as he deserves. In reputation, in rank, in fortune, in love candor requires his admitting he deserves Portia. (I do not call this boasting.) But perhaps, much as he may feel he deserves her, his deservings

> May not extend so far as to the lady.

He really cannot think of any reason why he should not choose the silver casket,

> What if I stray'd no farther, but chose here?

But ah! It is the *gold* casket that he is enamored of, so without explaining to himself why he turns from the silver to the gold, he adds,

> Let's see once more this saying grav'd in gold.

It promises what many men desire.

Why that's the lady!

Suitors come from the four corners of the globe to woo her. Moreover, only gold is fit to contain the picture of so heavenly a creature:

> Never so rich a gem
> Was set in worse than gold.

His expressed reasons for choosing the gold casket are a tribute, at least, to the depth of his esteem and affection for Portia.

He has chosen unwisely, and even Portia is touched by his failure after he has left:

A gentle riddance.*

The next scene (II, viii) with its account of Shylock's behavior after Jessica's elopement we have already considered. Here too are the earliest rumors of a wreck occurring in the English Channel. Finally, Salarino gives Salanio an account of Bassanio's parting from Antonio before leaving for Belmont. Antonio urged him not to hurry his visit to Belmont for Antonio's sake, but to be cheerful and concentrate on his suit for Portia's hand. Despite himself, Antonio could not forbear weeping as they said goodbye. (In Shakespeare's day men were not yet ashamed of their emotions.) Salanio and Salarino determine to see Antonio at once in order to encourage him to cast off his depression.

The following is the second casket scene (II, ix). Concerning Arragon, Craig is once more mysterious: he represents "love controlled by intellect." [47] I fancy Shakespeare meant the Prince of Arragon to represent a character called the Prince of Arragon.

---

* Her last line, "Let all of his complexion choose me so," might easily be overinterpreted. There is a play upon words here. *Complexion* = constitution, temperament, nature. e.g.:

It is the complexion of them all to leave the dam.

(III, i, 32)

Of that jealous complexion.

(*Much Ado*, II, i, 307)

This man is an irritatingly conceited one. Portia's first speech implies that she is already bored to death with him:

> But if you fail, *without more speech*, my lord,
> You must be gone from hence immediately.

As he recites the three things enjoined upon him by vow, his tone of voice must imply that he considers himself to be making a great sacrifice in having taken the oath, else why should Portia respond with a touch of irony?

> To these injunctions *every one doth swear*
> That comes *to hazard* for my worthless self.

After all, no one has sent for him! She dislikes him so much that she cannot resist the risk of throwing in his face the clue word on the leaden casket, *hazard!* But she is safe. Arrogant people like him never really listen to anyone else.

He too instinctively chooses against the right casket at once:

> Gold; silver; and *base* lead.

Portia is relieved. His reasons, as he advances them, paint him for the peacock he is. He will not choose what many men desire because he will not agree

> with common spirits
> And rank me with the barbarous multitudes.

He prefers the silver casket because it promises him as much as he deserves; and he cannot think of anyone in the world who deserves as much as he does. He concludes:

> I will asume desert. Give me a key for this.

He assumes too much. And Portia indulges her annoyance:

> Too long a pause for that which you find there!

When he finds, not her picture, but the portrait of a blinking idiot and reads again the inscription, he cries indignantly:

> How much unlike my hopes and my deservings!
> Did I deserve no more than a fool's head?
> Is that my prize? Are my deserts no better?

To which Portia replies quietly:

> To offend and judge are distinct offices
> And of opposed natures.

You cannot be in the prisoner's dock and on the judge's bench at the same time! We shall not be surprised that this young woman will presently take up the role of a judge herself.

When he at last goes, she cries with relief:

> Thus hath the candle sing'd the moth.
> O, these deliberate fools! When they do choose,
> They have the wisdom by their wit to lose.

[The scroll which Arragon finds within the silver casket tells him that the idiot is himself, so

> Take what wife you will to bed,
> I will ever be your head.

But his oath, as he has told us earlier was

> never in my life
> To woo a maid in way of marriage.

(12-13)

Halliwell suggested that the explanation of this inconsistency is that "the oaths were enjoined by Portia, and not by her father who prepared the caskets." [48] Some have suggested that perhaps Arragon is now free to marry a widow or a woman who is no longer a maid! Doubtless, the only satisfactory comment to be made was made by Samuel Johnson: "The poet had forgotten that he who missed Portia was never to marry any woman." [49] Shakespeare frequently enough makes slips of this minor cast. It is a matter of no importance to the play.]

The scene ends deliciously. A messenger arrives to tell Portia:

Madam, there is alighted at your gate
A young Venetian—

Portia requires no further designation. At last, at last! she rejoices within herself. Then, as if to clear the air of the unpleasantness of Arragon's presence, the messenger continues with a description of the arrival of Bassanio's courier, laden with rich gifts; his imagery breathes the freshness of Spring:

A day in April never came so sweet,
To show how costly summer was at hand,
As this fore-spurrer comes before his lord.

Portia, to mask the delightful confusion in her breast, sportively says to the messenger: Enough, enough! In a moment you'll be telling me he's some relative of yours, and excitedly cries to her companion,

Come, come, Nerissa, for I long to see
Quick Cupid's post that comes so mannerly.

This is the first time that Portia has shown any interest in a suitor's presence. Nerissa, who knows which way the wind is blowing, says teasingly:

Bassanio, lord Love, if thy will it be!

The third act opens with further talk of ships lost at sea, and goes on to the dialogues between Antonio's friends and Shylock, and then between Shylock and Tubal. These we have already considered.

The next scene (III, ii), one of the most beautiful in the play, is the crucial scene in the Bassanio-Portia story. Shakespeare, who has maintained our excited interest by varying the scenes between Venice and Belmont, now firmly ties his subplot to the main plot. Immediately after Bassanio chooses the right casket, word is brought of Antonio's life's being in jeopardy, and Portia persuades Bassanio to leave at once to be at his friend's side.

Quiller-Couch finds Shakespeare unconvincing: "A predatory young gentleman such as Bassanio would *not* have chosen the leaden casket." [50] Well, Shakespeare says that he does—and I'm sure that he ought to know. (But Quiller-Couch, who never tires of roasting Bassanio over the coals, says scornfully, "There is no need to expend ink upon such parasites as surround Antonio." [51]) Craig, who has given a symbolic label to Morocco and Arragon, naturally has one for Bassanio: he represents "love resting humbly on its own intuition." [52] This, if stripped of its symbolic emphasis is not far off. Stauffer is closer to the fact when he says that "Bassanio is almost pure instinct"; "he chooses the lead casket without hesitation" because "his natural sympathy responds to the motto." [53] I cannot quite agree that Bassanio is almost pure instinct, though certainly he is highly intuitive. He is too much the ideal gentleman, too much innately the elegant patrician to act solely on instinct. His exquisite manners must be, as exquisite manners are, somewhat the product of thoughtfulness too. But certainly his temperament does incline him, as Stauffer observes, to the casket that demands risking all. "Reckless" he is, I agree with Stauffer, in his affections, and this it is that helps bring him to the choice of the right casket, "for love is generous." [54]

In this scene we shall remember, by contrast, Portia's tense factualness of voice that gave no overtone to guide Morocco, and her irony with the overweening Arragon. For now she is in the presence of the man she loves. And like most of Shakespeare's adorable women, she comes very near to what could only be called a proposal of marriage. Of course, all young men (and many older men, who have learned nothing from experience or observation) know themselves to be the pursuers, and the girls to be the timid deer in flight. But Shakespeare was wiser than that. He knew that it is normally the woman who takes care of the little steps that lead to matrimony. The man indeed may say, at the very end, "Will you be mine?"—though one wonders how often that time-honored phrase has actually been uttered. But it is the woman who provides the possibility of such a declaration. She takes all the necessary precautions: she sees to it, as it were, that the lights are sufficiently dimmed, the soft music is in the background, the cushion is on the floor (should it be a proposer of the kneeling school), the Webster's Unabridged is handy on a nearby table (should the swain be deficient in appropriate vocabulary). And it is a good thing that women do take charge of these matters. Marriage is the best institution mankind has developed—provided it be the right man and the right woman—and if marriages were left to men there would not be any. Men always think of matrimony as something that will happen to them later; women have a sense of immediate urgency about it. So women must see to it that marriages do take place. And of course they do see to it, conscientiously—without need of any instruction from me.

I can find nothing lovelier in poetry than Portia's first speech to Bassanio before he makes his choice, unless it be the speech she speaks after he has won. They are completely womanly and endearing. Her powerful feelings force themselves into language; her maidenly modesty would arrest the flow of self-revelation. But the more she would retreat, the deeper she becomes involved in the declaration of her love.

Shakespeare manages all this not at all statically, but in a way completely pertinent to the dramatic moment at hand:

> I pray you, tarry. Pause a day or two
> Before you *hazard* . . .

(Ah, Portia, Portia—your vow not to reveal the correct casket to any suitor! There is the clue word, *hazard*, again! But this time you are not talking to a dense Arragon, but to a sensitive, high-mettled young man who, as you well know, is an adept at understanding even speechless messages!)

>   for in choosing wrong,
> I lose your company; therefore forbear awhile.
> There's something tells me—but it is not love—
> I would not lose you; and you know yourself
> *Hate* counsels not in such a quality.*
> But lest you should not understand me well—
> And yet a maiden hath no tongue but thought—
> I would detain you here some month or two
> Before you venture for me.

("Venture" is a not ineffective synonym for "hazard"!)

>   I could teach you
> How to choose right—

* fashion

(Surely here Portia pauses, actually considering whether she ought
not yield to temptation and teach him indeed. Hazards are well
enough for men. What woman ever had any use for them? But, then,
she remembers that she is Portia, and therefore, though a woman,
doomed to act honorably.)

> but then I am forsworn;
> So will I never be—

(She takes refuge in her pride for a moment. But what consolation
is pride to a woman if through it she run the risk of losing her
love?)

> so may you miss me;
> But if you do, you'll make me wish a sin,
> That I *had* been forsworn. Beshrew your eyes,
> They have o'erlooked me and divided me;
> One half of me is yours, the other half—yours,
> Mine own I would say—but if mine, then yours,
> And so, *all* yours. O, these naughty times
> Puts bars between the owners and their rights!
> And so, though yours, not yours. Prove it so*
> Let fortune go to hell for it, not I.
> I speak too long; but 'tis to *peize* the time,
> To eke it and draw it out in length,
> To stay you from election.

(She would like to extend the time before he chooses, to "peize"
it—that is, literally to retard it by hanging weights upon it [French
peser = to weigh]. And what is used to weight things, to make them
heavier, more often than—lead? Hazard, venture, peize. Portia
can, of course, console her conscience with the fact that she is not
actually telling him which casket he must choose!)

The women in Shakespeare are so entirely feminine, the men so
entirely masculine! Portia's declaration of love fills Bassanio with
such great hope that he cries out:

> Let me choose;
> For as I am, I live upon the rack.

* If it should prove so

She would have him wait; he cannot wait a minute. Women are happiest always in what to them must be the delicious zone which lies between inaction and action; they love to revel in the possibilities which precede commitment. Men, on the other hand, cannot breathe in that territory; the fools must always be *doing* something—anything—even if it means breaking their necks.

His image of the rack allows Portia to salvage her pride by indulging in some charming coquetry, which Bassanio's impatience terminates:

> But let me to my fortune and the caskets.

As he advances toward them, Portia in her excitement finds her eyes watering; her maiden attendants weep sympathetically—which overflow of feminine emotion she converts into semi-gaiety by comparing him to Hercules, herself to Hesione, her maidens to the Trojan women.* And, a modern Hesione, she cries the warning:

> I stand for sacrifice!

("Who chooseth me must give and hazard all he hath.") This is something more than a hint. And now:

> *A song, the whilst Bassanio comments on the caskets to himself.*
>   Tell me where is fancy bred,
>   Or in the heart or in the head?
>   How begot, how nourished?
>   Reply, reply.
>   It is engend'red in the eyes,
>   With gazing fed; and fancy dies
>   In the cradle where it lies.
>   Let us all ring fancy's knell;
>   I'll begin it.—Ding, dong bell.

Thaler says, with much point: "She lets music sound to give him his cue to choose not by the view." [55]

(Indeed this is one of the themes running through the play: do not mistake the appearance for the reality. Gratiano has warned

---

* Hesione was a daughter of Laomedon, King of Troy. To propitiate Poseidon she was exposed as a sacrifice to a sea-monster, sent by the god. Hercules killed the monster and saved her life.

(I, i, 88-99) against those who maintain deliberate silence in order to develop a reputation for wisdom and profundity,

> As who should say, "I am Sir Oracle,
> And when I ope my lips let no dog bark!"

Antonio has remarked on how the devil can cite Scripture for his purpose, and how evil can masquerade as goodness (I, iii, 99-103). And the three caskets reinforce the importance of not mistaking shadow for substance.)

But Portia does much more to help Bassanio than provide the music. The message of the song which Portia has caused to be sung while Bassanio is considering the caskets is: What is the nature of a love that is light ("fancy")? It is an emotion that is fed only by the appearances of things ("engend'red in the eyes"); such love is dead almost when it is born. In other words, Bassanio, if you love me you will not be taken in by the appearances of those caskets. This is more than a "speechless message," such as Bassanio had formerly received from Portia.

[Granville-Barker objects to such an interpretation that "Shakespeare was surely of a simpler mind than this. . . . Besides, how was it to be worked; how is an audience to be let into the secret?" [56] That Shakespeare was of a simple mind, anyone who knows him should be ready to deny. As for the second objection, Shakespeare's plays are full of a thousand wonderful small touches that no audience will ever perceive at a first hearing, exquisite nuances that only a reader saturated with the play can appreciate. That is why Shakespeare belongs to literature as well as to the theater. Brown further objects that "Portia has said she will not direct Bassanio (lines 10-13); she believes the lottery will find the right husband (line 41) . . . and it would belittle Bassanio and Portia and cheapen the themes of the play." [57] Portia has indeed said that though she could teach Bassanio the correct casket she will never break her oath not to do such a thing (lines 10-12); to that my answer, already implied, is that she is a creature of flesh and blood, not an abstraction; she is, moreover, a woman and reasons like one. So long as she does not *point out* the casket, she remains technically within the confines of her vow. (No *man*, of course, would know how to break a vow and keep it at the same time.) Her line, "If you do love me, you will find me out" (41) is not an expression of confidence that "the lottery will find the right husband," but an admonition to Bassanio to be careful in his choice. (Scholars are most stubborn in their deafness to the humane overtones of Shakespeare!) How it would belittle the lovers or cheapen the play, when it adds to their dimension as human beings and to Portia's womanliness, I cannot pretend to understand.]

That Bassanio received the message, though perhaps subconsciously, is proved by the next line he speaks; the first word, *So*, makes it a continuation of the thought of the song:

So may the outward shows be least themselves.

But the song has gone even further. How can the chime of its rhymes have failed to impress themselves upon his inner mind?

. . . fancy *bred*
. . . in the *head*
. . . nouri*shèd—*

(Choose the *lead!*) I have pointed out how Portia hinted with *hazard, venture,* and *peize.* I believe the rhymes in *ed* are to be taken the same way. I find that this peculiarly feminine way of helping her lover by overtones while keeping literally to her promise not to divulge the right casket, makes Portia all the more adorable and true to her sex.

Bassanio continues now to reflect on how fallacious it can be to judge by appearances, in a speech informed with his usual charm of language and elegance of mind. [But Quiller-Couch, a good hater: Bassanio talks here as though he were addressing "a Young Men's Christian Association." [58] When Bassanio speaks of the world as "still deceiv'd with ornament," the reader "feels moved to interrupt, 'Yes, yes—and what about yourself, my little fellow?' " [59] As for the first criticism—Spurgeon: "When the actual moment of choice arrives, the images crowd thick and fast"; in Bassanio's 32 lines there are 12 images, "each fast on the heels of the other, each taking light from the one before." [60]] Bassanio will not have the gold, "Hard food for Midas," nor the silver, [Goddard: his friend "Antonio is the silver casket. He got as much as he deserved: material success and a suicidal melancholy." (!) [61]] "pale and common drudge 'Tween man and man." But dull lead, which rather threatens than promises, is his choice. (Spoken like a soldier!) [Granville-Barker reminds the actor that when Bassanio begins to speak this speech, "the emotional ascent will have been half climbed for him" [62]— that is, by Portia and the song and music. I should like also to point out that the song has had the further technical advantage for Shakespeare of enabling him to dispense with a restatement of the inscriptions on the caskets. While the song is being sung, Bassanio is reading the mottoes to himself.]

Portia's reaction to his choice is a joy bordering on violence. At last the long waiting and anxiety are over. Opening the casket, Bassanio finds Portia's portrait within. Like most men truly in love, it is for him impossible to make amorous speeches to his beloved; the portrait enables him to make them, without immodesty, to the picture; the praises he bestows upon the painting are, of course, intended for her: the painter has done wonders in his work—

> But her eyes—
> How could he see to do them?

And thus gracefully he is able to turn from the portrait to the original.

> Yet look, how far
> The substance of my praise doth wrong this shadow
> In underprizing it, so far this shadow
> Doth limp behind the substance.

He reads the scroll found in the casket, which congratulates him and bids him:

> Turn you where your lady is
> And claim her with a loving kiss.

His manly embarrassment is delightful as he approaches her:

> A gentle scroll. Fair lady, by your leave;
> I come by note,* to give and to receive.†

---

* according to directions
† i.e., a kiss

He feels like a man who has won a wrestling-match, standing breathless and dizzy amidst the applause of the spectators,

> So, thrice-fair lady, stand I, even so,
> As doubtful whether what I see be true,
> Until confirm'd, sign'd, ratified* by you.

Portia's words of surrender are, as I have said, among the loveliest, most womanly in literature. It is every true woman's pleasure, no matter how superior to her lover she may be, to feel a self-abasement in her yielding to him. It is not necessary to draw a diagram to explain how such emotions spring from her very nature.

> You see me, Lord Bassanio, where I stand,
> Such as I am. Though for myself alone
> I would not be ambitious in my wish,
> To wish myself much better; yet, for you
> I would be trebled twenty times myself,
> A thousand times more fair, ten thousand times
> More rich;
> That only to stand high in your account,
> I might in virtues, beauties, livings, friends,
> Exceed account. But the full sum of me
> Is sum of—something, which, to term in gross,†
> Is an unlesson'd girl, unschool'd, unpractis'd;
> Happy in this, she is not yet so old
> But she may learn: happier than this,
> She is not bred so dull but she can learn;
> Happiest of all is that her gentle spirit
> Commits itself to yours to be directed,
> As from her lord, her governor, her king.
> Myself and what is mine to you and yours
> Is now converted.

We know that Portia is not an unlessoned, unschooled, unpracticed girl, but it is no false modesty that bids her make this sincerely intended confession. It is the eager surrender of her heart. When a man wins one of Shakespeare's girls, he truly wins a woman worth the winning!

* i.e., with the kiss promised in the scroll
† describe generally

[Yet how differently each of them manages a moment like this! Who could imagine Beatrice speaking in Portia's strain? Yet her way is like a restorative cordial too:

BENEDICK. (*Embarrassed*)   I do love nothing in the world so well as you. Is not that strange?
BEATRICE. (*Caught off guard*)   As strange as the thing I know not. It were as possible for me to say I loved nothing so well as you.—But believe me not—and yet I lie not. I confess nothing—nor I deny nothing. . . .
BENEDICK.   By my sword, Beatrice thou lovest me!
BEATRICE.   Do not swear by it, and eat it.
BENEDICK.   I will swear by it that you love me, and I will make him eat it that says I love not you.
BEATRICE.   Will you not eat your word?
BENEDICK.   With no sauce that can be devised to it. I protest I love thee.
BEATRICE.   Why, then, God forgive me!
BENEDICK.   What offense, sweet Beatrice?
BEATRICE.   You have stayed me in a happy hour. I was about to protest I loved you.
BENEDICK.   And do it with all thy heart.
BEATRICE.   I love you with so much of my heart none is left to protest.

(*Much Ado About Nothing*, IV, i, 269 seq.)]

Now, for a moment Portia feels a little sadness at the thought of parting with her freedom:

> But now I was the lord
> Of this fair mansion, master of my servants,
> Queen o'er myself—

But what are such privileges when measured with the riches of surrendering to love?

> and even now, but now
> This house, these servants, and this same myself
> Are yours, my lord.

Portia concludes this sweet gravity with a turn of merriment (which lays the foundation for more merriment in the last act):

> I give them with this ring;
> Which when you part from, lose, or give away,
> Let it presage the ruin of your love
> And be my vantage* to exclaim on† you.

Nothing could be more beautiful than this speech. The spoken word means much to women (sometimes quite fatally so), but alas for them! Though spoken words of rapture come easily from their lips, they do not trip from the lips of men of honor. Bassanio, as a man, cannot match her eloquence in speaking his love. He feels his love for her pounding in his blood, and, characteristically of the male, he asks her to hear that!

> Madam, you have bereft me of all words,
> Only my blood speaks to you in my veins.

No clairvoyant, he willingly swears

> But when this ring
> Parts from this finger, then parts life from hence;
> O then be bold to say Bassanio's dead.

Nerissa, quite the woman too, makes the opening, with a nudge, for Gratiano to declare that he and she are also to be wed. Gratiano is a good sport, but something of a vulgarian, and his vulgarity in speaking of his love underlines the refinement of Bassanio's for Portia. He no sooner has their congratulations then he must have his bawdy joke, though a good one:

> GRATIANO. We'll play with them the first boy for a thousand ducats.
> NERISSA. What, and stake down?
> GRATIANO. No! We shall ne'er win at that sport and stake *down.*

Just when the happiness of every one present is complete, Lorenzo, Jessica, and Salerio, "a messenger from Venice," come in.

[This sudden appearance of a new character in the person of Salerio, has occasioned much discussion. Some critics have thought

* opportunity
† reproach loudly

his name a misprint for Salanio or Salarino. (Salarino it could not be, for him we meet in the next scene as having been still in Venice.) J. D. Wilson is convinced that throughout the play "Salarino" is an error for "Salerio." [63] He substitutes the latter for "Salarino" everywhere in his edition of the play. Since the Quartos and Folios all introduce Salerio only at this point, and since I am not enamored of tampering with the received texts, I find no harm or great disadvantage in following tradition. As for the argument that "Salarino" must be an error since it is too much like "Salanio," I find it rather amusing that the two Venetian gentlemen who are constantly together and are more or less bystanders in the action should have similar names. For that matter, is not "Salerio" quite as much like "Salanio" as "Salarino" is?]

Bassanio's superiority as a human being at once declares itself. Having won lordship over Portia and her household, he does not, as many aggressive men would, forthwith begin to behave as though the place belonged to him. His modesty is what we should expect from him:

> Lorenzo and Salerio, welcome hither,
> *If that the youth of my new interest here*
> *Have power to bid you welcome. By your leave,*
> *I bid my very friends and countrymen,*
> *Sweet Portia, welcome.*

She welcomes them handsomely. Salerio hands him a letter from Antonio, about whom Bassanio inquires at once. The messenger is evasive, knowing that the letter he bore will discover the bad news without help from him.

While Bassanio is reading the letter, Jessica is made welcome by Gratiano. Portia, however, sees that Bassanio's cheek is changing color as he reads his message—

> Some dear friend dead; else nothing in the world
> Could turn so much the constitution
> Of any constant man. What, worse and worse!

She crosses to him. But these are gentlefolk, who carefully cultivate the art of beautiful living. She doesn't snatch the paper out of his hand; she does not pry. She understands the sacredness of private correspondence. Instead, with the greatest politeness, she says:

With leave, Bassanio; I am half yourself,
And I must freely have the half of anything
That this same paper brings you.

Half the sorrow, she means to imply.

The open honorableness of the man informs every syllable of his answer:

> O sweet Portia,
> Here are a few of the unpleasant'st words
> That ever blotted paper! Gentle lady,
> When I first did impart my love to you,
> I freely told you, all the wealth I had
> Ran in my veins: I was a gentleman.
> And then I told you true; and yet, dear lady,
> Rating myself at nothing, you shall see
> How much I was a braggart. When I told you
> My state was nothing, I should then have told you
> That I was worse than nothing; for, indeed,
> I have engag'd myself to a dear friend,
> Engag'd my friend to his mere* enemy
> To feed my means. Here is a letter, lady;
> The paper as the body of my friend,
> And every word in it a gaping wound,
> Issuing life-blood.

[The reader by this time may be feeling that no avenger treading the shadow of his intended victim ever pursued his man more remorselessly than Quiller-Couch, Bassanio. He remarks that Bassanio does not seem deeply affected by Antonio's letter.[64] It would seem that any impartial listener would find Bassanio's words eloquent enough of his distress. Does Quiller-Couch expect him to roar in King Cambyses' vein?]

Shylock is busy plying the Duke morning and night, calling into question the state's administration of equal justice if he is denied the forfeiture. Twenty merchants, the Duke, and noblemen of importance have been unable to move him from his intended cruelty.

Portia finds it hard to believe that the situation can be hopeless.

* absolute

How much is owing the moneylender? Bassanio will not allow her to forget that the tragic situation is his responsibility:

PORTIA.   What sum owes he the Jew?
BASSANIO.   For *me*, three thousand ducats.

It is one of those delicate touches, to be found everywhere in Shakespeare (and normally overlooked by "scholarship"), which are better than a volume of commentary in showing us the nature of the speaker.

Portia is truly astonished:

> What, no more?
> Pay him six thousand, and deface the bond;
> Double six thousand, and then treble that,
> Before a friend of this description
> Shall lose a hair thorough Bassanio's fault.

Her general compassionateness we know. But it is again woman talking here at her best: her quick sympathies grasp the anguish Bassanio must be suffering from a sense of guilt. It is for her lover's sake she wants Antonio rescued.

Not all women, however, would be equal to the sacrifice she is prepared to make. Portia is singularly unpossessive. Bassanio is to leave for Venice at once,

> For never shall you lie by Portia's side
> With an unqiet soul. You shall have gold
> To pay the petty debt twenty times over.

Every money matter is a petty one to her. However, she is womanly enough to think of another matter too:

> First go with me to church and call me wife,
> And then away to Venice to your friend.

She urges Bassanio to cheer up: she is certain that everything will turn out all right. Bassanio swears that

> till I come again,
> No bed shall e'er be guilty of my stay,
> No rest be interposer 'twixt us twain.

The next scene (III, iii), in which Shylock, Antonio, Salarino, and the Gaoler figure, we have already considered. It is interesting to remember that according to English law in Elizabethan times, creditors had the right to shut debtors up in the Fleet indefinitely. "The gaoler himself became personally responsible for his prisoner, so that if any escaped he was himself liable for their debts." [65] This will account for the Gaoler's presence in the scene. (See, too, *The Comedy of Errors*, IV, iv.)

Antonio shows not only courage but even a touch of wry humor in adversity:

> These griefs and losses have so bated me,
> That I shall hardly spare a pound of flesh
> Tomorrow to my bloody creditor.

In the next scene (III, iv), Lorenzo expresses his admiration for Portia's unselfishness in having dispatched her husband to Venice. Portia replies modestly that she has never had cause to repent a good deed. Moreover, she knows that Antonio must be well worth the thoughtfulness for, being Bassanio's close friend, he must have much in common with him. In those who are drawn to each other

> There must be needs a like proportion
> Of lineaments, of manners, and of spirit;
> Which makes me think that this Antonio,
> Being the bosom lover of my lord,
> Must needs be like my lord.

She bids Lorenzo and Jessica make themselves at home: she has a little journey to make. They are to think themselves master and mistress of her household. Though they have no place to go, and must welcome this hospitality, she offers it as though she were asking a favor of them:

> I do desire you
> Not to deny this imposition,
> The which my love and some necessity
> Now lays upon you.

The two lovers go out, and Portia informs Nerissa that they (she and Nerissa) will be seeing their husbands soon, though in such a guise that they will not be recognized. Portia is in high spirits—as women seem always to be at the prospect of donning men's clothes. She indulges in a racy little witticism: she and Nerissa will be so garbed that Bassanio and Gratiano

> shall think we are accomplished *
With that † we lack.

She has a gay time anticipating the manly stride and boasting of a young fellow. To Nerissa's surprised, "Why, shall we turn to men?" she makes a merry quibble:

> Fie, what a question's that,
> If thou wert near a lewd interpreter!

The final scene before the trial (III, v) contains some excellent fun between Launcelot and Jessica, who are presently joined by Lorenzo. The scene concludes with some charming love-banter between the newlyweds. Jessica has been praising Portia as the most wonderful woman in the world:

LORENZO.   Even such a husband
   Hast thou of me as she is for a wife.
JESSICA.   Nay, but ask my opinion too of that.
LORENZO.   I will anon; first, let us go to dinner.
JESSICA.   Nay, let me praise you while I have a stomach.
LORENZO.   No, pray thee, let it serve for table-talk;
   Then, howsoe'er thou speak'st, 'mong other things
   I shall digest it.

[J. D. Wilson: "Shakespeare had no hand whatever in the composition of III, v." [66] (!)]

We are now ready for the great trial, where the forces of greed and generosity, hate and love, literal justice and mercy will wage

* perfectly outfitted
† that which

war to the finish. A great creator with an important idea never furnishes a weak villain for an ethical combat. Milton knew this when he created his Satan, and Shakespeare when he conceived his Claudius. Shylock and Portia—no mean adversaries they—and worthy of the noble concept they must shadow forth.

7

The Trial:
Justice vs. Mercy

Yet in the trial much opinion dwells.—*Troilus and Cressida,* I, iii, 337.

::

Love gilds the scene, and women guide the plot.—Sheridan, Epilogue to *The Rivals.*

::

Yet show some pity!—
I show it most of all when I show justice.—*Measure for Measure,* II, ii, 100.

::

This even-handed justice
Commends the ingredients of our poison'd chalice
To our own lips.—*Macbeth,* I, vii, 10-12.

::

At this hour
Lie at my mercy all mine enemies.—*The Tempest,* IV, i, 264-5.

::

Virtue may be assailed, but never hurt,
Surprised by unjust force, but not enthralled,
Yea even that which mischief meant most harm,
Shall in the happy trial prove most glory.
But evil on itself shall back recoil,
And mix no more with goodness, when at last
Gathered like a scum, and settled to itself
It shall be in eternal restless change
Self-fed and self-consumed: if this fail
The pillared firmament is rottenness,
And earth's base built on stubble.—Milton, *Comus,* 288-98.

::

. . . . . . Like sleepers wide
From home in blindness blundering, we seek
The hand to lead us back, the voice to speak
The word that calls us to the shining dwelling
Towards which the love within us ever welling
Impels our steps.—A. B. Grinère, *The Twelfth Disciple.*

The great crucial scene of the trial in Act IV has been subjected to considerable scrutiny by legal experts and near-experts, with a view to determining just how authentic a trial is there presented. As early as 1792 an anonymous commentator protested against the legality of allowing Shylock "to take his debtor's forfeiture," yet punishing him "for not performing an impossibility in taking it." [1] The editor Campbell (1838) declared that Shylock loses his case "only by a legal quibble." [2]

Later the same year (1838) Richard H. Horne composed *Shylock, A Critical Fancy*, which was publicly presented May 16, 1850 at Sadler's Wells. It purported "to show what might have passed through Shylock's mind on listening to certain portions of Portia's line of defence, supposing the same trial . . . had occurred in the present century." The scene follows Shakespeare's up through Portia's admonition not to shed one drop of blood. From there Horne rewrites the scene:

SHYLOCK.   Peace, false Judge!
  There's no such thing as flesh devoid of blood!
  Flesh is made up of vessels, and they're filled
  With blood alone,—nay, blood is liquid flesh.
  Oh, thou false Judge! Most treacherous, wicked Judge!
  Send to your butcher for your daily meal—
  What will you say if he do sell a pound
  Of skin and empty veins? Till you can show me
  Flesh that is bloodless, be't what kind it may,
  My claim is good; one flesh alone exists,
  And that hath blood, for each includes the other.
  Doth all your wisdom in a quibble end
  Like bubbles blown by Law?
        (*The Duke and the Magnificoes look confounded. Portia
        stands troubled and perplexed.*)
PORTIA.   Yet—fear the Law!
SHYLOCK.   This bond holds blood!—out on your cullender wits!
  If Laws be folly, all are fooled by them.
  I am your fool in suffering these delays.
  But *he* is mine, by wisdom and by law.
  A Jew may be the dog
  That's hated by a Christian's charity,
  But not the dupe of *words!*
BASSANIO.   O Jew, forbear!
SHYLOCK.   Forbear!—I came here to be paid a debt.

BASSANIO.   Lash not thyself to fury, like a beast!

SHYLOCK.   'Tis ye who have lashed me thus: I'll have my bond!
Trifle no more—there is no power in Venice
To alter a decree established;
Said not the Doctor so?—then was he wise,
But afterwards he spake as doth a fool;
Nay, worse; he damned his soul with lies, to save
That Christian beast who spat upon my beard.
>*(The Court is thrown into utter perplexity, and remain silent.)*

PORTIA.   *(After a troubled pause)*   The Jew shall have all justice;
Therefore prepare thee to cut off the flesh;
Yet, Shylock, see thou cut not less nor more
But just a pound of flesh; if thou tak'st more
Or less, than just a pound, be it so much
As makes it light or heavy in the substance
Or the division of the twentieth part
Of one poor scruple;—nay, if the scale do turn
But in the estimation of a hair,
Thou diest, and all thy goods are confiscate.

SHYLOCK.   *(With deadly bitterness)*   I'll not take more; I'll take it *by degrees,*
Therefore not more,—since thou'd'st be so exact;
Be not thou hasty, treacherous young Judge;
I am not bound to take it all, at once.

BASSANIO.   O villainous Jew! thou'd'st torture him to death!

SHYLOCK.   *(Calmly)*   If in some days after the half be paid,
He chance to die—that is no fault of mine;
My bond doth say a pound; but doth not say
That I must take the whole immediately.
We're not compell'd to ruin thus our debtors.
I'll take it *by instalments*—would you jeer me?
Old Shylock hath his jest!

PORTIA.   But since the whole
Is offered and not taken, thou canst have
No claim hereafter.

SHYLOCK.   I do claim all, now.

PORTIA.   Take then the pound of flesh and blood, fierce Jew!
But see you spill not aught that is *not yours.*

SHYLOCK.   Why must I have this care—look *ye* to that;
It is the very nature of all flesh
When cut to bleed; and here my bond declares
That—from the Christian breast of one who scoffs
At me, my tribe, and ever used to mock

My prosperous dealings, I shall forthwith cut
A pound in forfeit! No more words,—prepare!
PORTIA.   His wasted blood shall yet bring ruin on thee.
SHYLOCK.   Let ruin come!—so I can once behold
That streaming breast, I care not if his blood
Swell to a second Galilean Sea,
And with its humming and abhorrent surge
Sweep away Venice! Now! now! stand aside!
DUKE. (*Rising*)   Restrain him!—sure some devil speaks in him!
    (*All rise*)
Keep back the bearded vulture!
PORTIA. (*As by a sudden thought*)   The ruin thou defiest shall
    fall upon thee!
Thy vengeance be thy sentence, e'en by the bond
Which thou so fiercely urgest! By its terms,
Purport and stratagem, thou seek'st the life
Of a Venetian citizen; for which *crime*
The Law unwinds itself from that man's neck
And with a terrible and just recoil
Springs back on thee! Shylock! one half thy goods
Are forfeit to Antonio! . . .

[Can Furness, normally a man with much taste and wit, have been serious when he described these lines as being written with "great vigour"? [3] Horne has successfully, it must be admitted, destroyed all that Shakespeare wished to convey in the scene.] The rest of the scene follows Shakespeare fairly closely, except for the stage-direction, later: "Exit Shylock wildly." [4]

In 1872 *The Albany Law Journal* contained a fanciful report of a decision by the Supreme Court of New York, on appeal, of the case of Shylock vs. Antonio; the author of the Report is supposed to be one Esek Cowen of Troy, N.Y. Antonio is described as mentally unsound because (this will appear to lawyers as good reasoning) he loaned money to friends without interest. In the appeal for the case, it is asserted by the counsel for the appellant that the referee, agreed to by all parties, was in point of fact a woman! Though she called herself Balthazar, her maiden name had actually been Mary Jane Portia, an oil heiress, and she was now married to Antonio's friend, Bassanio. The judgment pronounced by this referee was: 1. That the bond was valid; the plaintiff was entitled to a pound of flesh. 2. That he was entitled only to an exact pound, neither more nor less; if he took more or less or a drop of blood, he would be found guilty of murder. 3. That under a law dating back to the time of Peter Stuyvesant, the plaintiff was liable to the punishment of death "for practising against the life of a Christian." 4. That he could evade capital punishment only by giving half his fortune to his daughter and becoming a Christian. The plaintiff had no counsel, and was forthwith baptized. Upon first appeal, the judgment was confirmed.

The Supreme Court's decision follows: 1. The judgment pronounced upon Shylock was a truly feminine one—a decree half-civil, half-criminal, with the punishment half-commuted; it has no resemblance to any law or equity known to civilization. 2. The bond itself should have been voided since it provided for the commission of a capital crime. 3. It was further voided by the offer to Shylock in court of the amount of the loan. 4. No one can cut an exact pound of flesh, nor is it possible to cut flesh without drawing blood. 5. Hence, if the bond *was* allowed, the stricture about weight and blood was absurd. It is therefore the unanimous opinion of this court that Mrs. Bassanio's decree must be reversed.[5]

In the same law journal a correspondent later observed that the very absurdity of Portia's decree was proof that Bacon could not have written the play.[6]

In 1872, a "remarkable book" by the German Dr. Rudolph von Ihering, *The Struggle for Law*, eventually translated into sixteen languages, forcefully condemns Shylock's treatment. Shylock cries, "I crave the law." "In these four words Shakespeare has marked the true relation of law in its subjective sense to law in its objective sense . . . in a way no philosopher learned in the law could have done more strikingly. . . . It is not the claim of Shylock which is on trial, but the law of Venice. To what mighty, gigantic proportions does not the figure of Shylock dilate as he utters these words! It is no longer the Jew demanding a pound of flesh; it is Venice herself that knocks at the door of the court." Portia "nullifies law by a miserable quibble." Even in the days of the Roman Twelve Tables, this jurist reminds us, it was expressly declared that "the creditors should be unrestricted as to the size of the piece to be taken."[7]

In *Jurist and Poet*, A. Pietcher answered the argument (1881): No tears need be shed over Shylock. He was very clever—why did he not "anticipate the possibility of the objection which Portia after-wards actually made? Or else why did he not consult a jurist? . . . The clever man was not clever enough. . . . To overcome cunning with cunning, to take advantage of an opponent's weakness" is not a mockery of justice, but sound legal procedure.[8]

John T. Doyle in a letter entitled "Shakespeare's Law—The Case of Shylock," printed in *The Overland Monthly* (July 1886), says that the proceedings of the trial "are such as never could have oc-curred in any court administering English law. . . . No jury is im-panelled to determine the facts, no witnesses called by either side. . . . From my boyhood I regarded it as an instance of the failure of the cleverest men (not themselves lawyers) to introduce a lawsuit into fiction without violating the common rules of procedure. To make the situation dramatic they invariably make it impossible." But "subsequent experience" convinced the author that Shakespeare was not so ill-informed after all. In 1851-52, Mr. Doyle was in Nicaragua representing his company. His predecessor having entangled the af-fairs of the firm, Mr. Doyle became involved in a half-dozen law suits. One day he was accosted in Grenada by a "dapper little man" who called him by name and informed him that the alcalde had sent for him. Though inclined to put off the invitation because of its discourtesy, Mr. Doyle was informed by a friend that he "had been legally summoned to the alcalde's court," and urged to go at once. There he found himself participating in a trial whose pro-cedure was almost identical with what "Shakespeare had in view." Sometime later Mr. Doyle has come upon a similar instance in Mexico. Since both countries must have inherited their legal prac-tices from Spain, was it not the Spanish law which Shakespeare was mirroring in his play? [9]

Despite the weighty opinions of members of the legal profession, Mr. Fripp, life trustee of Shakespeare's birthplace, and authority on the records at Stratford-upon-Avon, is certain that on leaving school, Shakespeare "was articled for three years to an attorney." He feels that the dramatist's "experience as a lawyer" served him well for the Trial Scene.[10]

Doyle's justification of Shakespeare by reference to legal proce-dures in Nicaragua and Mexico, though well-intentioned, is quite beside the point. So is Fripp's defense of Shakespeare's legal knowl-edge. We are used in the twentieth century to plays which scrupulously adhere to the facts of court techniques, from "Do you solemnly swear . . . ?" etc., etc. (repeated conscientiously every time a witness takes the chair) down to "Will the prisoner rise?" etc., etc. I know of no such plays which make serious claims to being works of art. Normally, these plays are merely "thrillers," and perhaps the monotony of the naturalism of legal procedures in them has the salutary effect of modifying the sensationalism of what is being said.

To object to Shakespeare's Trial Scene on the grounds that it copies no known legal procedure is equivalent to objecting to a Matisse interior that it contains a chair one cannot sit upon, or a Redon still life in that it contains flowers one cannot smell. It would be small claim to merit in a painting that it showed a chair that one felt one could sit on or a bowl of flowers one could smell. That is not why a painting is made. Nor is it the business of a play to reproduce faithfully the legal methods of conducting a trial. A play is concerned with the human issues involved; and a great play will be more than a little impatient with engulfing those issues by a faithful reproduction of the dry facts of courtroom procedures. Shakespeare has reduced the law court to the quintessence of what is involved in a trial, and made that reduction credible to the imagination. Nothing more is required of a work of art.

For his Trial Scene Shakespeare may have taken some hints from one of Alexandre Sylvain's *Epitomes de cent histoires* as translated by Lazarus Piot (probably a pseudonym for Anthony Munday) in 1596 under the title of *The Orator*. The work consists of a hundred pieces, each of which contains an anecdote which is followed by a speech and a rebuttal. The ninety-fifth deals with this situation:

> A Jew unto whom a Christian Marchant ought nine hundred crownes, would have summoned him for the same in Turckie: the Merchant because he would not be discredited, promised to pay the said summe within the tearme of three months, and if he paied it not, he was bound to give him a pound of the flesh of his bodie. The tearme being past some fifteene daies, the Jew refused to take his money, and demaunded the pound of flesh: the ordinarie Judge of that place appointed him to cut a just pound of the Christians flesh, and if he cut either more or lesse, then his owne head should be smitten off: the Jew appealed from this sentence, unto the chief judge, saying:

Impossible is it to breake the credite of trafficke amongst men without great detriment unto the Commonwealth.* . . . It seemeth at the first sight, that it is a thing no lesse strange then cruel, to bind a man to pay a pound of the flesh of his bodie, for want of money. . . . But there are divers others that are more cruell . . . as to bind al the bodie unto a most lothsome prison, or unto an intollerable slaverie,† where not only the whole bodie but also al the sences and spirits are tormented. . . . Who ought then to marvile if a Jew requireth so small a thing of a Christian, to discharge him of a good round summe? A man may aske why I would not rather take silver of this man, then his flesh‡: I might alleage many reasons. . . . But I will onelie say, that by his obligation he oweth it me. It is lawfull to kill a souldior if he come unto the warres but an houre too late, and also to hange a theefe though he steale never so little: is it then such a great matter to cause such a one to pay a pound of his flesh? . . .

The Christian answers this plea:

This Jew is content to lose nine hundred crownes to have a pound of my flesh, whereby is manifestly seene the antient and cruell hate which he beareth not only unto Christians, but unto all

* He plies the Duke. . . .
  And doth impeach the freedom of the state.

             (III, ii, 280-1)

  The Duke cannot deny the course of law;
  For the commodity that strangers have
  With us in Venice, if it be denied,
  Will much impeach the justice of the state. . . .

             (III, iii, 26-9)

  If you deny it, let the danger light
  Upon your charter and your city's freedom.

             (IV, i, 38-9)

† You have among you many a purchas'd slave,
  Which, like your asses and your dogs and mules,
  You use in abject and in slavish parts,
  Because you bought them. . . .

             (IV, i, 90-3)

‡ You'll ask me why I rather choose to have
  A weight of carrion flesh than to receive
  Three thousand ducats.

             (IV, i, 40-2)

others which are not of his sect. . . . He would by sophisticall
reasons proove that his abhomination is equitie: trulie I confesse
that I have suffered fifteene daies of the tearme to passe, yet who
can tell whether he or I is the cause thereof, as for me I thinke
that by secret meanes he hath caused the money to bee delaied,
which from sundry places ought to have come unto me before the
tearm which I promised unto him; Otherwise I would never have
been so rash as to bind my selfe so strictly: but although he were
not the cause of the fault, is it therefore said, that he ought to bee
so impudent as to goe about to proove it no strange matter that he
should be willing to be paied with mans flesh, which is a thing
more natural for Tigres, then men.* . . .

(I should like to point out that in his discourse the merchant
accuses the moneylender of causing "by secret meanes . . . the
money to bee delaied." If I am correct in my suggestion that Shylock was responsible for spreading false rumors about the wreck of
Antonio's ships, Shakespeare may very well have got the hint from
this passage. The book was published only a short time before he
must have begun writing *The Merchant of Venice*.)
In connection with the Trial Scene it might be amusing to relate
a curious piece of chicanery. William Ireland, the late eighteenth-
century forger of Shakespeare plays and documents, came upon
an antique colored print showing an old Dutchman and a young
man in early seventeenth-century dress. Ireland purchased it, drew a
pair of scales and a knife for the Dutchman, and touched up the
face of the young man to resemble the portrait of Shakespeare in
the First Folio. He added the Shakespeare coat-of-arms, the initials
W. S., and the titles of some of Shakespeare's plays. "The two figures on this remarkable pastiche were at once interpreted by the
connoisseurs as representations of Shylock and of Shakespeare himself in the character of Bassanio." [11]
Quiller-Couch does not have much use for the Trial Scene. He
admits that because of it he "long hated the rest of the play." The
contest between Shylock and Portia is, to him, only "a set-to between
a Jew and a suffragette." Shakespeare, he thinks, had done a muddled
job of the play because Portia's plea for mercy is not reflected in

---

*   Never did I know
  A creature that did bear the shape of man
  So keen and greedy to confound a man.

                                             (III, ii, 277-9)

the verdict against Shylock.[12] (The answer to this, by no means a puzzle, will be crucial to an understanding of what Shakespeare was undertaking in the play.)

Zangwill, the novelist, sternly judges Portia as a disgrace to women in particular and the human race in general: "Obviously breaking the sartorial law of her sex, and armed with an untruthful introduction from an absentee judge, [she] is allowed to officiate at once as plaintiff, pleader, preacher, arbitrator, assessor, sentencer." [13]

Goddard, who misses entirely the meaning of the trial accuses Portia of delaying the saving of Antonio for the sake of torturing Shylock and "because she wanted a spectacle." [14]

Among the surprises in literary criticism is Furness' reverie on the trial. Furness is usually a well of common sense and good judgment, and one does not normally expect him to show such an unawareness of the creative process as his words imply. At the turn of the tide, when Portia says, "Why doth the Jew pause?" Furness makes this comment, all the more reprehensible because the charm of its mood might easily make one forget how plays are written:

> In this "pause" does Shakespeare intimate to us that the balance is trembling between Tragedy and Comedy? The choice between them lies in Shylock's power. Is he debating it? The end is not yet; he can yet make that end Tragic, and I am rash enough to say that I am not altogether sure he should not so make it. [Shylock, because of Portia's verdict becomes a victim of persecution] and compels our sympathy, when the law, which ought to have supported him, crushes him. . . . Cureless ruin has fallen on him; his life is gone, since there is no law for him in Venice. . . . Since his fall, then, is inevitable, let him redeem his vow ["An oath, an oath, I have an oath in heaven"] and drag down Anthonio with him. . . . No one of course can say with assurance why at this dividing of the ways Shakespeare decided in favor of comedy. If he objected to the many corpses on the stage, he got well over that aversion by the time he had written *Hamlet*. In my secret heart I like to believe that Shakespeare had fallen in love with Portia, as why should he not, with the most perfect of his creations? and though he might have thought that as a work of art the play should be a tragedy, yet that the vision of Portia's troubled, agonised face was more than he could bear, and her streaming eyes were more intolerable to him than Anthonio's streaming breast; it is to Portia, in more ways than one then, that I hope the Merchant owes his life.[15]

Such a reflection implies that when Shakespeare began a play he had no idea of where the work was headed. In his great plays—and this is one of them—we find exhibited a power of plot construction unsurpassed in world drama. And no one can hope to emerge with even a barely acceptable sort of plot if he should wait until the middle of the fourth act of his five-act play to decide what it is he is trying to say dramaturgically and ideationally. To suppose that any writer of stature, no matter how much he fell in love with his own characters, could allow them to pervert or determine his purposes, is to conceive the dramatist as the creature and instrument of his characters, not the author of their being. Even when, as some writers discover, the characters an author is writing about take on a life and will of their own, the creator of artistic conscience is on guard to see that they do not stray into unreasonable or impossible patterns. We are told that Dickens wept inconsolably after killing off one of his favorites. But he was careful to weep over her after he had killed her; the anticipated misery of being parted from her did not prevent his sending her to her doom.

Perhaps the gravest error that Furness makes is in forgetting that when a man like Shakespeare writes he has something to say, and that what Shakespeare had to say required the play's being a comedy, not a tragedy. It was not a matter that Portia, no matter how much he loved her, could decide for him. I cannot believe that he loved Juliet or Cleopatra less, but that love could not move him to ruin their plays by sparing their lives. It is a little outrageous to dare suppose that Shakespeare entertained the smallest doubt that he was composing a comedy when he began writing the first line of the play.

But to my mind the most amazing explanation of Portia's conduct at the trial is that of Margaret Webster, who has directed many of Shakespeare's plays under the most favorable auspices, in a style remarkable for the number of pretty stage pictures as well as for a total unawareness of the dramatic issues and meaning of each of those works. I suspect that many an innocent has been taught in the grade schools and high schools to look at the trial the same way. Portia, Miss Webster believes, when confronted by Shylock's document, hopes "there may be some flaw in the bond." She discovers that there is none. So "again and again she delays, while she frantically searches the wording of the bond. Her very repetitions ('You must prepare your bosom for his knife' and 'Therefore lay bare your bosom') are a desperate pretext for delay. She asks are there balances, . . . is there a surgeon, . . . hoping in each case to secure a respite." As the minutes pass, she becomes "panic-stricken that she may fail." Her speech,

> A pound of that same merchant's flesh is thine.
> The court awards it, and the law doth give it

is a "last desperate bid for time." Then "at the very last second the solution, simple and complete, flashes on her." Miss Webster suggests that the actress should make the line

> Tarry a little,

"blaze from her in an uncontrollable burst of passionate relief"; this would furnish "a new element of genuine and thrilling emotion." [16]

This incredibly school-girl conception of what occurs at the trial might do well enough for a melodrama but is certainly unworthy of a play which is to be taken seriously. We are apparently to assume that Portia, at the last ditch, suddenly has a divinely inspired intuition as to the content of the law-books, without ever having opened them. While I respectfully acknowledge the vast reliability of feminine intuitiveness on many matters where male logic is deaf and blind, I submit that this is pushing the claims of womanly inspiration rather too far.

We must certainly believe that if Portia has gone to the extent of coming to Venice to save her husband's friend, she, of all people, is not going to leave that to chance. She has consulted Bellario, an authority, on all the legal aspects of the case, and we may be sure that *from the moment she enters the courtroom she is armed with the knowledge of what she can do in law to rescue Antonio*, and for that matter, Shylock too. No decent lawyer would undertake to do otherwise. To imagine that she is able to save Antonio only by a sudden burst of feminine intuition as to what the law books say, is not only silly—it misses completely the dramatic meaning of the trial.

This, by very much the longest scene in the play, is one of the most dramatic Shakespeare ever penned. Before we examine it as it unfolds, let us take cognizance of another instance of Shakespeare's poetic skill.

We have noted how the words *love* and *hate* began their interplay from the very beginning of *The Merchant of Venice*. When the opposing forces come face to face in open trial in this scene, love will espouse the cause of mercy, hate the cause of "justice."

I believe that no one has remarked upon Shakespeare's artistic cunning in the manipulation of these terms. Once the time of forfeiture begins to approach, it is Shylock who is clamoring for justice. The word itself, whenever we hear it, is identified with him alone.

It first appears in the account of his raging in the streets after Jessica's elopement:

> Justice! the law! my ducats!
>
> (II, viii, 17)

and

> Justice! Find the girl!
>
> (21)

At Belmont Salerio reports that

> He plies the duke at morning and at night,
> And doth impeach the freedom of the state
> If they deny him justice.
>
> (III, ii, 280-2)

And it is added

> But none can drive him from his envious plea
> Of forfeiture, of justice, and his bond.
>
> (285-6)

At Antonio's head he flings:

> The Duke shall grant me justice.
>
> (III, iii, 8)

Some lines later Antonio concedes that if the forfeit is denied by the Duke it

> Will much impeach the justice of the state.
>
> (29)

Thus with accelerating frequency the word appears before the day of the trial, where it figures as one side of the ethical question at issue.

The word *mercy* appears but thrice before the trial begins. The first time, only a little before the trial, is when Antonio is out with the Gaoler, and Shylock cries:

> Gaoler, look to him: tell not me of mercy.
>
> (III, iii, 1)

The next time it comes from Jessica's lips, when she is pretending to complain to Lorenzo of the sermon Launcelot has administered to her:

> He tells me flatly there's no mercy for me in heaven.
>
> (III, v, 35)

Finally, just before the trial, it is used by the Duke himself to describe Shylock:

> Uncapable of pity, void and empty
> From any dram of mercy.
>
> (IV, i, 5-6)

It is to be noted, furthermore, that on each of these three occasions the word *mercy* is part of a negation. In short, there is to be no mercy.

Thus Shakespeare, subtle craftsman, threads the word *justice* through the earlier part of the play up to the very hour of trial; this justice is demanded by the sole person of hate and greed. *Mercy*, on the other hand, is never heard until the day before the trial, and then only negatively. Mercy is to figure as the other side of the ethical question at issue; but its voice is so faint before the trial that we are made unconsciously to feel that it cannot fail to succumb before the sterner demands of justice. In this way,

Shakespeare is in a position to make the trial scene all the more dramatic. The triumph of mercy will be all the more heartening because unanticipated.

We left Shylock at the threshold of the trial, defiantly telling the Duke that he cannot and will not give a reason for preferring Antonio's flesh to three thousand ducats (see pp. 210-13).

Bassanio is horrified at Shylock's blatant malice. His sensibilities seem hopelessly ineffectual against the iron of Shylock's will; and Shylock sweeps him aside with crushing arrogance:

> BASSANIO. This is no answer, thou unfeeling man,
>   To excuse the current of thy cruelty.
> SHYLOCK. I am not bound to please thee with my answer.

Antonio is by this time convinced that his fate is unalterable, and he is weary of these vain appeals to his enemy:

> Make no moe* offers, use no farther means,
> But with all brief and plain conveniency
> Let me have judgment and the Jew his will.

Bassanio offers six thousand ducats for the three due, and Shylock makes it clear that money cannot tempt him now:

> If every ducat in six thousand ducats
> Were in six parts, and every part a ducat,
> I would not draw them; I would have my bond.

And that is a vast amount of money.

It is now that the grand theme of the Trial Scene is introduced by the Duke:

> How shalt thou hope for mercy, rendering none?

Without being aware of the fact, Shylock begins to build his own funeral pyre in his retort:

> What judgment shall I dread, doing no wrong?

* more

He feels safe within the embrace of the law; why should he trouble himself with mercy? Throughout the play he has been posturing, though unconvincingly, as a noble defender of his faith —a man sinned against, not sinning. Now he has wrapped himself in the cloak of virtuousness. He is a good man. How? Because he does no wrong in demanding the fulfillment of a legal agreement. That the fulfillment of his bond involves the death of another man is for him apparently outside the present ethical consideration.

Shakespeare was later, in *Measure for Measure*, to write a play in which one of the wickedest men he ever created, Angelo, postures to himself as a model of rectitude—and convinces almost everyone else that he is too—only because he has never done anything in his life which is against the law. When his betrothed was left dowerless he jilted her and wrecked the girl's life. But there is no law against doing that, and hence he feels beyond blame for it. He has refrained from doing any act that might have landed him in jail: according to his lights, therefore, he is a good man.

This conception of virtue has always been far from uncommon. Yet a man might commit dreadful crimes every day of his life and still keep safely within the limits of the law. The greatest crimes are those against the souls of other human beings; for many of those crimes there are no possible legal punishments. This purely negative idea of goodness—that one is good as long as he does nothing illegal—enables many a scoundrel to look down his nose at his neighbor.

What is true virtue? Nobody could answer that question more eloquently than G. K. Chesterton has answered it: "Virtue is not the absence of vices or the avoidance of moral dangers; virtue is a vivid and separate thing, like pain or a particular smell. Mercy does not mean not being cruel or sparing people revenge or punishment; it means a plain and positive thing like the sun, which one has either seen or not seen." [17]

All of which is entirely apropos to the values which clash in the Trial Scene of *The Merchant of Venice*. Shylock, desiring to murder a fellow human-being, feels no need of mercy since he is being "just." But Shakespeare's villain is not a fool. To the Duke's plea for mercy, he has a ready answer. You have many slaves among you, he says. If you believe in mercy why don't you free them?

> Marry them to your heirs!
> Why sweat they under burdens? Let their beds
> Be made as soft as yours . . .

No wonder the Duke has no answer to this, for there is none. One must have clean hands before one can purge others of uncleanness.

Shylock knows he has scored a point, and quickly follows it up: Just as you've bought your slaves, I've bought this pound of flesh. It's mine and I will have it.

> If you deny me, fie upon your law!

Nerissa, dressed in a clerk's robe, comes in bearing a letter from Bellario. While the Duke is reading it, Shylock goes out of his way to increase the general happiness by whetting his knife. Shuddering, Bassanio asks his reason; Shylock answers contemptuously,

> To cut the forfeiture from that bankrupt there.

Gratiano's vulgarity is peculiarly evident in this Trial Scene; his affections are in the right place, but his fulminations mount in odiousness, much to the embarrassment of his friends. He begins to rage against Shylock, and concludes,

> Can no prayers pierce thee?

Shylock puts him down with a phrase:

> No, none that thou hast wit enough to make.

Gratiano raves on, accusing Shylock of having the soul of a wolf. Shylock's dignified reply makes Gratiano look almost foolish:

> Till thou canst rail the seal from off my bond,
> Thou but offend'st thy lungs to speak so loud.
> Repair thy wit, good youth, or it will fall
> To cureless ruin.

The letter from Bellario introduces Portia as his substitute, and informs us that she is well instructed in the laws pertaining to the case. And Portia comes in.

The Duke welcomes her and she takes her place. Naturally, she is a little nervous at first, and asks a question obviously superfluous:

> Which is the merchant here, and which the Jew?

They identify themselves.

The commentary which we have reviewed on this scene is incomprehensible after a careful study of what ensues. We are by now thoroughly acquainted with Portia's character and her philosophy of compassionateness. If we watch her with attention, it becomes quite clear what she is attempting to do. Her most important objective is to save Antonio's life, but she also wishes to achieve that without wreaking cruelty upon anyone else—this is her way of living, and she must feel that she owes it to herself to try to manage it that way. *She knows very well the law she can invoke, should it be absolutely necessary, to rescue Antonio. But she will do all she can not to invoke it, for doing so will bring the ax down on Shylock's neck. Being Portia, she would much rather give him her own money, thrice the sum due him—call it mercy in him to accept it, and not call in the law for support at all.* Therefore we hear her again and again pleading with Shylock to be merciful and take the money. As he refuses consistently, we watch her advance two steps toward freeing Antonio and always retreating one step by appealing anew to Shylock—appealing to him, in fact, not to force her to bring the rigors of the law upon his head. *It is Shylock who has most to gain by abandoning his desire for Antonio's life* in what he names a demand for justice. *It is himself he is sparing if he yields to her entreaties.* He has every opportunity to take thrice the money owing him, be hailed as a merciful man, retire with profit and esteem, and leave the court without the slightest jeopardy to his person or his fortune. But he is too much eaten up by hatred to see anything but the immediate satisfaction of that hatred.

Portia asks Antonio whether he acknowledges the bond. He does. She announces, meaningfully,

> Then must the Jew be merciful.

There is a great deal more in that "must" than Shylock guesses. He must show mercy not only because he is a member of the

human race, but also because his being merciful will enable Portia
to be merciful to him in a manner he need never know.

But he is too sure of himself. Blind with hate he demands,

> On what compulsion must I? Tell me that.

Since it is mercy she wishes him to show, not a bargain she wishes
to strike with him, she is not in a position to tell him what the
compulsion, so far as he himself is concerned, really is. Her answer
to his question is couched in such terms as ought to make any
murderer pause; it is justly one of the most celebrated speeches
Shakespeare ever wrote. Probably few of the many thousands who
have got that speech by heart have troubled themselves over the
meaning of its first line,

> The quality of mercy is not strain'd.

It is a direct answer to Shylock's "On what compulsion must
I?" The nature ("quality") of mercy, she reminds him, is that it
is *not* given by compulsion ("strained" = forced). Mercy is bestowed
as freely and fruitfully as the rain from heaven. It blesses giver and
receiver, and is most admirable when given by those who could
instead crush because they are in a position of power. It is a godlike
quality, and earthly power becomes godlike when mercy tempers
strict justice. Therefore, she entreats Shylock,

> Though justice be thy plea, consider this:
> That, in the course of justice, none of us
> Should see salvation.

[This is Hamlet's philosophy too:

> HAMLET.   Will you see the players well bestowed? Do you hear,
> let them be well used. . . .
> POLONIUS.   My lord, I will use them according to their desert.
> HAMLET.   God's bodykins, man, much better! Use every man
> after his desert and who shall 'scape whipping? Use them after
> your own honour and dignity. The less they deserve, the more
> merit is in your bounty.
>
> (II, ii, 545 seq.)]

If each of us were to be judged by God according to what we deserve, we should all be damned. We therefore, she continues, have need of God's mercy, we pray for it, and therefore must show it to our fellow human beings. This is the philosophy, as we have already seen, which is at the root of Portia's own character.

But Shylock is deaf to the call of humaneness, and cries prophetically, without knowing it:

> My deeds upon my head!

Portia now asks: Cannot the merchant pay the sum owing? Eagerly Bassanio offers twice the sum, and engages himself, if that will not do, to pay ten times as much. If Shylock will not agree, he cries in anguish, it is plain that his desires are murderous: let Portia turn aside the law this once—

> To do a great right, do a little wrong.

But to that Portia wisely cannot consent. If we are to settle this by law, she understands, then the law cannot be perverted. There is a threat in this for Shylock, but he, of course, does not hear it. Instead he interprets her to mean that his victory is assured. He hails her as another Daniel who has come to help him, just as the Biblical Daniel saved Susannah in the story told in the Apocrypha. (Again the devil is quoting Scripture to serve his purpose.) He feels he has a friend in court. He has, indeed, if only he knew!

Portia asks to see the bond; Shylock tenders it eagerly. The moneylender is plainly immovable, and Portia is inclined to proceed to judgment—which must be against Shylock. But she cannot:

> Shylock, there's thrice thy money off'red thee.

To this Shylock, suddenly anew the man of religion, responds:

> An oath, an oath, I have an oath in heaven!
> Shall I lay perjury upon my soul?
> No, not for Venice.

That is to say, Heaven will not forgive him if he does not murder Antonio.

Now Portia begins, very reluctantly, to move to a conclusion. The bond itself is legal enough, she says, in form. She hesitates again:

> Be merciful;
> Take thrice thy money; bid me tear the bond.

Bid me tear it for *your* sake, is what she means. But he is adamant. There is nothing on earth, he declares, that can alter him:

> Proceed to judgment.

Exhausted with waiting, Antonio seconds his request. Portia is forced to continue on the path she hates to tread. But, obviously, she hopes that at the last minute Shylock will be unable to execute the murder; she continues to give him a chance to withdraw. Perhaps the sight of Antonio's exposed flesh will work upon Shylock's humanity. Antonio must now prepare his bosom for the knife. Her words, which sound partisan to Shylock, are full of portent for him if he persists in his demand:

> For the intent and purpose of the law
> Hath full relation to the penalty. . . .

Shylock, lost in error, exults. Portia gives Shylock another opportunity to prove that he himself will be entitled to some mercy:

> Have by some surgeon, Shylock, on your charge,
> To stop his wounds, lest he do bleed to death.

Shylock, who will insist on the letter of the law, is busy piling his funeral pyre high:

> Is it so nominated in the bond?

The threat in Portia's words becomes graver:

> It is not so express'd; but what of that?
> *'Twere good you do so much for charity.*

[At this point we are inclined to cry to him in warning, Friar Lawrence's words: "This is dear mercy, and thou see'st it not!"] The charity would be toward himself, but he dismisses the plea:

> I cannot find it; 'tis not in the bond.

There is nothing more that Portia can do for him.

At this high point of tension, Shakespeare both provides a little comic relief and keeps us in further suspense. Antonio takes leave of Bassanio, and urges him not to be weighed down by guilt for his death, with a wry little jest:

> Repent but you that you shall lose your friend,
> And he repents not that he pays your debt;
> For if the Jew do cut but deep enough,
> I'll pay it instantly with all my heart.

Bassanio in anguish cries that though he loves his wife as dearly as he loves life, he would give up her and the whole world,

> I would lose all, ay, sacrifice them all
> Here to this devil, to deliver you.

Portia, too much the woman to remember her masquerade, cannot resist saying to this:

> Your wife would give you little thanks for that,
> If she were by, to hear you make the offer.

(No doubt Bassanio has not heard the last of his declaration!) Gratiano, not to be outdone by his friend, wishes his wife were already in heaven so she could move the heavenly powers to stop Shylock. To which Nerissa is impelled to retort:

> 'Tis well you offer it behind her back.
> The wish would make else an unquiet house.

If everyone were not so much agitated, it might have struck some of those present that quite suddenly these two young men were talking very much like two young women!

Shylock is impatient of the delay:

> We trifle time. I pray thee, pursue sentence.

Every expedient has failed Portia in her attempt to save Shylock the sentence awaiting him. As she speaks now it is as though she were herself the austere Goddess of Justice, slowly lifting her sword:

> PORTIA.   A pound of that same merchant's flesh is thine.
>   The court awards it, and the law doth give it.
> SHYLOCK.   Most rightful judge!
> PORTIA.   And you must cut this flesh from off his breast.
>   The law allows it, and the court awards it.

Shylock is in a delirium of delight. He advances to cut the forfeiture. As his hand is raised, the sword of justice descends like lightning to intercept it:

> Tarry a little; there is something else.
> This bond doth give thee here no jot of blood;
> The words expressly are "a pound of flesh."

Portia's voice becomes sterner with each phrase. The die is cast; nothing more can be done to save Shylock:

> Take then thy bond, take thou thy pound of flesh;
> But, in the cutting it, if thou dost shed
> One drop of Christian blood, thy lands and goods
> Are, by the laws of Venice, confiscate
> Unto the state of Venice. . . .
> SHYLOCK.   Is that the law?
> PORTIA.   Thyself shalt see the act;
>   *For, as thou urgest justice, be assur'd*
>   *Thou shalt have justice, more than thou desir'st.*

Shylock is quick-witted. At once he sees that the tide has unexpectedly turned against him: he offers to accept thrice the sum due him. Bassanio, with relief, gladly holds the money out to him. But Portia interferes:

> Soft!
> The Jew shall have *all justice*. Soft! no haste!
> He shall have nothing but the penalty.

Literal justice is what Shylock has ruthlessly demanded, and now he is made to see what literal justice can mean:

> Therefore prepare thee to cut off the flesh.
> Shed thou no blood, *nor cut thou less nor more*
> *But just a pound of flesh.* If thou tak'st more
> Or less than a just pound, be it but so much
> As makes it light or heavy in the substance
> Or the division of the twentieth part
> Of one poor scruple, nay, if the scale do turn
> But in the estimation of a hair,
> Thou diest and all thy goods are confiscate.

This is talking the language which Shylock understands; this is the literal justice for which he has stipulated. He himself had been offered, before he brought the case to trial, any amount of money by Antonio's friends as soon as they had been able to scrape it together, and he had refused it on the grounds that the exact day for payment was past. Now he hears what may happen to those who will insist upon the letter of the law. He has been blind to the truth that life has a way of tumbling mischief down on the inventors' heads, of forcing the cup of poison down the throat of the poisoner. In renouncing mercy he has found in the letter of the law only a false security, a false security which often drives men mad with a sense of power. The sense of power is the most dangerous of all human emotions; too often it causes a man to forget that he himself is only a frail mortal. As Isabella magnificently phrases it:

> Could great men thunder
> As Jove himself does, Jove would ne'er be quiet,
> For every pelting,* petty officer
> Would use his Heaven for thunder, nothing but thunder!
> Merciful Heaven,
> Thou rather with thy sharp and sulphurous bolt
> Split'st the unwedgeable and gnarled oak
> Than the soft myrtle. But man, proud man,
> Dressed in a little brief authority,
> Most ignorant of what he's most assur'd,

* paltry

His glassy essence,* like an angry ape,
Plays such fantastic tricks before high Heaven
As make the angels weep.

(*Measure for Measure*, II, ii, 110-22)

Gratiano, ever since Portia has arrested Shylock's hand, has been behaving more and more bumptiously—as though it is he who has saved Antonio's life:

Now, infidel, I have thee on the hip.

Shylock is cornered, but makes one last attempt to salvage something:

Give me my principal, and let me go.

Open-hearted Bassanio is only too willing to oblige:

I have it ready for thee; here it is.

But Portia, who has a better head, knows that it is too late for that:

He hath refused it in the open court.
He shall have merely justice and his bond.

Realizing that he is to get nothing, Shylock, no fool, is anxious to quit the place before further disappointments are visited upon him:

Why, then the devil give him good of it!
I'll stay no longer question.

But as he makes for the door, Portia halts him. Literal justice has not yet had its full say. Shylock, an alien, is manifestly guilty of conspiring against a citizen of Venice. There is a law for that too: the culprit's life is at the mercy of the Duke, one-half his goods is to be awarded his intended victim, the other half is to be confiscated by the state. This is what she has dreaded bringing down on Shylock.

* his brittle, fragile nature

As everything collapses about Shylock's ears, though he has fully merited the direst punishment, we cannot help being sorry for him in his total defeat. Shakespeare conceived him as a man of some dignity, and to reinforce our pity for him he causes Gratiano to exult over him in an obnoxious way that makes us squirm. The Duke, however, grants him his life before he asks for it; as for the half of his estate due to the state, the Duke is willing to commute that to a mere fine. Remembering Shylock's vast wealth, we are made to feel that he will thus be left still a very rich man. But once more his greed directs his tongue:

> Nay, take my life and all; pardon not that.
> You take my house when you do take the prop
> That doth sustain my house; you take my life
> When you do take the means whereby I live.

—a frank confession that money is dearer to him than his life.

But Antonio, in answer to this plea, renounces his half of Shylock's fortune on two conditions: that he will bestow the income of half his fortune on Jessica and Lorenzo while Shylock lives, deeding the principal to them on his death; and that, in exchange for this kindness, he become a Christian.

With the exception of this enforced conversion, Shylock is not, as Kittredge justly observes, "treated with undue severity. . . . He simply loses the income on half his property, which income he would not spend in any case. The other half remains his own. . . . The terms are sufficiently galling to Shylock's pride and self-respect, but from the merely monetary point of view they are much better than could have been expected. Their mildness is due, it will be observed, to Antonio's interposition." [18]

Monetarily, at least, Shylock will lose only as much of his money as the Duke will exact as a fine. This is clear mercy, when it is remembered what the law for his offense provides. Even Furness, so strong a partisan of Shylock, reflects whimsically: "I find relief in the assurance, which a knowledge of his character as revealed on the Trial affords, that it cannot be long before his financial prospects are as fair as ever. One half of his present property [Furness has forgotten that the Duke's promise to reduce the other half to a mere fine will leave Shylock with his fortune almost intact], which he is allowed to retain, is probably a much larger sum than he started with in life; and the wide-spread notoriety which will accrue to him from this trial, and which is believed in these modern days of advertising to be 'the soul of business,' cannot but stand him in admirable and remunerative stead." [19]

Shakespeare is so incredibly modern that one is constantly forgetting that he was writing nearly four centuries ago. Only once in a while do we come upon a point of view that brings us up short with the reminder that we cannot expect even the greatest of sixteenth-century poets to surmount the limitations of his time in every detail of his thought. One such instance is Antonio's requirement that Shylock become a Christian—the only moment in the play that throws us back to Shakespeare's day. Since only a Christian could expect salvation, the audience would have interpreted this stipulation of Antonio's as but another proof of the man's goodness: he was so much concerned about Shylock's soul that he wished to make him a candidate for eternal blessedness.

This, I say, is the way the Elizabethan audience would have taken Antonio's stipulation. It was simply an act of extraordinary kindness to bring the nonbeliever into the true faith. Boccaccio's Jehannot, it will be remembered, out of love for his Jewish friend, was unceasing in his desire to convert him (see pp. 34-7). The reader will recall that that delightful busybody, Tom Coryat, was also moved with like religious zeal (at Venice, too, by coincidence): "Truely it is a most lamentable case for a Christian to consider the damnable estate of these miserable Jewes, in that they reject the true Messias and Saviour of thier soules. . . . And as pitifull it is to see that fewe of them living in Italy are converted to the Christian religion." For which reason, it will be recalled, well-meaning Tom, argued at great length with a "learned Jewish Rabbin" and some fifty other Jews of Venice in a fervent attempt to convert them (see pp. 71-2). So, too, the scholar Musto was zealous to do the same (see p. 66).

This was the Elizabethan view of the matter, and it is the view of many a missionary-minded Christian today. But I am not at all sure that it was Shakespeare's. For certainly he allowed himself, earlier in the play, to poke fun at this zeal for converting everyone to Christianity. Launcelot Gobbo has been assuring Jessica that she is damned because of her parentage, and she has declared that she will be saved because her husband has made her a Christian. To which Launcelot replies:

> Truly the more to blame he; we were Christians enow before;
> e'en as many as could well live, one by another. This making
> of Christians will raise the price of hogs. If we grow all to be
> pork-eaters, we shall not shortly have a rasher on the coals for
> money.
>
> (III, v, 23 seq.)

In any case, what is important to our study of Shylock is not Antonio's point of view, but Shylock's reaction to the stipulation. At last and in a very thoroughgoing manner he makes it clear just how dear his religion has been to him. He can keep his religion and die proudly as the staunch upholder of his faith—as, every once in a while, he has pretended to be when it has suited his purposes. This is obviously what a Jew devoted to his religion would do, what countless numbers of Jews have done from time immemorial (e.g., the Jews of York, see p. 23). Or he can keep his money instead by the simple expedient of becoming a Christian. He unhesitatingly accepts the latter alternative, for money is truly the only god he worships:

> I am content.

With these words the conflict between literal justice and mercy is over. Shylock has but one more speech for the rest of the play:

> I pray you, give me leave to go from hence.
> I am not well. Send the deed after me,
> And I will sign it.

Shylock's "I am not well," though often interpreted tragically by actors was not so intended. We may feel a little sorry for him, but it is too late to make a bid for our deepest compassion. He has been called upon again and again to behave like a human being, and has refused. Our recollection of that is bound to limit our sympathies for him.

A well-known actor to whom I was introduced was telling me of his experiments on the road with *The Merchant of Venice*. Because Orthodox Jews conduct a service for the dead when one of their offspring marries out of his religion, this Thespian introduced such a scene to extend the story of Jessica's elopement, to show its effect upon Shylock, and to accentuate his "piety." But he went further than that in his own performance of the role. After Shylock's last words, he paused in the doorway before leaving the courtroom, and held out his arms in an attitude to suggest the Crucifixion! When I asked him how successful these "new ideas" had proved, he answered, with no hint of humor, "You know—I just couldn't put it across. Shakespeare stacked the cards too much against Shylock!" Upon that innocent reflection one could write a whole treatise entitled, "Modern Conceptions of the Actor's Function."

Quiller-Couch, naturally, is furious at the judgment meted out to Shylock; it renders Portia, Antonio, and their friends "just as heartless as Shylock without any of Shylock's passionate excuse." [20]

Allied to this point of view is a question I have been asked frequently: If Portia believes so profoundly in mercy, once she has saved Antonio from murder, why does she not let Shylock off scotfree? I have even been asked a more naïve question: If Portia is so generous, why doesn't she warn Shylock at the very outset that if he will not cease his demands for Antonio's flesh his own life will be in jeopardy?

Such questions, such points of view imply an ignorance of something quintessential to the great idea with which the trial is concerned. We have seen indeed how mercy, had Shylock permitted, could have blessed him, the bestower (together with a gift of six thousand ducats more in cash), quite as much as Antonio, the receiver—in fact, in the eventuality, a great deal more. We have seen, too, how as frail mortals none of us ought dare demand the letter of the law lest the letter of the law prove a boomerang. But the very nature of mercy, as Portia has said, is that it must be bestowed freely, without conditions or thought of recompense. Shylock would have earned the right to as great mercy as he gave, if he had been equal to giving it. But to have forewarned him that he might have to forfeit his own life if he were not merciful himself, would have been as ludicrous as the plea of the Ghosts, which is intentionally ridiculous, in W. S. Gilbert's *Ruddigore*. After torturing the latest heir to the title of the family, the Ghosts of his ancestors, about to leave him in peace, cry out:

> We want your pardon ere we go
> For having agonized you so—

294 :: *The Truth About Shylock*

> So pardon us, so pardon us, so pardon us—
> Or die!

To have so forewarned Shylock would have been to strike a shameful bargain, not to pave the way for his showing true mercy, whose quality is not strained. Mercy on his part under such conditions would prove itself a bawd, for as Isabella says tersely,

> Mercy
> Is nothing akin to foul redemption.
>> (*Measure for Measure*, II, iv, 112)

Mercy is no longer mercy when it is to be had only at a price.

I believe that no passage in the Bible has been so generally misunderstood as Jesus' injunction: "Whosoever shall smite thee on thy right cheek, turn to him the other also." (*Matthew*: V, 39) For Jesus also said: "Neither cast ye your pearls before swine, lest they trample them under their feet, and turn again and rend you." (*Matthew*: VII, 6) And the one is not contradicted by the other. The injunction to turn the other cheek has been cited to justify every kind of spiritual pusillanimity—as though it were a Christian's duty to bend his neck obligingly before the ax of a Hitler, a Stalin, or a Khrushchev. Why does one turn the other cheek? Surely, not to make *oneself* more holy. Jesus had small regard for those who use the world to puff up their own saintliness. One turns the other cheek for the sake of him who has struck one, to make him ashamed of what he has done. Even fine human beings are capable of striking out at others in anger or ignorance, and because they are essentially decent they may be more readily brought to a sense of the wrong they commit by meeting their blow, not by a blow in return, but by standing defenseless before them. It is because they are fundamentally good and for love of them that one turns the other cheek. But those who are strangers to goodness, those who live only to bend the world to their will, can profit nothing from such meekness: it is only an invitation for them to become more cruel and inhuman. They are the swine before whom one is not to cast the pearls of meekness and mercy, for they will only turn upon one and rend one further. There is no impracticality here in Jesus' teaching. That doctrine of turning the other cheek was hideously misapplied, after the collapse of the Nazi regime, with pleas for clemency for the ruthless inventors of nightmarish horror. Mercy but murders when it pardon those that kill for the sake of killing.

To extend complete pardon to Shylock after he has rejected again and again every shred of mercy is to make a travesty of mercy, to render it meaningless. Shylock himself signed his own death warrant before the trial ever began:

> DUKE. How shalt thou hope for mercy, rendering none?
> SHYLOCK. What judgment shall I dread, doing no wrong?

As it is, and though we are sorry for him only because he manages somehow to maintain dignity in the midst of savage cruelty, he has been granted more leniency than he was entitled to.

As he leaves the play, we are glad to have him go. But we cannot avoid a sense of tremendous waste that a man of such gifts should have perverted them all in the wretched service of greed.

8

Penultimate

Sir, the maid loves you, and all shall be well.—*The Merry Wives of Windsor*, I, iv, 127.

: :

Such tricks hath strong imagination.—*A Midsummer Night's Dream*, V, i, 18.

: :

Love talks with better knowledge.—*Measure for Measure*, III, ii, 159.

: :

Be cheerful
And think of each thing well.—*The Tempest*, V, i, 250.

: :

The accent is usually on the antepenult; but sometimes it falls on the penult.—A. Ingerber, *Indo-European Rhetoric*.

Shylock's forced conversion, as we have seen, was from the point of view of the Elizabethan audience "the greatest possible compliment and reward which the Christian can pay the Jew." [1] But what became of him after he was baptized? Thaler wonders.[2] Since Shylock is no more seen or heart of after the trial, Thaler's is a question not to be asked. Nevertheless, a number of writers have composed sequels to *The Merchant of Venice* in order to supply a full answer. These I shall conscientiously report in the last chapter.

Meanwhile for those who insist upon an immediate reply, I can only recount a little anecdote told in the days of Czarist Russia. A quiet-loving Jew in a small village was a good friend of the village priest, and was urged by him to become converted to Christianity in order to save himself from the recurrent wave of pogroms. As much to put an end to his friends's worry over him as for any other reason, the Jew allowed himself to be instructed in the new faith, and eventually became baptized, greatly to the priest's satisfaction. Some weeks later the priest dropped in upon the new convert on a Friday afternoon, and found his friend at dinner, relishing a fine juicy steak. The priest was alarmed. "Have you forgotten so soon, my good friend? This is Friday," he cried. "Yes, I know," the ex-Jew replied wearily. "But you are eating meat!" "Oh no! You are deceived," replied the other; "I am eating a good fish." The priest stared at him as though he had gone mad. His friend reassured him: "Don't worry, dear friend, I am quite sane. I suppose this looks like a fine steak to you, and I'll admit that as my wife began to prepare it for the oven, it looked like that to me too. Then I remembered it is Friday. 'Wait!' I said to her. Then I took a cup, ran to the church, and brought back a tiny bit of holy-water. I sprinkled it on this, and said, 'You are no longer a steak, but a fine fish.' And a fish it became—the best I ever tasted. Won't you sit down and have some?"

Radford too asks, How did Shylock end? and provides an engaging answer (merely, he says, as "a matter of conjecture"): "His conduct in court justifies us in inferring that he accepted the inevitable and made the best of it. Had he lived in our day we might conjecturally sketch his subsequent career thus: His baptism was performed with pomp in a historic temple by a distinguished ecclesiastic who knows that there is Eternal Hope for Jews. . . . His marriage later on with a Dowager Countess who largely endowed the Society for the Propagation of the Gospel among the Jews, made his social position impregnable, and the money he subsequently made by publishing a financial newspaper far exceeded anything ever acquired by him in his old profession of usury." [3]

Judging from Radford's gentle spoof, he is well aware that no one is ever truly converted to a religion, including the religion of his fathers, except by himself. The man who has never discovered his religion for himself, has no religion.

I am reminded here of W. S. Gilbert's irreverently sardonic satire at the expense of the meddling missionary spirit, *The Bishop and the Busman*. It is a merry piece which everyone should know, and therefore I happily quote it in full:

> It was a Bishop bold,
>   And London was his see,
> He was short and stout and round about
>   And zealous as could be.
>
> It also was a Jew,
>   Who drove a Putney 'bus—

For flesh of swine however fine
    He did not care a cuss.

His name was HASH BAZ BEN,
    And JEDEDIAH too,
And SOLOMON and ZABULON—
    This 'bus-directing Jew.

The Bishop said, said he,
    "I'll see what I can do
To Christianize and make you wise,
    You poor benighted Jew."

So every blessed day
    That 'bus he rode outside,
From Fulham town, both up and down,
    And loudly thus he cried:

"His name is HASH BAZ BEN,
    And JEDEDIAH too,
And SOLOMON and ZABULON—
    This 'bus-directing Jew."

At first the 'busman smiled,
    And rather liked the fun—
He merely smiled, that Hebrew child,
    And said, "Eccentric one!"

And gay young dogs would wait
    To see the bus go by
(These gay young dogs, in striking togs)
    To hear the Bishop cry:

"Observe his grisly beard,
    His race it clearly shows,
He sticks no fork in ham or pork—
    Observe, my friends, his nose.

"His name is HASH BAZ BEN,
    And JEDEDIAH too,
And SOLOMON and ZABULON—
    This 'bus-directing Jew."

But though at first amused,
    Yet after seven years,
This Hebrew child got rather riled,
    And melted into tears.

He really almost feared
    To leave his poor abode,
His nose, and name, and beard became
    A byword on that road.

At length he swore an oath,
    The reason he would know—
"I'll call and see why ever he
    Does persecute me so!"

The good old Bishop sat
    On his ancestral chair,
The 'busman came, sent up his name,
    And laid his grievance bare.

"Benighted Jew," he said
    (The good old Bishop did),
"Be Christian you, instead of Jew—
    Become a Christian kid!

"I'll ne'er annoy you more."
    "Indeed?" replied the Jew;
"Shall I be freed?" "You will, indeed!"
    Then "Done!" said he, "with you!"

The organ which, in man,
    Between the eyebrows grows,
Fell from his face, and in its place
    He found a Christian nose.

His tangled Hebrew beard,
    Which to his waist came down,
Was now a pair of whiskers fair—
    His name ADOLPHUS BROWN!

He wedded in a year
    That prelate's daughter JANE,
He's grown quite fair—has auburn hair—
    His wife is far from plain.

So much for Shylock's conversion, impossible for a modern mind to accept however the Elizabethans would have applauded it. We can no longer believe in the merit or permanence of salvation by compulsion. There is no point in evading the truth: the compelled conversion of Shylock must always be a blemish upon the beauty of the play.

As Shylock leaves the court-room Gratiano is more offensive than ever in the imprecations he hurls after Shylock, and thereby increases our sympathy for the departing moneylender. He is the only one who behaves in this way, and the failure of his friends ever to follow up his slurs against Shylock makes it plain that his behavior is an embarrassment to them. He is the only character in the entire play who can be accused of anti-Semitism.

[Frank Harris: Gratiano is "a gallant gentleman." [4] Goddard: his imprecations at the close of the trial result in our all identifying with him(!) as "a thrill of vicarious revenge runs up and down the spine of every person in the theatre." [5] Ridley: There is "something a trifle ill-bred about him." [6]]

The trial over, the Duke invites Portia home to dinner, but she politely declines, therein showing her womanliness again. She came to court for a woman's reason—to help her husband. That accomplished, she is anxious to return home. It is one of the topsy-turvy platitudes of the world that women are vain. The kind of vanity women have is purely superficial, a matter of hats and makeup and looking well in the mirror. It is a good thing, it makes the world a more agreeable place to live in—and more power to it! But the vanity of men, which is never mentioned! Where is the plumb line which can sound the depths of male vanity? Vanity is the Achilles' heel of every man who lives: few men will confront the fact, and all women know it. If it had actually been a man who had saved Antonio's life, he would have *expected* a testimonial dinner afterwards, with a crown of laurels and gold medals awaiting him there. He would think it only right that a brass band should be waiting for him at Belmont, playing, "Hail the conquering hero." Such public acclaim, the bread of life to men, means nothing to women.

Bassanio, in thanking the wise judge, reveals again the refinement of his nature. He wishes her to accept the ducats which were due

Shylock. (These post-Shylock days most men would start quarreling with the lawyer over his fees.) Antonio adds that beyond such a payment there remains a debt of gratitude which can never be paid. But Portia is anxious to leave, and declines the offer; she declares herself well-enough recompensed by the outcome of the trial. Now we see anew how money is a means for increasing the beauty of life among these people; Bassanio delays her:

> Dear sir, of force I must attempt you further.
> Take some remembrance of us, *as a tribute,*
> *Not as a fee.* Grant me two things, I pray you,
> Not to deny me, and to pardon me.

(Is it possible to imagine the average man today pressing a large sum on his lawyer, and begging pardon for his insistence?)

Here Portia has the inspiration for a charming *jeu d'esprit,* the outcome of which makes for much merriment in the last act. Since they insist:

> You press me far, and therefore I will yield.
> (*To Antonio.*) Give me your gloves. I'll wear them for your
>   sake.
> (*To Bassanio.*) And, for your love, I'll take this ring from you.
> Do not draw back your hand; I'll take no more. . . .

If such a request were made to a woman, she would have no compunction in saying, "I'm sorry I cannot give you this ring. It was given to me by my husband, and I cannot part with it." But, for some reason, no man can bear to admit publicly either that he loves his wife or that his actions are ever limited by his love of her—perhaps out of a dread of appearing henpecked. As a man Bassanio cannot expose himself:

> This ring, good sir, alas, it is a trifle!
> I will not shame myself to give you this.

(Shakespeare is rapidly drawing his play safely back within the precincts of high comedy.)

She is still wearing the robe of a man, but Portia's spirit has already thrown off the masquerade. Her response is purely that of a woman:

I will have nothing else but only this;

and, holding his hand, which he is anxious to withdraw, she adds,

> And now methinks I have a mind to it.

He begs her to excuse him from making that gift; he will find out the finest ring in Venice and gladly give it her. Secretly delighted, she feigns annoyance:

> I see, sir, you are liberal in offers.
> You taught me first to beg; and now methinks
> You teach me how a beggar should be answer'd.

Touched where he is most sensitive, Bassanio at last confesses that the ring was his wife's gift and that he has sworn to her never to part from it. Portia pretends not to believe him, and leaves in a simulated huff. Humiliated at being found wanting in that generosity which is a cardinal point of honor with him, Bassanio needs but a word from Antonio, and without a second's reflection sends the ring after Portia:

> ANTONIO.   My Lord Bassanio, let him have the ring.
>   Let his deservings and my love withal
>   Be valued against your wife's commandment.
> BASSANIO.   Go, Gratiano, run and overtake him;
>   Give him this ring. . . .

In the next little scene (IV, ii) Gratiano catches up with Portia and Nerissa and delivers the ring. He is asked to direct Nerissa to Shylock's house with the deed to be signed; Nerissa determines to get the ring she has given Gratiano:

> Sir, I would speak with you. . . .
> Come, good sir, will you show me to this house?

When approaching his last act Shakespeare faced one of the greatest challenges of his career. Although Shylock has appeared in but five of the nineteen scenes of the play, his powerful, almost heroic personality of somber dignity and unalterable purposefulness has cast its shadow, from the moment of his appearance in the third scene through the seventeenth, over nearly the whole extent of the play. Though he is a major figure in the plot, the play is not his play, and Shakespeare wisely banished him from the last great act. Greed, hate, and the letter of the law which will not countenance mercy have been vanquished with his quitting the stage. But the memory of that grand and terrible figure, somehow pathetic in his just defeat, still lingers. The victory of generosity, love, and compassion requires that the play be a comedy. The remaining strands of the story waiting to be knit together presented no formidable problem to a skilled dramatist: the very logic of the plot idea dictated their being interlaced for the happy ending of comedy. But it is eminently possible to write a happy ending which carries no conviction. How, in short, was he to cause the audience to *feel* that a play with Shylock in it is indeed a comedy? What were the tones which must be employed in the last act, tones which would interfuse acceptably and convincingly with the louring image of that grim presence? That was the crux of Shakespeare's artistic predicament, and I believe that no one but him could have solved it. The solution called for no mean magic, but he is literature's greatest magician.

The last act is one of the truly superb achievements in letters. It opens on a scene tremulous with the shimmering beauty of a moonlit night. Lorenzo and Jessica are walking in Portia's garden, and saying the sweet nothings that lovers dote upon whispering to each other, seeing themselves exaltedly in the tradition of the great lovers of history:

> LORENZO.   The moon shines bright. In such a night as this,
>   When the sweet wind did gently kiss the trees
>   And they did make no noise, in such a night
>   Troilus methinks mounted the Troyan walls,
>   And sigh'd his soul toward the Grecian tents,
>   Where Cressid lay that night.
> JESSICA.   In such a night
>   Did Thisbe fearfully o'ertrip the dew,
>   And saw the lion's shadow ere himself
>   And ran dismay'd away. . . .

What mattered it that the Elizabethan audience, in a period when the stage was yet happily a stranger to the scenery-cluttered set, beheld a pair of lovers walking on the bare planks of a rude and un-adorned wooden stage? What mattered it that that stage, which was supposed to represent a lovely moonlit garden in Belmont, was actually exposed to the same dull light of a late London afternoon and the same uncertain open sky as was the audience? By a few magical lines Shakespeare has the stage already swimming in moonlight checkered with the shade of trees.

LORENZO.   In such a night
    Did Jessica steal from the wealthy Jew,
    And with an unthrift love did run from Venice
    As far as Belmont.
JESSICA.   In such a night
    Did young Lorenzo swear he lov'd her well,
    Stealing her soul with many vows of faith—
    And ne'er a true one.
LORENZO.   In such a night
    Did pretty Jessica, like a little shrew,
    Slander her love—and he forgave it her.
JESSICA.   I would out-night you, did nobody come;
    But, hark, I hear the footing of a man.

How Jessica begins to blossom under the benign influence of love into a charming woman! Lorenzo softly challenges the newcomer:

Who comes so soft in silence of the night?

It is a messenger to announce the imminent return of Portia and Nerissa.

Now Shakespeare employs an exquisitely cunning device. Into the quiet mystery of the night penetrate the bawling shouts of the clown Launcelot, shattering the beauty and stillness:

LAUNCELOT.   Sola, sola! wo ha! Ho! Sola, sola!
LORENZO.   Who calls?
LAUNCELOT.   Sola! Did you see Master Lorenzo? Master Lorenzo,
    sola, sola!
LORENZO.   Leave hollaing, man; here.

Launcelot continues to shout as he delivers his news: Bassanio's courier has announced that his master will be home soon. The ear-splitting shouts end with Launcelot's return to the house, and the silence and wonder of the night envelop us again, all the deeper by contrast with Launcelot's momentary disturbance of them.

Lorenzo calls for music to welcome Portia, and when he speaks again to Jessica the beauty of his words gives new magic to the night:

> How sweet the moonlight sleeps upon this bank!
> Here will we sit and let the sound of music
> Creep in our ears. Soft stillness and the night
> Become the touches of sweet harmony.
> Sit, Jessica. Look how the floor of heaven
> Is thick inlaid with patines* of bright gold.
> There's not the smallest orb which thou behold'st
> But in his motion like an angel sings,
> Still† quiring‡ to the young-ey'd cherubins;
> Such harmony is in immortal souls;
> But whilst this muddy vesture of decay §
> Doth grossly close it in, we cannot hear it.

We have learned little about Lorenzo earlier in the play beyond the fact that his love for Jessica is deep and all he seems to be concerned with, and that his friends know him as a man of few words. But now he has revealed, in the happiness of a love fulfilled, the soul of a great poet. [Reese: Though this speech is "a splendid piece of poetic description" (There is no sort of writing more meaningless than description for description's sake!), it "does not proceed functionally from the characters . . . or add materially to our knowledge of them." ⁷]

The Musicians come in, and it is perhaps because suddenly the moon has been momentarily hidden by a cloud that Lorenzo says to them:

> Come, ho! and wake Diana with a hymn;
> With sweetest touches pierce your mistress' ear
> And draw her home with music.

Jessica reminds us of how young she must be with the pensive innocence of:

* small flat plates used in the celebration of the Eucharist
† forever
‡ singing in perfect harmony
§ i.e., while this earth-bound mortal body envelops our immortal souls

I am never merry when I hear sweet music.

Her wistful words form the occasion for one of the most remarkable tributes to music ever composed:

> The reason is, your spirits are attentive;
> For do but note a wild and wanton herd,
> Or race of youthful and unhandled colts,
> Fetching mad bounds, bellowing and neighing loud,
> Which is the hot condition of their blood,
> If they but hear perchance a trumpet sound,
> Or any air of music touch their ears,
> You shall perceive them make a mutual stand,
> Their savage eyes turn'd to a modest gaze
> By the sweet power of music.* Therefore the poet†
> Did feign that Orpheus drew trees, stones, and floods;
> Since nought so stockish, hard, and full of rage,
> But music for the time doth change his‡ nature.
> The man that hath no music in himself,
> Nor is not mov'd with concord of sweet sounds,
> Is fit for treasons, stratagems, and spoils.
> The motions of his spirit are dull as night
> And his affections dark as Erebus.
> Let no such man be trusted.

[It is interesting to recall that Shylock had no love for music. He forbade Jessica to listen to it, or to allow the sound of it enter his

---

* Only the man who does not know animals well will consider this an exaggeration. I had a cat for seventeen years, Joseph, by name (a most unusual cat, I will admit—but is there any cat who is not unusual?), who was a formidable music-lover. He was perfectly familiar with the idiom of each composer. He would stop whatever he was doing, and come close to the piano whenever it was being played, and settle down to listen. Beethoven was his favorite. To Beethoven he always reacted with a deep and steady purr, while his eyes blinked in rich contentment continuously. At the richer harmonies of Chopin the purr would become so loud as to fill the room. The lovely romanticism of Schumann would make him roll over, raise his paws in the air, and emit tiny sounds of satisfaction. Debussy and Ravel (I'm afraid he never really could distinguish between the two) made him very skittish, and he would keep dancing about the room, making a series of leaps and short dashes. I'm sorry to say that he had no use for the contemporary Soviet composers at all. He frequently emitted a series of wails and whines in protest against them. This is not fantasy, but solid fact.

† Ovid

‡ its

sober house. The sound of the fifer was to him a "vile squealing" (II, v, 29 seq.)]

Portia comes in, chastened in mood after her tense experience. Her first lines are radiant enough to have pierced through the densest fog overhanging the Elizabethan stage:

> That light we see is burning in my hall.
> How far that little candle throws his beams!
> So shines a good deed in a naughty world.

Once more it is the gracious woman of philosophic mind who speaks. She and Nerissa hear the music, and Portia remarks upon a mysterious truth—that music ever sounds lovelier at night. Nerissa adds with great point:

> Silence bestows that virtue on it.

(Had Shakespeare suffered, like all music-lovers, from the babble of talk in the audience while music was being performed?) Portia supplements the thought:

> The crow doth sing as sweetly as the lark
> When neither is attended, and I think
> The nightingale, if she should sing by day,
> When every goose is cackling, would be thought
> No better a musician than the wren.

Which explains why many a great poet has sung almost unheard by his contemporaries, who had ears only for the geese making their raucous music to the acclaim of the arbiters of current taste.

The two women are greeted by Lorenzo and Jessica. Soon Bassanio, Antonio, Gratiano, and their friends arrive. While Portia is busy welcoming Antonio, Nerissa has lost no time inquiring about the ring she gave Gratiano. He swears he gave it to the judge's clerk. In the heat of quarrel he wishes that the boy had been castrated, since Nerissa takes the matter so much to heart. She professes to believe (what is the truth) that he gave it to a woman. He protests:

> Now, by this hand, I gave it to a youth,
> A kind of boy, a little scrubbed boy,
> No higher than thyself. . . .

The comparison begins to endanger the fun. Lest Gratiano give further thought to the looks of that boy, Portia intercepts to take Nerissa's part. He was wrong to give away a ring he had sworn to keep, his wife's first gift; to shame him, she adds:

> I gave *my* love a ring, and made him swear
> Never to part with it; and here he stands.
> I dare be sworn for him he would not leave it
> Nor pluck it from his finger, for the wealth
> That the world masters. Now, in faith, Gratiano,
> You give your wife too unkind a cause of grief.
> An* 'twere to me, I should be mad at it.

Poor Bassanio probably draws the guilty hand behind him as he murmurs wretchedly:

> Why, I were best to cut my left hand off
> And swear I lost the ring defending it.

Gratiano, no heroic soul, does not wish to be alone in his trouble, and he at once defends himself by tattling: Bassanio gave his ring away too. Portia's pretended rising wrath and Bassanio's shame-faced abjectness are portrayed with delicious drollery by a hand that was past master at high comedy:

> PORTIA.   *What ring gave you*, my lord?
>   Not that, I hope, which you receiv'd of *me!*
> BASSANIO.   If I could add a lie unto a fault,
>   I would deny it. But you see—my finger
>   Hath not the ring upon it; it is gone.
> PORTIA.   Even so void is your false heart of truth!
>   By heaven, I will ne'er come in your bed
>   Until I see the ring.

A safe oath to make!

> BASSANIO.   Sweet Portia,
>   If you did know to whom I gave the ring,
>   If you did know *for* whom I gave the ring,
>   And would conceive for *what* I gave the ring,

* if

And how *unwillingly* I left the ring,
When nought would be accepted *but* the ring,
You would abate the strength of your displeasure.
PORTIA.   If you had known the virtue of the ring,
Or half her worthiness that gave the ring,
Or your own honour to contain the ring,
You would not then have parted with the ring. . . .
I'll die for't but some woman had the ring.

Bassanio swears by his soul that he gave it to a doctor of law, who would take nothing but the ring as recompense for saving his friend's life. Portia maintains an obdurate silence. He continues to plead. Had she been there, he assures her, she herself would have begged him to give the ring to the doctor. Portia feigns to become even angrier:

Let not that doctor e'er come near *my* house!
Since he hath got the jewel that I lov'd,
And that which you did swear to keep for me,
I will become as liberal as you.
I'll not deny him any thing I have,
No, not my body nor my husband's bed.
Know him I shall, I am well sure of it.
Lie not a night from home. Watch me like Argus.
If you do not, if I be left alone,
Now, by mine honour, which is yet mine own,
I'll have that doctor for my bedfellow.

[It would be a pity to miss the delightful, naughty *doubles-entendres* she makes throughout this speech, which she intends Bassanio to understand to vex him the more. No doubt they contribute too to the violence of Gratiano's explosion which follows. By the *jewel* she loved and which he swore to keep for her (alone) she has an anatomical detail in mind. *Liberal* also meant "licentious." She may be also using *know* in the sense of carnal knowledge. Gratiano's *pen* is obviously meant as a ribald pun in the outburst he presently makes.] Nerissa delivers a like threat, but Gratiano at the prospect is far from taking it as meekly as Bassanio:

NERISSA.   And I his clerk. Therefore be well advis'd
How you do leave me to mine own protection.

GRATIANO.   Well, do you so! Let me not take him then!
      For if I do, I'll mar the young clerk's pen!

Antonio is wretched to think himself responsible for this contention:

      I am the unhappy subject of these quarrels.

Quickly, Portia relieves him of any concern:

      Sir, grieve not you; you are welcome notwithstanding.

Bassanio continues to plead; she continues intransigent. Antonio moves to settle the quarrel, and takes an oath that Bassanio will never break his vow to her again. She now pretends to be conciliated for his sake:

      Then you shall be his surety. Give him this
      And bid him keep it better than the other.

She hands the ring to Antonio, who gives it to Bassanio.

      BASSANIO.   By heaven, it is the same I gave the doctor!
      PORTIA.   I had it of him. Pardon me, Bassanio;
        For, by this ring, the doctor lay with me.
      NERISSA.   And pardon me, my gentle Gratiano;
        For that same scrubbed boy, the doctor's clerk,
        In lieu of this last night did lie with me.
      GRATIANO.   Why, this is like the mending of highways
        In summer, where the ways are fair enough.

[Anyone driving an auto in the United States during the summer along the highways, when they seem forever to be undergoing repaving, may remember these lines with chagrin. Everything is to be found in Shakespeare.]

Portia at last briefly explains the roles she and Nerissa have played at the trial. Thus, in the last scene of the comedy, Shakespeare reintroduces the theme which figured in the casket scenes: One must never mistake appearance for reality. She and Nerissa seemed to be judge and clerk: they were but a pair of loving wives. The letter of the law seemed bound to triumph over compassion:

mercy won the day. Bassanio and Gratiano thought they were breaking their oaths in giving away the rings: they had only given them
into their wives' keeping. Back in Belmont circumstantial evidence
seems to indicate they had been unfaithful husbands: they are
proved to have kept faith.

In the glow of general happiness, Portia has good things to bestow upon the others too, gifts which complete this theme. Antonio has apparently lost everything: she has a letter for him informing him that three of his fleets have come home safe and richly
laden. [Shakespeare has her add,

> You shall not know by what strange accident
> I chanced on this letter.

Clever Shakespeare! He would have been hard put to it to account
for that. Not that he could not have devised something satisfactory,
for he was equal to every demand of his art. But he must have felt
that it would be only tedious for us to listen to explanations at this
last hour—tedious like those insufferable revelations in the last pages
of inferior detective novels. How she found the letter is of no consequence now, nor how his ships are safe after all. No one is going to
begrudge Antonio a return of good fortune.] Lorenzo and Jessica
have apparently a dubious future ahead of them: Portia delivers
to them the deed making them rich Shylock's heirs.

It is almost morning, and Portia suggests that they all go in.
With a light and final reference to legal processes, she bids the men

> charge us there upon inter'gatories,
> And we will answer all things faithfully.

[When a complaint was lodged against a person for a "contempt,"
he was sent before sentence was finally pronounced to the Crown
Office, and there was "charged upon interrogation" and asked to
swear that he would answer "all things faithfully." [8]]
Our great play, this treasure-house of high ideas, exquisite poetry,
tense drama, characters of flesh-and-blood reality, wit, and comedy
high and low, ends with a vivacious speech of Gratiano's, none the
less delightful for its ribaldry:

Let it be so. The first inter'gatory
That my Nerissa shall be sworn on is,
Whether till the next night she had rather stay,
Or go to bed now, being two hours to day.
But were the day come, I should wish it dark,
That I were couching with the doctor's clerk.*
Well, while I live I'll fear no other thing
So sore as keeping safe Nerissa's ring.

* In England the word is still pronounced "clark."

9

Other Men's Shylock

Then came each actor on his ass.—*Hamlet*, II, ii, 415.

: :

Interpretation will misquote our looks.—*Henry IV Part I*, V, ii, 14.

: :

More new-fangled than an ape.—*As You Like It*, IV, 1, 153.

: :

L'imitazione del bene è sempre inferiore.*—Guicciardini.

: :

C'est un bétail servile et sot à mon avis
Que les imitateurs.†—La Fontaine, *Clymène*, V.

: :

If he thinks imitation the sincerest flattery, let the fool flatter someone else!—Ebirgenär, *Hamletje*.

The Merchant of Venice in the text Shakespeare wrote was not presented, as has been said, for a century after the closing of the Elizabethan playhouses. But in 1701 an adaptation of the play written by George Granville and renamed *The Jew of Venice* was produced at Lincoln's Inn Fields, with Thomas Doggett, the comedian, as Shylock and the aging Betterton as Bassanio. From what is known about Doggett as an actor there is every reason to believe that he converted Shylock into a farcical character.[1] It is very likely that the tradition (which still persists among scholars) that Shylock was intended as a comic figure dates from Granville's perversion of the play, which held the stage for forty years. It has been forgotten that there was no connection between that adaptation and Shakespeare's conception of the play. On Doggett's death in 1721 the comedian Griffin inherited the role, continuing the same tradition.[2]

Granville's "improvements" on Shakespeare are too numerous to quote. But the sheer impudence of some of them cannot be overlooked here. Moreover, this perversion of the play is responsible for

---

* The imitation of what is excellent is always itself inferior.
† Imitators are a slavish herd and fools in my opinion.

many inherited misconceptions concerning it. In the scene where Shylock proposes his bond "in a merry sport" (I, iii, 145 seq.) Granville substituted this:

> SHYLOCK.   And that we may henceforth
> Be friends, no penalty will I exact
> But this, merely for mirth—
> If you repay me not on such a day, in such a place,
> Such sum or sums as are express'd—be this
> The forfeiture.
> Let me see. What think you of your nose,
> Or of an eye—or of—a pound of flesh
> To be cut off, and taken from what part
> Of your body I shall think fit to name.
> Thou art too portly, Christian!
> Too much pamper'd. What say you then
> To such a merry bond?
> ANTONIO.   The Jew grows witty; I'll seal to such a bond. . . .

Morocco, Arragon, Launcelot Gobbo, Salarino, Salanio, and Tubal are all omitted from this adaptation. When Jessica elopes with Lorenzo (II, vi, 58-9), we read:

> *Enter Jessica shutting the door after her.*
> JESSICA.   Shut doors after you; fast bind, fast find,
> These were his last words. Thus I avoid the
> Curse of disobedience! Be thou shut till I
> Open thee.
> LORENZO.   So whilst old Laban snor'd in bed,
> Jacob with sprightly Rachel fled.
> JESSICA.   His gold, and gems of price they took,
> And eke the flower of every flock. (*Holds up a bag.*)
> LORENZO.   But not one precious thing was there
> That could with Jessica compare.
>   *Enter Antonio.*
> ANTONIO.   Fly, fly, my friend, why do you loiter thus? . . .

[In Shakespeare's play—a fact which commentary has often forgotten—Antonio is in no way connected with the elopement of Jessica and Lorenzo.]

There follows a scene of the supper to which Shylock was invited.

(J. D. Wilson has argued that Shakespeare himself originally wrote such a scene which he later cut from the play.[3])

> *Scene opens and discovers Bassanio, Antonio, Shylock, and others, sitting, as at an entertainment. Music playing: during the music, Gratiano enters, and takes his place.*

ANTONIO.   This to immortal friendship. Fill it up.
　Be thou to me, and I to my Bassanio
　Like Venice and her Adriatic bride,
　For ever link'd in love.
BASSANIO.   Thou join'st us well, and rightly hast compared;
　Like Venice on a rock my friendship stands
　Constant and fix'd; but 'tis a barren spot;
　Whilst like the liberal Adriatic, thou
　With plenty bath'st my shores.
　My fortunes are the bounty of my friend.
ANTONIO.   My friend's the noblest bounty of my fortune.
　Sound every instrument of music there,
　To our immortal friendship. (*All drink. Loud music.*)
BASSANIO.   Let love be next. What else should
　Follow friendship?
　To love, and to love's queen, my charming Portia,
　Fill, till the rosy brim reflects her lips. . . .
　　(*Drink, and music again.*)
GRATIANO.   Mine's a short health: here's to the sex in general!
　To woman, be she black, or brown, or fair,
　Plump, slender, tall, or middle-statur'd—
　Let it be woman, and 'tis all I ask.
　　(*Drink again, and music as before.*)
SHYLOCK.   I have a mistress that outshines 'em all—
　Commanding yours—and yours though the whole sex:
　O may her charms increase and multiply!
　My money is my mistress! Here's to
　Interest upon interest!　(*Drinks.*)
ANTONIO.   Let birds and beasts of prey howl to such vows,
　All generous notes be hush'd. Pledge thyself, Jew!
　None here will stir the glass—　(*All rise.*)

Antonio confesses to Bassanio that music makes him melancholy, and Bassanio proceeds to deliver to him Lorenzo's speech intended for Jessica (V, i, 70 seq.) "The reason is, your spirits are attentive." There follows a Masque of Peleus and Thetis of some 150 dull lines, e.g.,

THETIS.   But see! the mighty Thund'rer's here,
   Tremble, Peleus, tremble, fly.
The Thunderer! the mighty Thunderer!
   Tremble, Peleus, tremble, fly.

Bassanio is about to depart for Belmont, and we are witness to the scene which Shakespeare only reported (II, viii, 36 seq.), here given in sickeningly sweet lengthiness. This is its conclusion:

BASSANIO.   One more embrace. To those who know not friendship
   This may appear unmanly tenderness,
   But 'tis the frailty of the bravest minds.
ANTONIO.   I ask but this, Bassanio:
   Give not your heart so far away,
   As to forget your friend.
   Come, is all ready? I must hasten you. . . .
BASSANIO.   Shylock, thy hand. Be gentle to my friend.
   Fear not thy bond. It shall be justly paid.
   We soon shall meet again,
   Always, I hope, good friends.
   Oh my Antonio! 'tis hard, though for a moment,
   To lose the sight of what we love.
SHYLOCK. (*Aside.*)   These two Christian fools put me in mind
   Of my money. Just so loath am I to part with that.
BASSANIO.   Gratiano, lead the way. Shylock, once more farewell.
   We must not part, but at the ship, Antonio.
   Lovers and friends, should they for ages stay,
   Would still find something left, that they would say.
                                                      (*Exeunt.*)

In the third act Bassanio is at Belmont, and he addresses Portia in a hodgepodge of lines originally written for Jessica (III, v, 84 seq.) and Morocco (II, i, 32 seq.):

   Why if two gods should play some heavenly match
   And on the wager lay two earthly beauties,
   And Portia one, there must be something more
   Pawn'd with the other, for the poor rude world
   Has not her equal. But alas the while!
   Should Hercules and Lichas play at dice
   Who were the better man? . . .

Some lines are allowed Portia from her own beautiful speech (III, ii, 1 seq.), though in a hideously garbled form. When she has decided that she never will be forsworn by telling him which casket to choose, she continues:

> For oh, what heavier curse for perjury
> Could Heaven provide than losing all my hope?
> I speak too much, though thought will have no bound.
> A virgin's tongue should shame to hint a thought
> At which a virgin's cheek should blush.
> Think it not love, yet think it what you please,
> So you defer a month or two. . . .
> BASSANIO. Doubt is the worst estate. 'Tis better once
> To die, than still to live in pain.
> Desire is fierce, nor brooks the least delay. . . .
> PORTIA. Yet let me persuade you. If for yourself
> You cannot fear, tremble for her—
> For her, to whom you have so often sworn
> More than yourself you love her. Think! oh think!
> On Portia's fate, who may not only lose
> The man by whom she wishes to be won,
> But being lost to him, remain expos'd
> To some new choice. . . .
> BASSANIO. To love, and to be lov'd, yet not possess,
> No greater curse could be, but what thou fear'st.
> Yet I will on. With double flames I burn,
> Knowing that Portia loves me; all my fear
> Was for her love. Secure of that I go
> Secure of the reward. Lead me to the caskets. . . .
> PORTIA. Thy courage is an omen of success.
> If love be just, he'll teach thee where to choose . . .
> Love that inflames thy heart inspire thy eyes,
> To choose aught where Portia is the prize.

The caskets themselves are offstage; naturally, therefore, the song in which Portia so endearingly plays upon Bassanio's subconscious thought so he may choose the right casket, is omitted. Bassanio reenters bearing in each hand a casket. He considers the motto on the silver casket and speaks the lines on the martlet which Shakespeare assigned to Arragon (II, ix, 28 seq.), and concludes:

> What may their merit be? again let me consider.
> (*Walks about thinking.*)

GRATIANO.   Take the gold, man, or the silver. Plague on't!
Would I were to choose for him!

Bassanio continues to quote Arragon's lines about the stamp of merit. Then:

> Let me not be rash,
> There yet remains a third. Well will I weigh
> Ere I resolve.   (*Exit.*)
>
> GRATIANO.   Take the gold, I say. Pox on lead, what is it good
> For but to make bullets? 'Tis the image of
> Death and destruction.
> (*Re-enter Bassanio with a casket of lead.*)

He speaks a highly corrupted version of the speech Shakespeare gave him, and chooses this casket.

> GRATIANO.   Undone, undone. I'll not stand to't, Nerissa, I'll
> Choose for myself.

Bassanio opens the casket and finds Portia's picture. He quotes a few of his authentic lines; then:

> The very odour
> Seems here express'd, and thus invites the taste. (*Kissing the picture*) . . .
>
> PORTIA.   Had choice decided, and not only chance,
> As fortune has dispos'd me, so had I.

She gives him the ring, saying that if he ever parts from it

> Let it presage the ruin of your love
> And stand, as a record, that you were false,
> A follower of my fortunes, not of me,
> And never meant me fair.
>
> BASSANIO.   Die first, Bassanio! My mistress and my queen,
> As absolute as ever shall you reign,
> Not as the lord, but vassal of your charms,
> Not as a conqueror, but acquisition.
> Not one to lessen, but enlarge your power,
> No more but this, the creature of your pleasure.
> As such receive the passionate Bassanio. . . .

(*Gratiano and Nerissa seem in earnest dispute.*)

GRATIANO. A bargain's a bargain, and I will have justice.

NERISSA. I say, we drew stakes.

GRATIANO. That was only in case I had lost, child.

PORTIA. A dispute between our friends! What's the matter, cousin?

GRATIANO. I'll tell you, madam, the matter in short, and you shall be judge.
I happen'd to say to this lady that it was her destiny to
Have me. She consented to put it to trial, and agreed
To be determined by the choice my friend should make. . . .

NERISSA. Ay! but he recanted, and said afterwards, he
Would choose for himself.

GRATIANO. Why sure so I can, now I know the right casket. . . .

Nerissa gives in, and Gratiano offers to bet the others a thousand ducats for the first boy.

NERISSA. Methinks this looks like the last act of a play:
All parties are agreed. There remains nothing but
To draw the curtain and put out the lights.

GRATIANO. A good hint, my love. Let you and I make our Exit
About that same last act. . . .

Bassanio congratulates him and thinks how pleased Antonio will be of their success:

Shylock shall now be paid, my friend is safe,
And happiness on every side surrounds us.

The news from Venice now arrives with Lorenzo, Jessica, and a servant of Antonio's. The text more or less follows Shakespeare. Portia bids Bassanio hasten to Antonio's side.

BASSANIO. O love! O friendship!
Was ever man thus tortured?

GRATIANO. What, not one quarter of an hour to pack up
My baggage?

NERISSA. Whereabouts is the last act now, Gratiano?

GRATIANO. Faith, child, I have the part ready
If I might have leave to play it.

PORTIA. Away, ye triflers!

Nay, then, Bassanio, I must thrust you from me.
'Tis hard for both to be divided thus
Upon our wedding-day. But honour calls,
And love must wait, honour that still delights
To tyrannize o'er love. . . .

They leave. Portia entrusts her household to Jessica and Lorenzo. There is the scene with Shylock, Antonio, and the Gaoler, badly garbled. Shylock makes Antonio responsible for Jessica's elopement, and invokes some of the curses upon her originally spoken to Tubal.

The fourth act is the trial scene, whose opening passages more or less follow Shakespeare with many amputations. After Gratiano's calling Shylock a wolf (IV, i, 128 seq.), Granville writes:

SHYLOCK. Thou but offends thy lungs to speak so loud.
    Thy curses fall on thy own head, for thus
    Ensnaring thy best friend; thou didst it, and not I.
    I stand for law. Thy prodigality brought him
    To this.
BASSANIO. Inhuman dog!

Portia and Nerissa come in. The "quality of mercy" speech is also altered; the "gentle rain" becomes "gentle dew"; several lines are omitted; "It is an attribute to God himself" is changed to "It is the first of sacred attributes." As the scene proceeds, Shylock hails Portia not only as a second Daniel but also as "a second Solomon." When Antonio takes his farewell of Bassanio, the second half is thus altered:

An age of poverty, from which lingering penance
She kindly cuts me off. Once more farewell.
Grieve not my friend that thus you lose a friend,
For I repent not thus to pay your debt
Even with my blood and life. Now do your office.
Cut deep enough, be sure, and whet thy knife
With keenest malice, for I would have my heart seen by
My friend.
SHYLOCK. Doubt it not, Christian; thus far I will be courteous.

Bassanio now rises to the occasion:

Stand off. I have a word in his behalf,
Since even more than in his avarice,
In cruelty this Jew's insatiable.
Here stand I for my friend, body for body,
To endure the torture. But one pound of flesh
Is due from him. Take every piece of mine,
And tear it off with pincers. Whatever way
Invention can contrive to torture man,
Practice on me. Let but my friend go safe.
Thy cruelty is limited on him;
Unbounded let it loose on me. Say, Jew,
Here's interest upon interest in flesh—
Will that content you?

ANTONIO.   It may him, not me.

BASSANIO.   Cruel Antonio.

ANTONIO.   Unjust Bassanio.   (*Jew laughs.*)

[Well he may!]

SHYLOCK.   To hear a fool propose! Thou shallow Christian!
To think that I'd consent! I know thee well:
When he has paid the forfeit of his bond,
Thou canst not choose but hang thyself for being
The cause, and so my ends are serv'd on both.
Proceed to execution.

BASSANIO.   Then thus I interpose. (*Draws and stands before Antonio. The Jew starts back. Antonio interposes.*)

ANTONIO.   Forbear, Bassanio. This is certain death
To both.

BASSANIO.   In one, both die, since it must be,
No matter how.

DUKE.   Before our face this insolence! And in a court
Of justice. Disarm and seize him.

PORTIA.   Spare him, my lord! I have a way to tame him.
Hear me one word.

SHYLOCK.   Hear, hear the doctor. Now for a sentence
To sweep these Christian vermin, coupled,
To the shambles. O 'tis a Solomon!

PORTIA.   Hark you, Shylock, I have view'd this bond,
And find it gives thee not one drop of blood.

She proceeds to warn him of his risk. "Shylock starts surprised," saying, "Humph." Bassanio appropriates Gratiano's lines mocking him,

"O upright judge" etc. The scene continues (with some omissions and alterations) more or less as Shakespeare wrote it, up through Shylock's exit. After Portia and Nerissa have left and Bassanio has sent Gratiano with the ring after Portia, Bassanio continues:

> Once more let me embrace my friend. Welcome to life,
> And welcome to my arms, thou best of men.
> Thus of my love and of my friend possess'd
> With such a double shield upon my breast,
> Fate cannot pierce me now, securely blest.

In the last act there are changes and omissions. But especially noteworthy are the additions after Portia gives the ring to Antonio to hand to Bassanio:

> BASSANIO.   By Heav'n!   (*Starts.*)
> This is the same I gave the lawyer.
> PORTIA.   Why so it is: I had it from him. You see
> How quick an operation is in magic.
> We have met already.
> BASSANIO.   Met? How have you met?
> NERISSA.   Met—why by art magic, to lie together.
> Ask that same scrubbed boy, the lawyer's clerk.
> GRATIANO.   Why this is worse and worse.
> BASSANIO.   Antonio! This was your doing! (*Angrily.*)
> ANTONIO.   Take your revenge and kill me.
> BASSANIO.   I am answer'd—Is it then true?
> And can it be?—that by secret workings
> Of mystic words and spells and dire compounds,
> Potions and invocations horrible,
> Nature can be so led. What then is Virtue?
> And what security has love or reason,
> Thus subjected to every Hell-born hag,
> Who by such conjurations can disjoin
> United hearts? Uniting the averse!
> How, wretched man, how can'st thou boast free will
> If this in very deed be true? I'll not suppos't—
> But then that ring! How could she have it? 'Tis witchcraft,
> Damn'd, damn'd witchcraft! And I will fathom Hell,
> But I will find a fiend shall counter-work
> The devil that has done this. (*Portia and Nerissa laugh.*)

[And well *they* may!]
Portia now reveals the facts, but in order to win Bassanio out of his
moodiness she must call upon Lorenzo and Jessica to substantiate
her leaving soon after Bassanio's departure for Venice. He, after all
his declamation now declares:

> Amazement has bereft me of all words.

Antonio reads the letter assuring him of the safe return of his vessels, and Portia delivers a little sermon:

> Doubt it not, Antonio. 'Tis most true,
> Virtue like yours, such patience in adversity,
> And in prosperity such goodness,
> Is still the care of Providence.

Gratiano has his little jest about keeping safe Nerissa's ring, but so
phrased as to rob it of its ribald humor. Granville's Portia, in her last
speech, cannot refrain from lecturing her husband in a style that
promises ill for his enjoyment of marriage:

> Cease your astonishment,
> My lord. By these small services to you
> And to your friends, I hope I may secure
> Your love, which, built upon mere fancy,
> Had else been subjected to alteration.
> With age and use the rose, grown sick and faint,
> Thus mixed with friendly sweets, secures its scent.

And Bassanio is allotted the final speech, depressing in its dreari-
ness:

> The sweets of love shall here forever blow.
> I needs must love, rememb'ring what I owe.
> Love, like a meteor, shows a short-liv'd blaze,
> Or treads through various skies a wand'ring maze,
> Begot by Fancy, and by Fancy led,
> Here in a moment, in a moment fled;
> But fixt by Obligations, it will last,
> For Gratitude's the charm that binds it fast.

It is fair to say that my having omitted whole portions of Granville's adaptation makes it seem, dreadful though it appear, actually better than it is. It must seem incredible that this, not Shakespeare's play, held the boards for forty years, and in twenty-five years went into six printed editions. It is, of course, an execrable performance. The verse is not only wretched but also pretentious, not merely clumsy and unmusical but inflated and without rhythm. Noble Bassanio is converted into a foolish mouther of empty rhetoric; Portia into a self-righteous pedant; Shylock into a piece of ridiculous confusion. To account for the long life of this abomination, however, one must remember that Shakespeare's play was unknown to the theaters and that only readers of the relatively few available editions of the play could have guessed the mayhem wrought upon the original.

Not that a familiarity with Shakespeare's play would necessarily have made a difference. The neo-classical era, now fashionable to admire ever since T. S. Eliot and his disciples have made it à la mode to sneer at Milton, Shelley, and Browning, raised a tremendous fuss about "good taste," but it is astonishing to see how little one can discover of it in the most representative writers of the period. [More recently Mr. Eliot decided to admit Milton into the narrow circle of acceptable poets; but his disciples seem not aware that the ban has been lifted.] By Granville's day the public were quite habituated to and pleased with dreadful "versions" of Shakespeare made by D'Avenant and others, and no one can be charmed with the tamperings which even Dryden permitted himself with Shakespeare's works. If Granville's piece is shocking in its vulgarity to us today, it was not so to his contemporaries. He was, according to his own and their lights, merely bringing Shakespeare up-to-date —a practice richly indulged by our own contemporaries. Jack Landau (who, in his direction of the plays at Stratford, Connecticut, at a theater presumably built to do justice to Shakespeare's works, has been staggeringly unrelenting in his avoidance of Shakespeare's meaning, play after play, by thinking of novel ways of presenting them) justifies this procedure in an article entitled, "The Key to Production Is the Present," written for *Theatre Arts*, August 1961: What is the point, he asks, of producing "Shakespeare's plays the way they were done for an Elizabethan audience? Doesn't it make more sense to find what the plays mean for us in our time?" If the answer to that question is to be based upon Landau's productions—

remembering how he has found the meaning for our time by converting the brilliant poetry and mordant satire of *Measure for Measure* into a slapstick farce, or by drowning *Troilus and Cressida* in the magnolia scent and rebel yells of the American Civil War, to mention only two of his original ideas—I should have to answer in the negative. It is hard to be severe with Granville for doing what many other directors have been doing to Shakespeare in our own time by bringing him up-to-date according to *their* notions.

The superficiality of such a doctrine has been demonstrated for some years now by Joseph Papp in his series of brilliant productions in New York, which have been tireless in their desire to extract Shakespeare's meaning. Papp's audience has no admission charge to pay; it represents the broadest possible sector of the public, as did Shakespeare's audience. Yet that public attends regularly in multitudes to witness performances that prefer honesty to cleverness or novelty. Papp worries chiefly about one thing that few Shakespearean directors trouble themselves about: he insists that his actors understand every word that they are saying, and hence the audience is in a position to understand what Shakespeare is saying. His credo is expressed in an article in the same issue of *Theatre Arts:* "The challenge for the director therefore is to achieve this modernity [i.e., presenting characters that are believable with whom the audience can identify] without sacrificing the form and poetry of Shakespeare, and without vulgarizing the period." Excellent theory, and conscientiously put, season after season, into practice. No wonder Papp's successes have been so phenomenal!

It has been worthwhile, I believe, reprinting as much as I have of Granville's miserable work for several reasons. To turn from it back to Shakespeare's play is to enjoy a livelier appreciation of how magnificent *The Merchant of Venice* is. It is instructive merely to see what might have been done with his material by another hand. Also it ought to be a salutary corrective for the hard-to-kill insistence upon viewing Shakespeare as merely a representative of his times. In George Granville we have a perfect specimen of what it signifies to be a representative of one's era and nothing more. In him we find everything his times approved of, from the silly gallantries of the lovers, through the absurd histrionics at the Trial Scene, to the colorless abstractions of Bassanio's final speech. He was simply no better than his times, and that will not do. To survive you have to be better than your times—as were Swift, Pope, and Addison. It is in addition valuable to know something of Granville's play because, in my opinion, one may trace in it the origins of many misconceptions, still current, concerning *The Merchant of Venice*, such as the oft-repeated notion that Shylock was intended to be comic, that Portia is a cold woman, that Bassanio is a contemptible man, that there is something too much about the love between Antonio and Bassanio. Forty years is a long time for a conception to have sway without a rival. And the history of Shylock on the stage reveals few instances of an attempt to present before the public the play Shakespeare actually wrote.

When Charles Macklin undertook, on February 14, 1741, to revive Shakespeare's own play at the Drury Lane from its century of slumber, he "encountered nothing but derision," for his colleagues "believed that a serious treatment of Shylock would be only an arrogant and presumptuous display." [4] On opening night the theater was filled in every location within minutes of the doors' being opened. By the middle of the play he was greeted with uproarious applause. [5]

Macklin's interpretation presented Shylock as a detestable monster. It was at least a healthy corrective to Doggett's acting him as a farcical character. He made him so venomous that rumor began to have it that Macklin himself was a kind of devil. This Irishman, born McLaughlin, had in fact killed a fellow-actor six years earlier in a quarrel, but had been acquitted. No doubt his Shylock was so much of a shock to that "polite" age that he himself was confused by the audience with the part he played, and the part he played had superimposed upon it the recollection of him as a murderer.

But the production's Kitty Clive, cast as Portia, played her role flippantly, and introduced various pieces of comic business to burlesque the well-known mannerisms of a famous lawyer, Lord Mansfield. The contrast between such conduct and Macklin's savagery must have made for absurd effects. At later performances various extraneous matters were introduced to please the tastes of the time, with a consequent halting of the movement. Since Portia had a song, Lorenzo and Jessica were each given one too. This was Jessica's:

> Haste, Lorenzo, haste away,
> To my longing arms repair;

With impatience I shall die!
Come and ease thy Jessy's care! . . .[6]

A divertissement called *The Belle of the Village* was interpolated at the end of the third act, and a dance, *The Arcadian Festival,* at the end of the fourth.

Nevertheless, Macklin's Shylock, which provided the tradition for the next sixty years, although he did not make the Jew credible as a human being, performed a real service to Shakespeare. He rescued the role from Doggett's farcical perversion of it, and his artistic seriousness in studying it was entirely admirable. Pope so much admired his performance that he composed for him, in advance, this epitaph:

> This is the Jew
> That Shakespeare drew.[7]

Macklin himself enacted the role for the next fifty years. After a lifetime of triumph in the part, his last appearance was a pathetic one. On May 7, 1789, when he was nearly one hundred years old—he is said to have been born in May 1690—he appeared in a performance for his own benefit. He prepared himself with his habitual care, and entering the green-room came up to Mrs. Pope to say, "My dear, are you to play tonight?" "Good God! to be sure I am, sir," she replied; "Why don't you see I am dressed for Portia?" "Ah! very true," he answered absently, "I had forgot. But who is to play Shylock?" Everyone present was mightily disturbed at his "inane look" while he spoke. Mrs. Pope forced herself to say, "Why you are, to be sure; are not you dressed for the part?" He then appeared to recollect himself, but putting his hand to his forehead exclaimed pathetically, "God help me—my memory, I am afraid, has left me." He nevertheless appeared on the stage. At first he delivered his lines almost meaninglessly, then seemed to rouse himself. But soon he could not continue, and came forward to apologize to the audience that he could not proceed any further, begging them to accept the understudy as a substitute. The audience applauded him with affection and pity.[8] He survived another eight years, but never attempted acting again.

The Shylocks after Macklin seem to have adopted his interpretation of a malicious, inhuman moneylender—with, of course, such little variations as all actors feel required to make to establish their individuality. Until well past the first decade of the nineteenth century Shylock was now a blood-chilling fiend, provoking the hatred and animosity of all the audiences who beheld him. Garrick, oddly enough, never attempted the part.

A new tradition for the role was introduced when Edmund Kean appeared as Shylock at the Drury Lane on January 26, 1814. He was only twenty-seven at the time. An actor since his childhood, he was nearly unknown to the London public. He had already performed a fiendish Shylock, in imitation of Macklin, in the provinces. As John Doran vividly recreates the young man's bold venture in London, Kean, still sorrowing from the death of his five-year-old son, to whom he had been passionately devoted, at Drury Lane "stood in that cold hall, a little, pale, restless, dark-eyed man, in a coat with two or three capes, and nobody noticed him! In Cecil Street his family were living on little more than air; and he was daily growing sick, as he stood, waiting in that hall, for an audience with the manager, and subject to the sneers of passing actors." Even the actors he had played with ignored him; no one would grant him an opportunity to show what he could do with Shylock. Several others, while he still waited, were granted the part, and failed. Finally, the management agreed to let him appear, but as Richard. " 'Shylock, or nothing!' was his bold reply. He was afraid of the littleness of his figure . . . [and] hoped to hide it under the gown of Shylock. The Jew, or nothing!" At last he was granted what he sought. There was but one rehearsal, the morning of the performance. At it his fellow-actors and the manager were unnerved by his originality, the latter exclaiming, " 'Sir, this will never do! It is quite an innovation; it cannot be permitted.' 'Sir,' said the poor, proud man, 'I wish it to be so.' " Up to the very performance almost no one had even spoken to him. On the way to the theater that night, " 'I wish,' he remarked, 'I was going to be shot!' " He dressed himself and went down to the wing. There he began to create a sensation by wearing not a red wig but a black one. The house was half empty. But during his very first scene, he was interrupted several times by increasing applause. By the third act there was "a very whirlwind of approbation," despite the fewness of the spectators.[9] From that night on Edmund Kean was for his times the undisputed genius of the London stage.

Instead of the Shylock his immediate predecessors had exhibited, "a decrepit old man, bent with age and ugly with mental deformity, grinning with deadly malice, with the venom of his heart congealed in the expression of his countenance, sullen, morose, gloomy, inflexible, brooding over one idea, that of his hatred, and fixed on one unalterable purpose, that of his revenge"—as Hazlitt described the pre-Kean moneylender[10]—Kean showed him as vigorous and handsome, and a man of intellect. At the conclusion of the Trial Scene, his very appearance seemed to change, and he was able by his brilliant control of his voice to alter the audience's feelings from hatred to pity. He managed to leave the stage with such dignity that he had made them even sympathetic to him. Some critics objected to such an innovation, but the public liked it very much. As the part grew on him Kean portrayed Shylock more and more as "a persecuted martyr who, through the forces of circumstances, finally became an avenger."

This is the Shylock who has not yet disappeared from the boards. Though they were not up to Kean's dynamic intensity—Douglas Jerrold compared his Shylock to a chapter of *Genesis*[11]—Kean's contemporaries began at once to imitate his performance. In 1817 Dowton attempted to add to the pathos. His Shylock appeared in court with some fellow-Jews. At the announcement that he would have to become a Christian, he fell into their arms in a faint.[12] The audience roared with laughter.[13]

In 1820 Kean brought the play to the United States, where it was produced under the title of *Shylock*. In New York he was a great success, and *The Post* hailed him as the most accomplished actor the metropolis had ever seen. But Boston was at first indifferent and then hostile to him. On the third night, perceiving that there were only twenty persons in the house, he canceled the performance. This conduct was at once construed as an outrage to the city, and the newspapers began to attack him. He went back to England and did not return to America until 1825. In that year Boston's animosity had been so well fed by his reputation as a tippler and the widespread rumors of his extra-marital liaisons, that he was forbidden by the city fathers to appear in that city at all. That gave the cue for the rest of America, and for a time the public was lukewarm in its approval of his acting. Indeed, it became something of a demonstration of a woman's respectability that she would not be seen at an Edmund Kean performance.

In 1823 William Charles Macready, one of the most prominent actors of the time, challenged the Kean interpretation by bringing back a harsh Shylock. But it was one of his least successful roles.

Edmund Kean's son, Charles, inherited his father's interpretation of the role, but he was deficient in acting ability. Possibly for that reason, he turned his attention more to the technical resources of the theater. With him began the lamentable practice of engulfing Shakespeare's plays in "effects," so that the play becomes less of a drama than a spectacular pageant. He developed a talent for handling large groups of people on the stage, and wherever he went it was his custom to advertise for scores of extras. Through his version of *The Merchant of Venice* "there passed throngs of nobles, citizens, inquisitors, traders, foreigners, water-carriers and flower girls." [14]

It is no doubt with such productions in mind that the editor of the New Cambridge Shakespeare could write such unscholarly claptrap as this to provide the reader a setting for the play:

> We are in Venice—with all Vanity Fair . . . in full swing on her quays; grave merchants trafficking, porters sweating with bales, water-carriers, flower-girls, gallants; vessels lading, discharging, repairing; and up the narrower waterways black gondolas shooting under high guarded windows, any gondola you please hooding a secret of love, or assassination, or both—as any shutter in the line may open demurely, discreetly, giving just room enough, just time enough for a hand to drop a rose. Venice again at night—lanterns on the water, masked revelers taking charge of the quays with drums, hautboys, fifes, and general tipsiness; withdrawn from this riot into deep intricacies of shadow, the undertone of lutes complaining their love. [15]

This is the Venice of grand opera, but not of Shakespeare, who, of all the world's writers, was least interested in "local color." He probably never in his life had crossed the English Channel. With only an unlighted, unadorned wooden platform for a stage, Shakespeare was concerned with the dramatic issues, not the scenic effects. And whenever it was important for his dramatic purposes to provide something like a scenic effect, he much preferred to evoke moonlight than gondolas on a canal. Unfortunately, as the nineteenth century progressed, the tendency initiated by Charles Kean became an obsession, until by the end of it Sir Herbert Beerbohm Tree was giving Shakespeare that was all spectacle and no play.

In 1858 Charles Kean opened the play with "a throng of picturesque Venetians, nobles, inquisitors, flower girls, water-carriers" and the Doge, before Antonio and his friends emerged from the crowd to speak. For the second act he used a set which included "a bridge, under which gondolas pass and repass." Later when Jessica eloped she was carried off in a gondola. At the end of the act, just before the curtain, there was a "rush of illuminated gondolas." [16] Irving later employed such a set, too.

Junius Brutus Booth, father of the celebrated Edwin Booth, was so anxious to extend the sympathy which Edmund Kean had been the first to win for Shylock, that he went so far as to attend a synagogue often in order to study Jewish ways. He probably delivered Shylock's speeches in a Yiddish dialect, in the interests of realism. Thomas R. Gould described his interpretation as that of "the *representative Hebrew:* the type of a race as old as the world. He drew the character in lines of simple grandeur, and filled it with fiery energy. In his hands it was marked by pride of intellect; by intense pride of race; by a reserved force, as if there centered in him the might of a people whom neither time nor scorn, nor political oppression could subdue." [17]

Edwin Booth, his famous son, in a letter to Furness gave an account of his own conception of the role:

> My notion of Shylock is of the traditional type. . . . Not the buffoon that Dogget gave . . . , but the strongly marked and somewhat grotesque character which Macklin restored to the stage, and in which he was followed by Cooke, by Edmund Kean, and by my Father. 'Tis nonsense to suppose that Shylock was represented in other than a serious vein by Burbadge [sic]. . . . Is there any authority for the assertion which some make that he also wore a long nose? What if he did? A clever actor once played the part of Tubal with me, and wore red hair and a hook'd nose. He did not make the audience laugh; 'twas not his purpose. . . . Not till Lansdowne's bastard [i.e., George Granville's] came did the Jew make the unskilful laugh and the judicious grieve. . . . [Shylock] must, to a certain extent, be repulsive, a sort of party that one doesn't care to see among the dainty revellers of Venice. . . . It has been said that he is an affectionate father and a faithful friend. When,

where, and how does he manifest the least claim to such commendation? [18]

Edwin Booth presented *The Merchant of Venice* at the Haymarket in 1861, after having shown it in Australia. His Shylock, says Lelyveld, was "a man so disappointed in his avarice and so gratified at the thought of revenge, that his utterance was choked when he attempted to express these sentiments." [19] However, he was roundly criticized in New York for the "fierce malignity and noise of his speech," which would, said *The Times* for February 4, 1867, "consign him inevitably to the Station House"; there were moments when he "positively ranted. . . . Throughout the piece there was a constant effort to make the character melodramatic."

In Shylock's first soliloquy, at the words, "If I can catch him once upon the hip," Booth caused his hand to clutch as "rigidly as a claw," and with an imaginary victim in his grasp, dashed "its prey toward a devouring maw." At his "to bait fish withal," Booth sometimes made a gesture "as if holding a fishing rod," but at others his gesture implied that he was "tearing the flesh, and throwing it into the sea." At Tubal's report of Antonio's losses, he flung his arms over his head, and came "staggering down in mighty strides to the footlights in a delirium of revengeful joy." In Booth's acting version, when Shylock draws his knife to take the pound of flesh, Antonio advanced to stage-center and kneeled, while all the rest shrank back. [In Charles Calvert's production at Manchester, at this point of the drama, the prompt-book read: "A tableau is formed, accompanied by an orchestral clash and the sound of a gong." Antonio then "retires into a dark recess conveniently exposed as the intended scene of the ghastly operation." [20]] At the judgment that he must become a Christian, Booth's Shylock uttered a sharp groan, staggered backward, and raised his face with a look of utter despair, and then collapsed.[21] Like some of his predecessors, Booth ended the play with Shylock's exit. This cavalier excision of the rest of the fourth act and all of the fifth did much, one imagines, to propagate the false notion that Shylock is the central character of the play.

The most celebrated of all Shylocks was Henry Irving. His success with *The Merchant of Venice* when he presented it in London at the Royal Lyceum Theatre on November 1, 1879, is one of the legends of theatrical history. He had no natural endowments. Of medium height, ungainly slender figure, weak voice, he compensated for these shortcomings by the care and thought with which he prepared his productions. Instead of forging a new Shylock, his method was to present an eclectic one, incorporating what he considered the best of his predecessors). If there was anything new about his portrayal, it was his deepening of the audience's sympathies for the Jew.

A fairly lively idea of his presentation can be had from the account in *The Theatre* for December 1879:

> Irving evidently believes that Shakespeare intended to enlist our sympathies on the side of the Jew. . . . The fierceness associated with the character since Macklin appeared in it is not absent. Except in the scene with Tubal, where passion will out, the bearing of this Shylock is distinguished by a comparatively quiet and tranquil dignity. . . . He feels and acts as one of a noble but long-oppressed nation. . . . In point of intelligence and culture he is far above the Christians with whom he comes into contact, and the fact that as a Jew he is deemed far below them in the social scale is gall and wormwood to his proud and sensitive spirit. . . . [He] appears under three different aspects. First of all he is the usurer, then the outraged father, and finally the vengeful creditor. Mr. Irving's appearance is in harmony with this view of the part. He comes forward as a man between fifty and sixty years of age, infirm enough to need the support of a stick, with an iron-gray wisp of beard. . . . A picturesque background is at the outset provided for this striking figure by a view of the Palace of St. Mark with a quay on which porters are landing bales of merchandise. Mr. Irving's acting here is studiously quiet in tone, but full expression is given to the religious fervour of the Jew, the sense of wrong which rankles in his bosom, the undercurrent of sarcasm in his affected humility. . . . In the Scene where the loan is agreed upon we have a fine illustration of the text; the Jew touches Antonio on the heart, [(!) See p. 196.] and, seeing Antonio recoil from him, apologizes for his error by a bow. . . . The background of the Scene of Jessica's elopement is formed of Shylock's house at night, with a bridge over the canal which flows by it, and with a votive lamp to the Virgin on the wall. There a barcarolle is sung by some Venetians in a gondola, and a number of masqueraders rush merrily past. The noise having subsided, the curtain drops, to be raised a few moments afterwards—a pleasing innovation—to exhibit Shylock returning without any suspicion of Jessica's treachery to his plundered and deserted home. [See p. 157.] . . . The Scene which follows . . . [shows] his reason seem[ing] to reel under the heavy

blow it has received, and the brief allusion to his dead wife is full of pathos and tenderness. The father is here more visible than the usurer. Then comes the fierce thirst for revenge. . . . By the time of the Trial, however, the storm has subsided into a dead calm. . . . In the Duke's Court,—a fine mediaeval chamber, with portraits of Venetian dignitaries of times gone by on the walls, and with a crowd of deeply-interested spectators, including Tubal and other Jews, at the back—he slowly and gravely comes in. . . . He stands there like a figure of Fate,—pitiless, majestic, implacable. . . . His face wears a hard, set expression, relieved at long intervals by a glance of bitter hate towards Antonio, or a faint smile of triumph. Nor is this superb calm less conspicuous when the cause turns against him. The scales drop from his hands, but that is all. . . . Eventually, crushed by the conditions on which his life is spared, he stalks with a heavy sigh from the Court, only stopping to cast a look of deep pity at the ribald youth who is barking like a cur at his heels.

All this is, no doubt, impressive theater, but it has small connection with the play Shakespeare wrote. No wonder George Bernard Shaw castigated Irving for disemboweling Shakespeare! [See p. 157.] This sentimental Shylock, perfect for most Victorian tastes, would have astonished Shakespeare. Nevertheless, its influence on later interpretations (including those of the critics) has persisted.

Among other touches added by Irving, these are of interest: After Antonio and Bassanio had left, the bond having been agreed to, Shylock remained on the stage, "raising his stick and shaking it menacingly" at them. During the trial, when Bassanio offered the ducats, Shylock tapped the offered coins with his knife. Ellen Terry, the Portia of the production—it was said to be her greatest role— when Bassanio had chosen the right casket, "crumbled some roses and allowed the leaves to flutter down into the leaden casket"; then she bent over it, and "seemed to consecrate it with a kiss." [22] (Apparently, as this production was staged, while Bassanio was choosing, Portia must have been breathing down his neck.)

Lelyveld notes that during the past fifty years, *The Merchant of Venice* has been produced more often than any Shakespearean play except *Hamlet*.[23]

The vast success of Irving was a tax on the ingenuity of the Shylocks who came after him. William Poel in 1898 brought back a comic conception of the character. Herbert Beerbohm Tree was content to accept Irving's as a model, but he was evidently not half so impressive. Alexander Woolcott found him too effeminate and given to too much tossing about of the arms. Beerbohm Tree was, as his younger brother, the incomparable Max Beerbohm, confided to S. N. Behrman, devoted to the huge and monumental;[24] his production featured the Jewish quarter of Venice, exhibiting linen hanging on lines to add to the realism; later the Jews were seen going into their synagogue in the second act, and their prayers were heard. Tree not only followed Irving in having Shylock return to an empty house, he tore into the house and raged through its rooms, "appearing now at this window and now at that," [25] until he collapsed. Then he dashed into the street again and began tearing his garments to ribbons. Then he sprinkled ashes upon his head—in case anyone had missed the point. Tree had many admirers and they loved to hear his celebrated roars and shrieks.

Richard Mansfield in the earlier decades of our century won great acclaim for his Shylock of the long gray beard. He seems to have moved over the years from the portrait of a sympathetic moneylender to a repulsive one. When Shylock first greets Antonio, at "Your worship was the last man in our mouths," he spat to express his loathing. In his scene with Jessica he tenderly embraced her and kissed her on the forehead. When, like Irving's Jew, he returned to find her gone, he came out of the house with a "yell of surprise and agony at his loss and rushed into the street amid the hoots of delighted Christians." At the Trial Scene, Shylock was again present with his friends; they inspected the offered ducats and pleaded with him to accept them; Shylock paused, and then dashed the gold to the ground.[26]

E. H. Sothern's production opened "with an operatic overture on a street scene crowded with singers, mandolin players, a fortune teller, a flower seller and two fruit stands." [27] Shylock himself was gotten up to look like Michelangelo's Moses.

Twentieth-century Shylocks have largely tried to outdo one another in finding new pieces of business or new effects to justify their claims to originality. Nat Goodwin, when he returned to Shylock's house to find Jessica gone, "was heard crying out within the house, then appeared once more, distraught and dishevelled, bearing in his hand a letter." [28] Robert B. Mantell, whom I saw when I was a boy and can still remember for his ability to tear a passion to tatters, appeared in Puritan costume. Walter Hampden cut Portia's first scene in order to emphasize the hatefulness of his Shylock; in its place was presented the scene in which Gobbo decides to leave Shylock's employ. The most anticipated Shylock of our century was David Warfield's, presented by Belasco in the early 1920's. It was a colossal failure. It outdid Tree's lavishness and vied with Granville in the wanton distortion of the text. Warfield's portrayal was of a petty, forlorn little Jew, lost in the extravagance of the sets. When, at his last exit, Shylock was about to leave the courtroom, a monk present lifted a crucifix before him, while the others jeered aloud at him.[29] George Arliss was, as ever, George Arliss in the role, urbane and faintly snobbish; he made no bid for sympathy. Parrott has described Gielgud's performance at the Old Vic in 1932 as "something like a fairy tale, through which the figure of Shylock moved like that of a big bad wolf in the Disney films." [30] To anyone familiar with Gielgud's genius as an actor in other plays this judgment is rather hard to accept. At Stratford-on-Avon Emlyn Williams more recently presented a Shylock "in dirty clothes and matted hair." [31] It was not a success.

Mrs. Toby Lelyveld, to whose brilliant *Shylock on the Stage* I have been happy to confess my indebtedness for many a detail in this chapter, lists a number of women who have undertaken to perform Shylock (though only God knows why they were encouraged to do so): Clara Fisher, Charlotte Cushman, Mrs. Macready, and Lucille La Verne. (The number of women who have undertaken Hamlet is much greater.[32]) To see photographs of these ladies fully bewhiskered is a rewarding experience for anyone. But more remarkable than any of these was the well-considered Shylock presented by Ellen Bateman when she was four years of age; her older sister Kate, aged six, was Portia.[33] That was a performance worth the missing!

Our summary of the leading Shylocks, while revealing here and there some semblance to Shakespeare's original, indicates no single performance that was an accurate representation of the moneylender Shakespeare created. Indeed, most of these actors seem to have been less concerned with what Shakespeare meant than with improving upon it. This, by and large, continues to be the rule in all of Shakespeare's plays; it would be fair to say that he is generally worse acted than any other important dramatist. That is because actors and directors almost never think of themselves as the medium through which Shakespeare is addressing an audience; it is their frame of mind to look upon his plays as a medium for themselves. To find an actor or director who is primarily concerned with delivering Shakespeare's ideas is as rare as to find a Toscanini among musicians, and for the same reasons. The traditions of Shakespearean acting have operated more in the direction of confusing the meaning of his plays than in elucidating them. What is badly needed is to discard the acting traditions and begin again with a fresh desire to understand the plays as Shakespeare wrote them, and to act them not for novel effects but for comprehensibility.

Shakespeare has also been tampered with by other writers. It is easy enough to understand how a man with a sense of fun might be moved to write a burlesque of something inane or pretentious, particularly if it has been acclaimed without desert. But it is very hard to understand why some people are constantly tempted to burlesque the magnificent. *The Merchant of Venice* has come in for its share of that.

Shylock, or the Merchant of Venice Preserved, "an entirely New Reading of Shakespeare by Francis Talfourd," was presented at the Royal Olympic Theatre in 1853 with Frederick Robson in the title role. The oddest thing about this performance is that Robson was connected with it, for he had been highly praised for his performances in tragedy. Allowing for omissions, Talfourd's piece follows the Shakespearean synopsis fairly closely. It is a puzzle to decide what is being satirized; the burlesque about "a Jew who does not on this occasion conduct himself as a Gentile-man," seems to have been written only for the sake of its unending, forced, and atrocious puns. Its first scene deals with the matter of the loan:

SHYLOCK.　Antonio's a good man.
BASSANIO.　　　　　　　　　Yes—do you know
　Aught contrary?
SHYLOCK.　　　　Oh, *tout au contraire*—No!
　At him, believe me, I don't mean a rap at all,
　But all his property is floating capital. . . .

SHYLOCK.　Who voided his rheum on my beard, I presume,
　In decency should have avoided my *room*. . . .
　On the rialto your *real toe* I've felt.

After the bond has been suggested:

SHYLOCK.   Nor were it worth my while to cut and run,
    And *carry off* what is but *carri-on.*

In the second scene we are at Portia's house, where Arragon, Morocco, and Bassanio are all present to make their choice of the caskets. The love-affair between Gratiano and Nerissa is elaborated far beyond the proportions Shakespeare allotted it.

BASSANIO.   Though *Portia portionless* should be my *portion,*
    I never did the *poor shun,* and I will
    Love her *till* death, and none shall rob the *till!*

The letter arrives from Antonio; it concludes:

    I've little hope of finding Shylock lenient,
    So come to Venice when convenient.

Bassanio and Gratiano leave. Portia decides to become the lawyer in the case.

The third scene deals with the elopement of Jessica.

JESSICA.   Now to prepare—Lorenzo, sweet, be true,
    And I to Shylock will bid *a-Jew.*

The fourth scene is between Shylock and Tubal, and the fifth scene, the last, is the trial.

SHYLOCK.   On what compulsion must I? Tell me that.
PORTIA.   The saying's *must-y* and is soon explained.
    The quality of mercy is not strained.
    It droppeth as the gentle rain—
SHYLOCK.   There stop.
    It drops itself, so please, we'll let it drop . . .

When Antonio bares his breast:

DUKE.   Yet stay. Is there no plan,
    No *panacea* for your cruel mood?
SHYLOCK.   You see the *pan is here* to catch the blood.

Shylock is defeated in the usual way. The piece ends with Shylock's conversion and his reconciliation with Lorenzo and Jessica. Jessica asks pardon.

> SHYLOCK. She's done for pa, and now she asks her *par-don*.

Lorenzo restores the jewels and the money, and there is general re-joicing and friendliness.[34]

This piece was considerably popular in both England and the United States during the height first of Kean's and, later, Booth's popularity. Its continued success sponsored a whole crop of bur-lesques on *The Merchant of Venice*. Of these we may note one, called *The Merchant of Venice*, "as performed by Griffin and Christy's Minstrels," and "arranged by George W. H. Griffin." This gem was performed in the 1870's, presumably in blackface. A few extracts will suffice. When Antonio approaches Shylock for the loan, Shylock says:

> If at the time he doesn't come and pay—
> I'll cut his *liver out*, the very day!
> If he's *a liver* then, he shall not prate,
> He must *die early*, so he sha'n't *di-late!*

At the end of the trial scene Portia comes in just as "Shylock ad-vances flourishing knife." She warns him to "draw not one drop of blood." Shylock, "shrinking back," is now allotted these concluding lines:

> The game is up, I cannot solve this riddle,
> I'm trembling like a cat-gut on a fiddle;
> I've lost my flesh, my *monish* and my *daughter*,
> Now I'll sneak out like a lamb to the slaughter.
> OMNES. No you don't.
> > (*They all rush after him, bring him back, crying out,* "Toss him in a blanket." *They get large canvas and toss him in air until*
>
> > CURTAIN.[35]

There have been a number of writers who have improved upon Shakespeare's play with intentions, at least, not comic. Granville and Horne (see pp. 226, 314) were not alone in showing him how the play ought to have been written, either in part or as a whole. John Cournos in a one-act play, *Shylock's Choice*, shows Shylock planning to spare Antonio at the very last minute of the trial in order to cause Antonio to be morally in his debt.[36]

But not even Granville's distortions can outvie the sober efforts of the popular Yiddish actor, Maurice Schwartz. In the mid-1940's he presented (in English) his drama, *Shylock and His Daughter*, to the apparent satisfaction of many in New York. The critics were pleased enough with it, and generally found it "interesting" or "absorbing." In our times there is always an audience for something new.

This incredible piece of melodramatic nonsense was dramatized by Schwartz from a Hebrew novel by Ari Ibn Zahav, who himself provides a highly ill-informed preface to the play. The novelist declares that his purpose was to "show the real Shylock"—an undertaking worthy of Cervantes' Don, since Shylock's only existence is in the play Shakespeare wrote. He finds Shakespeare's Shylock in violation of fact. In substantiation of this charge Ari Ibn Zahav blandly asserts that "there is no single instance" in the entire history of the Jewish people of a "Jew taking another man's life." The novelist apparently does not know his Bible very well. But, as we have seen, many modern commentators have made the same amazing pronouncement. With a kind of Alice-in-Wonderland confusion of reality with fantasy, Ari Ibn Zahav states categorically: because of his wrongs "Shylock *demanded* vengeance but he did not ta cause he was a Jew." Shakespeare's misrepresentations are due to herited prejudice; Shylock's soliloquies "can be taken as indisputable proof that had Shakespeare scrutinized closely the life of the Sixteenth Century Jew in Italy, he would have given us a Shylock who could have served as an eternal protest against the inquisition and persecution of Jews generally." [37]

The play which follows owes its existence to Shakespeare's, but its melodramatical perversities are beyond comprehension. Any writer is free to compose a work on a Jewish banker, his daughter, her Christian lover, and a circle of friends. But what purpose is served by identifying them with Shakespeare's creations? It might be retorted that Shakespeare himself improved upon works of his predecessors; but Shakespeare was running no risks, being Shakespeare. There is a kind of unadmirable audacity involved in attempting to improve on him.

In *Shylock and His Daughter*, Jessica's father owns a bank in the Ghetto. (In Shakespeare there is no Ghetto.) Shylock is a deeply religious and pious man. He is busy helping to free Jews in other cities from persecution, and would himself like to go on such a mission to Rome, but dares not leave Venice even for a day. If he did not bribe the German mercenaries with a bag of gold each week, they would "rob every Jewish home and burn the Synagogue." Without him the Ghetto would long ago have been demolished. Jessica is the apple of his eye; she is all that has been left to him of four children. Often he tiptoes into her bedroom in the middle of the night to see that she is properly covered.

In this play Bassanio, though mentioned once, does not appear. It is Antonio who is married to Portia. Sixteen years ago he had made the journey to Belmont, where Bassanio was one of the unsuccessful suitors. Their life together has been so happy that Portia feels the years have made their love grow all the "more poetic." [38] Antonio is so kind that his wife exclaims, "Oftentimes I think you are the Holy Son." Has he ever, she asks, shown "a wrathful countenance to anyone?" "To none, my dear," he replies, "except the Jews. No sooner do I see them on the Rialto than my heart becomes filled with exceeding hatred toward them." Because Shylock is a usurer he hates him most of all. He fears "the world will come to destruction because of the sins of the Jews." However, he adds poetically, "Love will evermore float in the space of the Heavenly Spheres" (whatever it says means).

There are numerous touches of local color. Jessica was born in a gondola. The Ghetto is sealed off by a heavy iron Ghetto-gate, in the keeping of two guards named Gratiano and Salanio. Gratiano loathes the Jews and his job, but Salanio has no complaints because they often bring him gifts of bread, pudding, stuffed fish, raisin wine, and nuts.

Launcelot, Shylock's servant, when we first meet him is an enthusiast for Jewish ritual and custom. Since the death of Shylock's wife he runs for the family a "kosher kitchen," and boasts of being able to go through the entire Passover service. "My Passover dishes," he avers, "can be equalled only in Paradise."

Lorenzo, an employee at Shylock's bank, a bitter Jew-hater, asks Launcelot if he has any Christian blood left in his veins. The servant replies that "Gentile Jew" though he is, "All my blood is strictly Christian!" Lorenzo has been wooing Jessica. Suddenly, and for no reason, Launcelot, the devoted servant, becomes a villain. He tries to blackmail Lorenzo into giving him a large sum of money if he is to hold his tongue about Lorenzo's courtship. He and a fellow-servant, Stephano, decide to quit Shylock's house. Now Launcelot intones Latin instead of Hebrew: "*Mea culpa, mea culpa.*"

Unlike her husband Portia pities the Jews, "who have driven away from amongst them the Son of God, Him whom you resemble even as a twin brother," she says to Antonio. She and he have no children, and when Lorenzo brings Jessica to their house she envies Shylock his daughter. She hopes that she and Antonio both can "lead this lovely Jewish daughter to the marriage-altar with our Lorenzo." [39]

Shylock plans to marry Jessica to Morro, a scholarly refugee whom he is befriending. She refuses to have him and faints. But it turns out that she has caught the grippe in the gondola on her visit to Portia. The doctor who attends her would prefer to live in the Ghetto instead of as the only Jew in the city proper, where "I must restore enemies of Israel to health so they can persecute my people." Jessica is left alone to recuperate, and while she sleeps there is a "musical interlude, suggestive of the burning of the Talmud. Wall in background is lit up with visions of bishops and cardinals in black and red robes, as they burn the Talmud. . . . Echo of wild laughter of spectators is heard, developing into musical crescendo." Troubled by this dream, Jessica asks her father to protect her from the "evil winds" which encircle her.

She hears that Cardinal Roberto at Rome has refused to see the messengers pleading for the Jews imprisoned there, and decides to go herself as soon as she has recovered from the grippe.

Antonio comes with Lorenzo to visit Shylock, who is more than gracious to them. Antonio is stiffly distant. He wishes to borrow three thousand ducats for Lorenzo (who needs the money to pay off the blackmailers), and offers to pay 10 per cent interest. Shylock reminds Antonio that Antonio has always treated him with "hatred and mockery," called him "dog, base usurer, exploiter," spit on his Jewish gaberdine, and threatened him with prison for taking interest. Antonio speaks of having himself loaned money gratis, even to strangers; Shylock appends, "With intent to rob Jews of their crust of bread." The banker suggests Antonio's palace as surety; at this Antonio is ready to leave in indignation: "My palace is a sacred temple." Shylock then kindly offers to lend the money without interest.

It is Antonio himself who suggests the pound of flesh because, as he says, "I do not want any kindness from Jews." He is so certain of repaying the sum that he asks for only a month. Shylock interprets Antonio's offer of the pound of flesh as a new insult, but Antonio is firm in demanding the clause in the bond. As Shylock goes into the house to fetch the money, Lorenzo chortles at the idea that Shylock will be repaid with his own money: when Jessica and he elope she will take much more than that amount. Antonio does not like this: he and Portia are interested only in converting Jessica to Christianity.

Launcelot and Stephano have been paid off in their blackmail by Lorenzo in installments; they now plan to leave Shylock's employ. The undecipherable Launcelot feels they "are behaving swinishly" toward their master, who has always treated them "as members of his own family." Stephano reminds him that Christ "is always ready to forgive what we do to Jews."

When Jessica is ready to depart for Rome, Lorenzo urges her to "empty" her father's chest, but she refuses. When she runs out Launcelot demands the rest of the blackmail money, and Lorenzo is forced to comply. Nevertheless, Launcelot is concerned that on Jessica's journey to Rome the "appetizing victuals" he has prepared for her may be stolen; since she is going to Rome, he moans, "for whom will I now bake and cook?"

Antonio is in low spirits. His ships are sinking in the Atlantic, and he is worried about his bond. Portia offers to sell her jewels, but he refuses to allow his enemies "see such vengeance on me." [40] She feels he has abased his pride in going to the Ghetto for a loan.

We are now in Rome. Jessica visits the prison where Jewish refugees are being held. She is unable to accomplish anything for them, and decides to return to Venice. The Cardinal is annoyed that she has resisted conversion, and will leave with "a soul still sinful, unwilling to be cleansed."

Back in Venice, Lorenzo and Jessica visit Portia; Portia invites the girl to stay with her a few days. Stage direction: "Jessica stares at everything as though in a dream. Suddenly screams with unnatural voice, 'I must leave!'" She has taken no gold or jewels from Shylock; Antonio says, "She is more than gold or jewels to us. She shall be a torchbearer to lead Jewish maidens from the Ghetto to the Church."

Shylock is worried at Jessica's failure to return: "In the luxurious homes of Cardinal Roberto, I have seen the ashes of burnt Jews in huge, golden vases." Lorenzo, too, has been absent from the bank for days, and Launcelot is leaving the house. Stephano lets the cat out of the bag by telling Shylock that Lorenzo has gone to Rome to bring back Jessica. Drunken Gratiano, guard of the Ghetto-gate, reveals to Shylock the blackmailing of Lorenzo to which he is also a party. When Shylock learns that Jessica is to become a Christian and will be married tomorrow, he tears her picture from the wall. Realizing now that the loan to Antonio helped undoing his own child, he dotes on the thought of revenge. Suddenly he remembers that the bond is already five days overdue. His friend, Tubal, urges him not to take revenge, for it will "bring ruin upon all the Jews of the Ghetto."

Still at Portia's, Jessica in her wedding-dress has not recovered from her mesmerized state. She murmurs, "Father is waiting for me," but Portia will not allow her to go. The bells for the wedding toll, and Lorenzo arrives, decked out as a bridegroom. The Cardinal explains, "The prison and the flames [which Jessica saw in Rome] have weakened her resistance." She allows herself to be led off to be married.

Shylock is busy destroying all of Jessica's possessions. He tears her pillow-cases, crumples her dresses. The Rabbi forbids him to take the pound of flesh; Shylock prefers to shun the synagogue hereafter, and is solemnly excommunicated.

After the wedding, Lorenzo tells Jessica how he has paid the black-mailers with money borrowed from Shylock.

Despite its wild divergencies from *The Merchant of Venice*, this play in its final pages assumes a knowledge of Shakespeare's master-piece. We are never told how Portia comes to Antonio's aid. Suddenly we are in the courtroom and Portia is the lawyer. She asks Shylock to be merciful. He is willing to tear up the bond if he can have his daughter back. No one will agree to that. Portia becomes a second Daniel. However, she loses the case: the Duke insists that Shylock must take his pound of flesh, and Antonio is sent off to prison until the deed be done.

But at the last, Shylock cannot take Antonio's flesh: "I cannot shed blood," he says. "I am a Jew." [41] Stage-direction: "Cardinal Roberto and the Bishops bend under these words. A ray of light plays about Shylock." Morro appears to announce: "Rejoice! Our

Jessica has returned to us. Forbidden to come back to her people, she drowned herself by the Ghetto-shore." Shylock has the last line of the play: "I praise thee, God, for thy loving-kindness."

One ought, in charity, to remember that this play was produced with the horrors of the Nazi regime all too fresh in everyone's mind. Only the worst kind of bigot would dare deny that the Jews have more to afflict the conscience of the Western world with than can ever be atoned. Still nothing of any moral value can accrue to anyone by ravaging Shakespeare's masterpiece. Nor is mankind served any more by painting every Christian as some sort of a villain than it is by so depicting every Jew. Perhaps the worst that can be said of *Shylock and His Daughter* is that, despite its good intentions, it already has defeated itself by reading like a nightmarish burlesque.

What would the world of music think of a composer who wrote, unsolicited, a fifth movement for Beethoven's *Eroica* or the *Fifth Symphony?* He would probably be judged mad. Nevertheless, a number of writers have written appendices to *The Merchant of Venice,* including in their ranks several with considerable literary reputation in the twentieth century.

Oscar F. Adams wrote a sequel which he actually called *The Merchant of Venice, Act VI,* to show Shylock becoming converted, still despised by Christians, still planning revenge, and still remaining a Jew at heart. St. John Ervine, who as dramatic critic was normally quite harsh in his judgment of his contemporaries, has written *The Lady of Belmont,* a play in five acts, which has been presented on several occasions. The story takes place in the space of one day at the home of Bassanio and Portia, ten years after their marriage. Bassanio, Lorenzo, and Gratiano are all inveterate anti-Semites; they weary of Antonio's frequent references to his great act of sacrifice for Bassanio's sake. Bassanio has run through all of Portia's money, and she comes to regret saving Antonio's life. Gratiano and Nerissa have a dreadful time of it with their constant bickerings; Gratiano's lechery has converted Nerissa into a shrew. Jessica loathes her Lorenzo and has an affair with Bassanio. Shylock, now Senator of Venice and intimate of the Duke, is in flourishing wealth, and has been privately practising his old faith. Portia and he meet again, and find they can deeply respect each other as the only truly decent people of their circle of acquaintanceship.[42]

Ervine no doubt felt himself adequately revenged on Shakespeare by writing this play (for offenses I can hardly imagine). But his revenge has been rather illusory, for there is not one of his characters who bears the slightest resemblance to those in *The Merchant of Venice*.

Louis Untermeyer, poet, anthologist, and literary critic, has written a piece which is also called *The Merchant of Venice, Act VI*. We discover Antonio and Shylock as business partners some years after the events of Shakespeare's play. Jessica has quit Lorenzo to return to her father. Shylock, now a practising Christian, tries to convert his old friend Tubal. Why not? There are no differences to be found in Jews and Christians—all are materialists, hungry for money and comforts.[43]

The best known of all the sequels to *The Merchant of Venice*— at least, it was much spoken of for a while—was Ludwig Lewisohn's novel, *The Last Days of Shylock*, which not only undertakes to finish off the lives of Shakespeare's *dramatis personae*, but also undertakes to correct some of the errors in his play.

The story begins right after the conclusion of the trial. Tubal and other members of the Jewish community have tried vainly to persuade Shylock to accept the money offered by Antonio's friends and forget the pound of flesh. Not that Tubal does not detest Antonio too: "On me too he has voided his rheum; I know as well as you that he was the informer and took a wage of four hundred lire when the accursed Trevisano caused all our sacred books to be burned in the Piazza." But policy dictated not insisting on the terms of the bond. Chus, however, knows that Shylock has been obdurate out of piety; he "never could reconcile himself to injustice; he dreams of a Messiah to right our wrongs."

Shylock, a "dark, bowed, slender figure," returns from the trial a broken man. He is outraged that a perfectly valid bond should have been declared illegal. Besides, he never intended to take Antonio's life; blood has always sickened him. He had planned that "his knife would not have gone very deep into the bosom of his adversary"—kind Shylock! He is bitter because he has been cheated of his supreme triumph, "that moment in which he could have felt uplifted above the thousand humiliations of his sacred nation," when he took the pound of flesh. He hopes, after his enforced baptism, to flee Venice and resume the faith of his fathers. His vow to heaven to take the pound of flesh he believes is registered with God. Now he must go home to "perform the ceremonies of the dead for Jessica. . . . It was not granted him to see her safe and dead at his foot."

At his house he opens chests holding caskets, jewel-cases, and purses containing gold and bonds of debtors, and hands all these to Tubal and Chus to hold for him. He feels safer that goods and securities "to the value of half a million ducats" are in their safekeeping: in any event he will not be reduced to "beggary." He is irked that he must make Lorenzo and Jessica his heirs; if he refuses to become a Christian and die "in the flames," he would at least be sure that nothing would be left for them to inherit. He eventually decides to become a convert so that he can "live in order to help right the balance of justice." [44] As he thinks over the trial, he sees again the Duke's sly, stern face; "the self-pitying mien of Antonio"; the "empty, handsome face of Bassanio, prodigal adventurer and gambler who cozened himself and his friends with fine, round, fluent words."

The next day Gratiano appears with a halbedier of the Duke's. "Art prepared, old owl?" he asks. "Ere noon comes thou'lt be a Christian, as thy daughter, well baptized and well-bedded with Lorenzo and so well sprinkled o' both ends, is even now!" Postponing revenge, Shylock feigns humility, but upbraids Gratiano that not one of Antonio's friends came to the rescue: "Is love not worth three thousand ducats here in Venice?" he asks witheringly.[45] Gratiano has no answer.

They join Antonio ("stroking his pointed beard with unctuous satisfaction"), the "plump" Bassanio (who is "careful to show the whole length of his shapely legs in over-tight hose"), Salanio, and Salarino. Antonio offers to end their old enmity now that Shylock is to be a Christian. They enter San Marco, where Shylock undergoes the ceremony of conversion, which requires his saying, "And I anathemize all Jewish heresies and heretics." His "tears of grief and shame and loathing" fall on the cross which he is made to kiss. After the baptism the priest says, "I have seen thy like ere now. Thy tears are but water, such as the crocodile exudes." Shylock is ordered to confess once a week. Moreover, he must attend daily mass and high mass and vespers on Sundays, or be punished. He is forbidden to consort hereafter with Jews or to take interest. The priest advises his entering a monastery as the safest step for him.

On the counsel of Tubal and Chus, he leaves Venice, boarding a ship flying the flag of the great Sultan Suleiman. After seventeen days he comes to the city of the Sultan. He prospers in the East and has many adventures.

At length at Cyprus he meets Jessica again. She has three children now, and is in great distress. He asks her, "Where is the Goy, Lorenzo, thy husband?" She does not answer.

Since her children have not been circumcised, Shylock has the operation performed on them. Jessica comes to his house and weeps "low and long" with her head against his knees. She acknowledges her sins. She admits that at first she loved the gay spendthrift life of Lorenzo and his friends. But when she knew she was to have her first child she yearned for a home of her own, and to depend no more on the bounty of Portia and Bassanio. Bassanio, wearying of his idle life, went off to the wars against the Turk with Gratiano and Lorenzo; Portia and Nerissa left for a convent to pray for their husbands' safety. Jessica found herself all alone at Belmont, and there in a "windy, solitary room" bore her child. Once in a while Lorenzo would return as an intermission from the wars. He was apparently still loyal to her, though he did not spare telling her of the "fair wenches" who had been kind to him while he was away. At the end of the wars Bassanio and Lorenzo quarreled "over a wench in Venice." A servant of Portia's, who loved his mistress, taunted Bassanio in her presences over his amorous escapades. Afraid to lose Portia's wealth, Bassanio accused Lorenzo of being the guilty person. Offended, Lorenzo took Jessica and their child to Naples, where they went to live in a hovel. After that they wandered everywhere. He appealed to Antonio in vain. Lorenzo began to complain that the world "was falling into its yellow leaf." At length he accepted a menial job at Verona. After that he grew cruel, and taunted Jessica with her "race and faith," and blamed his sorry conditon on her. Becoming involved in a drunken street-brawl in which a man was killed, Lorenzo fled town. Jessica, abandoned, made her way to Venice, where she gave birth to her third child "in a hovel among thieves and harlots." One of the harlots kindly arranged for her passage on a Greek ship, which took her to Cyprus, where Shylock has found her.

Contented at last in the reunion with his daughter, Shylock spends the closing years of his life in study and in conversing with his grandsons. When death comes for him, it finds him among his loved ones, "his white head against his daughter's bosom." [46]

*

The Elizabethan age was a hearty one, and Shakespeare was as hearty as any of his contemporaries. But one of the qualities which singles him out from his fellow-dramatists is that his ribaldry is never indecency for indecency's sake. An even more amazing fact about his plays is that, unlike many of even the world's greatest writers, despite the powerful emotions which move like lightning through his works, he never once degenerates into sentimentality —that is, emotion for emotion's sake. It may have been remarked from the excerpts quoted in this chapter, brief though they are, that their authors failed to possess his delicate awareness of where indecency begins and fun ends or of the sharp line which distinguishes pathos from bathos. These attempts to improve on him are remarkable for being either vulgar or heavy-handed or drooling with sham sentiment. It still remains a mystery why anyone has been tempted to a venture that is doomed to failure by its very nature.

It is certainly one of the aspects of great literary genius to manage profundity gracefully. The masterpieces of the world do not require the philosopher's long beard to impress us with their seriousness, for the cardinal sin in the arts is dullness. Our study began with the parable of the blind men and the elephant, and it is a sad truth that critical commentary has tended to overplate many of Shakespeare's light-footed plays with so many layers of heaviness that the comedy or tragedy emerges in the public mind as some sort of pachyderm. To this process Shakespeare's "improvers" have made their contribution.

Directors and actors of Shakespeare's plays are, with few exceptions, still racking their ingenuities in the frantic search for new ways of doing him. The greatest novelty of all would be to present the plays as their author intended them—not as sociological treatises, but as masterworks for the stage, which, like all dramatic masterworks, have certain universal ethical ideas to communicate in terms of drama. It is as a contribution to a re-awakening as to what *The Merchant of Venice* meant to its author that this work has been undertaken. As long as the play continues to be viewed as concerned primarily with "the Jewish question," it will not be understood that its real business is with matters quite different, quite as important, and even more universal—since they are above distinction of race or creed.

References

CHAPTER 1

To Begin with an Elephant

1. J. Q. Adams, *Hamlet* (Boston, 1929), p. 182.
2. A. C. Bradley, *Shakespearean Tragedy* (London, 1929), p. 169.
3. B. Grebanier, *The Heart of Hamlet* (New York, 1960), pp. 265-78.
4. J. M. Murry, *Shakespeare* (London, 1954), p. 24.
5. H. Golden, *Only in America* (New York, 1958), p. 175.
6. A. Harbage, *As They Liked It* (New York, 1947), p. 166.
7. For a discussion of these matters, see *The Heart of Hamlet*, pp. 15-16 and ("Text Edition") pp. 353-54; p. 13; pp. 240-44.
8. J. Palmer, *Comic Characters of Shakespeare* (London, 1953), pp. 54-55.
9. See E. Honigmann, in *Modern Language Review* XLIX (1954), pp. 293-307.
10. E. E. Stoll, *Shakespeare Studies* (New York, 1942), p. 280.
11. *Idem, Art and Artifice in Shakespeare* (New York, 1951), pp. 92, 93-94.
12. E. N. Calish, *The Jew in English Literature* (Richmond, Va., n.d.), p. 65.
13. L. L. Schucking, *Character Problems in Shakespeare's Plays* (New York, 1948), p. 235.
14. A. C. Bradley, *op. cit.*, p. 2.

CHAPTER 2

Prick Them and They Do Not Bleed: Englishmen and the Jews

1. A. Harbage, *As They Liked It* (New York, 1947), p. 167.
2. E. N. Calish, *The Jew in English Literature* (Richmond, Va., n.d.), p. 67.
3. H. B. Charlton, *Shakespearian Comedy* (New York, 1938), pp. 132-38.
4. W. A. Neilson and C. J. Hill, *The Complete Plays and Poems of Shakespeare* (Cambridge, Mass., 1942), p. 116.
5. H. Golden, *Only in America* (New York, 1958), p. 170.
6. Scherer, *Die Rechtsverhältnisse der Juden*, quoted in *Encyclopedia Britannica* (11th ed.), Vol. XV, p. 403.
7. *Idem.*
8. A. Sefanov, in *Jewish Encyclopedia*, Vol. III (New York, 1941), pp. 203-04.
9. Quoted by E. E. Stoll, *Shakespeare Studies* (New York, 1942), p. 281.
10. *Ibid.*, p. 282.
11. *Encyclopedia Brittanica* (11th ed.), Vol. XXIII, p. 373.
12. E. N. Calish, *op. cit.*, p. 35.
13. See I. Abrahams, *Jewish Life in the Middle Ages* (London, 1896), especially chapter 12.
14. Taken down from recital, R. Jamieson, *Popular Ballads and Songs from Tradition, Manuscripts, and Scarce Editions* (Edinburgh, 1806).

15. *Jewish Encyclopedia*, Vol. IV, pp. 636-67.
16. E. N. Calish, *op. cit.*, p. 48.
17. L. Cardozo, *The Contemporary Jew in the Elizabethan Drama* (Amsterdam, 1925), p. 329.
18. M. Holmes, *Shakespeare's Public* (London, 1960), p. 62.
19. L. Cardozo, *op. cit.*, pp. 85-140.
20. R. South, *Sermons*, Vol. II (1865), p. 228.
21. Quoted by M. Packard, *Shylock Not a Jew* (Boston, 1919), p. 49.
22. A. Quiller-Couch, in New Cambridge Edition of *The Merchant of Venice* (Cambridge, 1926), p. xiv.
23. E. Rosenberg, *From Shylock to Svengale* (Stanford, Cal., 1960), p. 15.
24. M. F. Modder, *The Jew in the Literature of England* (Philadelphia, 1960), p. 15.
25. E. Rosenberg, *op. cit.*, p. 22.
26. K. L. Bates, *The English Religious Drama* (New York, 1893), p. 146.
27. E. Rosenberg, *op. cit.*, p. 23.
28. H. H. Furness, *The Merchant of Venice* (Philadelphia, 1888), pp. 320, 321, 331.
29. A. W. Ward, *History of English Dramatic Poetry*, Vol. I (London, 1875), p. 188.
30. E. N. Calish, *op. cit.*, p. 66.
31. Dyce, quoted by H. H. Furness, *op. cit.*, p. 322.
32. M. F. Modder, *op. cit.*, p. 24.
33. Harleian Ms. 6848, fo. 185-86. Baines's whole indictment will be found quoted *in extenso* by C. Norman, *The Muses' Darling* (Drexel Hill, Pa., 1950), pp. 196-98.
34. A. Tretiak, "*The Merchant of Venice* and the 'Alien' Question," in *Review of English Studies*, V (Oct., 1929), p. 404.
35. G. B. Harrison, *Shakespeare at Work, 1592-1603* (Ann Arbor, 1958), p. 111.
36. *Coryat's Crudities*, published for the University by J. MacLehose (Glasgow, 1905), pp. 152, 165, 168, 169, 171, 197-8, 211, 267, 299, 272.
37. *Ibid.*, p. 16.
38. *Ibid.*, pp. 301-428.
39. *Ibid.*, pp. xvii-xx.
40. *Ibid.*, pp. 31, 35, 46, 48, 51, 63, 64, 70, 75, 85, 105.

CHAPTER 3
Jingler of the Guinea: The Usurer

1. See B. N. Nelson, *The Idea of Usury* (Princeton, 1949) for a full history of the concept of usury up to modern times.
2. *Politics*, I.
3. In *Encyclopaedia Britannica* (11th Edition), Vol. XXVII, p. 812.
4. B. N. Nelson, *op. cit.*, p. 4.
5. *Ibid.*, p. 6.
6. Quoted by B. N. Nelson, *op. cit.*, p. 9.

7. *Ibid.*, p. 13.
8. In *Summa Theologica*, quoted by B. N. Nelson, *op. cit.*, p. 14.
9. *Inferno*, cantos XI, XVII (translated by C. E. Norton).
10. B. N. Nelson, *op. cit.*, pp. 19, 20, 22.
11. *Works*, edited by J. Bowring, Vol. III (Edinburgh, 1843), p. 17.
12. Quoted by A. Quiller-Couch in the New Cambridge Edition of *The Merchant of Venice*, p. xiv.
13. B. N. Nelson, *op. cit.*, pp. 73-4.
14. S. Pufendorf, *De Jure Naturae et Gentium*, Vol. II (Oxford, 1934), p. 756.
15. 37 Henry VIII, cap. ix.
16. 6 Edward VI, cap. xx.
17. 13 Elizabeth I, cap. viii.
18. J. W. Draper, "Usury in *The Merchant of Venice*," in *Modern Philology*, XXXIII (August 1935), p. 40.
19. W. Besant, *Tudor London* (London, 1904), p. 238.
20. I. Disraeli, *Curiosities of Literature*, Vol. II (London, n.d.), pp. 158-71.
21. J. W. Draper, *op. cit.*, p. 41.
22. I. Disraeli, *op. cit.*, p. 159.
23. *The Pack of Autolycus*, edited by H. E. Rollins (Cambridge, 1927), p. 5.
24. *Pierce Penilesse*, edited by G. B. Harrison (London, 1926), pp. 13-14.
25. *A Cabinet of Characters*, edited by G. Murphy (London, 1925), pp. 86-87, 107-109.
26. C. T. Wright, "Some Conventions Regarding the Usurer in Elizabethan Literature" in *Studies in Philology*, XXXI (April 1934), pp. 176-97.
27. A. B. Stonex, "The Usurer in Elizabethan Drama," in *Publications of the Modern Language Association*, XXXI, no. 2 (June 1916), pp. 190-210.
28. B. N. Nelson, "The Usurer and the Merchant Prince: Italian Businessmen and the Ecclesiastical Law of Restitution, 1150-1550," in Supplement to *The Journal of Economic History*, VII (May 1947), pp. 104-22.
29. H. W. Farnum, *Shakespeare's Economics* (New Haven, 1931), p. 99.
30. *Ibid.*, p. 105.

CHAPTER 4

This Bond Is Forfeit: The Pound-of-Flesh Story

1. M. D. Conway, *The Wandering Jew* (New York, 1881), pp. 137-9.
2. J. L. E. Ortolan, *The History of Roman Law* (London, 1871), pp. 105-6.
3. A. Quiller-Couch, *Shakespeare's Workmanship* (London, 1918), p. 104.
4. M. R. Ridley, *Shakespeare's Plays* (London, 1957), p. 90.
5. T. Niemeyer, *Der Rechtspruch gegen Shylock* (Kiel, 1912), pp. 20-2.
6. G. Friedlander, *Shakespeare and the Jew* (London, 1921), pp. 26-7.
7. T. Niemeyer, *op. cit.*, p. 22.
8. G. Friedlander, *op. cit.*, p. 65.
9. W. S. Holdsworth, *A History of English Law*, Vol. III (London, 1932), pp. 413, 414.
10. E. C. Brewer, *Dictionary of Miracles* (London, 1884), p. 291.

11. M. K. Simrock, *On the Plots of Shakespeare's Plays* (London, 1858), pp. 50-1.
12. Quoted by H. H. Furness, *The Merchant of Venice* (Philadelphia, 1888), pp. 293-5.
13. See J. L. Cardozo, *The Contemporary Jew in Elizabethan Drama* (Amsterdam, 1925), pp. 279-83; also M. K. Simrock, *op. cit.*, pp. 56-7.
14. See A. Vambery, "Keleti Szemele" in *Revue orientale*, 1901, pp. 18-29.
15. M. Slauch, "The Pound of Flesh Story in the Germanic North," in *Journal of English and Germanic Philology*, XXX, (1931), p. 348.
16. B. N. Nelson and J. Starr, "The Legend of the Divine Surety and the Jewish Money-Lender," in *Annuaire de l'Institut de Philologie et d'Histoire orientales et slaves* VII (1939-44), pp. 289-338.
17. S. Pufendorf, *De Jure Naturae et Gentium*, Vol. II (Oxford, 1934), p. 433.
18. B. N. Nelson and J. Starr, *op. cit.*, p. 320, p. 323.
19. *Ibid.*, pp. 289-93.
20. Quoted by H. H. Furness, *op. cit.*, pp. 295-7.
21. Furness, *op. cit.*, pp. 320, 321, 331.
22. A. Quiller-Couch, Introduction to the Cambridge edition of *The Merchant of Venice*, p. xi.
23. J. D. Wilson, Introduction to the Cambridge edition of *The Merchant of Venice*, pp. 113-4.

CHAPTER 5

Shylock Himself

1. W. Hazlitt, *The Characters of Shakespeare's Plays* (London, 1906), p. 206.
2. Quoted by H. H. Furness, *The Merchant of Venice* (Philadelphia, 1888), p. 421.
3. H. Spencer, *The Art and Life of William Shakespeare* (New York, 1940), p. 239.
4. J. L. Cardozo, *The Contemporary Jew in the Elizabethan Drama* (Amsterdam, 1925), p. 236.
5. H. Granville-Barker, *Prefaces to Shakespeare, Second Series* (London, 1948), p. 67.
6. J. M. Murry, *Shakespeare* (London, 1954), p. 199.
7. M. R. Ridley, *Shakespeare's Plays* (London, 1957), p. 89.
8. L. Cooper, *Aristotle on the Art of Poetry* (Ithaca, 1947), p. 80.
9. S. C. Sen Gupta, *Shakespearian Comedy* (Oxford, 1950), p. 129.
10. W. J. Courthope, *A History of English Poetry* (London, 1911), Vol IV, p. 118.
11. E. Dowden, Introduction to *The Merchant of Venice* in *The Comedies of Shakespeare* (Oxford, n.d.), p. 589.
12. B. Stirling, *The Populace in Shakespeare* (New York, 1949), p. 55.
13. H. Spencer, *op. cit.*, p. 240.
14. *Ibid.*, p. 239.

15. E. N. Calish, *The Jew in European Literature* (Richmond, Va., n.d.), p. 75.
16. *Ibid.*, p. 78.
17. G. L. Kittredge, *The Merchant of Venice* (Boston, 1945), p. x.
18. A. Quiller-Couch, *Shakespeare's Workmanship* (London, 1918), p. 98.
19. H. Golden, *Only in America* (New York, 1958), p. 169, 172, 174, 176-7.
20. W. Hazlitt, *op. cit.*, p. 212.
21. In *The Saturday Review*, Dec. 14, 1895, Sept. 26, 1896.
22. E. Terry, *The Story of My Life* (London, 1908), p. 186.
23. W. Winter, *Shadows of the Stage* (New York, 1892), p. 183.
24. Quoted by H. H. Furness, *op. cit.*, pp. 449, 430.
25. W. Raleigh, *Shakespeare* (London, 1907), pp. 149, 150-51.
26. M. Packard, *Shylock Not a Jew* (Boston, 1919), pp. 18, 22-4, 25, 45.
27. E. N. Calish, *op. cit.*, pp. 72, 84.
28. In *Shakespeare-Jahrbuch*, XVIII, pp. 200 seq.
29. C. N. Coe, *Shakespeare's Villains* (New York, 1957), p. 52.
30. E. E. Stoll, *Shakespeare Studies* (New York, 1942), p. 452.
31. H. Granville-Barker, *op. cit.*, p. 95.
32. A. Harbage, *As They Liked It* (New York, 1947), p. 194.
33. H. C. Goddard, *The Meaning of Shakespeare* (Chicago, 1951), pp. 6, 94, 99, 100-01.
34. H. R. Walley, "Shakespeare's Portrayal of Shylock," in *Essays in Dramatic Literature*, ed. by H. Craig (Princeton, 1935), p. 235.
35. O. J. Campbell, *The Living Shakespeare* (New York, 1949), p. 265.
36. W. A. Neilson and C. J. Hill, *The Complete Plays and Poems of William Shakespeare* (Cambridge, Mass., 1942), p. 116.
37. M. Van Doren, *Shakespeare* (New York, 1939), p. 101.
38. E. E. Stoll, *op. cit.*, pp. 255-336, especially pp. 256-67.
39. Quoted by T. Lelyveld, *Shylock on the Stage* (Cleveland, 1960), p. 11.
40. E. E. Stoll, *op. cit.*, pp. 255, 271.
41. A. Harbage, *op. cit.*, pp. 23-24.
42. In *The Heart of Hamlet* (New York, 1960), pp. 60-65.
43. E. Gosse, "D'Avenant," in *Encyclopedia Britannica* (11th ed.) (Cambridge, England, 1911), Vol. VII, p. 852.
44. E. Rosenberg, *From Shylock to Svengali* (Stanford, 1960), pp. 3, 35, 37.
45. E. E. Stoll, *op. cit.*, p. 322.
46. H. Spencer, *op. cit.*, pp. 245-6.
47. E. Spivack, *Shakespeare and the Allegory of Evil* (New York, 1958), p. 146.
48. J. Palmer, *Comic Characters of Shakespeare* (London, 1953), pp. 75, 80, 88.
49. S. C. Sen Gupta, *op. cit.*, p. 143.
50. E. E. Stoll, *op. cit.*, p. 288.
51. E. I. Fripp, *Shakespeare, Man and Artist* (Oxford, 1938), Vol. I, p. 416.
52. A. Quiller-Couch, Introduction to *The Merchant of Venice*, New Cambridge edition, p. xxviii.
53. J. M. Murry, *op. cit.*, p. 197.
54. H. Spencer, *op. cit.*, p. 240.
55. F. Harris, *The Man Shakespeare* (New York, 1909), p. 196.
56. B. Stirling, *op. cit.*, p. 59.
57. M. Van Doren, *op. cit.*, pp. 104, 105.

58. C. F. E. Spurgeon, *Shakespeare's Imagery and What It Tells Us* (Cambridge, England, 1958), p. 281.
59. W. H. Clemen, *The Development of Shakespeare's Imagery* (Cambridge, Mass., 1951), p. 82.
60. C. F. E. Spurgeon, *op. cit.*, p. 285.
61. M. Van Doren, *op. cit.*, p. 98.
62. W. Raleigh, *op. cit.*, p. 150.
63. L. L. Schücking, *Character Problems in Shakespeare's Plays* (New York, 1948), p. 88, 89.
64. E. E. Stoll, *op. cit.*, p. 275.
65. L. L. Schücking, *op. cit.*, p. 91.
66. B. Grebanier, *The Heart of Hamlet* (New York, 1960), p. 194.
67. E. E. Stoll, *Shakespeare's Young Lovers* (Toronto, 1937), p. 20.
68. J. Palmer, *op. cit.*, p. 61.
69. L. Cooper, *op. cit.*, pp. 5-6.
70. B. Grebanier, *op. cit.*, pp. 133-34.
71. A. Quiller-Couch, Introduction to *The Merchant of Venice*, p. xx.
72. A. Harbage, *op. cit.*, p. 126.
73. H. Giles, *Human Life in Shakespeare* (London, 1868), p. 147.
74. A. Quiller-Couch, Introduction to *The Merchant of Venice*, p. xxi.
75. M. Webster, *Shakespeare Today* (London, 1957), p. 194.
76. C. B. Graham, "Standards of Value in *The Merchant of Venice*," in *Shakespeare Quarterly*, IV, No. 2 (April 1953), p. 150.
77. M. Packard, *op. cit.*, pp. 51-3.
78. J. M. Murry, *Shakespeare*, *op. cit.*, p. 194.
79. A. Quiller-Couch, Introduction to *The Merchant of Venice*, p. xx.
80. H. H. Furness, *op. cit.*, p. 131.
81. J. R. Brown, *The Merchant of Venice* (Cambridge, Mass., 1955), p. 75.
82. Quoted by H. H. Furness, *op. cit.*, p. 432.

CHAPTER 6

Who Chooseth Me Must Give and Hazard All He Hath: The Lovers

1. M. R. Ridley, *Shakespeare's Plays* (London, 1957), p. 90.
2. F. O'Connor, *Shakespeare's Progress* (Cleveland, 1960), p. 86.
3. J. D. Wilson, Introduction to *The Merchant of Venice*, New Cambridge Edition (London, n.d.), p. 109.
4. In *The Heart of Hamlet* (New York, 1960), pp. 15-16, 212-14, 219-20, 353-54, 382-83, 395-97, 398-99, 403-06, 420.
5. Quoted by H. H. Furness, *The Merchant of Venice* (Philadelphia, 1888), p. 2.
6. *Idem.*
7. *Idem.*
8. *Idem.*
9. J. Palmer, *Comic Characters of Shakespeare* (London, 1953), p. 61.
10. M. R. Ridley, *op. cit.*, p. 91.

11. H. Spencer, *The Art and Life of William Shakespeare* (New York, 1940), p. 244.
12. M. Van Doren, *Shakespeare* (New York, 1939), p. 97.
13. W. H. Clemen, *The Development of Shakespeare's Imagery* (Cambridge, Mass., 1951), p. 83.
14. F. O'Connor, *op. cit.*, p. 87.
15. K. J. Spalding, *The Philosophy of Shakespeare* (New York, 1953), p. 77.
16. J. Palmer, *op. cit.*, p. 61.
17. A. Harbage, *As They Liked It* (New York, 1947), p. 192.
18. A. Sewell, *Character and Society in Shakespeare* (Oxford, 1951), pp. 13, 42-43.
19. H. C. Goddard, *The Meaning of Shakespeare* (Chicago, 1951), p. 85.
20. H. Golden, *Only in America* (New York, 1958), p. 174.
21. A. Quiller-Couch, *Shakespeare's Workmanship* (London, 1918), p. 100.
22. In *Penn Monthly* (1880), p. 737.
23. M. R. Ridley, *op. cit.*, pp. 92-3.
24. A. Quiller-Couch, *op. cit.*, pp. 99-101.
25. *Ibid.*, p. 100.
26. M. R. Ridley, *op. cit.*, pp. 92-3.
27. A. Quiller-Couch, *op. cit.*, p. 101.
28. M. R. Ridley, *loc. cit.*
29. C. F. E. Spurgeon, *Shakespeare's Imagery And What It Means* (Cambridge, England), p. 281.
30. A. Jameson, *Characteristics of Women* (London, 1833), Vol. I, p. 66.
31. In *The Atlantic Monthly* (June, 1876), quoted by Furness, *op. cit.*, p. 440.
32. W. Hazlitt, *The Characters of Shakespeare's Plays* (London, 1906), p. 209.
33. M. R. Ridley, *op. cit.*, pp. 93-4.
34. J. Palmer, *op. cit.*, p. 60.
35. E. I. Fripp, *Shakespeare, Man And Artist* (Oxford, 1938), Vol. I, p. 416.
36. H. C. Goddard, *op. cit.*, p. 101.
37. A. Sewell, *op. cit.*, p. 43.
38. D. A. Stauffer, *Shakespeare's World of Images* (New York, 1949), pp. 60-2.
39. J. Palmer, *op. cit.*, p. 61.
40. A. Quiller-Couch, Introduction to *The Merchant of Venice*, New Cambridge Edition, p. xx.
41. H. Golden, *op. cit.*, p. 174.
42. M. R. Ridley, *op. cit.*, p. 90.
43. H. C. Goddard, *op. cit.*, p. 102.
44. T. M. Parrott, *Shakespeare: 23 Plays* (New York, 1939), p. 212.
45. M. R. Ridley, *op. cit.*, p. 91.
46. H. Craig, *An Interpretation of Shakespeare* (New York, 1948), p. 117.
47. *Idem.*
48. Quoted by H. H. Furness, *op. cit.*, p. 119.
49. *Idem.*
50. A. Quiller-Couch, *Shakespeare's Workmanship*, p. 101.
51. A. Quiller-Couch, Introduction to *The Merchant of Venice*, p. xxiii.
52. H. Craig, *loc. cit.*
53. D. A. Stauffer, *op. cit.*, p. 61.

54. *Ibid.*, p. 62.
55. A. Thaler, *Shakespeare's Silences* (Cambridge, Mass., 1929), p. 28.
56. H. Granville-Barker, *Prefaces to Shakespeare*, Second Series (London 1948), p. 74.
57. J. R. Brown, *The Merchant of Venice* (Cambridge, Mass., 1955), p. 80.
58. A. Quiller-Couch, *Shakespeare's Workmanship*, p. 102.
59. A. Quiller-Couch, Introduction to *The Merchant of Venice*, p. xxvi.
60. C. F. E. Spurgeon, *op. cit.*, p. 283.
61. H. C. Goddard, *op. cit.*, p. 92.
62. H. Granville-Barker, *op. cit.*, p. 77.
63. J. D. Wilson, *op. cit.*, pp. 100-4.
64. A. Quiller-Couch, Introduction to *The Merchant of Venice*, p. xxiii.
65. G. W. Keeton, *Shakespeare and His Legal Problems* (London, 1930), p. 80.
66. J. D. Wilson, *op. cit.*, p. 108.

CHAPTER 7

The Trial: Justice vs. Mercy

1. Quoted by H. H. Furness, *The Merchant of Venice* (Philadelphia, 1888), p. 404.
2. *Ibid.*, p. 405.
3. *Ibid.*, p. 400.
4. *The Monthly Chronicle*, Nov. 1838, quoted by H. H. Furness, *op. cit.*, pp. 400-03.
5. H. H. Furness, *op. cit.*, p. 409.
6. *Idem.*
7. *Ibid.*, pp. 409-11.
8. *Ibid.*, p. 413.
9. *Ibid.*, pp. 417-20.
10. E. I. Fripp, *Shakespeare, Man and Artist* (Oxford, 1938), Vol. I, pp. 138, 416.
11. F. E. Halliday, *The Cult of Shakespeare* (London, 1957), pp. 88-89.
12. A. Quiller-Couch, *Shakespeare's Workmanship* (London, 1918), pp. 102, 103, 111.
13. I. Zangwill, *The Voice of Jerusalem* (London, 1920), p. 228.
14. H. C. Goddard, *The Meaning of Shakespeare* (Chicago, 1951), p. 109.
15. H. H. Furness, *op. cit.*, pp. 223-24.
16. M. Webster, *Shakespeare Today* (London, 1957), p. 81.
17. From *A Piece of Chalk*.
18. G. L. Kittredge, *The Merchant of Venice* (Boston, 1945), p. 139.
19. H. H. Furness, *op. cit.*, p. 224.
20. A. Quiller-Couch, *op. cit.*, p. 75.

CHAPTER 8

Penultimate

1. E. Rosenberg, *From Shylock to Svengali* (Stanford, Cal., 1960), p. 32. See also, N. Coghill, "The Governing Idea," in *Shakespeare Quarterly* I (1948), pp. 9-17.
2. A. Thaler, *Shakespeare's Silences* (Cambridge, Mass., 1929), p. 39.
3. G. H. Radford, *Shylock and Others* (London, 1894), p. 26.
4. F. Harris, *The Man Shakespeare* (New York, 1909), p. 198.
5. H. C. Goddard, *The Meaning of Shakespeare* (Chicago, 1951), p. 109.
6. M. R. Ridley, *Shakespeare's Plays* (London, 1957), p. 94.
7. M. M. Reese, *Shakespeare* (New York, 1953), p. 498.
8. F. F. Heard, *Shakespeare as a Lawyer* (New York, 1883), p. 24.

CHAPTER 9

Other Men's Shylock

1. A. C. Sprague, *Shakespeare and the Actors* (Cambridge, Mass., 1948), p. 19.
2. T. Lelyveld, *Shylock on the Stage* (Cleveland, 1960), p. 19.
3. J. D. Wilson, Introduction to *The Merchant of Venice* (New Cambridge Edition), pp. 110-11.
4. T. Lelyveld, *op. cit.*, p. 21.
5. W. Cooke, *Memoirs of Charles Macklin, Comedian* (London, 1806), pp. 92-93.
6. T. Lelyveld, *op. cit.*, p. 24.
7. J. T. Kirkman, *Memoirs of the Life of Charles Macklin* (London, 1799), Vol. II, p. 427.
8. F. Gentleman, *The Dramatic Censor* (London, 1770), Vol. I, p. 291.
9. J. Doran, *Their Majesties' Servants* (New York, 1865) pp. 428 seq.
10. W. Hazlitt, *The Characters of Shakespeare's Plays* (London, 1906), p. 212.
11. T. Lelyveld, *op. cit.*, pp. 45, 51, 53.
12. A. C. Sprague, *op. cit.*, p. 29.
13. F. W. Hawkins, *The Life of Edmund Kean* (London, 1869), Vol. I, p. 342.
14. T. Lelyveld, *op. cit.*, pp. 54, 60.
15. A. Quiller-Couch, Introduction to *The Merchant of Venice* (New Cambridge Edition), p. xxii.
16. A. C. Sprague, *op. cit.*, pp. 19, 21.
17. T. Lelyveld, *op. cit.*, pp. 63, 65.
18. H. H. Furness, *The Merchant of Venice* (Philadelphia, 1888), pp. 383-84.
19. T. Lelyveld, *op. cit.*, p. 66.
20. A. C. Sprague, *op. cit.*, pp. 20, 23, 24, 28, 29.
21. W. Winter, *The Life and Art of Edwin Booth* (New York, 1894), p. 304.
22. A. C. Sprague, *op. cit.*, pp. 21, 25, 27.
23. T. Lelyveld, *op. cit.*, pp. 97, 99.
24. S. N. Behrman, *Portrait of Max* (New York, 1960), p. 46.
25. T. Lelyveld, *op. cit.*, p. 100.

26. A. C. Sprague, *op. cit.*, pp. 20, 22, 23, 27.
27. T. Lelyveld, *op. cit.*, p. 104.
28. A. C. Sprague, *op. cit.*, p. 23.
29. T. Lelyveld, *op. cit.*, p. 109.
30. T. M. Parrott, *Shakespearean Comedy* (Oxford, 1949), p. 140.
31. T. Lelyveld, op. cit., p. 113.
32. B. Grebanier, *The Heart of Hamlet* (New York, 1960), pp. 101-02.
33. T. Lelyveld, *op. cit.*, pp. 124-27.
34. F. Talfourd, *Shylock or the Merchant of Venice Preserved* (New York, n.d.), pp. 3, 5, 12, 14, 17, 27-9.
35. G. W. H. Griffin, *The Merchant of Venice* (New York, 1876), pp. 4, 8.
36. In *The Fortnightly Review* CXXIV (1925).
37. M. Schwartz, *Shylock and His Daughter* (New York, 1947), preface, p. 2.
38. *Ibid.*, pp. 23, 36, 40.
39. *Ibid.*, pp. 13, 15, 40, 41, 45, 49.
40. *Ibid.*, pp. 58, 69, 73-5, 80, 87, 92.
41. *Ibid.*, pp. 119, 122, 145.
42. St. John G. Ervine, *The Lady of Belmont* (London, 1923).
43. L. Untermeyer, *Selected Poems and Parodies* (New York, 1935).
44. L. Lewisohn, *The Last Days of Shylock* (New York, 1939), pp. 7, 12.
45. *Ibid.*, pp. 64, 94.
46. *Ibid.*, pp. 199, 209, 213, 221.

Index

ABOUT THE AUTHOR

BERNARD GREBANIER is the author of books, poetry, short stories, and essays. He is a scholar, an expert pianist, and an incorrigible collector of *objets d'art*. His courses in Shakespeare at Brooklyn College, where he is Professor of English, are legendary, and have for many years been the most popular in the Department. "All the scholarship in the world, valuable as scholarship is," he says, "is utterly useless as a guide to Shakespeare's meaning, if one approaches the plays without a quick sympathy for human relationships. We can learn more about other people and ourselves through an understanding reading of him than we could gather in ten lifetimes of personal experience. But we must come to him with some experience to begin with; and, above all, unless we come with our humanity ready to be touched and exercised, it is better not to come to him at all."

Shy. There I haue another bad match, a bankrout, a prodigall, who dare scarce shewe his head on the Ryalto, a begger that was ysd to come so smug vpon the Mart: let him looke to his bond, he was wont to call me vsurer, let him looke to his bond, hee was wont to lende money for a Christian cursie, let him looke to his bond.

Salari. Why I am sure if he forfaite, thou wilt not take his flesh, what's that good for?

Shyl. To baite fish with all, if it will feede nothing else, it will feede my reuenge; hee hath disgrac'd me and hindred me halfe a million, laught at my losses, mockt at my gaines, scorned my Nation, thwarted my bargaines, cooled my friends, heated mine enemies, and whats his reason, I am a Iewe: Hath not a Iewe eyes, hath not a Iewe hands, organs, dementions, sences, affections, passions, fed with the same foode, hurt with the same weapons, subiect to the same diseases, healed by the same meanes, warmed and cooled by the same Winter and Sommer as a Christian is: if you pricke vs doe we not bleede, if you tickle vs doe wee not laugh, if you poyson vs doe wee not die, and if you wrong vs shall wee not reuenge, if we are like you in the rest, we will resemble you in that. If a Iewe wrong a Christian, what is his humillity, reuenge? If a Christian wrong a Iewe, what should his sufferance be by Christian example, why reuenge? The villanie you teach me I will execute, and it shall goe hard but I will better the instruction.

Enter a man from Anthonio.

Gentlemen, my maister *Anthonio* is at his house, and desires to speake with you both.

Salers. We haue beene vp and downe to seeke him.

Enter Tuball.

Solanio. Heere comes another of the Tribe, a third cannot bee matcht, vnlesse the deuill himselfe turne Iewe. *Exeunt Gentlemen.*

Enter Tuball.

Shy. How now *Tuball*, what newes from Genowa, hast thou found my daughter?

Tuball. I often came where I did heare of her, but cannot finde her.

Shy.